PLAYING JAZZ IN SOCIALIST VIETNAM

PLAYING JAZZ IN SOCIALIST VIETNAM

———— ★ ————

Quyền Văn Minh
and Jazz in Hà Nội

Stan BH Tan-Tangbau and Quyền Văn Minh
Foreword by Yamashita Yosuke

University Press of Mississippi / Jackson

The University Press of Mississippi is the scholarly publishing agency of
the Mississippi Institutions of Higher Learning: Alcorn State University,
Delta State University, Jackson State University, Mississippi State University,
Mississippi University for Women, Mississippi Valley State University,
University of Mississippi, and University of Southern Mississippi.

www.upress.state.ms.us

The University Press of Mississippi is a member
of the Association of University Presses.

Copyright © 2021 by University Press of Mississippi
All rights reserved

First printing 2021
∞

Library of Congress Cataloging-in-Publication Data

Names: Tan-Tangbau, Stan BH, author. | Quyền, Văn Minh, 1954– author.
Title: Playing jazz in socialist Vietnam : Quyền Văn Minh and jazz in
    Hà Nội / Stan BH Tan-Tangbau and Quyền Văn Minh.
Description: Jackson : University Press of Mississippi, 2021. | Includes
    bibliographical references and index.
Identifiers: LCCN 2021040971 (print) | LCCN 2021040972 (ebook) | ISBN
    9781496836335 (hardback) | ISBN 9781496836342 (trade paperback) | ISBN
    9781496836359 (epub) | ISBN 9781496836366 (epub) | ISBN 9781496836373
    (pdf) | ISBN 9781496836328 (pdf)
Subjects: LCSH: Quyền, Văn Minh, 1954– | Jazz musicians—Vietnam. |
    Jazz—Vietnam—History and criticism. | Socialism and music—Vietnam.
Classification: LCC ML419.Q94 T35 2021 (print) | LCC ML419.Q94 (ebook) |
    DDC 788.7/165092 [B] —dc23
LC record available at https://lccn.loc.gov/2021040971
LC ebook record available at https://lccn.loc.gov/2021040972

British Library Cataloging-in-Publication Data available

CONTENTS

Foreword by Yamashita Yosuke vii
Acknowledgments ix
Preface xi

★ ★ ★

TRACK 1 Prelude 3

TRACK 2 Minh's Jazz Club 18

TRACK 3 Growing Up 50

TRACK 4 Interlude I 72

TRACK 5 Encountering Jazz Again 84

TRACK 6 Berlin, 1987 97

TRACK 7 Solo Recitals 111

TRACK 8 Vietnamese Jazz 132

TRACK 9 Teaching Jazz 151

TRACK 10 Interlude II 166

TRACK 11 *Birth '99* 182

TRACK 12 Minh's Jazz Club Reprise 211

TRACK 13 Postlude 227

★ ★ ★

Notes 245
Bibliography 259
Index 265

Figure 0.1. Yamashita Yosuke, Quyền Văn Minh, and Honna Tetsuji, 2018 (photo by Trần Trung Cường).

FOREWORD BY YAMASHITA YOSUKE

　ベトナムにジャズがあったのか!
　という発見をしたのは2009年、ベトナム国立交響楽団と初めて共演した時だった。私が演奏した「ラプソディ・イン・ブルー」にはサキソフォン・パートがあるのだが、そこに現れてくれたのがMr. Quyền Văn Minhとその息子さんや仲間の人達だった。
　ミンさんがベトナムジャズ界の重鎮で、ジャズクラブのオーナーでもあることを知り、早速彼の店 Bình Minh's Jazz Club を訪問した。素晴らしいジャズのライブを楽しむ内に、自然に呼び上げられて何曲か一緒に演奏することも起きた。その後はベトナムに行くたびに必ずこのジャズクラブを訪れている。
　それにしても、どうしてこういうことが実現しているのかという自然な疑問が生じる。ジャズは敵国アメリカの音楽のはずではないか。それがどうして?
　ミンさんはどのようにしてジャズを習得したのか? どのようにして仲間を得たのか? どのようにして今日の地位を得たのか? それらの疑問への回答がすべて本書に記されている。そしてその内容は、日本におけるアメリカのジャズの受け入れの歴史とも重なって、限りなく興味深い。
　世界中の音楽好きの人にとって必読の書だ。
山下洋輔

　I discovered jazz in Vietnam!
　In 2009, I performed in a concert with the Vietnam National Symphony Orchestra for the first time. I performed George Gershwin's *Rhapsody in Blue* on that occasion, and the piece contained some saxophone sections. Mr. Quyền Văn Minh, his son, and his colleagues joined us to play those sections.
　I learned that Mr. Minh is a leading figure in the jazz scene in Vietnam and that he owned a jazz club, Bình Minh's Jazz Club, which I visited after the concert. I enjoyed their wonderful live performance, and I was called up to the stage to jam with the band. After that, every time I went to Hà Nội, I would visit his club.
　One would naturally ask how this could happen here in Vietnam, because jazz must have been seen as the music of the former enemy, the United States! How did Mr. Minh learn to play jazz? How did he find fellow musicians who could play jazz? How did he achieve his present-day position in the jazz world? Answers to these questions are all addressed in this book. It is all very interest-

ing, because it is quite similar to the history of how we came to accept American jazz in Japan.

This is a book that every music lover, all around the world, cannot miss.

—Yamashita Yosuke
(English translation by Hiroaki G. Muramatsu, JamRice, Inc.)

ACKNOWLEDGMENTS

This book is written for Quyền Văn Minh and the musicians who gave jazz a life in socialist Vietnam.

I want to thank Quyền Văn Minh for this once-in-a-lifetime opportunity to write his story. Thank you for being so patient in the years it took for the project to come to fruition. I also wish to express my deepest love, sincere admiration, and heartfelt appreciation to my wife, Cecilia Koh-Maran, for her expert research assistance and unquestioning support, and for being a constant source of encouragement to help me finally finish this project. This book would never have been completed without the loving company of our daughter, Aubrey, who often sat next to me quietly doing her own schoolwork while I was immersed in the writing.

Honna Tetsuji introduced me to Hiroaki G. Muramatsu, manager for Yamashita Yosuke, and put forth my request to invite Yamashita-sensei to write a foreword for the book. Muramatsu-san has been most understanding and efficient in arranging for my draft manuscript to be read by Yamashita-sensei and instrumental in getting his agreement to write the foreword. A big thank you to Muramatsu-san for providing an accurate and sensitive translation of Yamashita-sensei's foreword, too! A world-famous jazz pianist in his own right, Yamashita-sensei's succinct and empathetic foreword is a huge testimonial to Minh's endeavors to give Vietnamese jazz an original voice in the world of jazz. Thank you, Yamashita-sensei and Honna-sensei!

Ms. Dương Hà Linh transcribed some of my early conversations with Minh and provided heartfelt feedback on the first draft. Dan Ruelle and Stephen Lindhorst gave the manuscript a thorough read to clean things up. Manouchehr Abrontan stamped a filmmaker's endorsement of the manuscript through the subtle angles he infused in the documentary film about jazz in Vietnam, *Sắc Màu Của Jazz* (*Colors of Jazz*).

Quyền Thiện Đắc arranged numerous sessions to speak with friends, relatives, and musicians who had played at the jazz club. He also spent a substantial amount of time sharing stories of childhood and jazz with me over the years. I fully appreciate Đắc's refreshing candor about his relationship with his father to help me produce a grounded account of Minh's story. I think that Minh must be a most successful parent and role model, having repeatedly heard firsthand from both his children candid appreciations of his efforts and sacrifice in developing jazz in Vietnam, and gratitude for his tough love and nurturing parenting.

Minh's wife, Deborah Jan Aronson, read through the entire first draft of the manuscript in one go and immediately wrote back:

> I wish I had the words to describe your book. I cannot wait for the final published version and to share it. Your way with words, writing, interviews, and research is, to me, the equivalent of Minh's performances, composing, and love of jazz. I have smiled, oohed in awe, and cried during my marathon of reading for the past nine hours.
>
> Thank you from the bottom my heart.
>
> I've recalled so many memories and conversations with Minh over the past 19 years, and am so grateful I was able to join Minh and the musicians in Singapore, Macao, and Hong Kong, as well as nearly all the performances you describe. And, you provide the "back story" to so many things that I have wondered about, especially our early days when our conversations were a bit limited by language (and time) challenges.
>
> I hope over time that Chi and Đắc, and our grandchildren will have an opportunity to read and understand this testament to life and jazz . . . as each of us only knows our own small part and experience in the life of Quyền Văn Minh.
>
> I am truly grateful for every word you have written.
>
> With love, admiration, and respect, Deb.

I am not sure I am deserving of these very kind words! Your endorsement assured me that I have done a minimally decent job. Thank you!

Deep in my heart, having lived with the responsibility of this project resting on my shoulders for so long, I know for sure that it could only have been completed by the grace of God. I would not have written the book in this way had I rushed through it in the first year or two after the idea was initially mooted. I guess this has all along been God's plan.

Earlier versions of some paragraphs in the preface, Track 1, Track 5, and Track 7, and the whole of Track 8 appeared in *Jazz Perspectives*.[1] Earlier versions of some paragraphs in Track 2 and Track 5, and the whole of Track 6 are published in the *Journal of Narrative Politics*.[2] I thank the editors and publishers of both journals for permission to include these earlier published texts in this book. Finally, I want to thank Lisa McMurtray and Craig Gill at the University Press of Mississippi for taking on this project and patiently guiding me along the way to see the manuscript to publication. I want to thank the anonymous reviewers for their detailed, insightful, and constructive comments. I know that the book is better because of such intellectual collegiality.

PREFACE

There is jazz in socialist Vietnam? How did jazz come about in this environment? Did jazz come to Vietnam because of more than half a century of French colonial rule and, later, two decades of American domination in South Vietnam? Did the communist government ban jazz? Who are the Vietnamese playing jazz in Vietnam? Are they really playing jazz? Can they improvise? How did they learn to play jazz? Where did they learn to play jazz? Are there places for them to perform? What is Vietnamese jazz? Who are the people that started jazz in socialist Vietnam? These are questions I have overheard countless times, asked by patrons at Minh's Jazz Club, tourists in the lobbies of hotels in Vietnam, and passengers on my flights to Vietnam browsing through pages of Vietnam Airlines' in-flight entertainment guide. These are likely the most basic kinds of questions I assume readers who pick up this book would ask.

Playing Jazz in Socialist Vietnam: Quyền Văn Minh and Jazz in Hà Nội is an account of how jazz came into being in socialist Vietnam told through the life story of Quyền Văn Minh. Specifically, this story is about jazz in Hà Nội, although when jazz first evolved there, there was no jazz to speak of in the rest of the country. Why should this book focus on a single musician, Quyền Văn Minh, in order to tell the story of jazz in socialist Vietnam? If I might be allowed to put it boldly, Quyền Văn Minh's life story in fact tells a good part of how jazz started in socialist Vietnam. In comparison, there has been no individual person whom we could credit for the *all-around development* of jazz into a proper mainstream music genre in any other country in Asia or in socialist Eastern Europe. In the case of socialist Vietnam, Minh's endeavors kick-started the momentum, from performing jazz in the public sphere to teaching jazz both formally and informally, contributing to efforts to shape an original Vietnamese voice to play alongside the diverse textures of sound in the world of jazz, and, most importantly, creating a public space for musicians to play jazz and for Vietnamese to listen to jazz. His endeavors lent credibility to efforts at the national conservatoire, at present formally known as Học viện Âm nhạc Quốc gia Việt Nam (Vietnam National Academy of Music), to eventually offer jazz as a subject up to the vocational diploma level and, later, the bachelor's degree level in the professional music education program. It makes sense to begin telling the story of jazz in socialist Vietnam with Minh's life story.

As the book focuses on the life story of one key individual musician who has devoted his life to developing jazz in the country, I must emphasize that this is by no means a comprehensive study about jazz in Vietnam from past to present. This detailed narrative of an individual's relationship with jazz in Vietnam is just the first step in telling a more comprehensive story.

While Minh's personal story stretches from 1954 to the present, the story of jazz in socialist Vietnam in this book gradually tapers off after 2001. As Minh endeavored to promote jazz as a musical art form beginning in 1988, many other talented and devoted musicians made significant contributions along the way, too. Two musicians at the national conservatoire should be immediately mentioned here: Lưu Quang Minh and Hoàng Tùng. Lưu Quang Minh, a senior faculty member and administrator at the conservatoire, led the effort together with Minh and Tùng to develop jazz as a study subject in the professional music education curriculum at that institution. The broader story of jazz in Vietnam carries much more complexity and color, and the inclusive participation of many other musicians, especially when the music began to take shape at the turn of the new millennia; this topic deserves a separate analytical treatment. However, a prior, intimate understanding of the struggles faced by individuals to play jazz and bring this music into the official soundscape of socialist Vietnam could prepare readers for a better appreciation of such a contextualized analytical study of jazz in Vietnam.

This book seeks to fulfill such a preparatory role by placing front and center the stories of an individual musician, to narratively flesh out how jazz could be heard, learned, and played in socialist Vietnam. I started writing this book as a simple biography, seeking to emphasize the voice of the protagonist so that readers could see how the complex political and social contexts of socialist Vietnam are actually experienced by real people. However, I realized that the complexity of life in socialist Vietnam required a fair bit of expository intervention, to help readers understand the challenges Quyền Văn Minh faced in trying to play jazz in Vietnam, not to mention in seeking to make jazz a respectable musical genre in the country. Thus, I have inserted strategic interventions between sections of Minh's original words to give context to his stories. Most of these interventions are based on my informal conversations with Minh over the years.

Playing Jazz in Socialist Vietnam is an exercise in collaborative narrative writing using the original words of Quyền Văn Minh that I pieced together like a jigsaw puzzle from the many conversations we had between 2009 and 2017. With our conversations taking place over several years, many specific issues and events were revisited in retrospect by Minh over and over again. Often, Minh ended up repeating stories he had told earlier in a particular context, finding relevance interconnecting them to a different event and a different context. I have tried to keep things the way Minh remembered and recounted them in piecing together his jazz life story using key watershed events. Indeed, life stories, if told as lived, are haphazard but interconnected through the serendipity of human interactions.

I take responsibility for organizing the myriad topics of our conversations over the years into, I hope, a flowing narrative to reflect the milestones that mattered to Minh and his philosophy in life as a Vietnamese jazz musician and teacher of jazz. I have tried my best to stay faithful to his original nuanced use of words and phrases from our conversations, frequent repetitions of events, cross-referencing with different events and issues that crossed his mind, and peculiar colloquial phrases. I have styled the text in the form of a collaborative narrative that is a mélange of our original conversations centering on the voice of Quyền Văn Minh and filled in by my contextual interventions. I have formatted Minh's original words, pieced together from many different conversations, *in italics*, while my interventions are formatted in a regular, nonitalic font. All our conversations were conducted in Vietnamese, and I alone am responsible for any shortcomings in the translation.

When the project started, Minh and I only knew each other superficially. I was just one among numerous faces he had come to know at the jazz club. Already an old hand at giving interviews to reporters, Minh had a standard narrative on hand ready to tell. But we never really conducted a formal interview for the project. Instead, we just continued how we had started, a "conversation between friends and brothers about the past" (*tâm sự về quá khứ giữa anh em*) over whiskeys and smokes. The usual narrative he gave to curious journalists (who had contributed to raising the profile of Minh and jazz in Vietnam generally) was very soon replaced by more personal stories told in extremely serendipitous fashion as we reacted to different artifacts lying around in his apartment or people we had met earlier in the day. In some sessions, we switched on the voice recorder and set it aside to record the whole conversation. In other sessions, we just talked.

The recorded sessions resembled little of a conventional interview. We had discussed many of the same topics and issues during our earlier unrecorded conversations. When we came to these recorded sessions, sometimes with just audio and other times with audio-video recording, it was entirely up to Minh to decide what he felt relevant to his life story and about jazz in Vietnam. The stories followed Minh's train of thought and the emotions invoked during our discussion the previous day and during the session itself, and they very much depended on his mood on that day rather than following a structured and topic-based format. Quite often, Minh picked up his guitar, saxophone, or clarinet to illustrate a story or two he was telling. Other times, he just talked. I asked only very few questions during the recorded sessions, usually only because I could not contain my curiosity anymore. Sometimes, these interventions turned into two-way discussions between the two of us before reverting to Minh's stories when our exchange arrived at a particular juncture at which Minh would pull out a particular story to illustrate the issue we were discussing.

Somehow, after a few sessions together, Minh was convinced that he could entrust me with his stories. Perhaps it was my love for jazz and my regular, quiet presence at the jazz club prior to mooting the idea for the book. Perhaps it was because Minh was very comfortable with my command of the Vietnamese language and my sensitivity to the social context of Vietnam. Or it could be a combination of both. We do not really know, although we discussed this issue a few times. But I do appreciate the many times that Minh confided in me about his relationship with his children, a topic I never recorded in any way in my notes. We talked mainly at his old place on Hàng Giấy Street. The first time we went there, Minh apologized profusely for the messy state of the apartment, saying that it was not the ideal place to invite guests. But it was the place where his jazz life story began, and he felt that it was the most appropriate setting for him to get into the zone to tell his story. Most of our early sessions for the project were conducted there.

The bulk of the stories contained in this book were collected in 2009 and from 2012 to 2016. The project encountered an unfortunate break between late 2009 and 2012. For personal reasons, a story for another time perhaps, I had to put aside most of the things I was working on until 2012. With generous research support from Ritsumeikan University in Kyoto, where I was serving as associate professor at the College of International Relations, I traveled to Hà Nội for between a fortnight and one month annually from 2012 to 2016 to spend time with Minh. Each trip to Vietnam was devoted to working on Minh's life story project. I continued to update the stories when I returned to live in Hà Nội from late 2017.

In the course of carrying out this project, Minh generously passed me all the newspaper and magazine clippings, old documents, and whatever memorabilia he had managed to keep over the years from his life in music. His wife, Deborah Jan Aronson, kindly sent me copies of DVD recordings of television programs featuring Minh, transferred from old and moldy VHS tapes; and a complete collection of Minh's CD and DVD albums. A very perceptive photographer, Deb also contributed several of the photographs included in this book.

As I mentioned earlier, Minh often told his stories by beginning with a story about a particular tune, or even by playing a tune or two (sometimes several!) in the middle of our conversations. These tunes are symbolic representations of particular phases of his life and the agency he embraced to play jazz in limited conditions. At the same time, these tunes also reflect the intersections between individual lived experiences and the backdrop soundscapes of the political and social contexts of Vietnam in different periods. As such, I find it appropriate to label each chapter of the book as "track."

Track 1 starts with a declaration that jazz is an official part of the proper mainstream soundscape in Vietnam. I provide a profile of Minh's career, setting it amid a brief survey of the context of music in modern Vietnam. Track 2 introduces readers to the central pillar of jazz in Hà Nội, Minh's Jazz Club. Track 3 provides the historical context in which Minh was born and grew up, namely the Vietnamese revolution and the Second Indochina War (or the Vietnam War for most Americans).

Track 4 gives a broader contextualization of jazz in Eastern Europe to help provide a more sensitive appreciation of the intersection between the cultural arts and politics in socialist societies during the Cold War. Track 5 tells of Minh's second and third encounters with jazz in the 1970s, the latter taking place after Minh left his full-time job as a musician. Track 6 tells of Minh's return to the professional music scene in the late 1970s, leading to the fateful trip to East Berlin that strengthened his resolve to play jazz in socialist Vietnam.

Track 7 unveils behind-the-scenes stories of how the very first set of public recitals delivered by Minh introduced the sound of jazz in the Socialist Republic of Vietnam in 1988 and 1989. Track 8 is a detailed account of Quyền Văn Minh's concert at the Hà Nội Opera House on April 12, 1994, which premiered three original jazz compositions written by Minh, marking the birth of Vietnamese jazz. Track 9 tells the story of Minh as a teacher of the saxophone and jazz both informally as an individual and formally as a tenured member of the national conservatoire.

Track 10 provides another contextual intervention to the story by teasing out a few common motifs that can be identified in the development of jazz in Asia and that are relevant to appreciating the story of jazz in socialist Vietnam. Track 11 examines the original jazz compositions by Minh as well as the albums he recorded as a jazz artist and saxophonist. Track 12 is fundamentally a monologue by Minh telling how he sees his jazz club as a place where musicians can learn to play jazz, gain the confidence to develop their own individual voice, and indulge in their passion for jazz. Track 13 temporarily sums up the state of jazz in Vietnam in parallel with Minh's life.

With the exception of the opening and closing tracks, as well as the two interludes, each track in the book opens with a brief summary of the context in which stories in the chapter take place.

PLAYING JAZZ IN SOCIALIST VIETNAM

Figure 1.1. *Father, Son, and Jazz II*, April 27, 2009 (photo by Deborah Jan Aronson).

TRACK 1

Prelude

A most heartfelt welcome to all respected guests! All of you present in the audience tonight are special guests of jazz in Vietnam. There is one story that I would like to share with all of you. About six weeks ago, a student from Tây Bắc University in Sơn La sent some money through the postal service to purchase tickets for tonight's concert.... I would like to sincerely invite Đỗ Chi Kiên [the student from Tây Bắc University] to come on stage to receive a small gift from Minh's Jazz Club.... To know there is a student from Sơn La city, a place in the distant regions and far away from Hà Nội, who is so interested in jazz is really a tremendous encouragement for all of us to continue to work harder and develop jazz in Vietnam. While waiting for Kiên to come to the stage, I would like to add a few more words. Jazz in Vietnam is something relatively new. We have been doing our best to develop our own voice, [one] that we can use to play alongside jazz music originating from all over the world. And this support of the new generation, such as students studying in universities currently, is something that I really treasure. Here he is . . . come . . . I am presenting a Minh's Jazz Club T-shirt with my autograph to Kiên. Later, all the musicians performing on stage tonight will put their autographs on this T-shirt for Kiên. For now, let's reserve the time for some music.
—**Quyền Văn Minh**, *Father, Son, and Jazz II*, Hà Nội Opera House, April 27, 2009

There is jazz in Vietnam.

Presented by Quyền Văn Minh, a saxophonist and lecturer at the prestigious Học viện Âm nhạc Quốc gia Việt Nam (Vietnam National Academy of Music), the concert *Father, Son, and Jazz II* at the Hà Nội Opera House on April 27, 2009, featured a repertoire of standard jazz tunes and original Vietnamese jazz compositions. Opening with Nat Adderley's "Work Song," the "father" (Quyền Văn Minh) and "son" (Quyền Thiện Đắc) exchanged solos on saxophones in lieu of brothers on trumpet and saxophone as performed in the original by the iconic Adderley brothers. Switching to clarinet, Minh exuded his melancholic sensitivities with Jimmy Van Heusen's "Here's That Rainy Day." With a change of pace, Đắc brought the audience into a meditative sophistication with his interpretation of Chick Corea's masterpiece, "Litha." Traversing an expansive range of jazz standards, Minh and band ended the first half of the concert with Hank Mobley's "Recado Bossa Nova."

This was in fact the second edition of a music program entitled *Father, Son, and Jazz* started by Quyền Văn Minh and featuring himself and his son, Quyền Thiện Đắc, a saxophonist also teaching at the national conservatoire. The first edition was delivered on April 6, 2008, at the Hà Nội Opera House and on April 14, 2008, at the Hồ Chí Minh City Municipal Theater. Both editions in 2008 and 2009, according to Minh, showcased the contrast between standard jazz tunes from around the world (mainly the United States) and original Vietnamese jazz compositions. Both editions also demonstrated two different approaches to the genre of Vietnamese jazz. Minh saw in these original Vietnamese compositions thoughts and cultural sensitivities belonging to two different Vietnamese generations, namely his generation, which started playing jazz during the late 1980s in socialist Vietnam, and his son's generation, which really got into jazz in the late 1990s after the Đổi Mới reforms. Guests who attended the night's concert on April 27, 2009, were treated to an array of original Vietnamese jazz tunes recorded on Quyền Văn Minh's *Đồng Cảm* album (released in 2001) and Quyền Thiện Đắc's *Shadow of My Homeland* album (released in 2004). These were original compositions written by Quyền Văn Minh, Quyền Thiện Đắc, and Lưu Quang Minh, Vietnam's most famous accordionist. According to Minh, each song was composed with an original melody to tell an original story, and set in a specific scale and framework of motifs inspired by different ethnic folk sounds found in ethnically diverse Vietnam.

As Vietnam prepared to enter the second decade of the new millennia, Quyền Văn Minh, Quyền Thiện Đắc, and their small ensemble were not the only musicians playing jazz in Vietnam. On April 6, 2009, Minh delivered the first Vietnamese big band concert, entitled *Quyền Văn Minh with His Friends and Jazz*, at the Hà Nội Opera House. For this concert, Minh assembled a full big band of Vietnamese jazz musicians, wrote his own arrangements of standard jazz tunes, and even featured an original Vietnamese tune, "Những Phút Giây Qua" (The Passing Minutes and Seconds) composed by Nguyễn Quốc Trường, who played trumpet and sang on the piece. There was already a group of active musicians playing jazz in the country.

Jazz in socialist Vietnam is not a dissident sound played in the shadows, not since Minh publicly performed the genre in two officially endorsed solo recitals in 1988 and 1989. Jazz concerts by Vietnamese musicians have featured at both the Hà Nội Opera House and Hồ Chí Minh City Municipal Theater since 1994, the two most prestigious concert venues in the country. As heritage buildings preserved from the French colonial era, only officially sanctioned and mainstream cultural performances can grace the stages of these musical halls. Almost all musicians who played at the concerts in 2008 and 2009 are, or have been, full-time music *cán bộ* (cadres) at state institutions such as the national music conservatoire, schools for the arts and culture, and state song-and-dance troupes. Quyền Văn Minh has been teaching at the national conservatoire since 1989. Lưu Quang Minh, one of the composers featured at both editions of the program and coproducer of the 2008 concerts, was deputy director of the national conservatoire then. In the opening of the *Father, Son, and Jazz II* concert, Quyền Văn Minh had the emcees convey his appreciation to several state institutions, namely the Ministry of Culture, Sports, and Tourism of Vietnam, the Vietnam National Academy of Music (VNAM), the Center for Music Performance of VNAM, the Hà Nội Opera House, and the Vietnam Television Corporation (VTC, the digital television broadcasting subsidiary of Vietnam's national radio broadcaster, the Voice of Vietnam), as well as reporters from state newspapers and radio stations. The concert was also jointly sponsored by several domestic and international companies such as Tin Tức Online, Heineken Beer, GM Daewoo, Indochina Airlines, and the Gami Group. Minh's *Father, Son, and Jazz* programs received full endorsement by state institutions and significant support from private corporations.

As noted by Minh in his remarks, "jazz in Vietnam is something relatively new." The officially endorsed existence of jazz as part of Vietnam's music soundscape in Hà Nội and Hồ Chí Minh City could seemingly be attributed to the presence of major music institutions such as the conservatoire; professional music ensembles such as the state song-and-dance troupes and national orchestra; the opening up of Vietnam through the Đổi Mới reforms; and globalization gradually penetrating Vietnam's two biggest cities. But Sơn La, the home province of the ethnic Thái people in Tây Bắc (northwestern Vietnam), is better known for its landscape of rice terraces carved into mountain valleys. It is a place where anthropologists flock to study the "exotic cultures" of mountainous ethnic minorities such as the Thái, Dao, and Hmong, and agrarian change brought about by half a century of migration and agricultural expansion through the Khai Hoang (Agricultural Pioneering) and Vùng Kinh Tế Mới (New Economic Zones) policies. Here, ethnomusicologists record, preserve, and study the folk sounds of various ethnic minority groups to present the unique cultural diversity of the Vietnamese nation. In Vietnamese parlance, Sơn La remains a *vùng sâu vùng xa* (out-of-the-way region). But jazz found its way into the heart of Kiên, an ordinary student living in this *vùng sâu vùng xa*. Quyền Văn Minh dedicated a tune he performed that night, "Núi Rừng Quê Ta" (Mountains and Forests of Our Homeland), to Kiên, the student from Sơn La. Originally recorded on his second jazz album, *Đồng Cảm*, Minh composed the tune by taking inspiration from ethnic Thái folk songs commonly heard in the northwestern mountains of Vietnam.

Jazz, somehow, could be heard across Vietnam by 2009.

Figure 1.2. Map of Vietnam.

Any trace of jazz introduced during the French colonial era disappeared entirely in the Democratic Republic of Vietnam with the end of the First Indochina War in 1954. Western music had arrived in Vietnam with the Christian missionaries as early as the sixteenth century, who brought in not only a new religion but also new music genres from Europe and new instruments such as strings, woodwinds, and brass to help proselytize the faith. In the late nineteenth century, as the

French deployed its armed forces to colonize Vietnam by force, military bands followed, bringing with them brass and woodwind ensembles and more genres of Western music. French colonialism in Indochina was also accompanied by a conspicuous demonstration of cultural soft power by means of transplanting Western arts through building concerts halls, staging concert performances, setting up music schools, and importing recorded sounds via Victor machines, records, and radio.[1]

Bùi Thanh Vân established the earliest Vietnamese brass band in Huế in late 1918 under the auspices of the Société des Amis de la Musique. The following year, King Khải Định established a Vietnamese royal brass band under the direction of Trần Văn Liên. In 1924, the Garde Indigène Hà Nội formed its own brass band, directed by the French officer Camille Parmentier with Đinh Ngọc Liên as his assistant. Bùi Thanh Vân's brass band, which had taken on the name Musique de la Garde Indigène de la Résidence Hue, performed at an international music festival in Paris in 1931 and won the gold medal in a music competition among France's overseas colonies.[2] In 1927, the Nhạc viện Viễn Đông (Conservatoire Française d'Extrême-Orient) was established in Hà Nội to bring formal Western classical music training to the French colony in the Far East.[3] Together, these were the earliest formal Western music establishments comprising Vietnamese musicians and students established under the French. If there were any Vietnamese capable of playing the swing music of that era, it would have to be from among these groups of musicians.

By the late 1910s and early 1920s, Western dance music had entered the luxurious European-styled hotels in Western enclaves in Vietnam (by then a part of French Indochina). Classical music, dance music, and some early jazz could be heard in places such as the Metropole, Batagelle, and Taverne Royale in Hà Nội and the Sài Gòn Palace, Majestic, Continental, and Reine Pedock in Sài Gòn, played by visiting European and Filipino musicians and dance bands.[4] But these traces of early jazz remained very much within the limited confines of such European enclaves.

Apparently, some jazz was heard on the radio besides European art music, French chanson, light orchestra music, and traditional Vietnamese music broadcast by Radio Hà Nội in the 1940s.[5] Vinyl recordings made by major labels such as Victor, Odeon, Columbia, and Pathé could also be found in Vietnam during the colonial period.[6] Vietnamese youths of that era enthusiastically received Western recorded music; some even recalled "standing outside record stores listening to a public victrola for hours."[7] But how much recorded jazz of that era actually found its way into Vietnam remains to be investigated.

While jazz did not really take off in French Indochina, the introduction of Western popular songs had a tremendous influence in the development of Vietnamese popular music. In the 1920s and 1930s, Western melodies were adapted for

Vietnamese settings and given Vietnamese lyrics.⁸ In time, original Vietnamese music adapted from Western forms was written and came to be recognized as "Vietnamese music in its own right," marking the early beginnings of *tân nhạc* (new music) or *nhạc cải cách* (reformed music).⁹ These early modern compositions included songs by the Myosotic group, the Tricea group, and Văn Cao (especially famous were his compositions "Suối Mơ" [Dream Stream], "Buồn Tàn Thu" [Autumn Sadness], and "Thiên Thai" [Paradise]). The popularity of *tân nhạc* made it a powerful tool for the burgeoning anticolonial movements, especially the Việt Minh (Việt Nam Độc lập Đồng minh, League for the Independence of Vietnam), a united front led by Hồ Chí Minh and the communists. Văn Cao was said to have composed "Tiến Quân Ca" (Song of Advancing Soldiers) following a secret request from the Việt Minh. The song was later adopted as the national anthem by the socialist state.¹⁰

The eminent Vietnamese music historian Nguyễn Thụy Kha sums up the relationship between the rising popularity of *tân nhạc* and the revolutionary movement: "The revolution embraced the new musical movement as if it were bringing under its wing a commando force."¹¹ Beginning in the early 1940s, composers such as Văn Cao, Lưu Hữu Phước, Thẩm Oánh, and Đỗ Nhuận composed song after song to urge the people to stand up together and fight for their independence. Nguyễn Công Luận noted in his memoir: "[T]he people's high spirit was greatly promoted by songs and plays, not only by political indoctrination."¹² Following Cách Mạng Tháng Tám (the August Eighth Revolution) in 1945 and until the end of the First Indochina War in 1954, these revolutionary songs played a major role in mobilizing the people to stand with the Việt Minh.¹³

Bringing all this music to the front lines to boost the spirit of the resistance forces, and garnering support among the masses on the home front, were the newly formed *đoàn văn công* (artists' troupes) such as Đoàn Văn công Tổng cục Chính trị (General-Directorate of the Political Commissariat Artists' Troupe, formed in 1950), Đoàn Văn công Nhân dân Trung ương (Central People's Artists' Troupe, formed in 1951), and many amateur artists' troupes made up of volunteers who went deep into the military zones and even the front lines to support the Việt Minh fighting units.¹⁴

With the end of the First Indochina War in 1954, all forms of cultural arts and performance considered unfaithful to the ideology of the revolution were restricted and even banned in the communist-ruled North, the Democratic Republic of Vietnam. These included nonrevolutionary *tân nhạc* composed before the August revolution. Even songs written by composers such as Văn Cao, who had contributed tremendously to the music of the revolution, were affected. Innocuous romantic popular tunes such as "Gửi Người Em Gái Miền Nam" (For a Girl in the South), "Chuyển Bến" (Moving to Another Port), and "Thu Quyến Rũ" (Seductive Autumn) by Đoàn Chuẩn were also severely restricted.¹⁵ Nostalgic and romantic ballads composed outside the thematic framework of the revolution, in particular songs from the South, were branded as *nhạc vàng* (yellow music) and banned in the North. One could even be jailed for the performance and dissemination of yellow music.[16] With the dawning of the Cold War in Southeast Asia and the outbreak of the Second Indochina War, all things deemed capitalist and belonging to the West disappeared from the public sphere in the communist North. As Nguyễn Thụy Kha puts it, "the arts were completely appropriated by ideology, and music became its most faithful instrument."[17]

Born in Hà Nội in 1954, Quyền Văn Minh's journey in jazz occurred in the context of the Indochina Wars and the Vietnamese socialist revolution. Jazz was practically unheard of among the masses in the North after the French left Vietnam and communists took over the government. Minh picked up the classical guitar in 1967 before learning the clarinet at the encouragement of his mother in 1968. Receiving only basic instruction in the clarinet, Minh was very much a self-taught musician. His chance discovery of a strange, mesmerizing music while playing with the family's transistor radio changed his life. He called it "mesmerizing music" at that time, because he knew of no genre that could categorize this music. He told himself, "I have to learn to play this! I have to be able to play like this!" Minh memorized every single note he could remember, made his own improvised notations on paper, and practiced and mimicked what he heard. Introducing variations and the feel of this new sound in the marches, polkas, and rumba he played for weddings and other celebratory occasions, Minh as a teenager became an in-demand musician for such gigs in his local community in Hà Nội.

That "mesmerizing sound" Minh heard on the transistor radio was jazz. Through our conversations over the years, we agreed that he had most likely chanced upon a program broadcasting jazz on Voice of America. The program was quite likely Willis Conover's *Music USA: Jazz Hour*. For Minh's father, however, that sound from the radio was the "music of the enemy" (the United States), because the Second Indochina War had begun years earlier.

Meanwhile, jazz, blues, and rock began to flood into the South as American intervention in the Republic of Vietnam reached its peak in the 1960s. As part of its global cultural strategy against communism during the Cold War, the US State Department sent "jazz ambassadors" to visit Southeast Asia.[18] In November 1961, the iconic jazz drummer Buddy Rich and his all-star sextet consisting of Rolf Ericson (trumpet), Sam Most (flute), Mike Mainieri (vibraphone), Johnny Morris (guitar), and Wyatt Ruther (bass) visited Sài Gòn at the invitation of the State Department. The Vietnamese drummer Huỳnh Anh was said to have engaged in a "drum battle" with Buddy Rich at Hưng Đạo Theater during this visit.[19] In 1966, the State Department sent Stan Getz to the South, where he performed for US servicemen at several military bases.[20] The music scene in

South Vietnam was fully plugged into the popular culture trends of the West. Vietnamese bands were formed, covering hit rock 'n' roll and Western popular songs of the day. Jazz was a minor sound played by a small group of Vietnamese musicians in nightclubs, dance halls, and bars. With reunification of the country under socialism in 1975, ideological alignment with the socialist revolution was applied to the cultural sphere in the former South. Jazz disappeared from the whole of the Socialist Republic of Vietnam (as the reunified country has been officially called since 1976).

Meanwhile, at the age of sixteen, Minh joined Đoàn Văn Công Quân Khu Việt Bắc (Việt Bắc Military Region Artists' Troupe) in 1970 to embark on his journey to become a professional musician. During Thời Bao Cấp (the Subsidy Period, the era of a centrally planned economy) in socialist Vietnam, joining state song-and-dance troupes was one of very few ways to become a respected professional musician. In fact, almost every professional vocation required official recognition by the state. To become a professional musician during the centrally planned economy era meant studying at the state music conservatoire or at a school for the arts and culture. Upon graduation and receiving a diploma, one's career track simply meant joining formal music ensembles established by the state, such as the National Symphony Orchestra, a military band, or a song-and-dance troupe. But Minh did not graduate from any of these schools, nor did he have a diploma in music. He joined the Việt Bắc Military Region Artists' Troupe as part of his family's obligation to send a male child for national service in the military. Over a short period of time, Minh was talent hunted from one troupe to another before ending up at Đoàn Ca Múa Thăng Long (Thăng Long Song-and-Dance Troupe), the top song-and-dance ensemble in Vietnam.

By the early 1980s, Minh had emerged as a notable clarinet and saxophone player in the music circle of the song-and-dance troupes. As a music cadre, he had access to channels and opportunities that could help him seek out better reeds, mouthpieces, and other accessories. And he could gain access to a wider range of music through opportunities granted by the state and an expanded network of people in the music circle, many of whom had the precious opportunity to travel both within the country and overseas (mainly to socialist Eastern Europe). Over the years, Minh persisted with his quest to source out what little materials he could obtain about jazz, and he continued to practice playing jazz behind the scenes. Colleagues and audiences were impressed by his lyrical accompaniments and sophisticated improvised solos on stage.

As the Đổi Mới reforms were officially and gradually introduced in 1986, the state's dogmatic grip on the arts began to loosen as well. The Đổi Mới reforms led to the steady decollectivization of Vietnamese society, the introduction of a market economy in the socialist state, and a subtle loosening of political control over every aspect of life. Nguyễn Văn Linh, then secretary-general of the Vietnam

Communist Party, who was considered a key proponent of the reforms, for a while even encouraged writers and artists to produce creative works that reflected the actual state of affairs in society. But the rehabilitation of music in Vietnam was no simple process to be taken for granted even as the reforms kicked in. The party and the state retained ultimate authority over what could be played, heard, and learned.[21] It was in this context that Quyền Văn Minh endeavored to play jazz in Vietnam.

In 1987, Minh performed in East Berlin with the Thăng Long Song-and-Dance Troupe. During this trip, Minh was fully exposed to the active jazz scene in East Germany, and the experience hardened his resolve to develop jazz in socialist Vietnam. In 1988 and 1989, Minh, still a cadre at the Thăng Long Song-and-Dance Troupe, delivered two separate solo recitals presenting jazz as part of the repertoire in officially sanctioned public performances. For the first time, jazz performed by a Vietnamese musician was heard in the public sphere in socialist Vietnam. Minh was nationally recognized as the premier saxophonist in Vietnam after delivering these two solo recitals at the Hội Nhạc Sĩ Việt Nam (Vietnam Association of Musicians). Jazz was endorsed by key figures in the official music circles. Both concerts were recorded and broadcast on national television. Jazz was heard across Vietnam as the country began its uncertain, baby steps on the path of political reform.

Following the 1988 and 1989 recitals, Minh was invited to join Nhạc viện Quốc gia Việt Nam, Hà Nội (Hà Nội National Music Conservatoire of Vietnam), which would later be known as Học viện Âm nhạc Quốc gia Việt Nam (Vietnam National Academy of Music). In this book, I shall follow Quyền Văn Minh and refer to this institution simply as *nhạc viện* or the conservatoire. In 1991, Minh's tenure as a professional music cadre was fully transferred from the Thăng Long Song-and-Dance Troupe to the national conservatoire, making him a full-time lecturer on the saxophone. From 1991 onward, through the combined efforts of Lưu Quang Minh, Hoàng Tùng, and Quyền Văn Minh, the classical music–focused conservatoire began offering jazz as a subject up to the diploma level. A Jazz Department was eventually formed within the Faculty of Accordion, Guitar, and Organ at the conservatoire in 1992. By means of being included in the professional music education curriculum of the national conservatoire, jazz was effectively accepted as a professional, respectable, and proper mainstream music art form.

Minh reached the second pinnacle of his career as a *nghệ sĩ biểu diễn* (performing artist) with an extremely successful solo concert at the Hà Nội Opera House on October 12, 1994. His original Vietnamese jazz compositions premiered at the concert were heard and seen nationwide on color television. The editors of the filmed concert made full use of the growing availability of color television in Vietnam by highlighting the vibrant lighting choreography that accompanied Minh's concert, which illustrated the different colors of jazz presented on stage that night. With this concert in 1994, Minh staked his claim as a bona fide Vietnamese jazz musician of a unified socialist Vietnam. He was a national star musician. More importantly, jazz was performed on the stage of Vietnam's most prestigious concert venue.

On the basis of his three highly recognized concerts in 1988, 1989, and 1994, his consistent contributions as a music cadre in the song-and-dance troupes, and his role as a lecturer who developed the saxophone discipline at the national conservatoire, Minh was conferred the order of Nghệ Sĩ Ưu Tú (Eminent Artist) by the Vietnamese government in 1997. This was a significant public recognition of his achievement as an artist and an affirmation of his contribution to state and society through his art. An emerging jazz artist received official recognition in socialist Vietnam.

The same year, Minh decided to open a jazz club in Hà Nội. On October 23, 1997, Minh's Jazz Club opened its doors on Giảng Võ Street in Hà Nội. The jazz club would become the premier venue where Vietnamese and foreign visitors could go to listen to live jazz in Vietnam, and it would serve as the training ground for Vietnamese musicians to hone their art in jazz. Minh saw the jazz club as a key pillar in his ambition to promote jazz in Vietnam.

To further develop the genre of Vietnamese jazz, Quyền Văn Minh began recording his compositions as a solo jazz artist, releasing his debut album of original jazz compositions in 2000. The album, *Birth '99 Ngẫu Hứng: Những Giai Điệu Dân Gian Việt Nam với Phong Cách Jazz* (Birth '99 Improvisations: The Traditional Folk Music of Vietnam with Jazz Style), contains eight original Vietnamese jazz compositions by Minh and a bonus track, "Misty." Between 2000 and 2017, Minh released a total of eleven CD/DVD albums consisting of studio recordings and live concerts recorded at the Hà Nội Opera House. Following the release of *Birth '99*, Minh was invited to participate at various jazz festivals and cultural programs in Asia, most memorably a nine-day concert tour in Singapore in 2001.

Indeed, after the concert in 1994, it was clear that Minh could no longer put all his time, energy, and resources exclusively toward being a performing jazz saxophonist and a jazz teacher; he had to take on concurrently more diverse and time-consuming roles as a composer, recording artist, and club owner. As Minh himself often puts it, "developing jazz music in Vietnam is the ultimate mission in my life."

On October 27, 2017, Quyền Văn Minh celebrated twenty years of managing his jazz club and fifty years of a life in music (Minh first picked up the guitar in 1967) with a concert extravaganza at the Hà Nội Opera House that went on for three and a half hours. The concert was entitled *20 năm Nhạc jazz và 50 năm Cuộc đời Âm nhạc NSƯT Quyền Văn Minh* (*Twenty Years of Jazz and Fifty*

Years of a Life in Music of the Eminent Artist Quyền Văn Minh). Students past and present, friends old and new turned up to play alongside Quyền Văn Minh. Some played new tunes to showcase what they had achieved as jazz musicians, to acknowledge Minh's tutelage. Others played old tunes, in particular Minh's original jazz compositions, to pay tribute to him. Some fifty musicians consisting of Minh's students and friends from across Vietnam gathered at the Hà Nội Opera House for this celebratory concert, broadcast live on YouTube by VTC Channel 3. This concert was a grand and public recognition of Minh's devoted efforts to develop jazz in Vietnam.

This prelude gives an idea about who Quyền Văn Minh is, but it barely scrapes the surface of his life story and the tremendous challenges that jazz in general faced in coming into being in socialist Vietnam. Table 1 presents a comparative chronology of key milestones in Minh's music career and socialist Vietnam's story of jazz and music.

Table 1. Chronology of Jazz in Socialist Vietnam

Year	Major Events in Vietnam	Music in Socialist Vietnam	Jazz in Socialist Vietnam
1954	End of the First Indochina War. Formation ofv the Democratic Republic of Vietnam in the North. Agrarian land reforms in the North.	Red music all over the North.	Jazz disappears from the North.
1955	Formation of the Republic of Vietnam in the South.		Jazz, rock 'n' roll, and Western popular music floods the South.
1958	Subsidy Period begins in the North.		
1960	National Liberation Front formed in the South.	Văn Ký composes the song "Bài Ca Hy Vọng" (Song of Hope) to commemorate fifteen years of the declaration of independence.	
1965	The United States begins bombing the North.		
1968			Minh's first encounter with jazz.
1970			Minh's guitar solo recital of "Bài Ca Hy Vọng" (Song of Hope) in school. Minh joins the Việt Bắc Military Region Artists' Troupe.
1971			Minh's second encounter with jazz. Minh joins the Hà Tây Song-and-Dance Troupe.
1975	Reunification of Vietnam.	Yellow music and other Western music banned in the former South. Emergence of the electric combo band in the North.	Jazz disappears in the South.
1976	Vietnam becomes known as the Socialist Republic of Vietnam.		Minh's third encounter with jazz.
1978	Vietnam's war with the Khmer Rouge's Kampuchea begins.		

Prelude

Year	Major Events in Vietnam	Music in Socialist Vietnam	Jazz in Socialist Vietnam
1979	The Sino-Vietnam border war begins.		
1980		Light music begins to be included in shows by song-and-dance troupes.	Minh joins the Golden Bell of the Capital Troupe.
1981			Minh joins the Thăng Long Song-and-Dance Troupe.
1986	Đổi Mới reforms begin.	Return of popular Vietnamese love songs.	
1987		Trần Tiến's *Đối Thoại* 1987 concert, which includes songs critical of the state of Vietnamese society.	Minh hears jazz in East Berlin.
1988			Minh's first solo recital; jazz performed publicly for the first time.
1989	Vietnam withdraws from Cambodia.	Western popular music heard in the major cities. Saxophone officially taught as a subject in the national conservatoire.	Minh's second solo recital; jazz performed publicly for the second time. Minh starts teaching saxophone and jazz at the national conservatoire.
1991			Minh joins the national conservatoire full time and permanently. The Faculty of Accordion, Guitar, and Organ formed at the national conservatoire. Jazz offered as a major up to the vocational diploma level at the national conservatoire.
1992			Minh headlines the jazz act at the Metropole Hotel in Hà Nội. Jazz heard regularly at the Metropole Hotel. The Department of Jazz formed at the national conservatoire.

Year	Major Events in Vietnam	Music in Socialist Vietnam	Jazz in Socialist Vietnam
1994			Minh's live concert at the Hà Nội Opera House. Minh premieres three original Vietnamese jazz compositions.
1995	Vietnam normalizes diplomatic relations with the United States.		
1996		Sting performs in Sài Gòn.	
1997			Minh is granted the Eminent Artist award. Minh's Jazz Club opens.
1998			Minh's Jazz Club moves to Lê Thái Tổ Street.
1999			Minh's Jazz Club moves to Lương Văn Can Street.
2000			*Birth '99*, the first Vietnamese jazz album, officially released.
2001			Minh's *Birth '99* Tour in Singapore. *Đồng Cảm*, the second Vietnamese jazz album, officially released. First European Jazz Festival in Vietnam.
2002			Minh performs at Vietnam's National Day reception in Hong Kong. Second European Jazz Festival in Vietnam.
2003			Third European Jazz Festival in Vietnam.
2005			Minh performs at the Jazz Festival for Peace in Okinawa, Japan. Herbie Hancock, Wayne Shorter, and delegates from the Monk Institute visit Vietnam.

Year	Major Events in Vietnam	Music in Socialist Vietnam	Jazz in Socialist Vietnam
2007			Jazz offered as a major up to the bachelor's degree level at the national conservatoire.
2008			Minh performs at the Taichung Jazz Festival in Taiwan. *Father, Son, and Jazz I* concert at the Hà Nội Opera House.
2009			*Quyền Văn Minh with His Friends and Jazz* big band concert at the Hà Nội Opera House. *Father, Son, and Jazz II* concert at the Hà Nội Opera House.
2013			Faculty of Jazz established at the national conservatoire.

TRACK 2

Minh's Jazz Club

On October 23, 1997, Minh's Jazz Club opened its doors in Hà Nội. It was the first jazz club to open in Vietnam under communist rule. Ever since then, Minh's Jazz Club has been the place for Vietnamese musicians to indulge in playing jazz for a live audience. Earlier, in 1992, the Metropole, the reopened colonial-era luxury hotel, had begun to feature a regular jazz act at the hotel's bar. That jazz act was a Vietnamese band led by Quyền Văn Minh. In 2001, Minh's Jazz Club was one of four venues that hosted the first European Jazz Festival in Vietnam. In the years that followed, a stream of international jazz artists including Herbie Hancock, Wayne Shorter, and Yamashita Yosuke visited Hà Nội. Almost every one of these musicians made a stop at Minh's Jazz Club. There is a bona fide jazz venue in Hà Nội. Jazz can be heard in the political capital of socialist Vietnam.

Hà Nội, 2017

You can walk into a Starbucks and enjoy a signature Frappuccino while listening to the music of Miles Davis in the background and watch the world go by. This signature ambience of aroma, style, comfort, and jazz, the archetypal café experience made popular by Starbucks, belies a contrasting street scene of a seemingly haphazard flow of motorbikes and cars, and a muted soundscape of deafening cacophony layered by revving engines and vehicle honks behind thick glass windows. You can indulge in the hip global café experience of coffee, dimmed lighting, sofa chairs, and jazz.[1] You can "Grab-bike" your way around, navigate through the traffic jams, and disappear into the narrow *ngõ* (alleyways) of this fast-changing historical capital city of Vietnam. All these amid the *phở* (Vietnamese flat rice noodles), *bánh mì* (Vietnamese bread), *cà phê sữa đá* (iced milk coffee), *nón lá* (conical thatched hats), yellow-star, red background T-shirts, and relics of war that are emblems of the twenty-first-century Vietnam tourist experience. Hà Nội has come a long way since the Đổi Mới reforms were carefully ushered in during the mid-1980s at the tail end of the Cold War. The

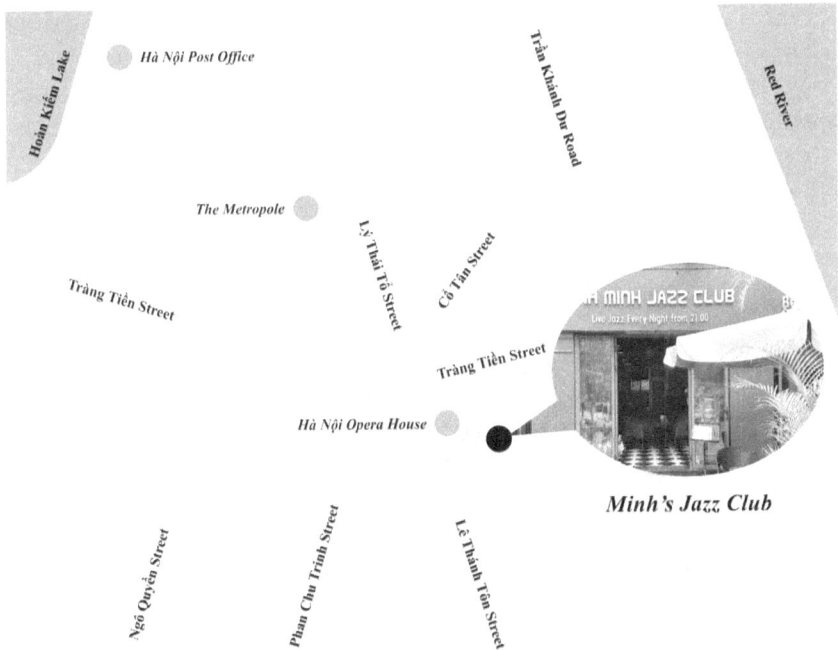

Figure 2.1. The location of Minh's Jazz Club.

sound of jazz as background music in the slightly more "hip" boutique cafés and lounges that augment major cities in Vietnam is quite the norm nowadays. This is very much in contrast to the days when Michael Learns to Rock, ABBA, and the Bee Gees ruled the airwaves of cafés and lounges together with the Viet-pop ballads sung by Hồng Nhung, Mỹ Linh, and Bằng Kiều in the late 1990s. And this is starkly different by many levels from the soundtrack of pre–Đổi Mới days. To speak of jazz in Hà Nội, or Vietnam in general, is no longer a jaw-dropping topic.

One would also not be surprised to learn that there is a dedicated jazz club with a resident band that plays nightly, seven days a week, located at 1 Tràng Tiền, just behind the Hà Nội Opera House. Opened by the Vietnamese musician Quyền Văn Minh, Minh's Jazz Club (called Bình Minh's Jazz Club now) has been around since 1997. Originally opened on Giảng Võ Street, the club has moved locations several times in the past twenty years, the longest being a full decade at 31 Lương Văn Can in Phố Cổ (the Old Quarter) of Hà Nội.

At 9:00 p.m. every evening, the jazz club comes alive with a quartet playing a mixture of contemporary jazz tunes by the likes of Steve Kuhn, Jaco Pastorius, and Herbie Hancock and jazz standards by Duke Ellington, Charlie "Bird" Parker, Miles Davis, and others. The club's glass doors can hardly contain the unbridled improvisations of the musicians. On a good night, there is only standing room for anyone walking in when the band starts playing. All available chairs are squeezed close to the stage to enable a view of the musicians as guests share tables, take selfies, and livestream a tune or two on Facebook. Seated inside, one is transported to the liminal world of jazz clubs devoid of city and country specificities, with the music punctuated only by bursts of applause and expressions of "Yeah!" and "Ooh" following an inspired improvised solo, occasional clinking of beer bottles as friends raise their drinks to toast one another, and smoke rising to the ceiling from contemplated drags of cigarettes, cigars, and pipes. It is not uncommon to hear visitors remark in English to Quyền Văn Minh between sets, "This place sounds exactly like any jazz bar in my hometown!" Only the occasional smattering of Vietnamese, to be more specific northern Vietnamese, among the audience or staff shouting orders to the bar through the live music reminds one that this is Hà Nội, Vietnam. With portraits of notable jazz musicians such as Sonny Rollins, Stan Getz, and Michael Brecker adorning the walls and pillars, Minh's Jazz Club makes no pretense about the owner's passion, jazz. Take a careful look and you'll see photographs of Quyền Văn Minh taken at the club with iconic jazz musicians such as Herbie Hancock, Wayne Shorter, and Yamashita Yosuke.

For those who grew up with the Cold War, who are familiar with Vietnam's painful experiences during Thời Bao Cấp (the Subsidy Period) and the Indochina wars, who witnessed the labored process of the Đổi Mới reforms, and who experienced the persistent cultural surveillance in Vietnam before the digital revolution changed the world, the existence and longevity of Minh's Jazz Club is something hugely significant.

With Every Breath from the Heart...

Just yesterday, I was at a Catholic parish in Nam Định [Province] to teach some members of the congregation. Some time ago, they had invited me to teach saxophone at their church. They told me, "We need someone to guide us, could you come and teach us?" I agreed and I went down to Nam Định to give them some pointers. From Hà Nội, I took the "xe đò" [interprovincial bus] and arrived there in the morning. In the morning session, I asked the students to play for me. I listened carefully to each and every one of them. Then I explained and showed them the correct ways to play or suggested better ways to play. In the afternoon, they practiced what I had taught earlier. I recorded their practice and we listened together, then I pointed out the problem with different aspects of their playing. I gave them further pointers to practice on their own until I returned the next time. The next morning, I took the xe đò back to Hà Nội, hopped on a "xe ôm" [motorbike taxi] at the bus station to get to the jazz club to check on things, and had breakfast. I had a bowl of phở. The guy who previously ran the kitchen at the jazz club when we were still at Lương Văn Can operated the kitchen in the morning to sell breakfast. The breakfast at the jazz club is quite good! Then I came over to meet you. I will return to Nam Định next month to teach them again. There is no money or any form of remuneration involved. Although they try to make up to me by other means, I tell them, "No, you don't have to do that." I just want to help them. In fact, I have been doing this for a while already. They are not trying to improve so that they can make more money or become famous. They are trying to play better music for their religious beliefs. They practice to play for the Sunday service. They play it for God. When they play well, the Heavenly Father is happy, and they find fulfillment. To hear them play well is, to me, priceless.

Besides teaching full-time students at the conservatoire, I also teach music to people who are not students at the conservatoire. Some of them are just beginners; I try my best to help them learn how to play music. Some of them have already learned the basics, so I try to guide them to become more proficient musicians. Most of these students are not full-time musicians; they have other professions. When I teach the amateurs or beginners, sometimes they just want to learn to play a song or two on the saxophone. They find happiness in doing that, so I teach them. This is a very simple and down-to-earth kind of happiness. I also teach many students studying at different schools, such as Trường Văn Hoá Nghệ Thuật Quân Đội [Military College of Culture and the Arts]. Teaching at different places and teaching different students call for different approaches. Students in other provinces, they do not have the same kind of learning environment as students in Hà Nội. But they are sincere and they are passionate, so I dote on them. I want to help them play better. I try to find ways to help them improve. They remind me of myself in the past, trying to play and nurture a passion in the context of limited access to information, lack of guidance, and overall limited conditions.

If I can bring something good to society with my music, I will do that. I believe that my music will always bring something good back to me, too. My mother taught me all these [things]. I will always remember because she said this to me when I started playing the clarinet, around 1968. That was a period of time in Vietnam when we all suffered from unthinkable hardships and constant hunger. It was unimaginable hardship; life was really tough! Unforgettable. Everyone wished and hoped that one day we could have a better life. Not a day passed by when we didn't wish that life could be better. Nonetheless, even in difficult times like that, my mother told me: "I don't need anything from you, my son. I only need you to play the clarinet well. When you play clarinet, the air circulates close to your heart, and thus every breath comes from the heart. With a good heart, one can produce beautiful sound. This beautiful sound will bring something good back to life. If you do anything good for life, life will bring something good back to you." My mother taught me this even though we were living in the midst of difficult times during the war years.

Although I was born in Vietnam, a country that basically did not know what jazz was, I have been in love with jazz ever since I heard it on the radio in 1968. I have been playing music for more than fifty years since 1967, and I started the jazz club over twenty years ago, in 1997. The fact that I could have the self-belief to play jazz is, I think, by itself already an achievement! In the limited conditions in which I learned to play jazz, I became a professional musician, and then I became a teacher of saxophone and jazz.

Then I came to open my own jazz club, a place for us to play jazz, and a place to nurture students to play jazz.

Minh opening the jazz club was both a major milestone in the story of jazz in Vietnam and a major chapter in his life story. Minh started teaching saxophone and jazz at the conservatoire in 1989. But there were limited opportunities for budding jazz musicians to perform for a live audience to hone their art. As far as music performances in Vietnam were concerned, Minh's concerts at the Hội Nhạc Sĩ (Association of Musicians) in 1988 and 1989 and the Hà Nội Opera House in 1994, which included jazz pieces in the repertoire, were exceptional occasions in the public sphere. Minh's own breakthrough with jazz was itself a singularity in the political and cultural contexts of socialist Vietnam. To make jazz an integral part of the Vietnamese soundscape, Minh had to create a new stage so that jazz could be performed regularly and be easily accessible to the public. Minh opened his own jazz club in 1997 and gave it a mission.

Playing Jazz at Hotels

The idea of opening his own jazz club was first planted when Minh started accepting gigs that gave him the opportunity to play jazz. These were mainly occasional engagements organized by foreign embassies, and more regular gigs contracted by major hotels in the early 1990s. These gigs were valuable opportunities for Minh and his friends to try their hand at playing jazz for a live audience. Beginning in 1991, Minh assembled and led an all-Vietnamese jazz band that played at bars and lounges of various major hotels, such as the Metropole and Thắng Lợi in Hà Nội.

After the solo recitals in 1988 and 1989, in which I introduced the sound of jazz to the Vietnamese public, the conservatoire officially requested that I put together a jazz band to perform at an official event organized by the French embassy. That was in 1991. So I started to build a proper band to play jazz. You see, I could only gather a makeshift ensemble of amateur players that included my siblings to play jazz with me for the recitals in 1988 and 1989. The year 1991 was when I first put together a group of professional musicians to play jazz with me for a gig. This group I formed in 1991 consisted of Quốc Trung, son of Trung Kiến; Vũ Hà, son of Văn Ký, he played bass; and another guy who studied drums in the Soviet Union and had just returned to Hà Nội. Experiences preparing for the solo performances in 1988 and 1989 and lecturing at the conservatoire taught me how to put together the very first jazz band in Hà Nội to take part in French Culture Day in Vietnam organized by the French embassy. We played at the French embassy on, I remember the date clearly, June 21, 1991. After the performance, the ambassador was so impressed and even remarked that I would be the first to be able to receive a scholarship to study jazz in France after Đổi Mới. However, somehow, when they finally announced the recipient of the scholarship, after going through rounds of deliberations and recommendations at different levels from the Ministry of Culture to the conservatoire, it was someone else's name! Before the ambassador returned to France, he told me that he was sorry that he could not intervene in that matter.

Soon after our performance at the French embassy in 1991, we started receiving invitations to play jazz at different functions. Together with Ban nhạc Phương Đông [Oriental Music Group], we were even invited to travel to Moscow to perform in the Vietnam National Day celebration program in 1993! Our band also participated in the National Light Music Festival in Đà Nẵng, and we came in first. Then we started receiving invitations to play at the lounges and bars of five-star hotels in Hà Nội. We were invited to sign a contract with the Metropole in 1992 to play jazz at the hotel's bar. In fact, I was the first local to sign a contract to specifically play jazz at the bar of the Metropole with my own band. It was for five nights a week at the bar.

Minh remained the premier act in the hotel gig circuit in Hà Nội for a good decade immediately after Đổi Mới. In fact, advertisements the Metropole ran in the *Saigon Times* throughout 1999 proudly declared that the hotel's bar "features one of the capital's premier jazz musicians, Quyền Văn Minh, on Friday evenings."[2] The Metropole is perhaps the most prestigious hotel in Vietnam and one of Southeast Asia's classic luxurious colonial hotels, on a par with the Raffles Hotel in Singapore, extravagant enclaves built during the golden age of colonialism in the region. Completed in 1901, the Metropole was a home away from home for Europeans visiting Hà Nội in the early twentieth century. Known for its exquisite boulangerie, its wide selection of imported liquor, spirits, and wine, and its European fine dining, the Metropole provided the comforts and ambience of high-society Europe within its enclave environment. Classical music could be heard from the in-house gramophone machine, and sometimes live acts by visiting musicians. And there were European popular songs, early dance-hall music, and some swing. In fact, the Metropole was known for its European popular music evenings during the First World War and in the years afterward.[3] At the Metropole in the 1990s, Quyền Văn Minh, a Vietnamese musician born and bred in Vietnam, was the featured headliner act playing jazz to a mainly expatriate crowd.

When I signed contracts with the hotels to play jazz in the early 1990s, I had to negotiate not only salary for the gig, but also the treatment of my musicians. For example, musicians must have the right to be given a complimentary drink, beer, or soft drink during the break. Musicians must be allowed to sit at the bar where we played during the interval so that we could socialize with the audience. I learned the importance of all these little things from the initial days of playing at the Metropole. I recalled how a manager criticized my musicians for sitting at the bar during the break, chastising us that the seats were reserved for paying customers, not employees! I protested and threatened to quit. Friends and guests came to the bar to listen to us play. During the break, they invited us to sit down for a chat. Could we tell our friends or customers, "Apologies, we are not allowed to sit here?" That was ridiculous! That was a French manager at the hotel. Later, I spoke to the deputy general manager of the hotel. I told him, basic courtesy and respect must be extended to musicians playing at the hotel. All the more so because only the four-star or five-star hotels appreciate the value of jazz in helping to give the place a more up-class ambience. When I make agreements with musicians playing at my own jazz club, I make sure musicians are given their due respect, and they learn that being accorded this respect is just as important as the payment for the gig.

The Eminent Artist Award (Nghệ Sĩ Ưu Tú)

I went to Paris in 1996 to play in a special concert with French musicians. I was specially invited to present the original Vietnamese jazz compositions I had premiered at the Hà Nội Opera House in 1994. In Paris, I managed to visit a few jazz clubs. During the trip, I wished that we could have such jazz clubs in Hà Nội, in Vietnam! When I returned from Paris in 1996, I felt that I had been too reliant on opportunities given by others. I had been too dependent on other people to give me opportunities to play jazz to a live, public audience. Sure, by then I could perform jazz at the hotels, but the hotels only wanted a repertoire made up of jazz standards or just light instrumental music. If I wanted to play "traditional Vietnamese folk music with jazz style," if I wanted to experiment, I had to have my own place to play in order to try out my musical ideas. After the Paris trip, I realized something else: I had been playing alone. I needed a group of people to play jazz with me and a group of people able to play together regularly. I had been playing with musicians who were not into jazz, most of whom did not understand jazz. I got stuck at that level. I felt that I had to develop a stream of professional

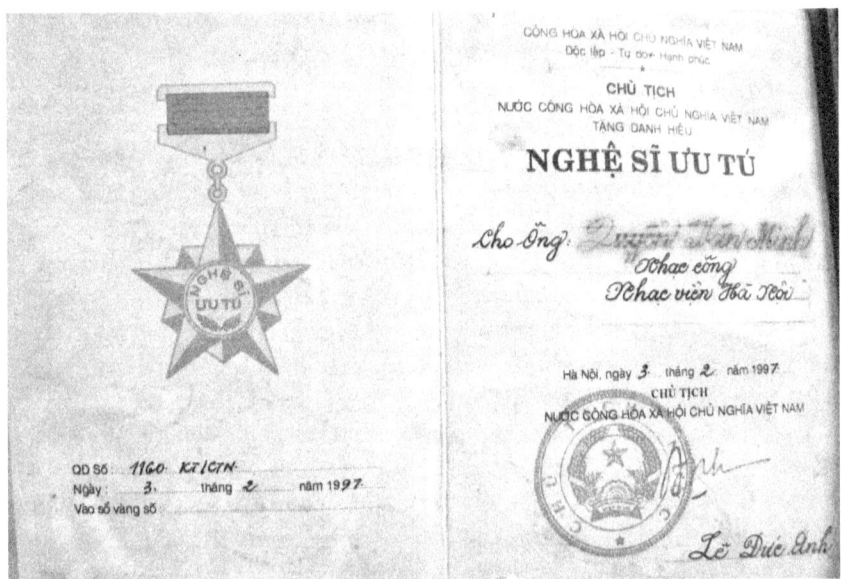

Figure 2.2. The Eminent Artist award.

jazz musicians to bring up the level of jazz in Vietnam. I had to have a place for people to practice, to train, and to get into jazz.

Soon after I came back from Paris, at the beginning of the following year, I was awarded the accolade of Nghệ Sĩ Ưu Tú [Eminent Artist] by the state. That was on February 3, 1997. That same year, on October 23, 1997, I opened my jazz club.

I started teaching at the national conservatoire in 1989. After my successful solo concert at the Hà Nội Opera House in 1994, the conservatoire asked me to prepare a dossier, because they wanted to recommend me for the Nghệ Sĩ Ưu Tú award. They had wanted to recommend me earlier, on the basis of my solo recitals in 1988 and 1989. But I felt I was not ready. This time, however, the dean of the Faculty of Wind Instruments and Percussion encouraged me, telling me, "Just go ahead and submit your dossier." To be honest, I would rather be recognized for my contributions as a teacher because from the day I joined the conservatoire, I effectively became a teacher; I was no longer a performing artist [nghệ sĩ biểu diễn]. Nonetheless, it was an important recognition! After several decades of hard work, driven simply by my love for music, I managed to develop my own sound as a musician. With help from my colleagues at the conservatoire, we successfully established the saxophone department. With endorsement and support of the directors of the conservatoire and the Faculty of Wind Instruments and Percussion, I was nominated to be awarded the title of Nghệ Sĩ Ưu Tú, a title conferred by the government of Vietnam. This award was a huge recognition of my work in the arts, and it was a huge encouragement for *me to continue to raise the level of my service to the arts and music education for the next generation. I received the Nghệ Sĩ Ưu Tú award at the Hồ Chí Minh Museum on February 3, 1997.*

After receiving the award, I felt the need to revisit my personal goal of developing jazz in Vietnam. Should I give another recital program to further showcase jazz as a worthy genre of music? I felt compelled to give another performance to demonstrate my worth for the award. At that time, I was thinking of doing a pure jazz concert. I started to write more tunes. I had started writing in 1993, and I premiered three of these compositions at the 1994 concert. I continued to write in bits and pieces over the years. I was thinking, I could do half the concert playing well-known international jazz tunes and half the concert featuring my own original compositions, jazz tunes from Vietnam. To organize a concert was costly; I would have to bear the cost for everything. I would have to invite people to come and listen to the music. It would be difficult to sell tickets to cover the cost of putting up a jazz concert. At that time, there was no available avenue to find sponsorship for another concert program. I would have to put in a large amount of my own money and resources for one performance. And it would be just one performance. Or I could do something else. At that time, I was already thinking about opening my own jazz club. I thought, why not invest my efforts and resources in opening a jazz club? I could cultivate a group of musicians; we could have a place to practice the pieces I composed; we could play together regularly to attain a better musical standard; and we would be ready, anytime, for another big concert when the opportunity arose. We could accumulate all these little things to do something big later. A jazz club would be the place where we could really play jazz for a live audience. I decided that I had to open a jazz club. I was determined. I took out the title deeds of my apartment on Hàng Giấy Street to get a loan to open the jazz club on Giảng Võ Street.

Hàng Giấy Street

Hàng Giấy Street in Hà Nội is where Minh grew up. His parents' apartment on the street is located near Đồng Xuân Market in the Old Quarter. Bit by bit, Minh saved up and was finally able to purchase a small unit with no windows in the same block as his parents' apartment around 1993, followed by a larger unit with a street view soon after.

In fact, Minh came up with the idea for the tune "Vấn Vương," one of three original compositions he premiered in the 1994 concert at the Hà Nội Opera House, at the Hàng Giấy apartment. According to the liner notes from Minh's debut CD released in 2000, *Birth '99*, that moment of inspiration came when he looked over Hàng Giấy Street from the window of his apartment, reminisc-

Figure 2.3. Minh's apartment on Hàng Giấy Street, the Old Quarter, Hà Nội.

ing about his life, striving to play jazz, and thinking about the future of jazz in Vietnam. Whether it was a reflective moment thinking about our mortal existence or just simply a moment's pause to appreciate the nicer things in life, one could indeed be easily absorbed in the multilayered soundscape of the streets in Hà Nội's Old Quarter during the 1990s. The interminable, gentle bursts of beeps and rings emitted by the ceaseless crawl of motorbikes and bicycles reverberating off the walls of abutting shophouse apartment blocks along the contours of the streets sounded like a magnificently unrehearsed but nevertheless coordinated a cappella performance of two-wheelers. The layerings of reverberation from similar productions on adjacent and parallel curving streets, peppered by the chattering and smattering of passing pedestrians and children playing on the streets, completed the soundscape. Ironically, it is the nostalgic cacophony of the Old Quarter's soundscape that releases bubbles of meditation space, allowing one to escape and indulge in one's thoughts. That was Minh's moment when he caught the inspiration for "Vấn Vương."

Located on the top floor of a wing facing the street, Minh's apartment on Hàng Giấy would be really quite spacious if not for the boxes of his own recorded CDs, books of music scores, parts of musical instruments, and old whatnots stacked across the floorspace; and the metal and wooden shelves flush against the walls holding boxes of trinkets. The interior of Minh's apartment belies the narrow, almost claustrophobic facade of the shophouse block when viewed from the main street.

The apartment on Hàng Giấy played an important role in my life. I lived a good part of my life here on Hàng Giấy Street. My parents lived here. I learned music here, I practiced my music here, and I taught music here, including teaching Trần Mạnh Tuấn, who used to come up here to study saxophone with me. All the students in the early phase of my career came up here to study saxophone with me in this apartment on Hàng Giấy Street. After my divorce, I sold my bicycle to build a small wooden shelter on the rooftop, above my parents' apartment. I lived in the shelter on the rooftop, and I put a small bed in there to sleep. My children would sleep in the apartment below with their grandparents. In the day, I cooked, and the two kids came up to the rooftop to eat with me; father and children as a family. In Hà Nội, it gets very hot in the afternoon during summer, so the kids played and did their schoolwork at their grandparents' place below, while I stayed there on the rooftop. Memories of difficult times stay with you.

Living on Hàng Giấy Street, when people called and asked me to play a gig "on call," at the last minute, I could just go. We called that "cấp cứu" [emergency help], which meant that I had to go immediately. I could go immediately because Hàng Giấy is right there in the heart of the city! Living on Hàng Giấy Street was really convenient in that sense. Over at Nghĩa Đô, where I was assigned an apartment in the "khu tập thể" [collective residence] built by the government for cadres in 1987, the place was rather spacious. But after moving there, we often wished that we could come back here to stay on Hàng Giấy Street, where I grew up. I saved up to buy this apartment. When I first managed to buy the small room next to the stairwell, it was a milestone in my life because I went through so much difficulty before that and ended up having to stay in a makeshift wooden shelter on the rooftop of my parents' apartment. To be able to buy an apartment of forty-eight square meters in total, including this main unit and that smaller one, right in the heart of the capital, from the labor of playing music, trying to play jazz, and not by solely performing popular music to cater to the market's demand, that was a real achievement! Memories of my childhood on Hàng Giấy Street, living here and working at this place after I started my own family, these are things that I treasure. I have a very strong attachment to this apartment on Hàng Giấy Street. Saving up to buy this apartment was quite a story on its own.

Figure 2.4. Bình An Villa in Sài Gòn, 1994.

The story began sometime in 1993, at the bar of the Metropole, where I was playing with my own jazz group. The bar was often crowded when we played. Many foreign guests came to the bar to enjoy our music. Most local people did not know about our music at that time. One fine day, there was this lady who had flown up from Sài Gòn, and she came to the bar. Initially I thought she was a Singaporean or a Filipino because even though she looked a bit like us, she just did not seem like a typical Vietnamese to me. Her outlook, demeanor, and characteristics did not seem like a local's. That was why I thought she was a Singaporean or a Filipino. Anyway, she came to the bar and heard us play. During the break, she came to talk to me. She asked, "Where did you folks learn to play this music?" That was when I recognized that she was a Saigonese, in fact she was a Việt Kiều [overseas Vietnamese]. I replied to her, "I learned from listening to vinyl and cassettes. I have been looking for books as well." She told me, "Hmm, I have a band in Sài Gòn, they are trying play some jazz, too. I want to invite you to join them, what do you think?" I said, "I would love to! But it will be costly to come and play with the band in Sài Gòn." "That is no problem at all, let me worry about that," she replied, and continued: "The important thing is you agree to come!" I called her Chị Mai. She loved jazz and played a little piano. In Sài Gòn, she had a villa outside the city and had invested money to set up a band to play jazz. Chị Mai was very impressed by our gig at the Metropole and wanted me to join her band and lead the musicians.

After agreeing to this invitation, from 1993 to 1997, I flew to Sài Gòn at least once or twice each week. I would fly down there, perform, and fly back the next day. That I could buy this Hàng Giấy place was simply because of the money I earned from playing jazz in those years. Of course, initially, I could only afford to buy part of it, the smaller room on the other side. You see, when I went to Sài Gòn for the gigs, I tried to save up as much as possible. After I disembarked from the plane, I would head straight to the "xe ôm" [motorbike taxi] drivers stationed at the airport. I could have taken a taxi from the airport, because in the envelope containing my air ticket, there would always be US$100 for my salary and VND200,000 for taxis and food. For every night I performed, the lady boss paid me US$100. In those days, this was a lot of money for a gig! With the taxi and food allowance she gave me for each trip, I could take a proper taxi, but I always chose to take a xe ôm. I would walk to a xe ôm driver and try to strike a deal with him. I would ask the xe ôm driver, "If you drive me to this place, I will pay you VND35,000. But if you let me drive and you sit behind me, I will pay you VND30,000. Which do you choose?" The xe ôm drivers would always tell me, "You are paying too little!" To which I always replied, "No, I've been there, I know the way and I know the price." The drivers usually chose the latter. I was happy to drive with the xe ôm driver pillion riding because I knew the route. This way, I could save a bit more money, and with each trip, the savings slowly added up. I could do a lot with that small amount saved up from each trip! With the money that I saved, little by little, I could finally afford to buy the smaller unit.

When the owner of this side, the bigger room, wanted to sell off the property, I did not have enough money to buy it. The lady boss, who employed me for the gigs in Sài Gòn, she knew about this, too. Chị Mai also played the clarinet, and she also came up here to study clarinet with me. My whole family, we were living in that small room, about fifteen square meters. My wife and I (I had remarried after my first marriage ended in divorce in 1984) slept on a loft that I installed inside the room, and the two children had a small bed each; that was the best we could do. For this side of the apartment, the larger room, the company (or rather the lady boss) provided me with a loan, which I paid back in installments. With every performance, she recorded in the accounts book, deducting US$100 from the loan amount with every gig. By 1997, I had paid off the loan.

Other than this fantastic long-term gig I had in Sài Gòn, and other gigs that I could take up, I also managed to bring home more income by learning how to repair saxophones. When I started teaching at the conservatoire, the students were not well off. They were actually quite poor. I started learning, on my own, to repair saxophones so that my students could have better instruments for their study. Because of this, I developed another source of income! The news about me being competent in repairing saxophones spread, and people from different provinces and different places started sending instruments for me to repair! But it was around 1995 or 1996 that I really came to learn how to repair saxophones properly from a Japanese teacher. He loves jazz, plays jazz, and he has a heart of

Figure 2.5. A collaborative autoethnographic session.

gold. He came to Vietnam, and when he saw the poor condition of the instruments used by musicians of the National Symphony Orchestra, he offered to help them repair their instruments. I came to know about him from my musician friends. I learned that he was very good and very proficient at repairing saxophones. I prepared some money to have him repair my saxophones. I went to visit him with a plastic bag filled with cans of beer in one hand and a few saxophones (in cases) in the other hand. When I arrived, he looked at me, broke into a smile, and said, "I am so busy now." I told him, "Okay, can I watch?" I sat near him, opened a can of beer, and invited him to have the beer. He hesitated and motioned that he already had beer from his fridge. I was persistent, "Just a can of beer, I won't bother you. I just want to observe." He drank the beer and let me watch him repair the instruments.

While observing him repair instruments, I immediately noticed something. Before, when I was repairing saxophones to check if the key pads could close properly, I would blow smoke into the saxophone to check for "leakage." If I detected smoke coming out from a specific key pad, then it meant the pad was worn out, the padding was loose, or the key could not close properly. The instrument would squeak when I played that key. I noticed how he put a small flashlight into the saxophone to see if light was coming out from any key pad when all the keys were closed. Gosh, I was so stupid! Why didn't I think of doing this? When I got home, I immediately did the same thing. I went out to the shops to find a small flashlight. Later, I went back again to watch him repair instruments, and we chatted. He asked where I was working, and I answered, "The conservatoire. I teach saxophone, classical music, Vietnamese traditional music, and jazz." When he heard the word "jazz," he was rather surprised!

I was playing that night, so I offered to bring him to see my gig. I took him on my motorbike. He was so happy, shaking his legs to the music, and drinking beer. After the gig, he told me, "Bring your saxophone to my place tomorrow morning, let me repair it. Your saxophone is leaky! You play well and you have a beautiful sound, but your instrument is letting you down!" When I went to his place again, I said to him, "I hope that you can show me how to do it, so that I can repair my own saxophones." He replied without any hesitation, "You are wise. Alright then." I sat next to him and observed. He showed me how he repaired different parts of the saxophone, and I practiced those methods on my own instrument. Once I had done it on my instrument, I let him check. He inspected the parts I'd repaired and advised me which part was okay and which part was not; and he explained how I should have treated that part. For that one week, I kept going back to him to study how to repair instruments as soon as I finished my official work at the conservatoire. I brought him to see the city and to my gigs. I spent the rest of the time studying with him. That was a story I remember from 1995 or 1996. I addressed him as my teacher. His name is Kenychi Hirose [sic]. I dedicated a song to him in the Father, Son, and Jazz II concert in 2009.

The apartment on Hàng Giấy Street is a time capsule of memories for me. I have a strong attachment to this place. Now, the room is like a warehouse! In the living room I keep all the souvenirs, leftover furniture, CDs, stock of my own recorded albums, and old instruments from the jazz club. The bedroom is where I hang out. I sit on the bed to write and arrange my music, using my old guitar. For months before the big band concert in 2009, I sat there in the afternoon arranging music. All the different parts for trombones, trumpets, and saxophones for my big band, I arranged using the old guitar. I bought the Hàng Giấy apartment entirely with my hard work, playing jazz, teaching music, and repairing instruments. That was how I could afford to buy the apartment. The Hàng Giấy apartment, including the wooden shelter on the rooftop, contains all my deep and precious memories. When I opened the jazz club in 1997, I used that apartment to take out a loan. That was how I got enough money to open the jazz club.

Minh's Jazz Club

"Câu Lạc Bộ Nhạc Jazz: Jazz Club by Quyền Văn Minh" is what the large fluorescent light board installed above the windows secured with metal grills announced to passersby and visitors. In 1997, such a large fluorescent light board was a luxurious investment in contrast to the usual hand-painted signboards that

Figures 2.6a, 2.6b. Minh's Jazz Club, Giảng Võ Street.

restaurants and shops in Hà Nội usually put up. It made sense, since the jazz club usually operated after dark. Giảng Võ Street was not exactly the most well-lit street in Hà Nội then. Right above the main entrance, the words "Jazz Club in Hà Nội" in neon lighting fixed on a brick wall welcomed visitors. A jazz club in Vietnam? One might wonder in 1997 Hà Nội. But there was no mistaking that one was walking into a local jazz club in Hà Nội a decade after Đổi Mới, with the syncopating rhythms and improvised solos that grabbed one's attention. Câu

Lạc Bộ Nhạc Jazz was a simple place without any fanciful interior decoration or designer furniture. It was properly renovated and furnished, nonetheless. But the music was no simple, easy-listening stuff for the uninitiated. This was the first Vietnamese jazz club in the history of Vietnam under socialism. Minh was aware of the challenges of keeping the jazz club alive in an environment where jazz was still perceived as new, strange, and difficult by Vietnamese audiences. In 1997, Giảng Võ Street was not exactly an area where foreign visitors to Hà Nội would generally hang out. In addition, foreigners did not come into Vietnam expecting to find jazz outside of tourist enclaves such as five-star hotels like the Metropole. An experienced and talented musician but a first-time club owner, Minh could only depend on building a solid musical reputation for the jazz club if it was to stand any chance of survival. And he would need time.

I opened the jazz club so that musicians who wanted to play jazz could have a place to perform and a place to practice. But for many musicians, if they could not receive a certain level of remuneration, they would not play at the jazz club. So, from the time I started the club, only musicians who were totally passionate about jazz would come to play there. From the time I stepped into the professional music world, I was just a musician and a public servant of the state. I did not know anything about running a business. At the end of the day, the jazz club is a business even though that was not what I had in mind.

The friend who introduced me to the location on Giảng Võ Street was also the one who invited me to form a band to perform in Moscow in 1993. Initially, I had found a place on Phùng Hưng Street, a piano bar, where I could set up the jazz club. But this friend recommended the location on Giảng Võ Street. I trusted him. He had treated us really well during that overseas gig in Moscow, so I trusted him. Given that he was from a revolutionary family and extremely well connected to members of the political leadership, even playing tennis regularly with a few leaders of the country, I believed his words. After all, he was no stranger; he was supposed to be an "anh em" [brother].

In October 1997, I opened my jazz club at the Giảng Võ Exhibition Center. But I was stupid and naïve; I gave total trust to this friend, blindly. I confided in this friend who helped me rent the place that "I don't need much, but I need time. A jazz club needs time for people to get to know the music so that they will come." He assured me, "Don't worry, there is no limit to how long you can lease the venue. The jazz club can stay there for as long as you like." Within three months of opening the jazz club, I was forced to close it down because the government took back the property for a new development. At that time, I remember inviting the director of the exhibition center where the club was located to come to the opening night, but he did not turn up! I suspected that something was wrong.

Anyway, in late December, I remember clearly it was December 22, I was playing in a program for a television station when the director of the exhibition center finally came to talk to me about the situation of the jazz club. I had earlier received notice that the Ministry of Culture would be taking back the land at Giảng Võ Exhibition Center. "Minh, I know you are a good man, I totally understand your difficulties. But you are also a civil servant, a lecturer, and an Eminent Artist; and we work under the same ministry. The land belongs to the ministry, and the ministry is taking back the land for redevelopment, so I think you should start packing up and move out of the place as soon as possible. I understand that it wrenches the heart. I can let you use block A6 at the exhibition center to store your things until you can find a new venue to continue with the music." *I told him,* "Yes, I have already agreed to move out. But I am asking you to help me with one thing: we have already advertised our program for Christmas and New Year's Eve, could you let us fulfill the advertised programs for these few days? I promise you, on the morning of January 1, we will move everything out." *But he told me,* "The cause is already a lost one; what's lost is already lost. Even if you play for two more days or three more days, it would not make up for whatever you have already lost. Instead, you would develop a bad reputation with the ministry for not moving out in a timely manner, and people would gossip about your recalcitrance." *I had no choice, so I agreed to move out the very next morning. I could only accept my fate. It was painful. I felt like I had just received a knockout punch!*

On December 23, 1997, we packed up and left the venue on Giảng Võ Street. I put up a notice to apologize to all customers that the jazz club had to move out because the authorities had taken back the place. After I left, building management cut off electricity to the place and locked it up. But guess what? The friend who had recommended the place to me, he removed the apology notice I'd put up. He brought in a mobile electricity generator, set up chairs and tables, and paid a group of musicians to perform for the evenings of Christmas Eve and Christmas Day! He continued to operate the place as if it were still the jazz club that I had opened. Well, he knew that customers who had been coming to the jazz club were expecting us to open and play on both nights! He knew that he could make some good money by selling beer with live music on those two nights.

Opening the jazz club on Giảng Võ Street was a huge lesson for me. Opened for three months only to have to close it down! Well, the authorities did not immediately demolish the building for redevelopment after taking back the place, as was the reason given to me. Someone else took it over and turned it into a "bia hơi" [local draft beer] place for a while! That was rather infuriating! You would think they could at least lease out the place to a cultural business or classy establishment. It was only a few years later that they tore down the building. The best part was, I still had to pass by that venue now and then when I traveled for work between Hàng Giấy and the conservatoire!

I did not go anywhere for Tết Nguyên Đán [Vietnamese Spring Festival] that year. Raised the flag for three months only to have to lower it! It felt like I had fallen off a horse, and people wanted to show sympathy and express concern for me, but it only made me feel more pained. It was customary to go visiting relatives and friends on the first day of Tết, but I did not go anywhere at all. People went around to celebrate Tết with well wishes; I did not go anywhere that year. Anyone who came to my home for Tết visits, I had my family tell them I was not at home. You know how I tried to get over it? How I prevented myself from going crazy? I rented stacks and stacks of videotapes of period heroic and kung fu dramas, such as the Kim Dung [金庸] stories that were filmed in Hong Kong.[4] In those stories, you always have a character whose family members are harmed and killed, leaving the character all alone. The character tries to learn martial arts, but he is beaten and forced into a really pathetic corner before he finds a proper martial arts master. And the master does not teach him how to fight but instead makes him carry buckets of water, cook rice, and do all kinds of irrelevant things. The master pushes him to the limit to train him before teaching him martial arts. Then he becomes a successful martial arts exponent and might even be capable of rescuing the master! Watching those dramas was therapeutic. At the end of the day, justice would triumph over conniving little people. I did not want to read the original novels; that would be too heavy. Watching television dramas was more lighthearted. I was already stressed out; I did not need any further stress. But the general story line is the same even when the story is dramatized into a motion picture, a simple story line of how perseverance ultimately wins the day. I would teach my students this, the importance of perseverance.

Chị Mai, the lady boss who flew me to Sài Gòn to play with her band every week from 1993 to 1997, spoke to me after I had to close the jazz club. She suggested that I relocate to Sài Gòn and work with her to build up the jazz scene there. She had resources and could set up a jazz club; I just needed to take care of the music side of things. She would take care of my family. There was no need for me to choose the more difficult path. I decided that I wanted to develop jazz here in Hà Nội and did not take up Chị Mai's offer. I explained to her that I was still a state cadre and so I could not just drop everything, leave, and join her in Sài Gòn.

I knew that I had an important role to play teaching saxophone and jazz at the conservatoire. It was a role that I could not abandon for my personal comfort and selfish ambitions. After the jazz club closed, the board of directors at the conservatoire told me, "Don't worry about the jazz club. Just focus on your work at the conservatoire. Complete all your certification and get promoted up the ranks at the conservatoire." However, I knew very well that I had joined the conservatoire in order to pass on what I knew and to cultivate the next generation of jazz musicians. My role there was to teach, not to rise up the ranks as an administrator. I understood very well that I had already forsaken the opportunity to rise up the ranks as a performing artist in the official arts and culture system when I joined the conservatoire. I made that decision because I wanted to put in place in the professional music education system a proper curriculum for saxophone, and because I wanted jazz to be accepted as a proper genre of music in Vietnam. I also knew that if I wanted to work on my own career to rise up the ranks as a full professor or become one of the directors of the conservatoire, I would have to compromise in my mission to develop a new generation of jazz musicians at the conservatoire and outside the conservatoire. I chose to focus on the mission of developing jazz in Vietnam. Let me put it this way: for classical music, the system and society were producing loads of talents for the genre. Classical music could select the best musicians to play in the National Symphony Orchestra and develop the genre. Every student who joined the conservatoire then aspired to be a successful classical musician. But not jazz. Jazz had nothing to begin with in Vietnam. Someone had to do it. I had to do it. I wanted to do it.

Tết had finished. That was already in 1998. I dug deep and searched wide. By chance, I met a friend who told me about an available venue. The venue, located on 16 Lê Thái Tổ Street by Hoàn Kiếm Lake, was leased to a restaurant called Sakura at that time, and the operator was planning to move to another location. 16 Lê Thái Tổ was a great location! I paid the middleman a sum of money to rent the place. This second venue where I set up the jazz club, 16 Lê Thái Tổ, was also owned by the Ministry of Culture. In Vietnam, in everything we do, there are always the hard formalities and the soft formalities. This has been something that I have had to live with since the day I started the jazz club in 1997. When I rented the space, it was in the name of a "joint" venture between the Vietnam-Japan Friendship Association and the jazz club. The association was renting the whole building at that time. By setting up the jazz club there, I contributed to the rent that the association was paying to the ministry for use of the building.

When I rented the Lê Thái Tổ place, I completely renovated the washroom to make it really clean and proper but only made minimal modifications to the original interior decoration. I was more careful this time; I did not put in too much money to renovate the place at the beginning. I just tried my best to play good music; I focused on the music. I had learned my lesson from Giảng Võ!

The association promised me that the lease was a guaranteed two-year contract. But in the middle of 1999, the ministry took back the place to house the Hội Khai Trí Tiến Đức [L'Association pour la Formation Intellectuelle et Morale des Annamites]. The place was classified as a heritage building and restored to its original architecture and interior decor of the French colonial era to celebrate 990 years of the founding of Thăng Long city [the old name of Hà Nội] in the year 2000. I had to go again! I had to accept my fate. For eight months beginning in late 1998, the jazz club operated at this superb venue right by Hoàn Kiếm Lake. I had invested only a little to spruce up the place, so when

Figure 2.7. Minh's Jazz Club, 16 Lê Thái Tổ Street.

we had to move, it was not so much of a loss, financially speaking. Because I had learned my lesson and just focused on the music, the most valuable thing that happened when I departed 16 Lê Thái Tổ was that we were ready to record my first CD, Birth '99.

From October 1998 to June 1999, Minh's Jazz Club was a fixture on the western bank of Hoàn Kiếm Lake. A charming standalone French colonial building constructed in 1919, 16 Lê Thái Tổ hosted the first National Assembly of the Democratic Republic of Vietnam in 1946 after Hồ Chí Minh declared independence from the French. Located on the second floor, the jazz club was smaller than what Minh had at Giảng Võ. The location was most advantageous, as local visitors and foreign tourists routinely gathered on the banks of Hoàn Kiếm Lake to enjoy the evening lakeside breeze and beautiful scenery that was a perfect blend of Vietnamese history, vestiges of French and Chinese cultural influences, and remnants of Soviet grandeur from the Cold War era. Minh made good use of the location by adorning the corridor overlooking the lake with a row of table and chairs for his guests to enjoy the music and the view. Jazz was the default evening soundtrack on this side of Hoàn Kiếm Lake after Minh's Jazz Club moved into the building. In his eight months of residency at 16 Lê Thái Tổ, Minh assembled his band, consisting of Quyền Thiện Đắc (soprano and tenor saxophones), Phạm Lê Phương (piano), Phạm Tuấn Hùng, (piano), Phan Trung Kiên (bass), Đào Minh Pha (bass), Hà Đình Huy (drums), and Lê Việt Hùng (drums) to practice the eight original tunes he had composed for his first jazz album, *Birth '99*. They practiced intensively and were ready to record by the time Minh was forced to hand the venue back to the Ministry of Culture. Minh and his band recorded the tunes at Dihavina Studio, Hà Nội, during August 12–14, 1999.

Not too long after we left 16 Lê Thái Tổ, I found another venue at 31 Lương Văn Can. This place at Lương Văn Can was owned by my former employer, the Thăng Long Song-and-Dance Troupe. Two business ventures, one after the other, had operated at 31 Lương Văn Can before I came to rent the place. The first business that rented the venue was operated by the son of a powerful politician. Together with a few friends, he had opened a seafood restaurant there. It did not do well. For a whole year, they did not receive enough customers, so they sold the lease to someone else. The second business was run by a guy who used to be a journalist, and he also owned several advertising agencies in the country. He took over the contract, renovated the place, operated it as a restaurant, and had people come in to perform ethnic folk music as well as popular music to entertain customers. But the venture was not successful, and he was ready to transfer the lease. I came to learn about the availability of the place and bought the lease from him. Two owners in two years! It certainly did not sound like a good venue. To be honest, when they were constructing the building, construction workers dug out skeletal remains of people who had probably died during the resistance war against the French. They might have been resistance fighters, or they might have been just ordinary citizens; we never found out. The building was constructed on such grounds. The two businesspeople who rented this place before me, these were very powerful people who had money, resources, and connections. Still, their businesses failed. Yet a nobody like me dared to rent the place to operate a jazz club!

By then, I already had some experience running a jazz club. Jazz music was already difficult to sell to Vietnamese. As for foreigners, they did not believe that there could actually be jazz in Vietnam or jazz played by Vietnamese. With the original objective of opening a place for musicians to play jazz, I persisted. When I bought the lease for 31 Lương Văn Can, it was rather costly. I needed a place for the jazz club, so I asked another friend to help. I managed to raise enough money to take over the lease at Lương Văn Can. As part of the deal, I bought everything in the restaurant: tables, chairs, kitchen equipment, and whatever else they had. It was a tough deal. The jazz club finally reopened at 31 Lương Văn Can on October 23, 1999.

Figure 2.8. Minh's Jazz Club, 31 Lương Văn Can (photo by Deborah Jan Aronson).

Located on the ground floor of the premises of the Thăng Long Song-and-Dance Troupe, Minh's Jazz Club at 31 Lương Văn Can was a short five-minute stroll from the most scenic circular junction in Hà Nội, Quảng Trường Đông Kinh Nghĩa Thục (Đông Kinh Nghĩa Thục Plaza) by the northern bank of Hoàn Kiếm Lake. Minh's Jazz Club was now a part of Hà Nội's Old Quarter, the city's chief tourist attraction. What the club lost in terms of scenery at the Hoàn Kiếm lakeside venue was made up by the nostalgic and inimitable charm of Hà Nội's Old Quarter. In general, shops in the Old Quarter were limited by the lack of parking space, as additional structures were quickly added to the front and sides of old buildings by owners to exploit both the property boom and commercial opportunities that came in the decade following Đổi Mới. Hanoians called these additions, thrown up on any available space adjacent to an original structure, *nhà dù nhảy* (parachute houses). At 31 Lương Văn Can, however, there was plenty of space at the entrance to the premises of the Thăng Long Song-and-Dance Troupe for customers, musicians, and staff of the jazz club to leave their motorbikes, which were parked in orderly fashion by the building's security guards. With a more spacious venue than at 16 Lê Thái Tổ, Minh could set up a bigger bandstand that was better elevated, and guests were seated at tables that were generously spaced out for a jazz club. For a period of time, Minh even offered a full menu of drinks and food, being able to operate a proper kitchen at the venue. Each table had an unhindered view of the bandstand. For a while, Minh's Jazz Club was even a fashionable dining place!

The observant patron would notice, however, discreetly placed by the left side of the main entrance near the bar, a small altar adorned with plates of fresh

Figure 2.9. Inside 31 Lương Văn Can (photo by Deborah Jan Aronson).

fruits, burned joss sticks dangling in an urn, and bottles of unopened whiskey and cognac. Minh might be pushing the frontiers of music, but he remained rooted in his cultural context.

When friends come and bring gifts to me at the jazz club, a simple bottle of whiskey, for example, I always make it a point to place it at the altar where I offer joss sticks daily. Every time a friend gives me a bottle of whiskey, I always tell him, "Let me place it at the altar and make some offerings first before we drink together." It is a way for me to be mindful and respectful of the place where the jazz club is located. At the same time, these are also reminders of the support and encouragement I receive from friends. These reminders always lift my spirits and motivate me to continue with my work. There is no question that I have already made the resolution right at the beginning, but it is always helpful to receive some motivation along the way. I guess you could call this a story of idealism and beliefs. At the end of the day, it seemed that my cycle of life [chu kỳ] with the Thăng Long Song-and-Dance Troupe was only good for ten years. I stayed with them as a musician for ten years, from 1981 to 1991. I actually started teaching at the conservatoire in 1989, but I only had my tenure fully transferred over officially in 1991. October 1999 was when I finally reopened the jazz club at 31 Lương Văn Can, which was the third venue that hosted the club. Ten years later, in 2009, we had to move again, ending the jazz club's tenure at the Thăng Long Song-and-Dance Troupe's premises. Well, the two operators before me lasted less than a year each, but we managed to stay at Lương Văn Can for ten years!

After we moved out of Lương Văn Can, I was still trying find a place, but the musicians had already called to ask when we could play again! After having

Figure 2.10. Altar and offerings at Minh's Jazz Club.

to move out of 31 Lương Văn Can, there was no way I could rent a place to operate the jazz club for US$2,000 or $3,000 a month in 2009. To rent a place that could host the jazz club properly would cost me at least $4,000 to $5,000 by then. To put it colloquially, I got "squeezed like a lime." I finally found a venue on Mã Mây Street, known for its little bars and restaurants catering to Western tourists. I had to come to an agreement with the owner on how to split the cost of operations and profits from hosting the jazz club. After we moved the things to that location, the owner wanted to change the conditions of our agreement! I rejected these new conditions, and so we did not set up the jazz club there. Then we moved to Trấn Vũ Street, just in front of Trúc Bạch Lake (right next to West Lake). We played there for three weeks, and after that we had to move again. Initially, we agreed to place the bandstand right by the window, so the band and music would be the focus of attention. A week later, right during the time I was on a business trip in Sài Gòn, the venue operators moved the bandstand to the back, so that during the day customers could sit by the window and view the lake. I could not agree with that. We immediately started looking for the next location. That was when an old friend, Bình, whom I met when I was working

Figure 2.11. Minh's Jazz Club, Quán Sứ Street (photo by Deborah Jan Aronson).

at Trường Thể Dục Thể Thao Từ Sơn [Từ Sơn College of Physical Education and Sports], offered to help. Bình had become a very successful businessman by then. This was also the reason that I added "Bình" to the name Minh's Jazz Club, and now it is known as Bình Minh's Jazz Club. We moved to Quán Sứ. At that time, we were choosing between two venues, both located on the third floor of the respective buildings. It was not really ideal, but those were the only choices available at that time. One was located at the corner of Phan Bội Châu Street, where Windows Café used to be. The other was located right next to Quán Sứ Pagoda. The advantage of the Quán Sứ venue was that it had parking space in the back. A huge parking space. By then there were already many cars on the roads in Hà Nội, so that was really advantageous. Again, we had to operate the club in partnership with the existing owner of the place, just like the ones at Mã Mây Street and Trấn Vũ Street. At Quán Sứ, we operated on the third floor. We had to procure our supply of drinks from the restaurant downstairs, the owner of the venue. I looked at the price of the drinks; it was too expensive! But what could I do? That part of the business belonged to the other partner, not me. There was nothing much that I could do to make the situation better. The venue at Quán Sứ was not desirable in the long run. Then in 2014, we finally moved to the present venue, 1 Tràng Tiền, behind the Hà Nội Opera House. I could now operate the jazz club as we did back at Lương Văn Can.

Over the years, Minh's Jazz Club has gradually grown in stature as a tourist fixture in Hà Nội; it is the best place to catch good, live jazz in Vietnam. Located just behind the majestic Hà Nội Opera House and next to Nhà Hát Kịch (Drama Theater), Minh's Jazz Club is now located among its peers in the cultural hub of downtown Hà Nội. The club established its reputation as *the place* for jazz in Vietnam during the decade at 31 Lương Văn Can, beginning in 1999. Within a few years, Minh's Jazz Club also became a venue for jam sessions, when international jazz musicians stopped in Hà Nội at the invitation or with the support of foreign embassies or development agencies stationed in the capital. The club hosted Australian jazz trumpeter Scott Tinkler's trio for a jam session after their concert at the Hà Nội Opera House in early June 2000. Chris Minh Doky, a Vietnamese Danish jazz bassist from Copenhagen, gave four performances at the club in late February 2001. Chris Minh Doky returned to Hà Nội with a bigger entourage of European jazz musicians in late November of the same year for the first European Jazz Festival in Vietnam, sponsored by the European Union's delegation in Hà Nội and Vietnam's Ministry of Culture and Information. Minh's Jazz Club was one of four official venues hosting that inaugural jazz festival.

In November 2002, the jazz club played host to the second edition of the European Jazz Festival in Vietnam. Earlier in 2002, Quyền Văn Minh also hosted Australian jazz musician Mark Isaacs at 31 Lương Văn Can. At the third European Jazz Festival in Vietnam in 2003, Minh finally met one of his idols from his early years of listening to jazz on vinyl and cassettes, Felix Slováček, a saxophone and clarinet master from the Czech Republic. As the premier place to be for jazz in Vietnam, Minh's Jazz Club has continued to host visiting jazz musicians over the years, whether for casual visits, jam sessions, or full performances. Among the jazz musicians who have visited the club are: Ismail "Pops" Mohamed (South Africa) in 2005; Amir Gwirtzman (Israel) in 2007; the Basadi Women of Jazz group (South Africa) in 2008; Joachim Mencel (Poland) in 2010; the Ari Roland Jazz Quartet (United States) in 2011; the Jarek Śmietana Quartet (Poland) in 2011; the P. O. Nilsson Trio (Sweden) in 2012; and the US Air Force Band of the Pacific-Asia's jazz combo (United States) in 2015, among many others.

Two visits to Minh's Jazz Club by overseas jazz musicians were particular memorable for Quyền Văn Minh. In December 2009, the Japanese jazz pianist Yamashita Yosuke (山下洋輔) gave his first concert with the Vietnam National Symphony Orchestra (VNSO), conducted by maestro Honna Tetsuji (本名徹次), in Hà Nội, performing George Gershwin's *Rhapsody in Blue* and other classic jazz pieces. Minh and his students filled in the saxophone section of the orchestra for the concert. Yosuke, a jazz giant in his own right, is a pioneer of avant-garde and free jazz in Japan and has recorded with jazz greats such as Hino Terumasa (日野皓正), Kikuchi Masabumi (菊地雅章), Cecil McBee, and Pheeroan akLaff.[5] After the concert, Yosuke visited Minh's Jazz Club and jammed with the band. Minh and his students also played in Yosuke's seventieth birthday concert with the VNSO, held in Hà Nội in February 2012, and Minh appeared

Figures 2.12a, 2.12b. Yamashita Yosuke's concert in Hà Nội, December 2009 (photos by Deborah Jan Aronson).

as a guest musician in Yosuke's subsequent participation as a featured soloist in the VNSO's classical jazz concerts.

Four years earlier, in late November 2005, Herbie Hancock, Wayne Shorter, and Nnenna Freelon had led an entourage of eight students from the Thelonious Monk Institute of Jazz to visit Vietnam. Hancock and Shorter are, of course, jazz

Minh's Jazz Club

Figures 2.13a, 2.13b, 2.13c, 2.13d. Yamashita Yosuke's seventieth birthday concert with the Vietnam National Symphony Orchestra (photos by Deborah Jan Aronson).

Figure 2.14. With Herbie Hancock, 2005 (photo by Deborah Jan Aronson).

Figure 2.15. With Wayne Shorter, 2005 (photo by Deborah Jan Aronson).

Figure 2.16. With Herbie at the jazz club (photo by Deborah Jan Aronson).

giants who need little introduction. Quyền Văn Minh hosted the jazz dignitaries at Minh's Jazz Club.

When I participated in the first European Jazz Festival in Vietnam in November 2001, foreign musicians who played at the festival came to the jazz club to jam after their scheduled performances. Ever since then, jazz musicians visiting Hà Nội would always drop by the jazz club. The club has hosted a number of really famous artists, such as Herbie Hancock, who sat right here and chatted with me, and we took photographs together. Among Hancock's entourage was Wayne Shorter and members of the Monk Institute. The night they visited the jazz club, the place was totally packed. There was no place to sit and hardly any standing room. Herbie Hancock was really surprised that a jazz club actually existed in Hà Nội and in Vietnam. As for me, I looked at the entourage and I asked myself if there would be a day when jazz in Vietnam could have the same learning environment as these students had, studying at the Monk Institute. I had never before dreamed that I could one day stand side by side with Herbie Hancock onstage. But we did! I had never before imagined that I could play my heart out on the stage with a jazz great and with due respect for each other. And that we might learn something about one another. I never imagined such a scene when, as a fourteen-year-old boy, I accidentally learned that jazz existed in this world!

TRACK 3

Growing Up

The socialist revolution began permeating every aspect of society in North Vietnam as the country came under communist rule in 1954. Jazz, once heard in the luxurious colonial enclaves in Hà Nội and included in the broadcast playlists of Radio Hà Nội, went silent. Revolutionary music, or "red music," dominated the official soundscape. In general, children who grew up in the years of the socialist revolution heard very little of other music in the public sphere. In the 1960s, the Second Indochina War extended into the North as the United States began the systematic bombing of major cities and military installations north of the seventeenth parallel. In the midst of the socialist revolution and war, Quyền Văn Minh accidentally encountered jazz through the transistor radio, igniting his passion for the music.

Hà Nội, 1954

Hồ Chí Minh's declaration of independence on September 2, 1945, was immediately challenged as the French refused to give up their colonial possession. As the Vietnamese fought for independence, the First Indochina War dragged on for a devastating nine years. The war ended with the battle of Điện Biên Phủ, where Việt Minh forces delivered a crushing defeat to the French. The Vietnamese finally gained their independence in 1954, but the country was divided between the communist-ruled North in the form of the Democratic Republic of Vietnam and the noncommunist South, which came to be known as the Republic of Vietnam in 1955. Peace returned to the country, but the country was divided, and a socialist revolution soon began in the North.

With the communist victory, noncommunist supporters and people wary of the intentions of the communists departed the North, if they could. Hence, the great Bắc Nam Tư (North '54) migration, during which almost one million people uprooted and left their homes of many generations in the North for the noncommunist-ruled South.[1] The rich and well-off in Hà Nội sold off their properties and took whatever possessions they could carry with them.² Even before the communists began implementing their ideological revolution in the newly independent nation, those departing Hà Nội had already lent a hand. In the words of Georges Boudarel, "Hanoi was emptied of the French presence, and it seemed to Western journalists to be a dead city. All machines, necessary supplies, files, and technical installations had been taken to the South."³ Not that the communists who had just taken over the country wanted much of any foreign or "unrevolutionary" legacy to stay behind. Hà Nội was ultimately the seat of the colonial administration. The city was filled with vestiges of colonialism, cultural artifacts of the imperialists, and aesthetics of the capitalists.⁴ The communists, after all, had won the war with a peasant army on the back of a promise to liberate the oppressed from colonialism and feudalism through a socialist revolution.

In the euphoria of being freed from French colonial oppression, the communists went about to liberate peasants from landlordism and the poor from class exploitation through the radical Cải Cách Ruộng Đất (Agrarian Land Reform). Land reform teams went about confiscating lands and properties from the wealthy property-owning class to redistribute to the landless and poor. Every household was categorized on the basis of their *lý lịch* (background) by assessing how much property they had, the professions of individual family members, for whom they had worked, and any role they had played in the resistance war against the French.⁵ The communist revolution penetrated every aspect of life, as the old society was turned upside down by this fervent attempt to redistribute land, property, and wealth. This radical reform was carried out as early as 1953 in areas liberated from the French and escalated with a feverish momentum after 1954. Cải Cách Ruộng Đất tapered down only in 1956 following strong public criticism, from even among loyal revolutionaries, against the violent nature with which it was implemented and the widespread abuse of authority by the land reform teams. At the end of the day, any criticism against the revolution was ultimately rejected, as demonstrated by the *Nhân Văn–Giai Phẩm* (*Humanities–Masterpieces*) affair (1954–1958). Taken aback by the ideology-driven radical change and violence, Vietnamese intellectuals and artists took to two journals, *Nhân Văn* (*Humanities*) and *Giai Phẩm* (*Masterpieces*), to demand freedom of expression so as to "speak truth to power." Hà Nội, after all, was both the political capital of the country and the intellectual center of Vietnam. In turn, the communist state clamped down on these criticisms, closed down the two journals, and finally imprisoned their writers and editors.⁶ Under the Democratic Republic of Vietnam (DRV), Hà Nội was the ideological center of the socialist revolution and was expected to serve as the ideological role model.

The socialist revolution was in full force when Quyền Văn Minh was born, picked up music, and encountered jazz.

I was born during wartime, on July 11, 1954. My parents named me Quyền Văn Minh. My mother gave birth to me in Hà Nội at a "nhà hộ sinh" [maternity assistance station] on Phùng Hưng Street at dawn [bình minh]. My childhood days were hard times. Those were the days when everyone in Vietnam had to go through tremendous difficulties. I was born in a family of amateur musicians. My father played the guitar and knew how to play the saxophone a little, but he was just an amateur musician. My mother was a singer; she was a very good singer. She had a beautiful voice. During the war, my parents had joined the resistance to fight against the French. My father served as an artist cadre in the cultural attachment of an infantry regiment that performed for combat soldiers to give them encouragement. My mother sang in the same cultural attachment. They were deployed to the battlefront in Thái Nguyên, where they married each other. In 1950, they gave birth to my elder brother and named him Quyền Văn Chương. Because he was born in difficult circumstances on the front line, my brother was undernourished and often fell ill. There was not enough food, and living conditions were tough. My mother was determined to keep my brother alive, so they had to put aside their work for the revolution. My father followed my mother's decision to leave the military zone and returned to Hà Nội. In that sense, they were considered as people who did not follow the revolution all the way to the end.

They found a better life back in the city. My brother's health gradually turned for the better, and he survived. But my mother knew that from the day they left the revolution halfway in Thái Nguyên to return to Hà Nội, things would not be easy after we won the war. Because when you join the revolution, you have to go all the way. But to save my brother, they had to return to Hà Nội. In the old days, people judged those who left the revolution halfway as "not fully righteous" people. Of course, even though my parents returned to Hà Nội, they did not work for the French at all! My father managed to buy a car to ferry passengers between Hà Nội and Hải Phòng. This was our family's main source of income. My father played the guitar, so he also opened classes at home and taught some students. He was just an amateur musician. By 1954, my father had accumulated some assets. Assets could be a real liability at that time; you could be labeled as a capitalist and classified as belonging to the class of exploiters! My parents arranged to send what little money they had to relatives who had already moved to France.

When our country was finally liberated in 1954, my mother told my father that it would be best if the whole family left the country. Many Vietnamese in Hà Nội left for France. But my father refused to listen, even though my mother had already managed to get plane tickets for the family to leave. At that time, I was still a baby in my mother's arms. Because my father refused to go, we had to give up our air tickets, and so we stayed behind. Having to stay back in

Vietnam, my parents were also worried about the political situation, because they had not followed the revolution all the way to the end. Politically, those were pretty grim years. Soon after liberation, the government launched the Cải Cách Ruộng Đất [Agrarian Land Reform] policy, and those were pretty volatile years. Even many good people lost their lives during those years of radical change and anxiety. Although my parents had not worked for the French, my family was perceived as belonging to an unfavorable social category from a political point of view. We were not categorized as belonging to the capitalist class, because you need to possess a lot of property to be categorized as such. Those were the days when the issue of political "colors" [màu sắc chính trị] could be really frightening and have dire consequences! We were classified as "tiểu tư sản trí thức" [petty bourgeoisie intellectuals] because we had a piece of property, my father's car, which he drove as a taxi to make a living. He joined the Thống Nhất Passenger Transport Cooperative of Hà Nội immediately after the war. By joining the cooperative, the whole family was allowed to stay in the twenty-five-square-meter apartment on Hàng Giấy Street. While my father served as a transport worker during the day, my mother stayed home to look after us.

I was born in such a context. I will always remember the hunger of those years. Everyone around was undergoing the same kind of suffering. Those were terrifying years. When I was packing things to move from Hàng Giấy to Nghi Tàm a few years ago, I came across an old French book with its cover torn off that belonged to my father. I remember my father telling me that he had to remove the cover because they could be arrested for possessing a French language book! That was how paranoid people were in those days. My father was fluent in French. When I was a kid, most of the adults spoke some French. We wanted to learn French, too. But my father absolutely refused to teach us or let us learn French. It was only when we started going to school, normal public school, that we started learning new languages. I learned some Chinese, or rather, Mandarin. Those were the days when relations between Vietnam and China were really close, so we were able to learn a little bit of Mandarin in school. Later on, we had to learn Russian in school instead. But I did not acquire much proficiency in either language, because they did not really teach us that much in the public schools anyway.

I am the second child. My brother was born in Thái Nguyên during the resistance war; he is the eldest. By the time my mother gave birth to me, the country was almost liberated. By then, our living conditions were also much better, so I was better nourished from the moment I was born. I was the healthiest among the four siblings, so I was able to help out with a lot of work at home. I have a younger sister, she later became a lecturer of cello in Hà Nội, but she left for Poland with her husband some time ago and settled down over there in the early 1990s. They have two children who studied there. Maybe when the *children are older, my sister and her husband might return to their homeland. Her husband is also a former music lecturer. My youngest brother was born in 1960; he also plays the guitar as an amateur musician. In fact, my eldest brother also plays the guitar. When you view the 1988 and 1989 solo recital programs, you can see both brothers performing with me. My youngest brother played guitar, and my eldest brother played bass guitar in the solo recital programs I performed at the Hội Nhạc Sĩ [Association of Musicians].*

Living in a Centrally Planned Economy

Under the Democratic Republic of Vietnam, inhabitants north of the seventeenth parallel lived in a centrally planned economy. Beginning in 1958, the communist regime rolled out nationwide policies to realize ideals envisioned in the communist revolution. Agricultural lands were collectivized and organized into agricultural cooperatives. In fact, all economic production and service units were organized into some form of cooperative managed by the "people" through the state and guided by the party.[7] Individuals were classified into specific professions: farmer, craftsperson, artist, technician, doctor, teacher, and so on. Goods and daily necessities were distributed according to needs painstakingly calculated by the state based on one's profession, age, and gender as well as leadership position in the communist party and state hierarchy. To implement this economic logic, the Vietnamese state issued ration stamps to control the exchange and flow of money and goods. The state was the only legitimate source for all goods exchanged. In Vietnam, this period of time is commonly referred to as Thời Bao Cấp (the Subsidy Period). As the journalist Ngô Minh's lively memoir about life under the Vietnamese centrally planned economy so correctly unveils, Thời Bao Cấp in the North began soon after the war ended in 1954.[8]

During my childhood days, it was the era of ration stamps [tem phiếu]. That was the Subsidy Period. You could only buy things if you had the state-issued ration stamps. My mother took care of all household matters. We were all still very young then. My mother also accepted some odd jobs at home to make sweaters for some cooperatives, which then exported them to other socialist countries. Other than attending school, my elder brother and I helped out with household chores and my mother's work making sweaters. My younger sister was also able to help out with the lighter aspects of chores and work at home.

My mother would usually task me and my brother to do the "shopping" for the family. She would instruct me the night before, "Son, early next morning, go and queue up at the trading shop [cửa hàng mậu dịch] for this item, then queue up at another trading shop for that item," and so on. My eldest brother had more schoolwork to do than me, and my two younger siblings were too small to help. I was usually the one who helped my mother with all kinds of household chores.

For these "shopping days," I had to wake up really early to be at the front of the line at the shop to purchase the items requested by my mother. There were two ways to queue up. One was to physically queue up at one shop and at the same time, stake a place with an object in the queue for the adjacent shop. Another was to write one's name and details on a piece of paper and post it at the shop to start a queue, so that other people who came later could write down their names one after another. I was born during a more peaceful time, so I was relatively healthy and strong, and could move faster than other people. Early in the morning, the truck carrying the food supply would arrive at the respective "trading" shops. I would volunteer to help the ladies at the shops, we called them "cô mậu dịch" [trade ladies], to carry all these heavy goods into the shop. The ladies working at the shops always appreciated my help and would let me make the first purchase.

It made a huge difference to be among the first at the shop. Being first in line meant a big deal! In those days, everyone wanted to buy fatty meat. With fatty meat, one could use the fat to fry other food in place of cooking oil, which was very limited in supply. If you were at the front of the line, it was more likely that you could purchase meat that had more fat. Pork ribs or the big bones for making soup might also not be available by the time you reached the counter if you were at the back of the line. Even though everyone was assigned a fixed amount for different items based on the ration stamps issued, the shops usually did not receive sufficient stock to be able sell to everyone. Possessing a ration stamp was no guarantee that one could get the goods. Only after I had finished buying all the things tasked by my mother, could I go home to wash up. My mother would then cook breakfast, and after having my breakfast, I would go to school.

Every Sunday, when everyone had their rest day, my mother always organized a gathering for the whole family. My mother would save up the week's money and stamps to buy a whole chicken or "bún chả" [barbecued meat skewers with rice noodles] for this family gathering. We used to call this family gathering "ăn tươi" [to "eat fresh"]. There would always be a whole chicken, or a whole fish, or more meat for ăn tươi. On normal days, there would usually be very little meat in our meals. The main course was vegetables. There could be a little bit of dried salted fish to give the food more taste. I would always remember the constant hunger we had to endure from day to day during that era, but there was no other way. We could only eat when we got home, and we could only eat during family mealtime. There was no extra food available. I was always waiting for my mother to come home. Because when she got home, she would prepare lunch or dinner for the family, and that meant that it was time to eat!

The 1954 Geneva Agreements that ended the First Indochina War split the country into North and South at the seventeenth parallel. It only brought temporary peace to Vietnam. The agreement also called for general elections to be held in 1956 on both sides to elect a unified government that would bring the North and South together. After Ngô Đình Diệm established the Republic of Vietnam in 1955 to replace King Bảo Đại's State of Vietnam south of the seventeenth parallel following a rigged referendum, the general elections meant to unify the country were never held. While the United States continued to pour in more support for Ngô Đình Diệm's regime in the South, the Vietnamese communists continued their insurgent activities in the South with the aim of reunifying the country under communist rule. The Cold War, which quickly enveloped the whole of Southeast Asia in the 1950s, would soon escalate into a "hot war" in Vietnam.

In 1960, the communist National Liberation Front for South Vietnam (NLF) was formally established with the goal of liberating the South from Ngô Đình Diệm's regime and the United States. Following the Gulf of Tonkin incident in 1964, in which the USS *Maddox* was engaged in a deadly skirmish with DRV navy boats, the United States became directly involved in the armed conflict against the Vietnamese communists. The United States launched Operation Pierce Arrow, which directly attacked military installations in DRV territory. The Second Indochina War had officially been "declared." In March 1965, US forces executed Operation Rolling Thunder, a sustained bombing campaign against North Vietnam's major cities and installations that would last until 1968.[9]

Residents of Hà Nội responded to the extended US bombing campaign by digging bomb shelters along the city's streets, where everyone would quickly take shelter upon hearing the public air raid alarm. Children and the elderly were evacuated from the city to rural areas in the Red River Delta and the midlands, while working adults continued with their daily lives to keep production going in the centrally planned economy. As Philippe Pappin reports, families were separated from one another during this period of time. For parents to be able to see their children evacuated to the countryside, they had to pedal bicycles for hours across many kilometers to where the children were staying and pedal back to the city during the weekend. Letters, written on thin pelure paper and delivered by friends, relatives, and even strangers traveling between the city and the countryside, became a primary channel for families to maintain contact during this period.[10]

The war came to Hà Nội, and we had to evacuate our home. During the war, warplanes rained bombs from above, and everything was destroyed. I remember it was particularly bad in 1967. We were evacuated from our home in the city. It was a very depressing time. A really difficult time. We were always hungry because we had to donate everything, almost everything, to contribute to the war effort. I still remember, our parents would come and visit us in the countryside during the weekends, and they usually tried to bring a bit more food for us to eat. You see, although the children were evacuated, the adults continued to stay and work

Figure 3.1. Quyền Văn Minh and family.

in Hà Nội. The children were evacuated to the surrounding rural areas, some twenty to thirty kilometers away from Hà Nội, such as Thường Tín or farther. We were even sent as far as Bắc Giang. We moved to different places so many times! That was because everyone was suffering during the war. We kept having to evacuate and having to rely on people, so sometimes they refused to shelter us. But we also had to be understanding. After all, there were four of us, and so it was really a huge burden on these very kind people, too! Just before the war arrived in Hà Nội, I had started learning the guitar at home.

Growing up, life in those days was tough. We just had to cope with the social context of that time period. I remember the hunger. But I also remember the joy of music from that era because of my mother. And I think that all her children felt that influence. Whenever she returned home from errands or work, she would sit down and listen to us play and practice music. We managed to pick up some music at home. Although all of us could play some music in my family, I did not come from a family of professional musicians. We were not professional musicians. It was only when I joined Đoàn Ca Múa Quân Khu Việt Bắc [Việt Bắc Military Region Song-and-Dance Troupe] that I embarked on the journey to become a professional musician. Even then, I received no formal musical training.

Learning Music

The first instrument I picked up was the guitar. That was in 1967. When I started playing the guitar, I had aspirations to become a proper guitarist, too! I practiced very hard. My father opened a guitar class at home, and students came to our *apartment to study with him. There were three guitars at home. My father used the better guitar among the three to teach during his lessons. The guitar was in good condition but was not exactly of exquisite quality. It was actually quite ordinary, and it was made in Vietnam. The other two guitars were for students to practice with when they came for lessons. Although my father was only an amateur musician, students could learn something about the guitar. I observed what they were doing, and I practiced on my own. We had a practice book for guitar at home, which my father used for teaching his students. I practiced following the instructions in the book, too.*

My father did not have time to teach me music. Everyone had to work in a specific vocation in order to earn a living in those days. My father only taught in his free time, which was primarily reserved for his students. I observed how my father taught his students, and I practiced on my own. That was how I learned the basics. I was able to follow the music notes on my own.

When I was small, we had the chance to attend lessons at a children's music club at the Ấu Trí Viên [a kindergarten], now known as Cung Thiếu Nhi [Children Palace], located on Lý Thái Tổ Street. At the music club, they taught young children simple musical knowledge such as learning to read notes and "do-re-mi," solfège. All the kids went there, and they taught us the black notes, the white notes, the sharps, and the flats. They taught for one hour each week so that children could read musical notes. I learned a bit of this, so I could read the notes in the practice book that my father used for teaching his students. There was really no one teaching me or guiding me in a formal way. It was entirely self-study. I would do my housework, rinse the rice, and wash the vegetables, and then I would practice the guitar. I listened to what he was teaching and observed what the students were practicing. After that, I would open the book and play according to the notes on the pages. Those weekly sessions at the children's club basically taught me how to read notes and listen to "do-re-mi."

Right from the beginning when I started playing, there was not a single proper music lesson that I ever had. When I managed to master a particular piece, I would go to my mother and play for her. My mother listened and would praise me, "Wonderful!," and encourage me to keep practicing. My mother was a very good singer who had a very beautiful voice. You could say that she was my first and only teacher. My mother taught me how to listen and encouraged me to put what I heard with my ears into what I could play on guitar, and later the clarinet. When I started taking up gigs and playing in the song-and-dance troupes, I was able to pick up new music very quickly. Over time, this ability made me into one of the most preferred musicians among the notable singers to accompany them on stage. They could sing what they wanted and the way they liked, impromptu, without worrying if the accompanying musician could keep up or not! Before every performance, they always asked who the musicians in the band were and would always smile if my name was on the list! I tried to pass on what I learned from my mother to my students, too.

My father thought that I was only playing for the fun of it, so he never thought about teaching me properly or anything about music. He would listen to my guitar, too, but he would only say, "Not bad. Keep practicing." I must admit, it was the combination of both the stringent discipline from my father and the accommodating love from my mother that contributed to my courage to pursue music. We had to live in difficult times and we had to accept that we had to live within all those limitations, so perhaps that harshness I experienced from my father was necessary.

My father was harsh and stringent about everything. We were not allowed to come home late after school. My father would ask, "Why did you come home late? You played football after school? Who gave you permission to play football after school?" The very next day, I obediently played during recess. I dared not stay back after school to play after that.

In the old days, people could be quite quick to judge, especially when it was time to bring home our "student record book." My results were quite good, and so I was often the top student in class. As a result, I was made the class monitor. But when it came to "moral conduct," I was only given an "average" evaluation. Why? Because I was often seen as the "enabler" of misbehavior! You see, in the past, when the teacher gave the class a short break, by right we should sit at our chairs, stay put, and rest in the classroom. But if I made everyone sit inside the classroom, the students would get restless and make noise! So what was the point of making everyone sit inside the classroom? As class monitor, I would let the whole class go out to the field to play every time we had a break! I instructed my classmates to go out slowly in pairs, so that students in other classes would not ask why we were leaving our classroom en masse. I would always be the last to leave. We would only return to the classroom when break time was over. As a result, I was given an "average" for moral conduct. But when it came to arts and cultural activities, I would always be tasked to lead my classmates.

When my father was out working, I sometimes took out his guitar, the good guitar, and practiced on my own. My father found out that I was using his guitar, and he got angry with me. He chided me for practicing with the instrument he used for making a living by teaching students. My mother doted on me, and she decided to buy a separate guitar for me. My mother took out forty đồng to buy a guitar for me to practice with. Forty đồng in those days was a large sum of money! But my mother wanted to buy a new guitar for me, because she saw that I was quite talented at it. I was fourteen years old then, according to the Vietnamese way of counting age; it was 1967. I had only practiced for about six months by then, but I could play really well. I was able to learn real quickly, and I practiced very hard. When we were evacuated from Hà Nội to the countryside,

Figure 3.2. Minh playing guitar on the rooftop.

I brought along the guitar, too. Every time we had to evacuate, I tried to bring along the guitar and the practice book. I tried to practice even though we were evacuated from home. My mother really loved the sound of my guitar. Although I did not continue to pursue the guitar afterward, it became an instrument that I use when I compose and arrange music.

I played the guitar well enough so that when I was in grade nine, the school gave me an opportunity to perform a solo recital in front of everyone during one of the morning assemblies. I practiced very hard to prepare for that big day. I remember, the piece I played was "Bài Ca Hy Vọng" [Song of Hope]. The day before my performance, I got very anxious and could not sleep, so I woke up, climbed down from the bed, and picked up the guitar. I started practicing. I was worried about my performance, so I practiced all night. At about 2:00 a.m., my father climbed down from the loft where he and my mother slept. My father was angry: "Are you crazy? Still practicing the guitar at this hour? What time is it now? Are you bent on not letting anyone sleep?" I explained that I had a solo recital in the morning. My father retorted, "Nevertheless. Put away the guitar. You should not practice at this hour and disturb everyone!" So I had to put away the guitar. My father thought I was crazy.

Under communist rule, music had to be ideologically correct to promote the socialist revolution or to drum up patriotism among the citizens to support the war effort in reunifying the country. Composed by Văn Ký, the song "Bài Ca Hy Vọng" was awarded the Hội Nhạc Sĩ Việt Nam (Association of Musicians) Prize in 1960. Written to commemorate the fifteenth anniversary of the 1945 declaration of independence, "Bài Ca Hy Vọng" came out at a time when it was clear that the country could not be unified by peaceful means.[11] At the same time, Ngô Đình Diệm's government in the South had just introduced the draconian Law 10/59, which allowed for military court proceedings to be meted out to suspected communist agents and for such proceedings to be completed within three days. Those deemed guilty by the military court for engaging in treasonous activities against the Republic of Vietnam were sentenced to death and executed by means of the guillotine.[12] "Bài Ca Hy Vọng" received much airplay through the communist radio channels and literally became a song of hope for communist insurgents fighting in the South. According to Nguyễn Thụy Kha, "Bài Ca Hy Vọng" was considered one of the most revered songs about Hà Nội in that era, along with "Quê Hương Tôi" (My Home Village), "Sông Hồng Reo Ca Hà Nội–Moscow" (The Red River Rings Hà Nội–Moscow), "Hà Nội Mùa Xuân" (Spring in Hà Nội), and "Trời Hà Nội Xanh" (The Blue Sky of Hà Nội). The song was so popular that it was even arranged into an instrumental piece for solo guitar by Hải Thoại and became a standard tune for anyone learning to play the guitar in the 1960s.[13]

In the old days, during wartime, the adults woke up very early to get ready for work. My parents woke up at about 5:00 a.m. to get ready for work, while the children could usually sleep until a bit later. We only needed to go to school at 7:00 a.m., so we usually woke up at 6:30. I woke up, brushed my teeth, washed my face, and went to get my guitar. But the guitar was gone! I asked my mother, who was getting ready to go to out, "Where is my guitar?"

My father had taken away the guitar. He told my mother, "This fella is too stubborn. He is crazy. I am taking away the guitar to sell it. I am not letting him play the guitar anymore!" Even though my mother tried to persuade my father not to do this, it was to no avail. My father had already taken away the guitar by the time I woke up. I felt sad and lost. I thought I should just go to school, explain, and apologize to everyone. But who would believe such a ridiculous story? So I asked my friend studying in the same class to let me borrow his guitar for the performance. With his guitar I could still give the solo recital, but I was not used to a different guitar. I was not exactly a professional guitarist then, so I was rather hesitant. But even a professional guitarist would all the more prefer his own usual instrument! Anyway, the performance was quite successful. After class, I went home, and then I went over to visit the friend who had lent me the guitar. I saw my guitar in his house! My father had sold the guitar to his family. That was in 1970, and I was in grade nine. By then I had already started learning the clarinet. I lost my guitar, but I still had the clarinet. From then onward I decided to only focus on practicing the clarinet.

When I started learning the guitar, I would play to accompany my mother's singing. My mother doted on me. First, it could be because of our beliefs. You see, my mother was born in the Year of the Horse in 1930, and I was also born in the Year of the Horse, in 1954, exactly two zodiac cycles after my mother. My mother and I naturally got on really well with each other. Second, I helped out with a lot of the work at home; I was essentially my mother's right hand! Often, I would wake up early in the morning, earlier than my siblings, to help my mother with household work. I would go to the market on behalf of my mother to buy beans and vegetables, then stand in line at the shops to buy meat and other things for the family. I did everything. I was a most capable assistant to my mother! I was also quite good when it came to studying the arts and music. My mother really loved listening to the sound of my guitar. Maybe it was because I was talented, intelligent, and also the healthiest. Perhaps it was because I was blessed with all these factors that my mother suggested I should try to play a woodwind instrument, either a clarinet or a saxophone. She told me, "My dear son, your guitar sound is good, but it sounds a bit sad. When one plays music with the human breath, the air circulates near the heart and as a result produces a beautiful timbre that cannot be replicated by other instruments." I later learned of another possible reason why she suggested I should pick up the clarinet or saxophone.

At night, my parents would go out to find extra work for additional income. They took up some informal gigs. My mother was an excellent singer. She had a beautiful voice, and people would invite her to sing for events and special occasions. When she was invited, she had to ask for my father's permission. She also had to negotiate with people to invite my father along to play the saxophone to accompany her. But my mother never found artistic satisfaction on stage with my father. My father played the guitar and saxophone, but only as a hobby. You could not excel in music by playing as just an amateur musician. My mother was rather frustrated because she could not deliver a fulfilling performance together with my father. She had a beautiful voice, but the sound of his saxophone was weak, like a tickling whisper! When they heard people talk about how well my mother sang and how weak his playing was, my father got upset. The professional performing groups invited her to join them; even the radio station invited her to join them. My mother had to reject all these opportunities that would develop her career. Because if she went, then there would be no one to look after the four young children. We were still very young then, so we could not take care of ourselves. My mother sacrificed a possible career for us. Seeing that I was talented in music, my mother hoped that I could take to the stage with the clarinet or saxophone and be a proper musician. This was probably the other reason she encouraged me to pick up the clarinet. Among my siblings, I was the one who had the health to really play a wind instrument. As a result, I picked up the clarinet and started studying it, mainly through self-study. That was in 1968. I was still fourteen years old then.

Choosing Music as a Vocation

My mother decided to buy a clarinet for me. That was a huge decision. She took out one cây [37.5 grams] of gold to buy the clarinet for me. At that time, this was an enormous sum of money! My father tried to stop my mother from buying the clarinet, but my mother was determined to buy one for me. When my mother put the clarinet in my hands, she told me, "I only want you to play it really well. Even when you only earn one đồng from playing the clarinet, that would be worth to me more than one billion đồng from other people." In those days, when you started learning a musical instrument properly, it meant that you were already choosing a vocation to earn a livelihood.

I was very enthusiastic about the clarinet, and I started practicing industriously. Those days, we could hardly find any accessories for the instrument, such as reeds. But I practiced very hard, nonetheless. In the morning I went to school to study, and immediately after school I took out the clarinet to practice. In the evenings, I followed my father wherever he went to for his gigs such as weddings and gatherings. Sometimes I joined in to perform together with him. With that kind of real-life exposure, I developed a "thick skin" when performing in public. I was not nervous and not afraid at all.

Later, when I started teaching, I would do the same for my students. Whenever they could play one or two songs, I would make them take a place next to me on stage and try to play along. This was something I managed to learn from my father, the importance of gaining the experience of actually playing for a real audience. Following my father's gigs in the evenings, I gained the very rich experience of performing for a live audience, and it helped me develop as a musician. In one to two months' time, I was able to improve, and I progressed to a different level of playing on the clarinet.

I started taking up gigs at weddings soon after. Those days in Vietnam, we had function rooms set up specially for people to organize weddings. People getting married would rent such a room to hold a simple banquet for friends and relatives. Often, the hosts would arrange for a band to come and play at the wedding to give it a lively atmosphere. After one year of practicing and following my father and his friends around, I started playing on my own at the weddings. In fact, I started receiving my own gigs. I was just about fifteen years old, but I knew that if I played really well, people would invite me. I did not have a regular "band" then. People just informed us that there was a wedding gig at this place and on this date and that they required four instruments: one clarinet, one accordion, one guitar, and one set of drums. When I got the gig, I would then recruit other people who could play these other instruments. The musicians who accepted the gig would turn up at the venue and play. When the gig was over, we were paid on the spot. Quốc Trường, one of the musicians who played in the big band for the Quyền Văn Minh with His Friends and Jazz concert, studied music properly with a teacher, but he also developed musically from taking up such gigs, just like myself. Back then, we often roped in one another to play at wedding gigs to earn extra income.

In those days, the main avenue for ordinary people like us who wanted to become professional musicians was to join one of the song-and-dance troupes. There was simply no other way for us to become professional musicians if we did not study at the conservatoire. I was fortunate to be able to join a song-and-dance troupe later. But there were very limited opportunities for budding musicians like us to actually try playing on a proper stage. Playing for weddings was a major avenue for us to hone our musicianship.

One evening, I was playing at Hoa Bình Wedding Hall [Phòng Cưới Hoà Bình], located on Bà Triệu Street. The place has since closed and the building torn down. When I finished the gig and was leaving the function room, a young boy, about two years younger than me, was standing at the door. He approached me, asking, "Brother, I want to learn to play the clarinet like you. Could you teach me to play like you?" I was practicing on my own, trying to learn things on my own, so I could empathize with him. The young boy did not have his own instrument, so I told him that he would have to come over to my place. We could take turns practicing the clarinet at my place. My mother had bought the clarinet for me, so I was reluctant to lend it to anyone to take home and practice. The young boy cycled to my place; he would cycle from Bạch Mai, near Chợ Mơ, all the way to my place on Hàng Giấy, near Chợ Đồng Xuân. The two of us would climb to the rooftop and practice together. He was very hardworking. For one year, the two of us practiced together almost every day. Sometimes, he cycled to my place; sometimes he took the city tram.

After practicing together for some time, he started following me around to take up gigs; just the two of us. I taught him the guitar as well. Sometimes he played the clarinet, while I accompanied him on guitar. Other times, he played the guitar to accompany me on clarinet. I also gave him some guidance on how to accompany me on the accordion. So he started going with me for wedding gigs. Although there were two of us, we only received payment for a headcount of one, because he was considered as just "tagging along." He was very humble and acknowledged that by right he was not on the payroll at all, so if he could, he would only ask for two "hào" [cents]. "We are hungry just the same, let's share it equally!" I insisted. We did this together for a while. By then, he was playing quite well already.

I joined the Việt Bắc Military Region Song-and-Dance Troupe in 1970 and left for Thái Nguyên. Around 1972, I found out that my musical partner had also left Hà Nội. His family had gone up to Tuyên Quang to pioneer a Vùng Kinh Tế Mới [New Economic Zone]. In those days, I remember, families that did not have a steady breadwinner or adequate living conditions in the city were mobilized by the local administrative wards to go up to the mountainous regions to pioneer new agricultural lands in the New Economic Zones. His family went to Tuyên Quang. After that, we lost contact.

In the late 1950s, the Democratic Republic of Vietnam began putting together a plan to expand agricultural production in the sparsely populated northern uplands and to alleviate population pressure in the cities and lowlands by means of organized migration to pioneer new agricultural lands. This began as the Khai Hoang (Agricultural Pioneering) program in the late 1950s, in which the government mobilized thousands of people living in villages and cities in the Red River Delta to migrate to the northern uplands. The Khai Hoang program was specifically put in place to help realize the first Five-Year Plan (1960–1965), which aimed to pioneer 550,000 hectares of new agricultural land nationwide.[14] This government-organized agricultural migration was later referred to as the Vùng Kinh Tế Mới (New Economic Zones) program in the 1970s. From 1961 to 1975, the government moved about one million people from the Red River Delta to the northern uplands.[15] There were people who actually volunteered to join such programs. However, a significant number of people, such as those who did not have enough agricultural land, the unemployed in the city, the socially disadvantaged, and the socially outcast were in fact mobilized by local governments to "sign up" for the program in order to meet the planned number of migrants to send to the uplands. Not all who went stayed in the newly established settlements. Many left.

Sometime in 2006, I was playing at the jazz club, and one of my staff brought over a glass of wine to the stage: "An Uncle Long in the audience bought this wine for you." I was in the midst of a song, and I thought to myself, "I know like a thousand 'Long's; which one is this?" I could not recognize a face among the crowd that I knew went by the name "Long." I smiled to the audience, drank the wine, and finished up the song. I told my students on stage to continue with the session, and I went down to look for this "Long." My staff directed me to the table of the said guest, but I could not remember if I knew this person at all! I was very frank and said to the man, "I am sorry, but I cannot recall where we met." The man was about my age but looked slightly younger, and he replied, "Certainly. It was a long time ago. I studied with you!" I was more surprised, because I only remembered taking in students after I had established myself in the music circle in the late 1970s. Technically speaking, the first student I took in was Trần Mạnh Tuấn. "Long, my music student?" I still could not remember.

"Long Bạch Mai! Long, who studied clarinet and guitar with you!" It was then that I remembered Long, my long-lost friend. Long, it turned out, had managed to migrate overseas after his family relocated to Tuyên Quang in the New Economic Zone program.

I thoroughly understood in those days that if I wanted people to invite me to play at weddings, I had to be outstanding. Even if you knew people who could do you favors, you still had to be really good. There was no other way. Put it this way: if I was not an excellent musician, if I did not perform to my best, no one would ever invite me to gigs. As such, I practiced very hard. In those days, you could find ten groups fighting over one available gig. You have to be truly excellent in order for people to offer you a gig. It was only because people recognized that I was an outstanding musician that I received those offers. I was young, I did not have a strong social network, and I did not know many people. In fact, other than playing music, I was not savvy about many things, socially speaking. But that was also a time when reputation was mainly established through word of mouth. If people had already heard you play, heard you play good music, and learned from others who had heard you play, then they would be willing to pay for your music. And they were willing to pay well, too. And if you play well, you must have the self-confidence to ask to be paid better, too!

When I followed my father around, I was just like a little chick tailing the rooster around. I received no money for my efforts. Several months later, some people actually began to take a liking to the sound of my clarinet, and they began to invite me to gigs separately. When they invited me separately, I knew that I could not ask my father or his friends, the older musicians, to come along because the audience expected newer things from younger musicians. When my father found out, he was unhappy and in fact rather angry with me. "How could you be so selfish? The uncles let you follow them around for gigs and now that you have gigs on your own, you do not invite them?" I could only explain to him: "The uncles do not know the newer songs, and when people invite me to gigs, they expect me to perform these newer tunes, so I cannot invite them to join me for the gigs." My mother intervened and explained to my father, "You know that is how society works. They invited him because they expect a certain kind of performance from him. He is not undercutting anyone, and he is not going behind anyone's back. He brings the money home to me to help out the family."

There was a particular gig I received that led to a heated argument with my father. I was invited to perform for someone we knew, but my father forbade me to take the gig. He was insistent that I follow his order, but the reason he gave me initially was simply that he did not like the person! But if I was paid for a gig, then naturally I had to turn up and play the gig. What had happened was that this person had previously invited my father to play a gig, but my father could not form a complete band to play at the gig, and the guy was upset with *my father. As a result, he refused to invite my father to any gigs after that. My father was angry with that man and, as such, refused to let me accept gigs from him, too! I explained to my father that even if I did not take up his invitation, others would. If he was paying a fair salary, then I had no reason to refuse his gig offer. With my father, things had to be his way. When he issued an order, we had to follow. He would not accept otherwise. When I started working and living independently from the family, I became the one who resisted my father. I dared to speak up because I was already an income earner in the family. Every month, I contributed my income to the family to help take care of everyone. I was like the right hand of my mother. One time when I had an argument with my father, I reasoned with him. I told him, "If I am wrong, you can punish me, make me kneel down, and admit my wrong; I have no complaints. But if I am not in the wrong, then there is no way I will kneel down and apologize." My mother took sides with me in that argument, because she understood the situation. That was in 1972, I remember. At that time, I was already working full time for Đoàn Ca Múa Hà Tây [Hà Tây Song-and-Dance Troupe] and receiving a professional musician's salary.*

Minh's First Encounter with Jazz

As I did not have the opportunity to study in a music school, I had to be more resourceful in order to pick up more knowledge about music. In those days, not anyone could enter the conservatoire simply because one was good, unfortunately. When I started learning the clarinet, I listened to all kinds of music and played all kinds of music that was available at that time. In some ways, that was beneficial to me, musically speaking. I listened to a lot of music, and I paid attention to what was playing on the radio and broadcast through the "loa phường" [neighborhood speakers]. Around 1968 or 1969, when I really got into music, I was listening to a lot of revolutionary music, or red music as it was also called. When I started following my father on his gigs and later taking up my own gigs, I played a lot of revolutionary music such as marches to encourage the warriors on the front line. Artists like us who stayed on the home front, we tried to provide support for the revolution through our arts and music to encourage the soldiers fighting on the front line.

    We would go around the neighborhood to play music in processions organized by the local neighborhood grassroots committee to uplift the spirits of the general public during the war years. We would be seated in the back of a truck going around the streets, and we kept looping the same tune as the procession kept going. When we did such gigs, we only required a very simple setup. It could be as simple as just having a drummer provide a consistent rhythm and a saxophonist playing the melody. These marches were very short and simple. Those were the days when I would follow the older Vietnamese like my father, who were just amateur musicians, to play in events organized by the local neighborhood grassroots committee.

I think many young musicians today do not even know these songs anymore. Sometimes, when my old friends visited me at the jazz club and reminisced about our childhood days, I would play a few of these tunes for memories' sake.

For wedding gigs in those days, we played mainly light instrumental music, including some old international pieces. We played at weddings quite a lot and we played mainly old tunes, old French tunes, Soviet tunes, and Chinese tunes. Those days, there was even a regulation that restricted the total number of foreign tunes that could be played for each occasion to just seven tunes, and the rest had to all be Vietnamese tunes! For Vietnamese tunes, we played folk songs such as "Trống Cơm" [Rice Drum], "Người ơi! Người ở đừng về" [Stay, My Beloved], and other popular "quan họ" folk tunes. Among the most popular Russian tunes was "Moscow Evenings," and among the memorable Chinese songs was "Chim Yến" [燕子]. Old songs! There were also some tunes from Cuba such as "Simone" and "Paloma" that were quite fun to play, songs from the 1940s and 1950s. All were songs from our socialist allies. People also played some old instrumental tunes that people used to dance to during the French colonial era. Old tunes that were considered ideologically acceptable. That was the kind of music we played for such gigs in those days.

When I started learning the clarinet, I was hungry for all kinds of music. I listened to all kinds of music, and I played all kinds of music available during that era! Whenever I heard something interesting, I would try to play it. Every time I learned something new, I practiced very hard to master it. Whatever I could play on the guitar, I would try to play it on the clarinet, too.

I even cycled all the way to the music conservatoire, stood at the gate, and tried to listen to what the students were practicing in their classes. Those days, the security guards would not let anyone without a proper permit enter the conservatoire. I focused on the different sounds I could pick up at the gate and tried to discern through the cacophony of music played by different students practicing different scales, different songs, and different instruments. I realized that they were practicing really sophisticated and technical exercises that I could not simply pick up through that faint, overlapping cacophony from outside the gate. I went home.

I went home and thought to myself, maybe I could find other music on the radio as well. Like many families, we had one radio at home, too. It was made in China and had Chinese words on it. I thought that there must be some music on the international channels, too. Perhaps international music would be more interesting. That evening, after doing my homework, I took out the transistor radio at home to find some music. I had to finish my homework first because my father would check our work, so I could only practice the clarinet after doing my homework. I did my homework quickly and practiced the clarinet. After practicing the clarinet, I waited for the whole family to go to bed, and I carried the transistor radio into bed and hid under the thick blanket. It was summer and so it was really hot, yet I covered myself under the blanket as if I were ill! I started tuning the radio to find channels broadcasting music. By luck, I came across a channel playing this "type" of music. I did not know that it was called "jazz" then. I trembled listening to the music. I thought to myself, if I could play like this, then I would have nothing to worry about!

Since I could not attend a proper music school and receive a formal music education, I had to constantly worry about not being as good as others who were able to study music properly. I had to give way to others, because they knew more and they could play better. But listening to that sound from the transistor radio, flowing like cascading water and moving like floating clouds, I knew if I could play like that, I would never have to worry about anyone else. I listened to that music very carefully and tried to remember every note I heard. It was probably an American radio channel. I did not even know whether the presenter was speaking English, because I did not understand the language. I did not even know what language it was. I only focused on the music.

That night, I went to sleep only after listening to the entire program. I could hear the music still playing in my head as I slept. Even in my dreams I was moving my fingers as if trying to play along to the music. The next evening, when it was time to practice clarinet, I tried to play every note I could remember from the night before. I told myself, I must write down the notes tonight. The problem was, I had never learned how to transcribe music properly, even though I could read simple music scores. Anyway, I went back to that channel on the transistor radio at the same time in the evening and listened to the same music program. I listened carefully and tried to make as many notes as I could. Of course, I could not notate the entire length of each song, but I managed to note together chains of phrases that could be found in a song. That was enough for me. I made a promise to myself that I had to prove that I was musically competent by playing this kind of sound.

The third time I tried to listen to the same radio program and note down the music, my father pulled away the blanket and warned me, "You cannot listen to this channel! Other people will consider that you are listening to the enemy's radio program!" Even when I explained that I did not understand what they were talking about since I did not know that foreign language and that I was only listening to the music, my father would not accept it. Even the music was considered the enemy's music, because that was American music and we were fighting the Americans at that time.

There was no way I could, or even knew how to, reason with my father at that time. I could only do what he said. The very next day, my father took away the transistor radio and sold it to someone. He was worried that if he kept the radio at home, I would try to listen to the music again. I was still only fourteen years old then, when I first heard this music.

Back then, the whole family of seven—my mother, my father, myself, my three siblings, and my paternal grandmother—all stayed under one roof in that twenty-five-square-meter apartment. Within the tight confines of the tiny apartment, every breath you took, anything you did, would be found out straightaway! There was no way I could do anything without being found out by my father.

I was still attending school, and I had a schoolmate who lived just a few doors down the street. In those days, my school gave out bread, just a small piece of bread, to each student in the morning. When we arrived at school, we would receive the bread. I made a deal with this schoolmate that I would give my bread to him in the morning, and in return he would let me go to his place to listen to music using the radio there. Although I knew I would go hungry in school, I still proposed this deal to him. He agreed straightaway! His family lived in relatively better conditions than mine, and they had a big radio that was made in China. It was such a luxury to be able to listen to music with this kind of radio in those days! That afternoon, I went over to his place, lifted up the thin mattress, and hid under the bed frame with the radio. He, too, was worried that others could hear what I was listening to with the radio, so I had to hide under the mattress to listen to the radio. I lay there and listened. I managed to note down in my mind some phrases of music here and there. I went over to his place a few more times until his mother discovered what I was doing and forbade him from having me over to use the radio. I told him, "Don't worry. This is enough for now. Thank you!" Deep inside, I hoped that I could listen to this music again or find materials to learn more about this music. Whatever I managed to note down from the radio, I tried to practice. I just kept practicing on my own to try to emulate what I had heard on the radio.

Concerns about being found out listening to radio channels from overseas were real in those years. During the war, each family that had a radio, by right, had to register the device with the postal communication authority, which would then issue a small certificate. Printed at the bottom of that small certificate, I was told, were the words *cấm nghe đài địch* (listening to enemy's radio channels prohibited).

Quyền Văn Minh found out, almost two decades later, that he had heard Benny Goodman during his first encounter with jazz through the transistor radio. Minh has told this story to many journalists, domestic and foreign, over the years since the late 1990s. In some of these earlier accounts, although Minh said that it was probably a BBC channel, he was not sure exactly which program and on what channel he caught jazz on the transistor radio. During our autoethnographic sessions between 2009 and 2016, Minh came to the conclusion that he most likely caught the program on Voice of America (VOA).

If that was the case, the program Minh heard was most likely *Music USA: Jazz Hour* produced by Willis Conover for VOA, broadcast worldwide and received by millions of listeners.[16] As I illustrate in the next chapter, *Jazz Hour* was indeed a product of the Cold War in which the Americans attempted to deploy jazz as a cultural instrument to gain an advantage in their ideological competition with the socialist bloc. In turn, however, socialist states in Eastern Europe and the Soviet Union also adopted a similar tactic to "de-Americanize" this popular music art form. As a result, jazz persisted. Behind the Iron Curtain, jazz even flourished in some places. Jazz was not officially endorsed in socialist Vietnam during the Cold War, but it existed within the larger context of the socialist world.

TRACK 4

Interlude I

Minh's early encounters with jazz in socialist Vietnam invite a broader contextualization of jazz during the Cold War, in particular the stories of jazz "behind the Iron Curtain." In Eastern European socialist countries during the Cold War, as Marta Domurat-Linde so succinctly sums up, "all facets of life were politicized and ideologized, [and] musical preferences could also be interpreted as a political statement."[1] Ladislav Tropp, a Slovakian drummer active in Prague during the 1960s, was considered persona non grata by the Czechoslovakian Ministry of Interior, which issued a warrant against him in 1963 on the basis of ideological disagreement with the ruling party. His crime? Frequent music collaboration with jazz musicians from Western countries, in particular, Laco Déczi (trumpet), Jan Hammer (piano), Miroslav Vitouš (bass), and Jira (George) Mraz (bass), all Czechoslovakian jazz musicians who had left the communist state for the United States.[2]

Jazz was caught in the ideological struggle between the Eastern socialist world led by the Soviet Union and the Western capitalist world led by the United States. In the Soviet Union during 1920s and 1930s, the state switched from criticizing jazz as the cultural excess of the bourgeois West to singing its praises as the music of the proletariat created by working-class African Americans in response to oppression by the dominant white capitalist class.[3] In April 1928, the Russian novelist Maxim Gorky published an essay entitled "On Music of the Gross" in the official newspaper of the Communist Party of the Soviet Union, *Pravda*. Jazz was declared "bourgeois" and "the music of the degenerate," a position that was strongly supported and pursued by the powerful Association of Proletarian Musicians.[4] Jazz, in particular the foreign Tin Pan Alley classical jazz of that era, was considered as going against the values of the revolution and therefore prohibited. One could even be punished with a fine and imprisonment for playing or bringing in American jazz records.[5] This position changed in the 1930s when the Communist International (Comintern) decided to expand the ideological struggle to North America and threw its support behind the formerly enslaved African American population to help them achieve political self-determination over the white capitalist ruling class of the United States. As a result, jazz, for a while, came to be seen as "proletarian music" in the Soviet Union.[6] Despite its use in the ideological competition, jazz would always face resistance from the Soviet state. Penny Von Eschen succinctly explains this cultural intransigence: "Given the widely acknowledged excellence of Soviet classical music and ballet, Soviet officialdom promoted a rigid hierarchy in art. Classical forms were deemed the only true art and any modern form was considered not simply inferior but degenerate and decadent."[7]

Ideology determined the fate of jazz, and what Domurat-Linde observed in the case of Poland fundamentally applied to all Eastern European socialist states in varying degrees: "It was the state that decided what was allowed and what was not, and it was the state that determined what was to be regarded as artistically valuable and what did not quite (or did not at all) meet this standard."[8] In Poland, jazz was not officially banned, but passion for the genre was perceived as dissidence and therefore disloyal to the revolution. Jazz records were trashed, and the music disappeared from the public sphere during the period between 1949 and 1956.[9] In Łódź, the YMCA's jazz collection was burned when the authorities declared the YMCA an illegal organization.[10] However, some people managed to secretly keep their jazz collections, and they gathered in private to listen to jazz, to discuss jazz, and to play jazz.[11] No one would outright declare, "I play jazz." The pianist Krzysztof Sadowski recalls hiding in school to wait for everyone to leave before studying jazz with his teacher. Saxophonist Jerzy Matuszkiewicz tells of playing the saxophone only in private because it was considered an "outlaw instrument" for its close affiliation with jazz. He adds, "We were playing dance music for young people at parties . . . mostly dizieland [sic] music, but we also played what I would term pure jazz at private sessions. These underground sessions were dubbed catacombs, because their very existence was known to a very small group of people."[12] This was the era of "catacomb jazz" in Poland, when all activities related to jazz were carried out underground either in secret or subtly snuck into the occasional open recital and public broadcast.[13]

In Hungary, just like elsewhere in Europe, jazz bands had already emerged on the music scene during the 1920s. By the 1930s, Hungarian jazz ensembles were playing in the dance halls and bars of Budapest. By 1944, the combination of war, the persecution of the Jews, and rise of the Arrow Cross Party led to the decline of jazz. With the end of the war, jazz returned to the soundscape of Hungary in what Hungarian music historians called the very brief "golden age of jazz" in the years 1945–1949. But with the rise to power of the Magyar Dolgozók Pártja (Hungarian Working People's Party), jazz was subjected to the state's strict cultural control via the Trade Union of Music Artists, the Hungarian Association of Musicians, and the National Center for Musical Entertainment. In Gergő Havadi's words: "Communist cultural policy saw in jazz the dance music for the entertainment of the 'immoral' pre-war bourgeoisie."[14] The state took over the entertainment sector, the record production industry was nationalized, and only approved ensembles such as the Budapest Radio Dance Music Band were allowed to give public performances.[15]

In Germany, the Nazis tried to ban jazz, seeing it as a form of decadent music invented by "unrespectable" African Americans and commercially distributed by Jews. With the end of World War II, jazz enjoyed a brief revival in the Soviet-occupied zone of Germany.[16] For a few years, jazz flourished, as it was "in no way suspected of being fascist" in the immediate postwar period. Popular dance orchestras such as the RBT Orchestra and Walter Dobschinski's Orchestra revived the music. Jazz clubs such as Hot-Club Berlin, opened by Hans Blüthner in 1945, provided a place for people to listen to jazz records and share their interest in jazz.[17] According to Christian Schmidt-Rost, a "sharpened Stalinist cultural policy" was introduced in Soviet-occupied Germany beginning in 1948, and jazz musicians and fans began to encounter severe restrictions in their pursuit of their musical interests. Ensembles playing jazz such as the RBT Orchestra were disbanded, and jazz was severely curtailed in the public sphere such as in concert halls and restaurants. Instead, new radio programs playing songs such as "Kleine Volkspolizistin" (Little Policewoman), articulating the goals of socialist realism, filled the soundscape of East Germany.[18]

On the other side of the Iron Curtain, jazz was indeed perceived by the Americans as a cultural instrument that could be deployed in the Cold War.[19] Voice of America (VOA) was launched on July 13, 1942, with the purpose of broadcasting news and updates about World War II to the rest of the world.[20] Immediately after the war, VOA's radio programs indeed contributed to the flourishing of the jazz scene in East Germany. Schmidt-Rost notes that these radio programs were produced primarily for the Allied forces.[21] Included in the daily broadcasts was popular American music such as jazz. As early as 1952, Leonard Feather hosted a program featuring jazz music called *Jazz Club USA*.[22] A study of the effects of VOA broadcasting conducted by US embassies concluded that jazz was a powerful instrument for attracting new audiences. Charles Bohlen, the US ambassador in Moscow during 1953–1957, suggested creating a new nightly jazz program to attract more listeners. US diplomats hoped that the popularity of jazz, an art form originating in the noncommunist world, would help to weaken people's support for the communist states. Beginning on January 6, 1955, *Music USA: Jazz Hour*, hosted by Willis Conover, broadcast nightly beyond the Iron Curtain a meticulously selected playlist of jazz music from Conover's private collection of thousands of jazz records.[23] *Jazz Hour* was a huge success, with an estimated nightly audience of thirty million.[24] The US State Department was convinced that jazz could indeed serve as a means to convey American cultural soft power in the Cold War. However, it was only a particular type of jazz as imagined in the narrow mindsets of the politicians and bureaucrats.[25]

There was indeed a receptive audience for jazz comprising musicians and music lovers in Eastern Europe. The first generation of musicians who played jazz in Poland and laid the foundations of the genre were mainly amateur musicians, self-taught musicians, and trained musicians grounded in classical music. They learned to play jazz from jazz records that circulated in Eastern Europe, and the arrival of jazz music broadcast on the radio was a tremendously rich and valuable resource for these musicians.[26] Through *Jazz Hour*, Willis Conover communicated the diverse range of jazz and the most up-to-date developments in the genre to his audience. Conover was perceived as a teacher and "trusted companion" who showed his audience what jazz was really like with his nightly show. Fans of the program even formed "listener clubs" in ninety-four countries to show their loyalty to the show.[27] Many jazz musicians were openly indebted to Conover, as they claimed that his show provided them with an avenue to learn new jazz styles and arrangements.[28] Polish artists told Keith Hatschek, "The only contact we had with contemporary jazz was the [*Music USA*] hour with Willis Conover. This was our real jazz academy. . . . Jazz blew in [on the airwaves] from America and we adored it. Conover really taught us what jazz is and how it sounds, [and] the theories of jazz."[29] In Hungary, communist cultural policy effectively ensured that jazz disappeared from the official airwaves in the 1950s. However, foreign radio programs such as the BBC, Radio Free Europe, Rundfunk im amerikanischen Sektor (RIAS) Berlin, and especially Voice of America through its *Music USA: Jazz Hour* program, kept jazz alive on the unofficial airwaves.[30]

Discovering jazz to be a powerful cultural weapon in the Cold War, the US government mobilized jazz stars of the era including Louis Armstrong, Duke Ellington, Dave Brubeck, Dizzy Gillespie, Benny Goodman, and a host of others as cultural ambassadors to perform in the socialist world and regions deemed susceptible to communist ideology. Jazz, according to Von Eschen, was perceived as "the ideological heart and soul of the tours" and presented as "a uniquely American art form."[31] However, the promotion of jazz beyond America was not restricted to narrow ideological deployment by the US government. Jazz stars such as Louis Armstrong had already embarked on cross-Atlantic tours to promote this original art form as early as 1932, and in 1955 Armstrong performed in Stockholm, Paris, Barcelona, and Frankfurt before the State Department launched even its first state-sponsored concert tour. As a result of Armstrong's pioneering outreach beyond American soil, producer George Avakian of Columbia Records released an album called *Ambassador Satch* in 1956 that included live recordings from Armstrong's European tour in 1955.[32] In the Cold War years, some of Armstrong's prominent tours, both state sponsored and privately organized, included his travels to Ghana (1956), Latin America (1957), twenty-seven cities on the African continent (1960–1961), and East Berlin (1965).[33]

Among some of the most prominent early jazz ambassador missions were Dizzy Gillespie's Middle East tour in 1956, Benny Goodman's seven-week tour of Southeast Asia (Thailand, Singapore, Malaya, Cambodia, and Burma) and East Asia (South Korea and Japan) in 1957, and Dave Brubeck's tour behind the Iron Curtain in East Germany and Poland in 1958.[34] In 1962, Benny Goodman became the first jazz ambassador to tour the Soviet Union.[35] Under the Richard Nixon administration, jazz ambassadors were even more actively deployed, in particular to Eastern Europe. The outspoken Charles Mingus and the eccentric Thelonious Monk and Ornette Coleman traveled to Belgrade on behalf of the state. The elder statesman of jazz, Duke Ellington, even played in little-known, landlocked Laos and toured America's chief ideological opponent, the Soviet Union.[36]

In 1958, when Brubeck crossed into East Germany without a visa for his journey to Poland, as the jazz giant recounted to Von Eschen, he waited for hours before an official approached him with all the necessary travel documents and a Polish newspaper article advertising his visit to Warsaw. Brubeck recalled the official's first words: "'Are you Mr. Kulu?' He got out a 'cool jazz' piece from a [Polish] newspaper that had a picture of me, Mr. Kulu." Brubeck's quartet delivered twelve concerts in Warsaw, followed by a tour to several other cities in Poland.[37] The Dave Brubeck Quartet left a strong impression with jazz musicians in the host country. For the first time, Polish musicians saw how American jazz musicians performed in person and witnessed possible styles they could emulate.[38]

By the time Duke Ellington performed in the Soviet Union, jazz was already played in the open in that country. Prior to his opening concert on September 13, 1971, in Leningrad, jazz fans in the city had already organized their own concert celebrating Ellington's music. The Duke was a recognized jazz hero in Leningrad before his visit;[39] his tour of the Soviet Union even received rave reviews in many Soviet newspapers, including *Pravda*, which had formerly declared jazz "music of the degenerate" during the Stalin era.[40] And it goes without say that, as with any traveling jazz musicians, jam sessions were the order of the day after officially scheduled performances. Members of the Ellington Orchestra engaged in a legendary, unofficial jam session with local musicians at the Byeliye Nochi (White Nights) café, which attracted a huge audience.[41]

These encounters between "jazz ambassadors" and local jazz musicians, while unveiling certain shortcomings among musicians from the East in comparison with the seasoned jazz stars from the West (read America), served to encourage a stronger resolve among local musicians to find their own voice in jazz in order to be successful and respected in that world.[42] Furthermore, as Von Eschen suggests, the American jazz ambassadors complicated "the characterization of jazz as America's music" because they saw jazz as "an international and hybrid music combining not just African and European forms, but forms that had developed out of an earlier mode of cultural exchange" arising from the slave trade, racial relations, and migration.[43] Jazz, while originating from America's historical global interdigitation, was seen as a music for all. Although transmitted with a purpose to the Soviet Union and its allies through radio, the jazz ambassadors, and other sponsored cultural activities, jazz intermingled with existing Eastern European sounds and gradually developed distinct styles in these places.[44]

Jazz was not used as a cultural instrument in this ideological battle by the United States alone; it was also used by the Eastern European socialist states. The competing use of jazz as a cultural instrument in the ideological war actually helped to create conditions for jazz to develop its own voice in different Eastern European countries. Soviet critics had briefly turned this cultural chess play on its head in the early 1930s when they interpreted jazz as "proletarian music" that grew out of the oppression of African Americans by the white capitalist class.[45] In Poland, following Stalin's death in 1953, this attempt to reinterpret jazz as aligned with socialist ideology, as the "music of the suppressed Black working classes," brought jazz out of the "catacombs" such that it could now be played within the framework of the state.[46] Jazz concerts that featured local jazz artists were organized at the prestigious Warsaw Philharmonic Concert Hall, not unlike the Jazz at the Carnegie concerts in New York. Not only was jazz accessible to the public, it was accessible via the state, it was jazz played by Polish ensembles, and it was ideologically sanctioned by the state.[47] From the mid-1950s onward, East Germany had its own jazz evangelist, Reginald Rudorf, who wrote about jazz and hosted radio programs broadcasting jazz. Promoting jazz along the lines of official ideology, Rudorf argued that "authentic jazz" (according to him being mainly blues, Dixieland, and spirituals) was aligned with East Germany's "search for an authentic German national culture."[48] Rudorf was ultimately jailed when he aroused the socialist state's paranoia about his activities in West Germany and for organizing jazz performances at Protestant churches.[49] Jazz in East Germany, however, continued to flourish. Journalist Günther Huesmann even goes so far as to claim that jazz was seen as a "creative cultural value in its own right" in the German Democratic Republic.[50] In other words, for a period of time, Eastern European socialist states even attempted to "create, propagate, and encourage an 'own jazz' and an 'own jazz life'" to counter the powerful cultural influence of jazz from the United States.[51]

Beyond the state, however, jazz musicians in the Soviet Union and Eastern Europe had, on their own accord, been trying to develop their own voices to play jazz with or without state endorsement and support. Two musicians stood out.

Leonid Utesov could be considered the earliest music pioneer in the Soviet Union who tried to give jazz a distinctive original voice. Utesov was an early champion of jazz music in the Soviet Union during the Stalinist period and a celebrity known for his original "Thea-Jazz" performances, a combination of jazz and theatricality (a form of theatrical performance found in Russian circus acts). Utesov openly challenged the government's stance toward jazz music at a time when it was perceived as "music of the gross."[52] According to Benjamin Beresford, Utesov promoted jazz at every available opportunity and would even deliver short speeches to defend the genre as the "merry, cheerful, buoyant music of the industrial epoch."[53] For playing jazz, Utesov was often at the receiving end of attacks by the Soviet press, with some critics even declaring his music "a form of prostitution."[54] In the 1930s, following the Comintern's attempt to reach out to African Americans so as to export the socialist revolution, jazz was officially seen as music of the proletariat and tolerated in the Soviet Union. As a result, the attacks on Utesov softened, although he was still ostracized because of his Odessa origins.[55] Utesov rose in popularity after his band appeared together with actress and singer Lyubov Orlova in the 1934 film *The Merry Guys*.[56] Utesov eagerly promoted local jazz by performing only Russian compositions, while other Soviet jazz groups included works by foreign jazz artists.[57] However, Utesov received no formal recognition from the Soviet leadership despite his popularity and service as a performing artist. It was only in 1942, after making extensive tours performing for soldiers fighting on the brutal Eastern Front of World War II, that Utesov was finally recognized for his cultural contribution. Utesov was awarded the title "Honored Artist of the Russian Soviet Federative Socialist Republic."[58]

Krzysztof Komeda Trzciński is often credited for pioneering a distinctive Polish jazz sound in socialist Poland during the 1960s. Komeda, a jazz pianist and film music composer, encountered jazz at a friend's apartment during the "catacombs" period. At that time, the communist government in Poland, directed by Soviet Union, saw jazz as "ideally foreign," of questionable "class values," and fundamentally representing a "bad American role model."[59] Although not officially prohibited, jazz was forced out of the public sphere. Nonetheless, jazz enthusiasts continued to listen to and play jazz. A practicing physician with a classical music background, Komeda was fascinated by the music he heard and gradually developed his mastery of the genre. Jazz was partially rehabilitated in Poland after the end of the Stalinist era.[60] In 1956, Komeda formed the Komeda Sextet, often recognized as the first Polish jazz group that played modern jazz openly after the "catacombs" era. The Komeda Sextet opened the way for jazz in socialist Poland. During this period, Komeda composed his first film score and after that rose to become one of the most notable European film score composers in the 1960s. But Komeda's ultimate achievement is found in jazz. As Marta Domurat-Linde puts it, Komeda is fundamentally credited for creating "his own original and unmistakable musical language, which is characterized above all as lyrical, romantic, and deeply rooted in the Polish tradition."[61] The Komeda sound is generally recognized as the original source of Polish jazz. As a result, jazz heard in Poland could no longer be just referred to as "jazz in Poland," but it would be more appropriate to call it "Polish Jazz."[62] Rather than the socialist state appropriating jazz as part of its ideological language, Domurat-Linde argues that the development of Polish jazz as its own unique genre through the grounded and creative efforts of Polish musicians such as Komeda was fundamentally a statement against the authoritarian grasp of communism.[63]

Jazz did not always successfully develop local characteristics behind the Iron Curtain. In the case of Romania, jazz was already present prior to World War II, played by a small group of musicians at luxurious restaurants in Bucharest. After the communists came into power, jazz and rock 'n' roll were portrayed as "symbols of Western decadence" by the official press until the early 1960s. The Romanian Workers' Party then initiated a period of political "relaxation" as part of its effort to gain some distance from the political influence of the Soviet Union and autonomy from the economic control of the Council for Mutual Economic Assistance (COMECON).[64] As a result, the Romanian public could access jazz without much difficulty, compared to the earlier period. Although jazz had entered Romania prior to communist rule, there were apparently no original compositions with identifiable local characteristics in the music played in the country. Musicians who embraced the music in the 1960s turned to American jazz for inspiration.[65] When the communist regime tightened its authoritarian rule in the 1970s, jazz was somewhat tolerated and continued to exist in small clubs under the cultural houses, even outside of Bucharest.[66]

We can safely conclude that there was a significant jazz scene behind the Iron Curtain despite attempts by the state to ideologically define and shape culture in the socialist world. In Czechoslovakia, the talented trumpeter Ladislav Martoník was playing with jazz ensembles at the Traditional Club in 1961, and in 1963 he joined the Revival Jazz Band. These jazz ensembles gave public performances at the Tarta Revue.[67] Ladislav Tropp drummed with Karel Velebný and his Spejbl and Huvínek Quintet (SHQ) in Prague. With the Reduta Quintet, Tropp even performed in Egypt, Tunisia, Paris, and West Berlin.[68] In fact, Tropp spent the 1970s playing jazz professionally with a coffeehouse orchestra and also with his own trio in East Germany.[69] In East Germany, the pianist Theo Schumann successfully blended jazz into his compositions, recordings, and performances throughout the 1960s.[70] The Komeda Sextet was perhaps the best-known jazz band in Poland from the late 1950s onward. Stan Getz was accompanied by a Polish rhythm section during his performance at the Warsaw Philharmonic Concert Hall as part of the Jazz Jamboree of 1960.[71] There was even a Polish Jazz Federation that was actively involved in the 1970 Jazz Jamboree, which saw the return of Dave Brubeck to Poland after his debut behind the Iron Curtain in 1958.[72] In Hungary, the Sándor Benkó Band, the Bergendy Band, János Gonda, Aladár Pege, Béla Szakcsi, and György Vukán were some of the active artists and jazz groups playing in the music scene.[73] In the early 1960s, the Hungarian jazz pianist Kertész Kornél was able to establish the Youth Jazz Club, located at the Dalia Café.[74]

In 1956, Poland held its first jazz festival in Sopot, which was attended by more than twenty-five thousand people. The 1957 edition even included several international jazz musicians. The American clarinetist Albert Nicholas played with a Polish ensemble; Big Bill Ramsey was the event's other featured American jazz musician. The All Soul's Day Jazz Festival was also particularly popular with Polish youths. In Warsaw, jam sessions at Tyrmand's were well-known regular events, and Club Hybryby was another place known for its nightly jazz performances, which began in 1957.[75] In Hungary, jazz festivals outside of Budapest such as in Debrecen, Szeged, Nagykanizsa, and Székesfehérvár (the Alba Regia Jazz Festival) were organized in the late 1960s. In the late 1980s, foreign jazz bands also played in the Mediawave Festival in Győr.[76]

In Czechoslovakia, the Jazz Section of the Czechoslovak Musicians' Union organized eleven Pražské Jazzové Dny (Prague Jazz Days) festivals between 1974 and 1982. Two of these events were supposedly organized without official permission from the government! The Prague Jazz Days festivals brought together professional jazz bands, experimental ensembles, and experimental groups that were often made up of amateur musicians as well as musicians who were not officially endorsed by the government's cultural committee. These events organized by the Jazz Section were seen as an open platform for performances of a wide variety of musical forms that were not necessarily supported by the communist regime such as jazz rock, alternative rock, freestyle avant-garde, experimental music, punk rock, and "happening experiments." According to Peter Motyčka, Prague Jazz Days provided the space for "another side of jazz music" showcasing the emerging variants of jazz.[77]

Eastern European countries were also actively engaged in releasing jazz recordings. Polskie Nagrania (Polish Recordings) began releasing a record series known as Polish Jazz in 1964. By 1989, the label had released some seventy-six albums.[78] Recorded in 1965, Komeda's album *Astigmatic* is still considered the most influential Polish jazz album.[79] In Czechoslovakia, the Supraphon and Opus record labels released jazz albums. Drummer Ladislav Tropp played on eleven LPs released by these labels in the years 1965–1971.[80] In Hungary, the MHV company controlled the market for jazz records, and their recordings were readily available.[81] Jazz enthusiasts in East Germany published journals and magazines that disseminated information about jazz events and discussions about jazz theory and history. The AG Jazz Halle published three issues of jazz journals in 1955. The Jazz Klub Eisenach published a magazine called *Posaune* (*Trombone*) beginning in 1959, albeit irregularly.[82]

Jazz was even officially taught in some of the socialist states. In Hungary, jazz was included as an accredited music subject shortly after 1961.[83] At the

Béla Bartók Musical Arts Vocational School, a jazz department was established in 1965, thus including jazz as part of the state-sanctioned professional music education curriculum.[84] In Bratislava, Czechoslovakia, Bohumil Trnečka began teaching jazz harmony and jazz arrangement at the city's conservatoire in 1980. The Slovakian jazz guitarist Matúš Jakabčic studied jazz with Trnečka as a distant-education student before enrolling as a full-time student. Following the fall of the Iron Curtain, Jakabčic formed the Matúš Jakabčic Tentet, which was known for experimenting with modern jazz sounds, and joined the Gustav Brom Big Band, arguably the best-known Czechoslovak ensemble. The Gustav Brom Big Band featured swing music in the styles of Duke Ellington and Count Basie; Miroslav Zahradník notes that Jakabčic's addition inserted a "sonoric colorfulness" to an already tight jazz orchestra.[85]

After the end of the "catacombs" era, the first Polish jazz radio program was broadcast to the public in Szczecin in 1957, followed by another one in Warsaw.[86] In 1958, the Polish government started a new Polish radio program, *Ze Świata Jazzu*, which broadcast music played not only by popular American jazz ensembles but also by new Polish ensembles.[87] In Budapest, Imre Kiss, a trained organist, began producing jazz programs and organizing jazz festivals for Radio Budapest in the 1960s after the restriction on jazz was lifted in Hungary.[88] While promoting jazz through state-sanctioned channels, Kiss was also tasked to "keep order in the jazz field." As a result, he managed to build a network of jazz musicians and music experts in order to run the radio programs. Eventually, such endeavors created opportunities for Hungarian jazz musicians to meet American jazz stars such as Louis Armstrong, Ella Fitzgerald, and Charles Mingus when they were invited to perform in Budapest.[89] In East Germany, Karlheinz Drechsel produced some short jazz programs for the East Berlin broadcasting services as early as 1952. These programs were banned at the end of 1952 but made a return two years later. This pattern repeated continuously for a few years until 1959, after which Drechsel's jazz programs would remain running for thirty years.[90]

In Romania, the public radio station, which had previously exclusively broadcast dance and patriotic music, began to include jazz in its music program during the early 1960s. Public television also began broadcasting performances by Romanian jazz musicians. In 1965, according to Adrian Popan, the term "jazz" appeared officially in the radio program schedule to introduce the program of April 18, 1965: "Jazz Music with Michel Legrand and His Orchestra." Dedicated jazz shows of between twenty and thirty minutes were scheduled daily on Radio Romania after this. On certain days, there were even up to three jazz shows available on the radio. These shows had a variety of names, including *Jazz Music*, *Jazz*, *Jazz at Night*, *Jazz Panorama*, and *The Parade of the Syncopations*. Jazz was seen as a musical art form compatible with socialist societies.[91]

Toward the end of the 1970s, Willis Conover established another radio program entitled *Music with Friends* using mostly music he had recorded from jazz festivals and other live performances in Eastern Europe. Surprisingly, there was sufficient jazz behind the Iron Curtain for Conover to make such a program! Conover produced and recorded *Music with Friends* in his studio in Washington, DC, and he then sent it to employees at state-owned radio stations in Poland, Czechoslovakia, Hungary, the Soviet Union, and elsewhere, who would then air the program. Ritter Rüdiger suggests that the primary reason Eastern European socialist states allowed the broadcasting of *Music with Friends* via official channels was because these governments preferred to air the programs through their own stations, since it was ultimately impossible "to eliminate the American jazz presenter and his programs."[92]

Although in some ways appropriated and used by socialist states to prevent people from completely associating this popular art form with America, jazz was always placed in a rather ambiguous position in these states. According to Rüdiger, "jazz musicians and jazz listeners never could know if listening to jazz was labeled as positive or as criminal."[93]

A most chilling reminder came with the invasion of Czechoslovakia by Warsaw Pact troops in 1968 to crush the Prague Spring. Following the invasion, jazz was once again perceived as a questionable genre. During this period of "normalization" in Czechoslovakia, which marked the return to a repressive communist system, many hobby and cultural organizations including the Czechoslovakian Jazz Club were shut down. Jazz fans responded by trying to set up a new association, Česká Jazzová Unie (the Czech Jazz Union). Karel Srp and two other signatories supported by Jindřich Kautský from the Department of Culture of the National Committee of the Central Czech Region submitted their request for the Czech Jazz Union's approval. The Ministry of Interior finally rejected the request because the state would not allow the coexistence of different organizations that focused on the same interests during the "normalization" period. Instead, Srp compromised by agreeing to place the Czech Jazz Union as a Jazz Section within the existing Czechoslovak Musicians' Union in 1971. In reality, however, the Jazz Section operated independently from the main union,[94] and it became a member of the International Jazz Federation at the UNESCO International Music Council in 1978. In 1984, the Jazz Section was deemed an illegal entity when the Ministry of Interior discontinued the Czechoslovak Musicians' Union. The homes of the Jazz Section committee members were searched, personal belongings were confiscated, and individuals were charged under the Czechoslovak Penal Code for "unjust enrichment."[95]

During this uncertain period, jazz artists such as Jan Jakeje, Jan Hammer, Miroslav Vitouš, and Jira (George) Mraz left Czechoslovakia to pursue jazz outside the Iron Curtain. Jakeje was banned from returning to his home country until the 1980s, even though political reforms brought on by the Soviet Union's glasnost and perestroika policies had already emerged in Czechoslovakia.[96]

In Hungary during the 1970s, the Communist Youth League supported the activities of jazz musicians and gave them opportunities to perform. However, music still remained under the constant control of the state. Secret agents were even deployed to spy on these musicians. According to Gergő Havadi, one agent reported on alleged smuggling activities by Hungarian musicians when traveling overseas for performances. Apparently, musicians were bringing home goods that were in short supply in Hungary such as musical instruments, record albums produced in the West, and everyday consumer goods.[97]

In spite of the ups and downs of such political ambiguity, jazz lived on in the Eastern European socialist states.

In Vietnam, as in the European socialist countries during the Cold War, the state determined what was culturally acceptable and what was not. Jazz, having originated in and having developed in the United States, leader of the capitalist world, was always perceived as ideologically suspect. In Vietnam, only revolutionary music was acceptable under the communist state until the Đổi Mới reforms. Adopted as a cultural instrument by both sides in the ideological competition of the Cold War, jazz was ironically able to persist and even developed its own individual characteristics in different countries behind the Iron Curtain. Indeed, there was jazz in the socialist states after the Stalinist era. But in socialist Eastern Europe and the Soviet Union, where classical music was deeply rooted and flourished, and where folk music was deemed a rich source of national pride, jazz was always placed a tier or two below the mainstream arts.[98] Nonetheless, jazz continued to persist behind the Iron Curtain. Caught up in the Second Indochina War and in its own socialist revolutionary fervor, the Democratic Republic of Vietnam made no room for jazz. But the story of global jazz in the context of the Cold War prevented Vietnam from being entirely insulated from the genre's circulating sounds. And what little contact Quyền Văn Minh had with jazz in such a global context was sufficient to plant the seeds of growth for Vietnamese jazz through Minh's passion for music, unquestionable pride in his national identity, and patient resilience.

TRACK 5

Encountering Jazz Again

Revolutionary music continued to dominate the soundscape of socialist Vietnam throughout the 1970s. From the 1950s onward, Vietnamese from the North were sent to Eastern European countries for vocational training and further education. Socialist Vietnam was not totally isolated from the rest of the world. Meanwhile, rock 'n' roll and other Western popular music flourished in the South during the Second Indochina War. As the whole of Vietnam came under communist rule in 1975, a centrally planned economy and radical socialist ideology was applied from north to south. The dance halls and nightclubs in Sài Gòn went silent, and what little jazz was once heard in the South completely disappeared from the public sphere.

The Việt Bắc Military Region Artists' Troupe

In 1970, I joined Đoàn Văn Công Quân Khu Việt Bắc [Việt Bắc Military Region Artists' Troupe] as an apprentice clarinetist. The unit was also called Đoàn Ca Múa Quân Khu Việt Bắc [Việt Bắc Military Region Song-and-Dance Troupe]. I had yet to even start grade ten when I joined the troupe; I was sixteen, going on seventeen. Of the four siblings, there were three boys in our family. At that time, my eldest brother was studying in college. If no one else from our family contributed to the compulsory military service, he would have had to disrupt his studies to serve in the military. I was the next in line, and so I joined the military. Although I was serving in the military, I did not have to carry a rifle. Instead, I carried a clarinet serving in a military song-and-dance troupe! I served as an apprentice musician in the troupe. It was then that I started to learn how to read a full score, how to follow directions of the conductor, what a proper music ensemble could look like, how music could be properly played in a group, how to get things organized in a band, and so on.

I still remember the challenges I faced when I first joined the Việt Bắc Military Region Song-and-Dance Troupe. One evening during a performance, I lost count during a rest section of the score, and I got really flustered. The next day, during our practice break, I approached the bandleader and asked him to let me take a look at the full score so that I could make notes. At that time, I was still "xanh" [green], and I knew very little about anything. To be honest, I did not even know what a full score looked like before that, so I was quite lost when I tried to read one for the first time! It was much bigger and a lot more complicated than I thought, and it contained all the different parts of a composition. I compared my clarinet score with what was written in the full score. In a drama and dance piece, the woodwinds part could rest for even a hundred beats! I could count, but it was easy to lose track every now and then. I studied which instruments would come in and play before my part toward the end of the extended rest section and made notes. I copied these parts to my own score. When I finished making notes from the full score, the bandleader, who did not in the first place offer any advice about what I should do to overcome my difficulty, asked me, "Have you managed to solve your problem?" I explained to him, "The flute player comes in one bar before me by playing this melody toward the end of my extended rest section, and I have made notes on that." The bandleader smiled at me and did not say anything.

The bandleader of the song-and-dance troupe's music ensemble was getting old by then and was ready to retire, so he was quite easygoing and allowed me to copy music from the full scores so that I could practice on my own. Those days, it was extremely precious for anyone to have music scores in one's possession. The only way to have a copy of the music score was to copy it by hand, and you had to copy it carefully. To be able to copy the music score, you had to make friends with and persuade the person who had the score to lend it to you. It was no straightforward matter at all!

When I got my hands on any music material, I practiced like crazy! I practiced so much and so diligently that when we were based in the mountains, fellow troupe mates had to ask me to climb farther uphill, so that others would not be disturbed by my practicing! So, early in the morning, I would climb up the mountain, some twenty to thirty meters above where we were based, to find an isolated corner to practice in. I kept practicing. I copied as much music as I could from the conductor's library of full scores into my music notebook. But in those days, there were not too many blank music books, blank music sheets, or even blank paper available. The troupe also did not issue much of these supplies, anyway. I had to go around to ask if anyone had any unused pages to spare. Even if I could get my hands on partially used pages or scribbled pages, that was fine. I cut out the unused pages or unused parts and pasted these together. With these loose pages, I compiled my own music practice book.

Because of my employment at the troupe, I had the opportunity to sell my clarinet to the troupe, and I returned the money to my mother. Although I sold the clarinet to the troupe, I was actually the one using the instrument. It was quite a good deal. My mother had used one "cây vàng" [bar of gold] to buy the clarinet for me. I managed to sell it for 1.5 cây vàng and returned the money with interest to my mother! Of course, that clarinet was priceless to me, if you ask me. But I was selling it back to the troupe, and the troupe used state funds to buy the instrument, so I could not ask them to pay a really high price for what it was really worth to me.

Moving to the mountainous Việt Bắc region was a huge change for Minh. The Việt Bắc uplands are characterized by distinct and diverse social, cultural, linguistic, and agrarian landscapes, compared to the Red River Delta, being the home abode of the ethnic majority Kinh (Việt) people such as Minh himself. Consisting of the provinces of Cao Bằng, Bắc Kạn, Lạng Sơn, Tuyên Quang, and Thái Nguyên, the Việt Bắc region was mainly populated by ethnic minority groups such as the Tày, Nùng, Dao (Dzao), Hmong, and Sán Chay before the large-scale migration of Kinh people from the plains that began with the Khai Hoang program in the 1960s. Việt Bắc ethnic minorities speak a wide variety of languages that are generally incomprehensible to the average ethnic Kinh, and each group possesses beliefs, customs, and cultures that are very different from one another as well as from the lowland Kinh population. Most ethnic Kinh living in the Red River Delta did not know or interact much with the ethnic minorities living in the uplands. Between 1956 and 1975, these provinces were governed under a special administrative unit known as the Việt Bắc Autonomous Region (Khu Tự Trị Việt Bắc). Having received the support of the ethnic minority groups in Việt Bắc and the neighboring Tây Bắc Mountains during the First Indochina War, and to ensure their continued loyalty to the new regime, the Việt Minh (Việt Nam Độc Lập Đồng Minh Hội, League for the Independence of Vietnam) had agreed to demarcate the mountainous regions as autonomous administrative units to allow for a higher degree of self-governance and self-representation by the ethnic minorities. However, these autonomous regions existed as such only from 1956 to 1975.[1] The mountainous region and its people left a lasting impression on Quyền Văn Minh and served as a chief inspiration for his first original composition, "Tiếng Khèn Gọi Bạn" (The Call of the *Qeej* [Hmong reed pipe]), which he would write and debut two decades later.

The Hà Tây Song-and-Dance Troupe

I stayed with the military song-and-dance troupe in Thái Nguyên Province until 1971. Together with the troupe, I performed in various provinces within the Việt Bắc Autonomous Region. In 1971, during a trip back to Hà Nội, I took part in a performance for one of the labor unions, playing the clarinet. A senior musician cadre from Hà Tây saw the performance, and he loved my playing! It turned out that he was the deputy head of the troupe and bandleader of the Hà Tây Song-and-Dance Troupe [Đoàn Ca Múa Hà Tây] music ensemble. He came to talk to me and asked, "Where are you playing now?" I told him that I was playing with the Việt Bắc Military Region Song-and-Dance Troupe. "I know the leadership of your troupe. I will ask them to transfer you over to join the Hà Tây Song-and-Dance Troupe. Do you want to join my troupe?" I told him, "Yes!" That was how I came back to the delta plains.

With the Việt Bắc Military Region Song-and-Dance Troupe, I was receiving the salary of an apprentice. The bandleader of the Hà Tây Song-and-Dance Troupe, who had offered me the opportunity to join his troupe, gave me a grade 2 salary! A grade 2 salary was worth forty-eight đồng, and an apprentice's salary was only five đồng! In those days during the Subsidy Period [Thời Bao Cấp], a grade 2 salary could also involve further benefits. For artists, we received rations of sugar, milk, and meat! That was an absolutely attractive offer. Cadres who were placed in higher salary grades would receive more rations for different types of daily necessities, food, cloth, stationery, and other things. Of course, there was no certainty that we would receive the stipulated rations due to shortage of supply. Every time I received mine, I set aside a small portion for myself and brought back the rest in a gunnysack for my family. All artists received this kind of privilege, and their families were very proud of them.

I stayed with the Hà Tây Song-and-Dance Troupe for three years. Starting as an ordinary member of the orchestra, I worked hard to become one of the key musicians in the ensemble accompanying singers on the stage. Six months later, I was promoted to a grade 3 salary because I was formally recognized as a full-time member of the troupe. I worked very hard to improve myself. My efforts were rewarded with the confidence of musicians and singers in my ability to play the clarinet. We delivered very successful shows in the provinces and cities in the North. I also participated in social outreach work when the Hà Tây Song-and-Dance Troupe collaborated with the musician Nguyễn Hữu and poet Bế Kiến Quốc to stage performances in the rural areas and camps for invalids. When the Hà Tây bandleader invited me to join him in the Hà Tây Song-and-Dance Troupe, he also advised me that there would be more opportunities to take up additional unofficial performances if I returned to the plains. Up in the mountainous region of Việt Bắc, other than playing in the official program of the troupe, there was almost no opportunity to pick up additional gigs.

Minh's Second Encounter with Jazz

While Minh relocated to the uplands and then returned to the plains as he began his professional music career, some of his friends and acquaintances traveled outside Vietnam as they embarked on their career path. Belonging to the socialist bloc, Vietnam received tremendous aid and support from socialist allies in Eastern Europe during the Cold War. Beginning in the 1950s, tens of thousands of Vietnamese from the Democratic Republic of Vietnam (DRV) were sent to socialist countries such as East Germany, Czechoslovakia, Poland, and the Soviet Union. These Vietnamese were sent to Eastern Europe for two specific purposes: vocational training and further study.[2] For example, Czechoslovakia and the DRV had agreed in 1967 that 2,100 Vietnamese would be sent to Czechoslovakia to be trained in specific industry-related skills for between three and five years. Vietnamese participating in such programs were called *praktikanti* (trainees). In 1974, the agreement with Czechoslovakia was extended and expanded. Another cohort of more than 5,000 Vietnamese *praktikanti* arrived in the host country during the 1970s.[3] These Vietnamese in Eastern Europe worked and studied in much better living conditions than they had back home, including the functioning infrastructure of these more developed socialist countries. As one of Christina Schwenkel's informants who had worked in East Germany remarked, "We used to say that East Germany was a paradise [*thiên đường*]."[4] Despite attempts by Vietnamese embassy personnel to isolate, surveil, and control interactions by compatriots in the destination countries, Vietnamese workers in Eastern Europe lived and interacted with members of the host country's wider society nonetheless.[5] Upon their return to Vietnam, these migrants not only brought back money and goods in short supply in the DRV; they also brought back cultural artifacts, including vinyl records circulating in Eastern Europe. And, as detailed in Interlude I above, there was jazz in Eastern Europe.

Sometime in 1972, soon after I joined the Hà Tây Song-and-Dance Troupe, I had an unforgettable encounter while playing at a wedding. One of the guests at the wedding, who had just returned to Vietnam after studying overseas in Eastern Europe, approached me after listening to my playing. He came over and said to me, "I have a vinyl record of music, featuring the clarinet, very interesting music. Would you like to listen to it?" I went to his place to listen to the vinyl on a record player; it was similar to the type of music I had heard on the transistor radio several years before! It was the same type of music that I had tried to transcribe and practice on my own. By now, I had already learned that it was called "jazz." But I dared not ask him to let me borrow the vinyl record. It was too valuable. Besides, I did not have a record player. I asked him to let me come back the next day to listen again and that I would come at any time that he could be available. We fixed the time at about 5:00 p.m. to 6:00 p.m. the next day. I went back at 5:00 p.m. the next day as agreed, and I listened for a full hour, but I could only write down a portion of the music from the entire record. I kept moving the needle back to repeat, but I was also worried that this would irritate my host. I was also reluctant to stay over into dinnertime, which would be most inconvenient for his family. I asked him to let me come back the

Figure 5.1. Vinyl record from Eastern Europe (from Lưu Quang Minh's collection).

next day to listen again, because I wanted to write down more of the music. For three afternoons, I went to his house to listen to the record, and I wrote down as much of the music as I could.

Three afternoons, I probably exhausted the hospitality and patience of my host. I was very grateful because I managed to transcribe one full song! I went home and practiced this song. I tried to perfect it, so that I could play exactly what I had heard on the vinyl record. I was elated! I could finally play jazz! When I was practicing it, my friends at the Hà Tây Song-and-Dance Troupe were puzzled by the music I was trying to play. They asked, "What is that music you are playing? It sounds strange. In fact, it sounds rather nonsensical!" By then I knew that the music that captivated me was called jazz, so I told them, "This is jazz." I told them that it was really difficult to play, but I was happy to let them practice together with me. "Practice for what? Who would want to listen to this nonsense?" Those were the reactions I received from my fellow musicians.

I practiced alone and I just kept practicing to play what I had heard. I practiced classical music, too. In fact, whatever song, whatever practice book, whatever anyone else could lend me, I practiced them all! I continued with the work ethic that had started my journey in music, practicing and trying to master whatever music I encountered. I became an extremely versatile musician because I practiced and studied all kinds of music that I could obtain or borrow. 1972 was also the year that I began to pay more attention to the saxophone. I think I could say that when I was playing for the Hà Tây Song-and-Dance Troupe, I was already one of the leading clarinetists in this country.

Leaving a Music Career

I moved back to Hà Nội in 1974 because my father wanted me to come back home. By then, I was receiving a grade 3 salary with the Hà Tây Song-and-Dance Troupe, the salary grade of a soloist. Together with nonmonetary benefits, I was receiving a very comfortable income for that time. Every month, I could bring home a whole gunnysack of sugar, milk powder, and meat. It was a huge thing during the Subsidy Period to be able to receive stipulated rations of these items! I tried to be more frugal so that I could bring back more money, sugar, milk powder, and meat for my mother and to support my family. At that time, my father advised me that, working out there in Hà Đông [the capital city of the old Hà Tây Province], there were only limited external gigs I could pick up outside my official work. As such, I should try to come back to Hà Nội, where I would have more opportunities to make extra income to help out the family. My eldest brother was still studying, so the responsibility of helping out the family fell on my shoulders.

My father arranged for me to join Đoàn Ca Múa Thăng Long [Thăng Long Song-and-Dance Troupe] in Hà Nội. Guess what? They wanted to know where I had studied music and asked if I had earned my music diploma! They could not accept a musician without a music diploma into their troupe.

That attempt to join Thăng Long failed, so my father arranged for me to try to join Đoàn Xiếc Hà Nội [Hà Nội Circus Troupe], to play music for the circus! True, I was very versatile and could play all kinds of music! I joined in the performance with the band straightaway when I went over to meet them. They were full of praise and compliments after that. They recognized that I was in control of the entire performance, even though that was only the first session in which I had joined them. The circus troupe was ready to take me in, but they could only pay me the salary grade of an apprentice musician. They insisted that I had to have a diploma in order to receive a performing artist's salary grade! I told my father that there was no way I could accept the salary grade of an apprentice musician. I was leading the music! I had been receiving the grade 3 salary of a soloist musician in Hà Tây! How could I accept the salary grade of an apprentice musician? If I accepted that, how many more years would it take for me to get promoted back to salary grade 3?

My father chided me for being stubborn. I said to my father, "No, I am not being stubborn." I was already a young adult, although I did try to listen to my father's advice and suggestions, which was why I had moved back to Hà Nội in the first place. I explained to my father that I knew the standard of my music and that I was not being proud. I knew that I deserved a better job, so in the end, I was left jobless since I had already left the Hà Tây Song-and-Dance Troupe. I read at home and practiced my music. I focused on my music. Even though I was already a young adult, I was still a little intimidated by the authority of my parents! But my mother was very understanding. She explained to my father that he could not blame me or reprimand me and that I had gained my own self-respect playing music in two different song-and-dance troupes, and that I had even been promoted to the position of a soloist musician in Hà Tây on my own. There was no way that I could go back to receiving an apprentice salary after I had already been the leading musician in the Hà Tây Song-and-Dance Troupe.

At that time, on the street in Hà Nội where I was staying, the local neighborhood committee was issuing a "sổ lao động" [labor booklet] to keep a record of who was working, who was not working, and what in professions people were working in the neighborhood. It happened that I had already resigned from my position with the Hà Tây Song-and-Dance Troupe and had just returned to Hà Nội. I reported to the neighborhood committee that I was "currently waiting to join another troupe." My father told the leader of the neighborhood committee that he had actually found me a job in Hà Nội, but that I had rejected that position. As a result, I was singled out to be criticized by the neighborhood! In the evenings, I had to attend self-criticism sessions with other youths who were considered unprogressive or unproductive, who were not being conscientious members of society. I went along, kept silent, and accepted all the criticisms laid on me, night after night.

Two days later, coincidentally, I came across an old classmate, the one who had let me listen to the radio in exchange for my ration of bread. He was working for Trường Thể Dục Thể Thao Từ Sơn [Từ Sơn College of Physical Education and Sports]. At his workplace, there was an arts ensemble that wanted to participate in a performance festival in Bắc Giang. He had told the leadership of his college that he knew a friend who was an excellent musician, could perform all kinds of music, and could play any song on the clarinet. He came back to Hà Nội to invite me to join them for the festival. I went along, arranged the music, helped them get ready for the performance, and played clarinet for them. We got a gold medal at the festival, and as a result the school asked me to join them. Having been criticized by the neighborhood committee, I agreed to join the school straightaway.

In 1975, I officially joined the propaganda department of the Từ Sơn College of Physical Education and Sports to help develop arts and cultural programs for both faculty members and students. During the day, I would play a bit of piano to accompany the students doing their exercise and practice routines. These were just simple pieces played to give them a rhythm for the exercises. Whenever there was any arts group preparing for a performance, I would practice with them. I managed to work there for three years. When I was working at Từ Sơn, around 1976, I took out my father's saxophone and started practicing with it regularly. I had time, and the place where I worked was spacious, so I was not disturbing anyone. In fact, I practiced even harder when I was at Từ Sơn. During this period, I continued to support the various government agencies, factories, and cooperatives that organized cultural performances for their cadres and members in the capital city. While working at Từ Sơn, there was not a day when I did not wish that I could go back to performing music on the stage.

Minh's Third Encounter with Jazz

When I was working at Từ Sơn, I joined the Hà Nội City Youth League [Thanh Đoàn Thành phố Hà Nội] and participated in the music group of the Youth Club [Câu Lạc Bộ Thanh Niên] under the direction of lecturers and musicians such as Vũ Nhật Thăng and Trịnh Kính. The music group brought together young musicians living in the city, including musicians in the various song-and-dance troupes and musicians not associated with any professional groups, and gave them the opportunity to play music together in a community music club. At that time, the Youth League sent a music ensemble to perform in Sài Gòn and Lâm Đồng (one of the provinces in Tây Nguyên [the western plateau, commonly referred to as the Central Highlands]) for the migrants pioneering new agricultural lands in New Economic Zones. I was one of the members who participated in this trip to the south. That was in 1976, and it was my first trip to Tây Nguyên. After finishing the scheduled performances in Sài Gòn, I thought that I should look around. Sài Gòn had been under American influence for over twenty years, so there must be some jazz materials lying around. I walked an entire street known for selling cassette tapes and vinyl records, but I could not find any jazz music.

America's intervention in the Second Indochina War permeated the musical soundscape of South Vietnam. Rock 'n' roll music, in particular, flourished in the South as soon as it was introduced to Vietnam in the 1950s. Amateur Vietnamese bands sprouted up in the music scene and performed this trending Western rock and popular music in the bars, dance halls, nightclubs, and military bases, and in live stage shows and music festivals organized for the general public. By the early 1970s, Vietnamese musicians in the South were writing original lyrics and music that reflected their attempt to find their place in the world, then marked by the disorder and violence of the Second Indochina War.[6] The soundscape of South Vietnam, however, was very much dominated by the ballads of local Vietnamese songwriters, creating a nuanced genre of *tân nhạc* (new music), who fundamentally sang of love, war, and philosophical musings on life in the complicated war years. The songs of Trịnh Công Sơn, Vietnam's most famous songwriter living in the South at that time, very much characterized the musical soundscape of South Vietnam.

But there was a tiny, almost insignificant jazz scene, too. Playing Western popular songs, rock, blues, and some jazz in the nightclubs, dance halls, and hotel bars of Sài Gòn were peripatetic musicians from the United States, the Philippines, and other ally countries of the Americans. Professional Vietnamese musicians worked the scene, too. Among the more prominent Vietnamese musicians was the legendary band leader and pianist Lê Văn Thiện, who led his own band in the nightclubs and played some jazz. In this Sài Gòn circle of musicians who played jazz were Đỗ Văn Ngọc (trumpet), Đan Thọ (saxophone), Đinh Văn Hoàng (saxophone), Nguyễn Văn Hạnh (double bass), Huỳnh Anh (drums), and Marcel Sang (vocals), among others.[7] This very insignificant jazz scene in South Vietnam, however, faded out with reunification under the communist regime in 1975.

After 1975, music in the reunified country was subjected to more stringent state control and was categorized by colors. *Nhạc đỏ* (red music) refers to revolutionary music that tells of the endeavors and ideals of the socialist revolution and patriotism for the nation. *Nhạc xanh* (green music), which emerged after reunification in 1975, refers to youthful music that tells of the peaceful era under the communist regime. *Nhạc nhẹ* (light music) and *ca khúc chính trị* (political songs), which began to gain popularity in the late 1970s, were included under the umbrella of *nhạc xanh*. Red music and green music were officially endorsed and encouraged by the communist state. These two categories of music could be freely performed and broadcast.

Nhạc tiền chiến (prewar music) refers to the romantic ballads composed by Vietnamese musicians such as Văn Cao, Phạm Duy, Đặng Thế Phong, and Đoàn Chuẩn prior to 1945. Prewar music was subjected to the state's scrutiny, censorship, and approval; it could not be performed or broadcast without explicit approval by the state.

Nhạc vàng (yellow music) refers specifically to the category of music composed in the South during the republican or "American puppet" regime era (*thời chế độ Mỹ Ngụy*) in the 1950s and 1960s; this music was considered reactionary, negatively romantic, and decadent.[8] This category included most of the songs composed by Trịnh Công Sơn.⁹ Together with foreign music such as rock and jazz brought in from the capitalist world, yellow music was specifically singled out by the communist government as reactionary cultural artifacts that should be eliminated in the effort to develop socialism in the reunified country.¹⁰

Jazz, according to Philip Taylor, was marked as a decadent foreign influence and was to be discouraged.¹¹ Taking aim at musicians in the South who had been influenced by American cultural poison, one Vietnamese critic (cited by Taylor) declared:

> [H]earing this music, one thinks it rich, for it involves many instruments, many complex melodies and arrangements; however, on analysis, it proves to be the higgledy-piggledy collection (*kết hợp hỗn độn*) of different kinds of varieties and methods. . . . The principal result of this kind of music is a barbarous shrieking (*tiếng gào thét màn rợ*) and arousal (*sự kích thích*), betraying the infiltration of jazz music—the diseased style (*phong cách bệnh*) marking nearly all musicians who call themselves avant-garde.¹²

Popular pre-1975 southern Vietnamese music and foreign music were banned outright or restricted from public broadcast. In private, people were afraid of being discovered listening to this unapproved music. Pre-1975 music artifacts such as cassette tapes and vinyl records that contained "unrevolutionary" music were disposed of, confiscated, or stored in secret.¹³ Immediately after reunification, many southern Vietnamese sold their electrical equipment such as cassette players, television sets, hi-fi equipment, electric fans, and even refrigerators at very low prices, as they sought to raise funds to meet their daily living expenses, or finance their eventual departure from the communist-ruled country. All this equipment began to rise in value in the black market from 1976 onward.¹⁴

I was about to give up looking when I walked into a store owned by an elderly man and asked, "Do you have any music cassette tapes of Black musicians?" The elderly owner took a very careful look at me, and I knew he was wary because he could tell that I was clearly a northerner by my accent. I explained myself a bit more: "I am just a musician; I play the saxophone and clarinet. I have nothing to do with politics at all. I want to listen to that type music so that I can learn." With this explanation, the owner opened up and told me that he might have one such cassette. He went to the back of the shop, and fifteen minutes later he came out with a cassette tape. I looked at the cassette cover: a band of Black musicians with a Black lady singing into a microphone. I knew that was it! I immediately said to the elderly owner that I would buy it. "It is not worth much money now, you can just take it"; the elderly owner was very kind. But I insisted that he let me pay for it. I asked that he play a bit of the cassette tape for me to listen to, simply because at that time I did not own a cassette tape player!

The elderly owner popped the cassette tape into a small cassette player. After listening for maybe half a minute, I asked the owner, "How much would this cassette player cost? If it is not too expensive, I would like to buy it, too. But I do not have much money to afford it." Seeing that I was really enthusiastic about the music, the elderly owner replied that it only cost ten đồng. I counted the money I had in my pocket; I only had eight and a half đồng. I asked the owner to hold the cassette player for me and promised that I would come back the next day with the rest of the money, after borrowing from my friends. "You can have it for eight and a half đồng, since you like the music so much. Let me help you." I was so grateful! I wrapped the cassette tape and the cassette player in my raincoat and carefully put the bundle inside my backpack. I was very careful to ensure that nothing knocked or pressed against my backpack on the way back to Hà Nội.

When I got back to Hà Nội, I carefully unwrapped the music cassette and cassette player. I sat down by myself to listen to the music and totally immersed myself in it. By the time I finished transcribing all the songs, the cassette tape was totally damaged. It was so difficult to transcribe the music, especially the solo sections, I kept rewinding and playing, rewinding and playing. The music was too sophisticated; I had to listen over and over again to catch every note and phrasing. It was a pity that by the time I was done, the cassette tape was damaged. I consoled myself that it was fine because I already had the "capital" to develop further.

Later, when I moved home from Nghĩa Đô back to Hàng Giấy, my second wife got rid of many of my old notepapers, books, records, and cassettes. She sold the lot by weight, by kilogram! That was how I lost these early materials that I had transcribed. You know how people used the old books and papers that were sold by weight? They cut out the paper and used it as lining for bird cages to collect bird excrement. What a waste of my notes and books! It was a pity indeed.

I got married in 1977. That was my first marriage. My first wife and I met in the Hà Tây Song-and-Dance Troupe, where I worked from 1971 to 1974. We worked together in the same troupe. I was born in 1954, and she was born in 1952, so she was two years older than me. In Hà Tây, I was young and easygoing; I came from Hà Nội and stood out as an outstanding musician. Many of the ladies in the troupe were very nice to me. My first wife, who had joined the troupe earlier than me, took very good care of me. Well, before meeting my first wife, I was going out with a dancer from Sơn Tây. There was much potential in that relationship, but she was transferred to the Hoà Bình Song-and-Dance Troupe, and I had to accept my fate. Because we would be living in different places far from each other, she suggested that we break up so that she could go on with her life in Hoà Bình. I had to accept that outcome. Anyway, for me, the most important thing was always music, so the end of that relationship did not trouble me too much. After that breakup, my future first wife took the initiative to approach me, and she consoled me. At that time, I felt that this lady was worth considering. I was a young man full of self-confidence. I was not well off, but being a musician, what really mattered to me was that I could play really good music. That was all I cared about as a musician. I might have to walk from place to place, since I did not own a bicycle at that time, but I was brimming with confidence because I knew that I was among the best clarinetists in the North. I had a regular job with a regular income, so I knew that when I started a family, my kids would not go hungry. Then I left Hà Tây in 1974 and ended up in Từ Sơn.

Our wedding was not a grand affair, but we had a proper wedding. In those days, the labor union provided a car for me to fetch the bride and gave us other kinds of support to get married. We had a band playing at our wedding, and of course it was not playing jazz music, since no one knew anything about jazz then! As I was in the music circle, my friends naturally came to play at the wedding. We rented a function room that belonged to the Department of Education, which was big enough to host all our invited guests. I remember that it rained very heavily that day, but our guests still came, and the ceremony was properly celebrated with friends and relatives. We did not invite too many people, just our friends in the music circle and our relatives. It was only at the ceremony for my second marriage that I was able to have a larger party, because by then I was already a member of the conservatoire.

I thought that that was all my life was going to be about at that time! Get married, start a family, and it would not be too bad a life.

We got married at the beginning of 1977, and by the end of the year my wife gave birth to Chi, my first child, my daughter. Then we had Đắc, my son. Working at Từ Sơn College, I received a state salary and was officially a state cadre. I was not making a good income, but I continued to play music and took up gigs as and when I could. When I finished work in the evening, I took the bus home and accepted any extra work available to make some extra income to take care of my children. Those days, I would accept extra gigs to provide background music for amateur groups to sing. These amateur groups belonged to various associations, agencies, or cooperatives. They would pay for musicians to come and play for them so that they could put up performances every now and then. Sometimes, they would pay me with items such as meat or even rice! And sometimes, I would suggest that they could pay me with a specific item that I needed. Those were the days when we could only purchase certain things with ration stamps. And it was not easy to buy fatty pork in those days. People very much preferred to buy fatty pork instead of lean meat. It was the most important item. With fatty pork, one could use the fat to stir-fry vegetables or tofu, or to make fried rice. It was the key ingredient. I know that I am repeating this information, but these were the kinds of things that really stayed with me and with the people of my generation.

Anyway, I finally decided to leave Từ Sơn so that I could refocus on my music.

TRACK 6

Berlin, 1987

After 1975, electric combo bands began to emerge in Hà Nội. *Nhạc nhẹ* (light music), which had largely disappeared from the official stage after 1954, gradually resurfaced in the North. Song-and-dance troupes began including an electric combo band playing light music in shows, giving Quyền Văn Minh the opportunity to flourish in the music scene. Toward the second half of the 1980s, popular Vietnamese love songs returned to the music scene as the Đổi Mới reforms were introduced. But jazz was yet to be found in the official soundscape. In 1987, Minh visited East Germany and heard jazz in the city of East Berlin.

The Golden Bell of the Capital Troupe

By the time Minh was ready to leave his stable job at Từ Sơn College of Physical Education and Sports, the music scene in Hà Nội was experiencing a subtle change, with the liberation of Sài Gòn in 1975. *Nhạc nhẹ*, generally understood as easy-listening music with or without lyrics, which was popular before 1954, had begun to slowly return to the scene. With the war over and the country reunified, the atmosphere relaxed a little, and light music gradually assumed a role in the peacetime development of leisure and artistic activities. Along with light music, the concept of the electric combo band, consisting of a drum set, keyboard, rhythm guitar, lead guitar, bass guitar, and saxophone (or trumpet), already common in the south, began to catch on in the capital. According to Nguyễn Thụy Kha, upon completing a performance tour in the South in 1975, the military band of Bộ Tư lệnh Thông tin (Information Headquarters) brought back to Hà Nội a drum set, two electric guitars, and a Yamaha keyboard. In 1977, the musician Khắc Văn formed the first official light music band for the recently established Nhà hát Tuổi trẻ (Youth Theater). More significantly, musicians in this band were officially included in the tenured head count of the theater and treated as *cán bộ nhà nước* (cadres of the state). The communist government even officially endorsed the electric combo band as an accepted format for

Figure 6.1. The Golden Bell of the Capital Troupe.

music performance by organizing combo band competitions singing *ca khúc chính trị* (political songs).[1] As Jason Gibbs notes, rock music developed in the South managed to travel north (ideologically speaking), having been quickly "rehabilitated through a musical movement called *ca khúc chính trị*" in support of the communist government's massive, organized migration program to create "New Economic Zones" by developing agricultural pioneer fronts in the forested uplands.[2] The rise of light music and the electric combo band in Hà Nội brought Minh back into the circle of the song-and-dance troupes.

It was in 1980 that I joined Đoàn Chuông Vàng Thủ Đô [Golden Bell of the Capital Troupe] to help them develop a light music band as part of the Chương trình Tân Cổ Giao duyên [New and Old Crossover program]. It was Trần Mạnh Tuấn's brother-in-law who introduced me to the troupe. The Golden Bell Troupe specialized in performing "cải lương" [reformed opera]. In Tân Cổ Giao duyên, there were two sets of musicians in the ensemble: traditional instrumentalists playing traditional folk sounds with the "đàn nhị" [two-string bowed instrument], bamboo flute, and other instruments; and "new" instrumentalists playing an accordion, a saxophone, and a drum set, making "new" sounds. In Tân Cổ Giao duyên, there was always a prelude using tân nhạc to introduce the traditional cải lương part. During the main performance, new and traditional sounds were featured in alternating sections. Before the performance began, a combo band would warm up the crowd. The Golden Bell Troupe's combo band, however, was not familiar with nhạc nhẹ, an emerging genre of music at that time. I was invited to join them to lead the band and the tân nhạc part of the Tân Cổ Giao duyên program. The working environment was very good. The way I performed on the saxophone and led the music—the troupe members and leaders, as well as the audience, were all very happy with my contribution. The musicians at Golden Bell really respected me, and I was treated like their musical leader, the conductor of the ensemble.

It was a good job. The basic salary from the troupe by itself, however, would not be enough to take really good care of my family. We had to take up performances here and there to have more income. Immediately after 1975, life in Hà Nội and in the north had begun to change. Things started to change for musicians, too. There were more music tea lounges with live music, more stage shows, and even places for people to dance! Men began growing longer hair, and young people began wearing bell-bottoms. There were more gigs available; people began to organize dances [vũ hội], and wedding occasions generated a bit more atmosphere than in the past. Friends and acquaintances who really enjoyed my playing invited me to perform at these gigs. It was a way to have more income for my family, especially after having children. There were more opportunities than before. With the troupe, we traveled far and wide to give many performances in the Hà Nội metropolitan area and various provinces in the north. The advantage of working at the Golden Bell Troupe was that during the day I had a lot of time to practice. But we traveled so much, it was difficult to take care of my children. With the Golden Bell Troupe, I was simply on the road all the time! Musically, it was very fulfilling. I was bringing home a decent income, but the troupe took on too many gigs, and we were on the road all the time! This was also at a time when I had to take on more responsibilities at home to help take care of my young children. I just could not be on the road all the time.

The Thăng Long Song-and-Dance Troupe

It was with Đoàn Ca Múa Thăng Long [Thăng Long Song-and-Dance Troupe] that I really furthered my career as a professional musician. With Thăng Long, I was fully plugged into the circle of professional musicians and artists.

Sometime in 1980, a group of musicians from Sài Gòn were giving a performance in Hà Nội. The musicians invited me to join them for the performance. It was a very successful performance, and the bandleader for the Thăng Long Song-and-Dance Troupe, the troupe that had refused to accept me a few years earlier because I did not have a diploma in music, was present at the performance. In fact, this was the very same man who had asked if I had a diploma! Anyway, after

Figure 6.2. The Thăng Long Song-and-Dance Troupe.

the performance, he approached me. "That was exceptional playing! Where did you learn to play like that?" I reminded him, "You don't remember me? I came to audition to join your troupe several years ago, but you could not accept me because I did not have a diploma in music!" He was surprised by my reminder. "Well, now I am ready to employ you as a musician, so will you come? I will give you a grade 4 salary, agreed?"

My mother had always hoped that I would play for an ensemble based in Hà Nội, especially the Thăng Long Song-and-Dance Troupe, which was considered the top ensemble in the country. She had always wished that I would come back to Hà Nội and play with Thăng Long. In Vietnam, the Thăng Long Song-and-Dance Troupe was the premier musical group to play with. They were the best. They even had a better reputation than Đoàn Ca Múa Trung ương [Central Song-and-Dance Troupe], because they had all the outstanding musicians playing with them. They had such a reputation then. At that time, Thăng Long wanted to set up an electric combo band consisting of guitar, bass, drums, keyboard, and saxophone. They had a clarinetist in the band, but he was not used to playing the more rhythmic and lively music that was required in a combo band. I was the missing piece of the puzzle.

In 1981, the Hà Nội Department of Culture and Information officially transferred my tenure from Từ Sơn College to the Thăng Long Song-and-Dance Troupe. In a

Figure 6.3. The Thăng Long Song-and-Dance Troupe, Cambodia, 1988.

very short time with Thăng Long, I earned the soloist's chair in the band. I also became the lead musician for the combo band accompanying singers on the stage. I was very hardworking. Whenever there was free time, I practiced. I was also very versatile. I could blend in with any performance genre the troupe put together. At that time, I already had some decent materials to properly practice playing jazz. Jazz is such an advanced form of music! By practicing jazz, I found it very easy to play the different kinds of music the troupe was performing. In Vietnam, if you could play jazz, I would say that you were most probably a more adept musician than even a classical musician. To improvise, you had to be technically adept, and you had to be creative. Naturally, you could play in any demanding situation.

Life at the Thăng Long Song-and-Dance Troupe was not very hectic; it was not like with the Golden Bell Troupe. We also formed our own group to take up contracts to perform for occasions outside the official program, so my income was quite good. I also came into prominence as a much sought-after musician, and I was often invited to perform with notable singers from the Central Troupe and other ensembles in Hà Nội. With Thăng Long, I also participated in many sound recording sessions for stage plays, motion picture soundtracks, and backup tracks for professional and amateur singers. I also performed with Thăng Long in different provinces around the country. A most notable trip was when our combo band participated at the arts festival held in Đà Nẵng in 1988.

I also had the opportunity to travel to other countries. In 1986, the Thăng Long Song-and-Dance Troupe visited Vientiane in Laos, where we gave a light music concert. Then, there was our most memorable trip to East Berlin in 1987 [see below]. In 1988, Thăng Long performed in Phnom Penh, Cambodia, and I was a member of the contingent. I would return to Cambodia with my own band to perform in my own solo concert later, after I released my first jazz album, Birth '99.

While Minh was working at the Thăng Long Song-and-Dance Troupe, the Đổi Mới reforms were officially introduced at the Sixth Party Congress of the Vietnam Communist Party in 1986. The Đổi Mới reforms were essentially Vietnam's version of the Soviet Union's glasnost policy reforms, serving to reopen Vietnam to the world and officially reintroduce a market economy. The reforms also applied to the cultural arts, reaffirming the leadership role of the party in developing the arts to a "higher stage" while acknowledging the importance of "freedom of creativity" to allow individual artists and musicians to create "true values in culture, literature, and the arts."[3] Musicians and artists were suddenly released from the tight leash that had bound artistic expression in the North since 1954, and in the South after reunification in 1975, to weed out the undesirable and decadent influence of yellow music and other Western music. Audiences could finally begin to listen to different genres of music without fear of being persecuted. By the late 1980s, Vietnamese popular love songs began to return to the scene, and people began to openly listen to yellow music and the Western popular music of the late 1970s and 1980s.

Toward the second half of the 1980s, the cultural arts scene changed almost overnight. It was a time when the government began to loosen control over the arts. The arts scene suddenly exploded with all kinds of activities. This created an environment that made it possible for artists to have a very good income. Playing popular music, especially "tình khúc" [love songs], became a lucrative activity. You could earn very good money playing popular Vietnamese love songs in the late 1980s and 1990s. At that time, a single unofficial performance could earn you even up to twenty times more than what you would receive from an official performance! It was a very high income. In one day, you could do four or five gigs! With this unofficial source of income, I could take very good care of my kids. If I had just focused on doing this at that time, I could have become relatively well off. If I had put my jazz ambitions aside and just focused on performing Vietnamese popular love songs and recording these songs to make albums for sale, I would really be very well off! In those days, I received a lot of outside gigs. I had the reputation of being the "top cat" in the business.

At the Thăng Long Song-and-Dance Troupe, I always tried to encourage my friends to come play jazz with me. The response was underwhelming. We were very much controlled by our living circumstances and bound by the restrictive shackles of our generation, so to speak. We always tried to improve ourselves, but once we achieved something, we would use it to try to earn a better income. No one dared take the risk to invest in something immaterial to achieve a higher goal.

When I read about the great artists and the people who pioneered new pathways in their artistic endeavors around the world, I felt that I was insignificant. I did not want to spend my time just trying to earn more money. I wanted to do something different. We had a lot of our own time at Thăng Long. People call it a social calamity. After performances, the time was all ours, one could do anything as one wished! Some people just indulged in drinking, smoking, gambling, and the like. Some people indulged in music. As for me, I indulged in my music. I kept practicing my music. But when you practiced so hard, where were you going to showcase your music? And I really wanted to play jazz.

Music and Family

Upon joining the Thăng Long Song-and-Dance Troupe, Minh began to grow in stature as a respected professional musician in the context of postwar socialist Vietnam. Through the early years of playing professionally with the song-and-dance troupes, beginning with the Việt Bắc Military Region troupe and later with Hà Tây, Minh was able to hone his musical skills on the clarinet and saxophone by playing in a variety of music ensembles. Following Minh's third encounter with jazz, he finally began to understand how jazz could sound instead of relying merely on his own imagination based on the bits and pieces he had encountered earlier. The reemergence of light music and the rise of the electric combo band format in the late 1970s gave Minh, by then an adept saxophonist whose playing was strongly influenced by jazz, the opportunity to flourish as a much sought-after musician. In his personal life, he had also grown into a mature adult, taking charge of his own life by securing a stable job and starting a family of his own. Unfortunately, during this time Minh had to constantly calibrate his decision to pursue jazz in socialist Vietnam with his desire to find a better, more lucrative, and stable means of taking care of his family.

When it comes to music, you must be willing to labor. You must be willing to put in the effort. Yes, I admit in some ways I was gifted, but hard work was just as important. If I wanted to be an outstanding musician, my head had to be clear so that I could work toward my goals. I have no need to hide the fact that my first marriage failed and I had to go through a divorce. But I had no choice. It was a last resort. I could not accept this kind of wayward lifestyle that could ruin my children's future. The situation with my first wife totally ruined my focus in music. I had to end the marriage. That was with my first wife. I married my first wife in 1977, but in 1984 we divorced and concluded that marriage. Chi, my daughter, was seven years old and Đắc was five years old at that time.

My first wife loved playing cards; she loved gambling. Life in the song-and-dance troupes, we had a lot of free time. I used my free time to practice music, but there were others who used their free time to gamble: cards, tiles, dice, and all kinds of games. It was quite common for artists and cadres to spend their free time playing cards. That was fine, but please don't overindulge! The excitement that came with gambling kept the addiction going, and the betting went higher and higher. My first wife got into gambling. She gambled too much, and that led to all kinds of problems. Not long after joining the Thăng Long troupe, I discovered that my wife's gambling had caused serious problems at home. It led to our divorce.

I can tell you one particular story. In the 1970s and early 1980s, the "sổ gạo" [rice booklet] was extremely important to every individual, every family. I remember, each adult was entitled to thirteen kilos of rice, and each child was entitled to seven or eight kilos at that time. When we bought the stipulated ration of rice each month, the amount was recorded in the book; you could not buy more, even if you had the money. With that book, you could buy rice, flour, cassava, and other staples. The sổ gạo was the most important document during that era. People actually used it as collateral in gambling. I could not tolerate such irresponsible behavior, and when something like this happened, I decided to end our marriage. But my father-in-law came and persuaded me to give further thought to our marriage for the sake of our two children, who were still very young. He promised that he would guide his daughter and asked me to give her a second chance. I understood where he was coming from, so I agreed. Yes, she had made a mistake, but if she could learn from it and henceforth take better care of the children, I believed that I could forgive her.

I thought about giving up my tenure at the Thăng Long Song-and-Dance Troupe in Hà Nội. Given the situation, I thought it would be better for my children if I transferred back to Hà Tây so that I could keep an eye on my wife. She was still working in Hà Tây then. I discussed the matter with the bandleader, the person who had hired me for the position at Thăng Long. The bandleader informed me that the city government had just introduced an initiative stipulating that if a husband was working in Hà Nội, it was possible to transfer his spouse to a working unit in the city, too! My first wife was a theater artist in Hà Tây, so technically speaking it would be all right for her to join another drama theater or song-and-dance troupe. But she was not considered an outstanding artist such that a theater group in Hà Nội would accept her at that time. I spoke to Đoàn Kịch [Drama Troupe] in Hà Nội. At that time, I had performed for them and made a number of recordings for them. But they could only offer my wife a position in the costume department. She could take on some small stage roles if they did not have enough actors. She was unwilling to accept this position. Later, my bandleader helped her find a position at Đoàn Múa Rối Nước [Water Puppet Troupe], which was a newly established unit then. And he helped me with the paperwork and to make the necessary arrangements. But at that time, I simply did not have the means to ensure a smooth transfer. The bandleader was very understanding, and he went all out to help make the transfer for my wife. My bandleader wrote to the Department of Culture and the city administration, and finally they managed to arrange for her transfer to the Water Puppet Troupe.

Although I had managed to change her working environment, I could not change her. We legally ended our marriage in 1984.

When the court summoned us, during the hearing, the judge looked at me and commented that I must be the one who had misbehaved and thus caused the breakdown of our marriage. At that time, I was slim, considered quite good looking, and exhibited the flair of what people at that time saw as an artistic outlook, so the judge naturally thought that I was the one at fault. I replied to the judge's comment, "I only have two things to say. One, please conduct a thorough investigation of my background with the song-and-dance troupe where I am working. In fact, check with the song-and-dance troupes and the department that I worked for in the past, and the current troupe that I am working for right now. You will get a better idea of my personality and the context of this divorce. Two, I am applying for full custody of the two children following the divorce." In those days, the regime always tried to protect the rights of women to make sure they did not lose out in the event of a divorce. I also knew that if I separated the two children, then I would totally lose my connection with the child who would be assigned to my wife. I wanted to have full custody of both children.

The judge, after reading our case report, immediately decided to grant me full custody of Chi and Đắc. He even wanted my ex-wife to contribute to the monthly expenses of taking care of the children! I suggested to the judge, "I can support the children myself. In the first place, I don't want her contribution. And, second, she does not have that kind of money. I am only a musician at the theater, so every time I receive a summons letter from the court, I have to put everything aside to attend the session. Every time she fails to contribute to the children's expenses as ruled by the court, I will have to come in to attend the necessary proceedings. I simply cannot afford to keep disrupting my rehearsals and performance schedule. I shall bear all the expenses for taking care of the children myself."

1984 was perhaps the lowest point in my life. Those were hard times. When my marriage ended, my father took me to task: "I warned you before about this marriage, but you wouldn't listen!" I could only quietly reply that I would look after everything myself.

I sold my bicycle to build a wooden shelter on the rooftop of my parent's place on Hàng Giấy. The shelter was only six square meters, enough for myself and my two children to sleep. My mother, she was very understanding, in particular about the tense relationship between my father and me. My father, he was advanced in years, and beyond the age at which he could change his temperament. As for me,

Figure 6.4. Wooden shelter on the rooftop of the Hàng Giấy apartment.

for me to adapt back to him after all these years as an independent adult would take some time. My mother said to me, "It is okay for you to stay on the rooftop; I support your decision. But the two children, they are still young, and there is no way they can bear the hardship of living on the rooftop as you can. Let them stay with me in the family's apartment." That was the toughest and most difficult period for me and my children. I agreed with my mother's suggestion. The children could stay with their grandparents in the family's apartment, but they had to come up to the shelter on the rooftop to eat with me during mealtimes. I would cook and take care of their meals. In the morning, I would cook rice and stir-fry vegetables with some pork fat and maybe one or two slices of meat. We would eat a portion of this for breakfast and save the rest for lunch. Of course, there would have been just a little meat left for lunch, and sometimes none at all! I tried to save a bit more meat for my two children, because they were still growing and needed better nutrition. I usually let them eat first. In 1984, I ended up staying on the rooftop, the very place I used for practicing guitar and clarinet when I was a kid.

Seeing the difficulties I was facing, some friends suggested that I put music aside and take up another, more lucrative opportunity to earn a better income. At that time, the Thống Nhất Railway was in full operation transporting passengers and goods between north and south. I had played some gigs for the railway agency. A friend who was working at the railway agency suggested that I participate in the business of buying and selling goods via the railway. People would buy goods in bulk and repackage them in smaller portions to sell elsewhere. Then they would transport these goods via the railway to different destinations along the line. They would also purchase supplies from different regions where the railway line passed and sell them in other regions. It was a very lucrative business! My friend asked me to join him full time to do this. It was an attractive offer; these kinds of opportunities were really attractive at that time. Those days, I even went so far as to skip lunch just to take up lunchtime gigs to earn a little bit more money! In the morning, we had our own meetings and rehearsals at the troupe, and we would do the same thing in the afternoon, meetings and rehearsals. During our lunch break, I could choose to go home and eat or accept a small gig to earn a little bit more money. I often went hungry just to take up such gigs. The opportunity to go into the trading business on the railway was very tempting, but I was already a tenured cadre with the Thăng Long Song-and-Dance Troupe. I chose to stay with music.

To be honest, I was later tempted by yet another opportunity for a more lucrative income and perhaps a better, more stable life, but I would have to give up my dream of playing jazz in Vietnam. In 1989, the Vietnam-Hungary Friendship Association invited me to perform in Budapest. After the performance, my friends who were already working in Budapest asked me to stay behind and make a living by starting a small business or something. I had gotten my divorce a few years earlier and was juggling to develop my career, make more money, and take care of my children, all at the same time. I gave some thought to my friends' suggestion. Naturally, I also went around to see Hungarian jazz musicians play. Hungary had a fabulous jazz scene. The musicians were fabulous! And I asked myself, "Could I stand among these Hungarian musicians and play jazz with them, side by side?" But I also understood that at that time, if I chose to stay in Hungary, I would not be making a living with my music or playing jazz. I would be selling things in the markets! Those days, people would bring cigarettes and all kinds of other items to sell in the markets overseas. You could earn a lot of money doing that. I could get rich and have a better life. Before the trip, my director spoke to me: "I am rather concerned about signing the papers for you to go to Hungary alone. I fear that you might not want to come back to Vietnam." My reply was very simple: "My life is intertwined with playing the saxophone. That is the only thing I want to do, play music. I am a very principled person; when the program is over, I will return. That is my promise." When I came back to Hà Nội, I went to the post office to call the director immediately to let him *know that I was back in town already. I wanted to play jazz. I was determined to play jazz in Vietnam.*

Berlin, 1987

1987 was a very significant year for me. I was invited to perform as a soloist at the testimonial concert of the musician Đỗ Hồng Quân. The concert was held at the prestigious Hà Nội Opera House. He was conducting the National Symphony Orchestra, and I was invited to perform two classical pieces featuring solo alto saxophone, namely "Song of the Indian Guest" by Nikolai Rimsky-Korsakov and "The Little Shepherd" by Claude Debussy. To be invited by Đỗ Hồng Quân, who was already a very respected composer then and would later become the chairman of the Hội Nhạc Sĩ [Association of Musicians], to perform with the National Symphony Orchestra was essentially a recognition of my competence as the leading saxophonist in the country.

In the same year, 1987, the Thăng Long Song-and-Dance Troupe was deciding on who to allocate a "căn hộ" [flat] in the "khu tập thể" [collective residential area] belonging to the Hà Nội Department of Culture. I was on the short list because of merit in terms of my work performance. That was a period when the country's various government bureaucracies were allocating living quarters to their own cadres. The list of criteria to select cadres who qualified to receive a flat in the khu tập thể was quite comprehensive, taking into account one's contribution as a cadre and one's family situation. The selection committee recognized my specialization as an outstanding saxophone artist and my contribution to the arts. As such, I was given some priority in the selection. At that time, I was also in a situation where a father and two children were all living together in a wooden shelter on a rooftop. The Department of Culture sent people to evaluate my living situation and agreed that the existing environment was not ideal for my children, and that I should be given further priority on the basis of individual living circumstances in the selection process. I was granted a flat located in Khu Tập thể Nghĩa Tân [Nghĩa Tân Collective Residential Area] in Nghĩa Đô. It was on the fourth level and slightly more than forty square meters. There were two rooms in the apartment; the children slept in the bigger room, and I slept in the smaller room. There, the children had to go to school on their own. It was not easy, because their schools were still near Hàng Giấy. But we finally got our own place!

Those days, to receive such an apartment was a huge deal, because people would evaluate its worth in terms of monetary value! Everyone saw this as a huge present given by the state! At that time, the city was constructing very few new buildings; the Hà Nội Department of Culture was only allocated six apartments, and I received one of these six apartments. I knew very clearly at that time that if I had no specialization, if I was not excellent in what I did and had no achievements, I would not stand a chance of being selected to receive this apartment.

In 1987, together with some members of the ethnic song-and-dance ensemble under the Thăng Long Song-and-Dance Troupe, I performed in East Berlin, in the Democratic Republic of Germany, to celebrate the 750th anniversary of Berlin. I played the clarinet as a member of the ethnic music ensemble. The trip to Berlin was by itself a most significant one, which led to the 1988 and 1989 solo recitals introducing the sound of jazz in Vietnam. This trip to East Germany was also a controversial one. The directors of the troupe had originally made the decision to send me but later changed their minds and decided to send another cadre who also played clarinet in the troupe. This other musician had graduated from the conservatoire, so he had a proper diploma in music. He had questioned our supervisors: "Why was Minh selected for this overseas trip when Minh has no diploma from a proper school?" He reasoned that because he had proper paper qualifications, he should be the one selected to go to Berlin. Others in the troupe felt that in terms of musical proficiency it was only right that the directors selected me for the trip. It created quite a controversy in the troupe. Some colleagues supported him, while others reasoned that I was the better musician and therefore deserved to go. Others suggested that we should organize a contest to see who was the better musician to travel to Berlin for this trip.

At the same time, a number of people argued that since I had been given the apartment, this was already a "lộc to" [huge fortune], because the house was worth a lot more than the trip, so I should give up the opportunity to go overseas and let someone else benefit from it. The controversy was quite sad, because in those days, people tended to reduce everything to money. I was upset because the other clarinetist and I played music together, and now because of an overseas trip we developed this kind of friction. I refuted all these positions. I stated that I had been granted the apartment because of my family situation and because of my contribution to the troupe. I could return the apartment to the Department of Culture if anyone felt I was not deserving. As for the issue about being selected to go overseas to perform, that decision had been based on my professional competence as a musician. And for me, music was the most important thing! Well, the directors agreed with my argument. In the end, the Department of Culture and troupe directors decided to send both of us to Berlin.

Those days, traveling overseas was a big thing. It was a most precious opportunity to make some quick extra income. For some, it was an opportunity to get rich. I did not know much about these things. I just followed what other people told me. Those days, people traveling overseas, mainly to Eastern Europe, would take all kinds of items from Vietnam that they could sell for a good price *in Eastern Europe. All who heard about my pending trip chipped in with advice and support—what to buy to take over there, how to take these things over, and what things to buy over there to bring back and sell in Vietnam. I took things like winter jackets, eyeliner brushes, lipstick, and colorful peacock figurine keychains to sell over there. One item that was quite valuable at that time in Vietnam was motorbike headlight bulbs! I brought some of these light bulbs back to sell. With that trip, I managed to earn enough extra income to buy a color television set for my mother! She had had a fall earlier that year, hurt her back, and was rather immobile at that time. She could only sit by the side of the bed, so I bought the color television set for her. I also managed to earn enough from that trip to buy a moped, a Babetta. I was able to use it to take my kids to school and to go work in the Old Quarter. Nghĩa Đô was quite far away from Hàng Giấy, so the Babetta made traveling a lot more convenient.*

When I was in Berlin, I could hear jazz everywhere. I could hear it riding the escalator; I could hear it in the hotel lobby; I could hear it when I returned to my room and switched on the radio; and I could hear it on several channels when I turned on the television. I saw musicians playing jazz on the saxophone or clarinet almost everywhere. And I knew that I had to put together a solo recital to introduce jazz properly when I returned to Vietnam. I told myself, I must definitely perform this genre of music, jazz, when I get back to Vietnam.

There was indeed jazz behind the Iron Curtain. While jazz disappeared in Vietnam with the rise of socialism, it persisted in Eastern Europe partially because of the ideological struggle between the socialist East and the capitalist West. Ironically, it was precisely because Vietnam was part of the socialist bloc that Quyền Văn Minh was able to listen to jazz on vinyl records and cassette tapes brought back to Vietnam from Eastern Europe during the 1970s and early 1980s. When Minh traveled to East Berlin in 1987, he heard the sounds of jazz reverberating in the city throughout his sojourn, and it hardened his resolve to play jazz in the public sphere in Vietnam. As Vietnam gradually reopened its doors to the market economy and the world with the Đổi Mới reforms beginning in 1986, opportunities for Minh to introduce jazz in the public sphere gradually arose.

After I came back from the Berlin performance tour in 1987, I started planning for a solo recital. I knew that, for sure, to be able to convince my audience, I needed to show them that I could perform classical music on the saxophone, and I had to perform Vietnamese music on the saxophone, before I showed them jazz. I knew that if I did not do this there and then, I might never do it. I was motivated to present jazz in a recital that was "đàng hoàng" [right and proper] in all respects.

TRACK 7

Solo Recitals

As Vietnam officially embarked on the road to reform in 1986, the music scene, as recounted by Minh in the previous chapter, dramatically changed. Musicians were playing popular Vietnamese love songs at gigs, and such opportunities were frequent and lucrative. The reforms rehabilitated the "freedom of creativity" for musicians and artists, even though the state was not yet willing to fully relinquish its control over what could be expressed in the arts. After his trip to East Berlin in 1987, Quyền Văn Minh was determined to showcase the saxophone and jazz as *chính thống* (proper mainstream) music. In two back-to-back concerts in 1988 and 1989, Minh performed jazz live in the public sphere.

The Hội Nhạc Sĩ Việt Nam, 1989

In a small column of the newspaper *Báo Hà Nội Mới* of October 14, 1989, there was a brief announcement:

> Saxophone Recital
> The artist Quyền Văn Minh will be presenting a recital program featuring classical, modern Vietnamese, and international compositions at 19:30 p.m. on October 16, 1989, at Câu lạc bộ Hội Nhạc Sĩ Việt Nam [Music Club of the Vietnam Association of Musicians] (51 Trần Hưng Đạo, Hà Nội).[1]

A small column it was, but to get anything printed in a newspaper in Hà Nội in 1989 was a big deal (see fig. 7.1). The audience attending the recital would receive a brochure printed on A4-sized paper, on only one side on a single sheet, in black lettering on a white background, folded into three panels. Right on top of the front panel, "Câu lạc bộ Hội Nhạc Sĩ" (Clubhouse of the Association of Musicians) is printed, the venue hosting the event; and just below that, "Đoàn Ca Muá Thăng Long," the agency responsible for presenting the program. The title of the brochure reads, "A performance by the artist QUYỀN VĂN MINH

Figure 7.1. Announcement, *Báo Hà Nội Mới*, October 14, 1989.

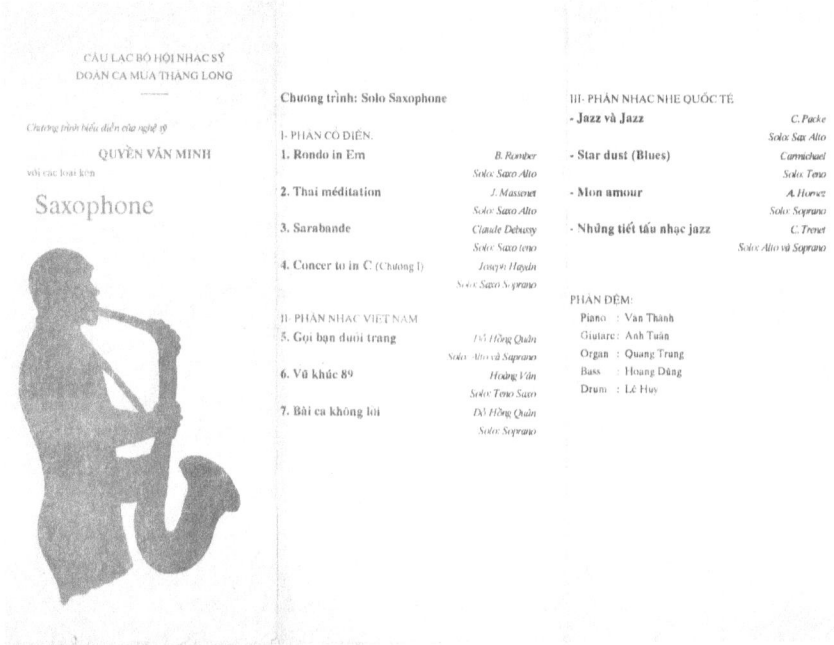

Figure 7.2. Solo recital program, October 1989.

on various types of saxophones." The name is printed in uppercase letters, in bold, and on a separate line that effectively draws the attention of the reader to the name. A silhouette graphic of a man playing a saxophone is the only artwork, and it takes up two-thirds of the print surface of the front panel (see fig. 7.2).

The performance took place in Hà Nội, right in the political heart of Vietnam, a city that had generated more than three decades of socialist, collectivizing, conforming ideology. At the same time, Vietnam in 1989 was experiencing an embryonic attempt at political liberalization with the Đổi Mới reforms.

In Quyền Văn Minh's 1989 recital program, we have an understated public performance featuring the solo talents of an individual in place of a collective. Amid a short period of fervent Vietnamization of the Vietnamese vocabulary to remove commonly used Han-Viet words and phrases from the language, we have the word "saxophone" spelled as it would be in any English-language document, rather than the Vietnamized version, *sắc-xô-phôn*. Every printed item intended for public distribution during that time was scrutinized and sanctioned by relevant authorities. The late 1980s in Vietnam were years of balancing on a knife's edge with regard to any performance in the public sphere, when the Đổi Mới reforms were still being carefully and gradually tested and contested.

The musician Trần Tiến experienced firsthand the ambiguity of the reforms in the mid-1980s when he wrote a number of songs with lyrics that served as critical commentaries on Vietnamese society, such as "Trần Trụi 87" (Naked '87) and "Rock Đồng Hồ" (Rock about the Clock). Tiến performed these songs with his band Trắng Đen in a concert program entitled *Đối Thoại 1987* in November 1987. It did not take long for the government to ban any further performances of the songs. Tiến's music was also subjected to further scrutiny.[2] The Trần Tiến incident was a reminder of how the ideological dogmatism of the socialist revolution still permeated every aspect of life in Vietnam, and that musicians had to continue to tread with care in the midst of this euphoric but uneasy time of change.

Vietnamese artists were at the tail end, albeit a rather drawn-out one, of a period when any form of cultural manifestation had to be state approved—before, during, and after. It was a time when mainstream classical music and Vietnamese music were ideologically defined, and foreign music had to be ideologically sanctioned. The minor details on the front panel of the brochure could be read as a subtle micro-relaxing of the cultural atmosphere in Vietnam during those watershed years.

On National Television in 1988 and 1989

For those *not* among the live audience privileged to witness that groundbreaking performance in 1989 at the Hội Nhạc Sĩ, Vietnam National Television (VTV) was there to record the concert, which would be broadcast later as part of VTV's *Chương trình Câu lạc bộ Nhạc* (Music Club Program). We have Đàm Linh, the eminent composer and then deputy secretary-general of the Hội Nhạc Sĩ, introducing Quyền Văn Minh to a national audience at the beginning of the program:

> Brother Quyền Văn Minh, through two performance programs, saxophone solo recitals, to grace the occasion of the Fourth Congress of the Hội Nhạc Sĩ Việt Nam, before and after, has unveiled a genuine talent. With regard to music, with regard to the saxophone, he is passionate and treats the saxophone as intertwined with his life. As a result, he has been able to overcome numerous challenges and difficulties presented by life. He has worked industriously to attain a higher level of music with each passing day and produced a pinnacle level of performance in the recital, which he has just played with huge affirmation and respect from the audience, including both domestic and foreign guests. Respect for the music, innate curiosity, and his own personality have combined to help Minh create an individual style that is unique, and it gives promise of a beautiful tomorrow.

This was no political statement or polite testimony as typically delivered by senior cadres in communist Vietnam on the occasion of a public broadcast.

Đàm Linh, a highly respected composer who was trained at the Tchaikovsky Conservatoire in Moscow, was the deputy secretary-general of the Hội Nhạc Sĩ. Quyền Văn Minh was but a self-taught musician holding the saxophone chair at a state-owned music troupe called the Thăng Long Song-and-Dance Troupe. The two were worlds apart in terms of social and political stature.

Đàm Linh had had an illustrious musical and revolutionary career. At the age of twelve, in 1944, Đàm Linh already started participating in the communist revolution. From 1960 to 1964, he studied at the prestigious Tchaikovsky Conservatoire in Moscow. After graduation, Linh was immediately delegated to Laos to help develop the cultural troupes of the Pathet Lao and support the revolutionary effort in that country. Back in Vietnam, Linh composed numerous soundtracks, ballet suites, choral works, theater pieces, symphonic and chamber music, and so on, many of which received prestigious national awards.[3] He was elected deputy secretary-general of the Hội Nhạc Sĩ Việt Nam for two consecutive terms, from 1983 to 1989 and from 1989 to 1995.[4]

Đàm Linh and Quyền Văn Minh had mutual respect and appreciation for each other's musicality. The following is Minh's recollection of these performances. These words relate the stories that culminated in the twin solo recitals by Quyền Văn Minh in 1988 and 1989, which brought jazz to the public sphere with official endorsement.

In 1988, none of the other saxophonists in Vietnam, even the seasoned ones, had attained the kind of standard needed to consider staging a saxophone solo recital. It was a pioneering event, and I put in a lot of effort thinking of the model for the recital. The title of my proposed recital was The Different Types of Saxophones with Three Genres of Sound; *and I performed on three types of saxophones: the alto, the tenor, and the soprano. I must have been the first to perform with the soprano on the public stage in this country; before that, I had not heard anyone do so. Or there might have been someone who played the soprano in the Catholic parishes, playing it in a simpler context. But I was the first to perform the saxophone with a serious conception featuring big compositions. The studio at the Hội Nhạc Sĩ could seat maybe 120 people or so; the maximum was 150 people. And the performance itself was kind of a private event with invited guests only, but I was proud to be able to perform there, and VTV, the national television broadcasting station, recorded the recital in 1988. For the second performance, in 1989, Đàm Linh, the deputy secretary-general of the Hội Nhạc Sĩ, passionately went on television before the broadcast of that performance to introduce it. At that time, I was still with the Thăng Long Song-and-Dance Troupe. Unfortunately, I could not find a copy of the performance from my first recital. In these two recitals at the Hội Nhạc Sĩ, I performed three classical pieces, three Vietnamese pieces, and three jazz pieces. The recitals at the Hội Nhạc Sĩ were very successful.*

In his curriculum vitae submitted for conferment of the Eminent Artist award, Minh reported:

> On September 25, 1988, I had the opportunity to present a solo concert featuring three types of saxophones:
> Soprano: mainstream classical music
> Alto: Vietnamese chamber music
> Soprano and Tenor: international light music
> For classical music, I performed compositions by:
> J. S. Bach
> Antonín Dvořák
> Camille Saint-Saëns
> For Vietnamese chamber music:
> "Giai Điệu Quê Hương," composed for the saxophone by Hoàng Vân
> "Trăng Sáng," composed by Đặng Hữu Phúc
> "Tên Hội Em Về," also by Đặng Hữu Phúc
> Part 3: international light music
> The concert was recorded by the Vietnam Broadcasting Station, aired via the program *Music Club*, and introduced by the musician Hồ Quang Bình.

Minh did not use the term "jazz" at all in the first recital, neither in his recollection nor in his report on the first performance.

I dared not use the term "jazz" then. In those days, no one would dare to proclaim, "I play jazz!" Those years in the 1980s, music in Vietnam was subjected to very strict censorship. We had to follow very strict regulations set by the Ministry of Culture. We could not simply play anything we liked on stage. In the first section, I presented "saxophone with classical music," "chính thống" [proper mainstream] music. I have to emphasize the use of the term "chính thống" here. In the second section, I presented "saxophone with Vietnamese chamber music." I played pieces composed by Vietnamese musicians. Those days, when people composed Vietnamese chamber music, they used melodies found in traditional folk music in Vietnam, composed according to the framework of classical music, such as the concerto or sonata, to give the music a formal structure. I had to make sure that I used the words "international light music" in place of "jazz" to present the pieces I intended to play in the third section, such as "In the Mood" and "Stardust." But what I played was indeed jazz music. The first few steps were the most difficult, especially in a society where the genre of jazz, a musical genre from America, was treated as "âm nhạc phản động" [reactionary music]. In the second recital in 1989, I also played a piece by Debussy in the classical section. And part 3 featured standard jazz pieces.

In the program brochure for the second recital in 1989, the following was printed:

Program: Solo Saxophone
I. Classical Section
Rondo in E Minor, B[ernard] Romberg; Solo: Saxo Alto
Thái Méditation, J[ules] Massenet; Solo: Saxo Alto
Sarabande, Claude Debussy; Solo: Saxo Tenor
Concerto in C (First Movement), Joseph Haydn; Solo: Saxo Soprano
II. Vietnamese Music Section
"Gọi bạn dưới trăng" [Calling a Friend under the Moon], Đỗ Hồng Quân; Solo: Alto
"Vũ Khúc '89" [Dance '89], Hoàng Vân; Solo: Tenor Saxo
"Bài Ca Không Lời" [Song without Words], Đỗ Hồng Quân; Solo: Soprano
III. International Music Section
"Jazz and Jazz," C[harlie] Parker; Solo: Sax Alto
"Stardust" (Blues), [Hoagy] Carmichael; Solo: Tenor
"Oui mon amour," A[ndré] Hornez; Solo: Soprano
"A Few Jazz Rhythms," C[harles] Trenet; Solo: Alto and Soprano
Rhythm Section:
Piano: Văn Thành
Guitar: Anh Tuấn
Organ: Quang Trung
Bass: Hoàng Dũng
Drums: Lê Huy

What was intended to be the section featuring a repertoire of jazz pieces was again merely subtitled "International Music Section," although the word "jazz" appeared three times in the song titles.

In the broadcast of the recital on VTV's *Music Club* program, the host introduced the classical section: "Although it has a brassy, yet seductive sound, many classical music composers use the instrument [the saxophone] effectively in their compositions, for example *L'Arlésienne* by Bizet, *Iolanta* by Tchaikovsky, and *Bolero* by Ravel. Coming up, let's listen to *Súy Tượng* [*Méditation*] by Massenet, performed by Quyền Văn Minh on the alto saxophone." Wearing an impeccably pressed and smart white suit, a black tie with slanted white stripes, and hair length just dropping below the ear but neatly combed, typical of Vietnamese artists of that era, Minh was styled for a somber performance. He looked the part of a serious artist, as expected from the clichéd "classical musician in a classical music recital" setting, but with a slight flamboyance that could not be contained. In contrast, the accompanying pianist, who dressed the part of a classical musician, completely exuded the somber movements of a classically trained professional musician and seasoned performer on the grand piano. But there was no mistaking the perfect classical timbre in Minh's alto saxophone, adding only a barely detectable flair perhaps with his use of a metal mouthpiece. A serious listener would be totally ensnared by Minh's focused delivery, perfect memorization of the score, and flawless execution of the instrument. Clearly, Minh was leading the performance, but he also demonstrated a subtle musical understanding with the pianist. Together, the exchange brought out a meditated flow of emptied thoughts, and toward the end of the piece, the emotions issued forth on the stage seemingly rose to the ceiling of the venue and dissipated with the instruments' soft fade-out.

In the first recital in 1988, Minh performed Bach's Violin Concerto no. 1, which he had transposed from an arrangement for the oboe. In the second recital in 1989, he performed an equally challenging piece, the first movement of Haydn's Oboe Concerto in C. Demonstrating an effortless, pitch-perfect articulation on the soprano saxophone of the intense opening, which traverses the expanse of the key in which the movement was composed, Minh immediately took charge of the performance after a brief introduction by the pianist. Minh's leadership, confidence, and perfect execution instantly transformed an orchestral composition rearranged for the piano and oboe into a native duet between piano and soprano saxophone. Oh, was this piece originally composed for the oboe? You could not tell from the way Minh took ownership of the concerto with his fluid execution on the soprano saxophone. Man and instrument were one recombinant entity, and one might be tempted to claim that any composition Minh channeled through his saxophone could immediately become his own.

When it came to the Vietnamese chamber music section, the television program host introduced an original composition, "Vũ Khúc '89" (Dance '89), which Hoàng Vân had composed for the tenor saxophone using the melody from an ethnic Thái folk song. Amid a stepped staccato rhythm punctuated with open spaces played on the piano, Minh poured out the winding flow of a melodic motif textured with the full-bodied timbre of his tenor saxophone. The music was like a poetic painting depicting villages surrounded by rice fields cascading along the gradients of mountainous valleys carved out by rivers—the landscape of the ethnic Thái in the northern uplands of Vietnam. Demonstrating a contrasting sound during the Vietnamese chamber music section, Minh performed "Bài Ca Không Lời" (Song without Words), a light music piece composed by then rising star composer Đỗ Hồng Quân for the alto saxophone and combo band. With Minh changing clothes and bringing on a band featuring rhythm guitar, drums, keyboards, and bass guitar, the opening tone of the piece paralleled the relaxed stage presence of the performers. Having jettisoned his jacket and tie for a more laid-back look, Minh filled the room with the sound of his saxophone, radiating the ambience of a therapeutic chanson without words. The saxophone was clearly the singer here, while the able rhythm musicians provided steady layers of tracks to shine the limelight on Minh.

Introducing the third section of the recital, "International Music," the television host carefully enunciated: "Now we invite the audience to try some jazz, the home of the saxophone, with a piece entitled 'Jazz and Jazz' by Parker, performed by Quyền Văn Minh on alto saxophone." Jazz aficionados would not need more than three notes to recognize one of the signature tunes of Charlie "Bird" Parker, "Bloomdido," although the host introduced it as "Jazz and Jazz," as was also printed in the brochure distributed during the live performance. Minh played the song at a slower speed than any recorded rendition by Parker, and with a quartet of backup musicians on piano, drums, guitar, and bass guitar playing a steady, by-the-score rhythm, his saxophone explored the different possibilities afforded by the bebop piece, yet holding back on any overly complicated licks and all the while maintaining a catchable melody—for his uninitiated audience, I would presume—amid his logically thought-out improvisation.

The year was 1989, and it was most likely the first time in the history of Vietnam that the word "jazz" was uttered during a public broadcast without ideological disdain. And it was probably the first time that the sound of jazz was performed by a Vietnamese musician on a public stage in the years since the socialist revolution first penetrated every facet of the country's cultural life.

I would say that it was only after the 1988 and 1989 recitals, when VTV broadcast the performances on national television, and the national conservatoire invited me to join the faculty, that a pathway was opened for jazz to be performed publicly, "danh chính ngôn thuận" [right and proper in name and speech], in Hà Nội. Before that, all along the saxophone had been seen as a musical instrument that was not serious. It was not an instrument used for serious music. People could see from the recitals that the saxophone was in fact a mainstream and proper musical instrument. They heard my solo recitals, and they could see that "chả có gì tội lỗi" [there was nothing criminal] about jazz music. Some of the lecturers at the conservatoire, who were teaching classical music and had the opportunity to be trained overseas, also understood that jazz was already a global phenomenon then; and they gave support. But I was aware that support for jazz was very limited.

In fact, the VTV broadcast began by stating: "We would like to introduce a musical instrument that plays an important role in jazz music, the saxophone. Before going into the program, let us invite maestro Đàm Linh, deputy secretary-general of the Hội Nhạc Sĩ, to say a few words." And then came the strong words of endorsement by Đàm Linh about Quyền Văn Minh, the saxophone, and Minh's musical endeavors. Đàm Linh's public endorsement of Minh's performance was a significant, uplifting moment, because it was indeed a most arduous task for Minh to bring jazz into the public sphere in that particular historical context.

*There were so few people who dreamed about developing jazz in Vietnam; there was me and, later, a few lecturers at the conservatoire. I had to find my own way and try things out on my own. Lecturers at the conservatoire were able to study overseas; they were exposed to the music; they could listen to the music; and they could get reference materials. I had to embark on my own, and **I had to prove** [emphasis in the original] that I could play jazz. And I came to realize one thing: I had to be really good, it was that simple! Nothing else would help, even if you knew people. If I was not good, if I could not play well, no one would come and invite me. I practiced very, very hard. I dreamed of performing a solo recital, and that opportunity came in 1988.*

Instruments for a Full Recital

But putting together Minh's envisioned solo recitals in 1988 and 1989 was no easy task. He had to literally do everything himself in order to prepare for these performances. Mere ideas and vision do not a successful path-breaking performance make, not to mention two recitals. Putting on a top-class performance for any artist requires, first and foremost, the right tools, materials, and support. Just in terms of the music side of things, Minh would have to dig deep to seek out suitable instruments, accessories, equipment, and materials, as well as committed personnel who would dare to embark with him on such a risky adventure in the socialist Vietnam of the late 1980s.

At that time, I had to "tự lực cần kiệm" [be very frugal and do everything on my own]. I had just finalized my divorce and, in order to save up, I had to take on many gigs so that I could afford to buy the three saxophones that I would use for the recital: the soprano, the tenor, and the alto. I managed to purchase the soprano, an instrument that I was the first to play in a public performance [in Vietnam]. When I finally managed to get ahold of all three types of saxophones, I could put up the performance: A Solo Saxophone Recital with Three Genres of Music. *In the repertoire, I presented the saxophone with classical music, Vietnamese chamber music, and international light music.*

The first saxophone I ever held in my hands was, I remember, a Linton saxophone. It was a saxophone that someone had purchased in Sài Gòn, from a Catholic parish, and brought up north, which they later sold to my father. That was the very first saxophone I ever held. I had to borrow my father's saxophone when I began switching to that instrument. Later on, I learned from my father, when he was still alive, that he had loaned the saxophone to a friend and never asked for it back. The friend had passed away already. I found the address and the family, but the saxophone could not be located anymore. Now, the saxophone I use is a Super Action (Selmer); before this I was using a Mark VI.

By the 1990s, I had accumulated a good collection of saxophones, but I had sold all but one when Đắc went overseas to study. I was able to buy some of these saxophones in Sài Gòn from the Catholic parishes. In fact, I found several Mark VIs, Mark VIIs, and even older premium models, which I bought from the locals. They sold me these saxophones because the instruments were really in poor condition, and many were unplayable! So, they wanted to exchange these for other instruments brought back from Eastern Europe that were newer and playable. I bought these instruments. To be honest, when I tried out these instruments then, it was almost impossible to produce any proper notes, at best maybe one or two proper notes on the instruments! But I found the sound produced from the one or two notes totally hypnotizing! I had to have them, even though I did not know the actual worth of these instruments then. I bought them. People did not know the value of these saxophones, and I also did not know their true value. We just negotiated the price with each other according to their worth in the market at that time. In fact, many people would bring their saxophones to me in exchange for something else! That was how I got the rare Czechoslovakian saxophone! I would exchange with them, and afterward, I would fix the instruments myself. I only learned about the actual worth of the saxophones I collected much later.

I remember listening to a recording by a musician from Czechoslovakia, Felix Slováček; he played both jazz and classical music, on both clarinet and soprano saxophone. I was inspired to play the soprano saxophone after listening to a cassette of his music! I immediately decided that I had to get a soprano saxophone. At that time, no one wanted to buy a soprano saxophone. There was only one available in Hà Nội; someone had brought it back from the Soviet Union, and it was originally made in East Germany. No one wanted to buy it! But I really loved the sound of the soprano saxophone. The guy who had brought it back, he was bored with the instrument, so I approached him to buy it. But I did not have the money to pay for it! When I went home, I told my mother about the soprano saxophone, and I asked if it would be possible for her to help me so that I could practice and improve myself further, and that I would repay her later. Just like the story of my first clarinet, the one that I had sold to repay my mother and bought back after I joined the troupe. My mother gave me a loan to pay for that soprano saxophone. It was a B&S brand saxophone, from East Germany. People do not think much of that brand now, but it was really very valuable at that time. I gave the solo recitals using that soprano saxophone. And that was the only way I could get that saxophone; no other way.

Getting hold of a soprano saxophone was difficult. Finding good saxophone reeds in the Subsidy Period and the early days of Đổi Mới was just as difficult. Getting enough reeds to sustain a disciplined practice ethic required resourcefulness and innovation.

In those days we got our reeds supplied by the Eastern European countries in COMECON such as the Democratic Republic of Germany, Czechoslovakia, and the Soviet Union. You could buy from the Germans, who would buy from the musical units that were supplied with these accessories. The musicians in these units saved up their assigned supplies and would sell them to willing buyers. And somehow these reeds ended up in Vietnam. With these reeds from Germany, I could use one reed for six months. But I cannot remember the name of the brand. I also used reeds from Czechoslovakia, a brand called Vibraphone.

We would practice and play using these reeds for a long time, until the reed became too soft. But in those days, we did not have a reed cutter. So when that happened, we used a coin to press against the reed and a lit matchstick to burn the head of the reed; then we shaved away the charred part. After that, we could continue to use the reed! I practiced a lot, so I just kept burning the reed in this way to extend its life. It was difficult; I could make sound from the reed, but it took more effort because the reed got heavier with each burn. There was no other option, because I could not afford more reeds or find more reeds. You burn with the coin, then you use a knife to shave it away. I had to learn how to repair my reeds in this way, so I could play longer. In the old days, I practiced every day for about two hours when I went to school, then in the evening I practiced for about one and a half hours. I tried so many different types of reeds, and it was a costly endeavor, trying so many different types. But the result was good.

After liberation, we learned that there was a large number of reeds, heaps of reeds, in Sài Gòn. People who went down to the South brought these reeds back. 1975 was the year of liberation, so around 1977 or 1978, we were able to get our hands on reeds made in the United States and France. But it was only around 1986 or 1987, when I was teaching the saxophone to foreigners in Hà Nội, that I could ask them to buy reeds from overseas for me. It was only then that I learned what a US dollar looked like! These foreign students studied with me, and they paid me in US dollars. It was around 1986 that I first started having foreign students. When I first bought the soprano saxophone, there were no soprano reeds available. So I had to use clarinet reeds! Later, I was able to ask a foreigner friend to help me buy the correct soprano saxophone reeds. I could practice properly after that and have the confidence to perform the concerto by Bach. It was only in 1986 that the reeds I used were relatively good, but the saxophones were still not of a very high quality. At that time, I began to use Vandoren reeds, no. 2. Nowadays I use both Rico and Vandoren reeds, no. 2.5.

There was, for a while, a plan for Vietnam to produce its own reeds, but the venture failed. There was a Vietnamese who went overseas to study, in Poland, and he even brought back a machine to produce reeds, an old machine that was used to make Vandoren reeds, French reeds. His name was, I think, Văn Liêm. The brand of that reed was called Văn Đô Liêm, but it was unusable! You blow three songs with it, and you have to throw it away! Your saliva would get stuck inside the reed, and you had to squeeze it out! So, the venture was a failure, and there were only imported reeds.

The first saxophone mouthpiece I bought was from Germany. The B&S saxophone mouthpiece was made of plastic. There were various brands that supplied the troupes [overseas], so when the players got their hands on mouthpieces from France or the United States, they would sell off the mouthpieces from [East] Germany, and we would buy those mouthpieces. After Vietnam opened up, we could get better mouthpieces. I could get a catalog and see which one I want to order. I like the Selmer mouthpieces. The Selmer mouthpieces are not categorized by number; the brand uses alphabet letters, for example, C, D, E, and so on. I like the E mouthpiece. I also use a metal mouthpiece; of course I like the metal mouthpiece. I used the metal mouthpiece quite a fair bit, but now when I play the alto, I use a plastic mouthpiece. When I play the tenor, I like the metal mouthpiece. When playing tenor, the metal mouthpiece brightens the sound of the tenor. And when using a plastic mouthpiece, it gives the sound more depth. I could give it an airier sound, but I would have to notice the volume so as to better balance with the other instruments at play. If you want to produce a refined sound with a metal mouthpiece, that would be most arduous! But if you wanted to produce a big sound for popular music, it was very effective. I have tried many types. In terms of experience in choosing mouthpieces, I could only learn from my own experience. In terms of the various types of saxophones, I am a pioneer in my own right; I would try the instrument and find the best way to produce a good sound. Before me, it was common for people who played saxophone to use either the tenor or alto. For the soprano, I was the first to perform it formally on the public stage [in Vietnam]. Before, people would only perform with the alto or the clarinet. From 1968 all the way to the 1980s, I was using very ordinary instruments that were very old, and often broken. Even reeds, those days, without a reed cutter—either I used scissors to cut or pressed a coin to the edge and burned the edges just so I could extend the life of the reed.

Putting Together a Vietnamese Music Repertoire for 1988 and 1989

A saxophone solo recital is, technically speaking, not a solo individual performance. Rather, the saxophone is the featured solo instrument. To find musicians who would come together to support such a performance in Vietnam was no easy affair. Inevitably, musicians would ask, what kind of music would Minh be playing? If Minh were merely going to perform the usual repertoire, then the recital program would not be a big deal and probably would not receive any attention or even be supported by the authorities. Such a mediocre program by a mere saxophone chair of a song-and-dance troupe would not have been allowed to grace the occasion of the Fourth Congress of the prestigious and influential Hội Nhạc Sĩ. It could not and would not be the usual repertoire. When Minh decided to present the three genres of music he ultimately settled on, he was posing a challenge both for himself and for the audience, in particular for the dignitaries of the music scene in Vietnam.

Minh would be scrutinized in every aspect to see if he could do justice to the national genre, Vietnamese chamber music. These were original compositions that presented, both to the Vietnamese audience and to the world, the national sounds of Vietnam. Hoàng Vân (the composer of "Vũ Khúc '89") defines in a theoretical paper three types of compositions in this genre. The first type utilizes both materials and approaches based on traditional folk music. The second type borrows base materials and approaches that originated from outside of Vietnam. And the third type combines base materials and approaches both from within Vietnam and from outside of Vietnam. In the 1960s, these compositions revolved around themes related to the Vietnamese socialist revolution and Vietnamese folk culture such as *quê hương* (home village) and *tổ quốc* (the motherland); politically significant regions such as Điện Biên (site of the famous victory over French colonial forces in 1954 and heartland of the ethnic Thái communities) and Tây Nguyên (the strategic Central Highlands, crucial to ultimate unification of the country in 1975); and socially significant topics such as *nông thôn đổi mới* (agrarian "renovation") and *dân ca* (ethnic folk songs). The dominance of these theme-based compositions would gradually loosen after 1975, and especially in the early 1980s, when a younger group of composers led by Đỗ Hồng Quân began to emerge on the scene.[5] Đỗ Hồng Quân, the rising star composer, would graduate from the Tchaikovsky Conservatoire in 1985 and later become chairman of the Hội Nhạc Sĩ.

Vietnamese chamber music was the very genre defined and shaped by this key group of people in the audience, the composers; and they dominated the Hội Nhạc Sĩ. Hoàng Vân himself was a pioneer Vietnamese chamber music composer who had already been elected into the Central Executive Committee of the Hội Nhạc Sĩ back in 1963.[6] Performing musicians had little influence in what defined Vietnamese chamber music, and in fact they were poorly represented in the Central Committee of the Hội Nhạc Sĩ. Bùi Gia Tường notes that while there were fourteen performing musicians out of a Central Committee of twenty-four in the Second Congress in 1963, this had dropped to four out of twenty-six in the Third Congress in 1983 and one out of thirteen in the Fourth Congress in 1989.[7] Minh recognized the influence of the Hội Nhạc Sĩ.

To prove that I could play jazz, for jazz to be recognized, and to get people to look at the saxophone with a different perspective, that it was not a frivolous instrument, I had to do it in front of people who had the ability to recognize jazz as a proper form of music and the saxophone as a serious instrument. At that time, it meant performing on the stage at the Hội Nhạc Sĩ [referring to the clubhouse]. The Hội Nhạc Sĩ Việt Nam [referring to the institution] was the center of the Vietnamese music scene, where composers and leaders of the scene gathered.

Minh put much thought into the pieces he wanted to perform for the recitals and even asked notable composers such as Đặng Hữu Phúc, Đỗ Hồng Quân, and Hoàng Vân to write pieces featuring the saxophone specially for the recitals. As a reputable saxophonist in the Vietnamese music circle, Minh had come to know these luminaries in the Hội Nhạc Sĩ. Earlier in 1987, Minh had performed a few classical pieces on saxophone in a concert conducted by Đỗ Hồng Quân. In his own recitals, Minh attended to both the thematic-based and nonthematic-based schools of Vietnamese chamber music when he presented a contrasting set of compositions that featured both dominant themes (e.g., "Vũ Khúc '89") and emerging trends (e.g., "Bài Ca Không Lời") in the genre.

Endorsement by the Music Dignitaries of Vietnam

For the 1989 recital, Minh would be scrutinized by the leadership of the Hà Nội National Music Conservatoire of Vietnam. The recital was an overwhelming success, because the conservatoire eventually awarded Minh a certificate of *trung cấp đạt cách* (intermediate level proficiency achieved; a high school qualification) soon afterward, which allowed him to teach at the conservatoire (see chapter 9). Performing for the dignitaries of the Hội Nhạc Sĩ required Minh to ensure that his performance be exceptionally precise, at the same level as that of any world-class classical music artist, and effectively bowl over the audience with his talent. Indeed, many of the leading figures in the Hội Nhạc Sĩ at that time had been trained in prestigious music conservatoires in the Soviet Union and Eastern Europe. Classical music was at the pinnacle of what defined a proper, serious, and high-standard musician. As Minh himself emphasized, classical music was perceived as *chính thống* (mainstream and proper) music. Minh would have to demonstrate his competence, and the seriousness of the saxophone as an instrument, by performing classical music.

For the first recital, I was worried because there had never been a precedent of anyone giving a solo recital in this fashion, in this country. Not on violin, not on piano, not on any woodwind or brass instrument, and not even by music lecturers at the conservatoire who had been educated overseas. And yet I dared to stand up and put together a saxophone solo recital playing Bach's concerto and pieces by Haydn, Mozart, and others. In the first recital, I used the soprano saxophone to play a concerto piece, the first movement of Bach's Violin Concerto in A Minor. To perform these pieces, I had to borrow books to copy; to copy with paper and pencil! The first movement of Bach's concerto was composed for violin. There was a book—a musician who was also a lecturer at the conservatoire teaching the oboe, he had the book. It was only through my sister and her husband that I was able to borrow that book. And I sat down to copy it by hand, because in those days, where could one find a photocopy machine? So, I sat down to make my copy; I copied the melody, and I copied the piano accompaniment. After that, I practiced the melody, and then I practiced with piano accompaniment.

When the Bach piece was arranged for oboe, such as in the book I borrowed, it was already abridged and rearranged for that instrument. Even then, when you play the arrangement on soprano saxophone, there are still many complicated problems. But I was determined to perform the piece, because I wanted to prove that the saxophone could play a diversity of music and that I could present that diversity. I will tell you a story about what happened during the 1988 program. The first piece I played in that recital was Bach's concerto for the violin. Back in the old days, when I was playing for weddings, when I was growing up, I never had to fully prepare for gigs. But for that first recital, psychologically speaking, I was nervous. The committee members seated with the audience evaluating the performance, they were experts. I played a few bars of the piece, but my mouth was totally dry! I had to stop. I apologized to the audience: "Sorry, I need to drink some water first." After that, I managed to finish the piece without any problems. That was a memorable lesson for me. Later on, when I was teaching, I would tell my students that on big occasions, drink a lot of water before going on stage. So now you see my students, before going on stage, they are always drinking water [pointing to the musicians seated by the stage sipping glasses of ice water and nonalcoholic drinks during the music interval at the jazz club]. Later, I would perform this piece again during my third solo recital, held at the opera house in 1994. When I returned to that big stage in 1994, my performance still was not perfect, but I managed to present it with a string quartet.

Assembling a Band to Play Jazz in 1988 and 1989

For the International Music section of his program, Minh played jazz, but he felt that he was on a knife's edge with this decision. What would be the point of the recital if he were not going to do something drastically different from a typical program? Would he win over the audience by showcasing his technical sophistication through the improvisation that was required of a jazz performance? Would he be able to convince critics that jazz was no "reactionary music" but really a proper genre of international music? Would the audience be able to accept the sound of jazz? Would he be able to convince the critics, using classical music, Vietnamese chamber music, and jazz, that the saxophone was a serious musical instrument that should be respected, just like any other solo orchestral instrument? To do all this, would he be able to put together a group of musicians sufficiently capable and willing to perform with him?

There were so many constraints. My experience in looking for musicians to play with me for the recitals has really stayed with me. In 1988, I was a soloist in the Thăng Long Song-and-Dance Troupe. The band that I was playing with was a light music band; we called our repertoire "extra music." We played additional gigs at many places, such as the music tea lounges where people gathered to dance. So I approached my fellow musicians in the band, telling them that I had a solo recital in the works and would be able to compensate them for their time and effort. And I asked them to rehearse with me. At first, everyone I approached agreed to play the gig. But when I brought out the scores, they shook their heads and backed out! Yes, the scores were difficult. At that time, these individuals all had their own reputations in the music circle; for example, I was the best saxophonist, one of my colleagues was the best guitarist, and so on. And they would not take the risk to do something that might not turn out well, for fear of harming their own reputations. Another thing was that when they heard the way I was playing, they could not follow, but they could not oppose. Since they could not agree with the music, they chose not to play. Each step was small and difficult. Then, there was no one who wanted play for the recital. Everyone refused, because it was really too difficult and too new. If people did not like the sound, in Vietnam we have this concept called "ngang tai" [piercing to the ear], they reject it outright. I had to fulfill these two recitals by myself.

That was why I ended up having to persuade my elder brother and younger brother to play for me. I assured them: just play like this, and it would be fine. They did not have to do more. Well, they did it because they loved me and were willing to give in to me, although they were really worried. You can see in the video of the 1989 concert at the Hội Nhạc Sĩ, I have my youngest brother on guitar and my elder brother on bass guitar. For the first recital in 1988, I had my elder brother, my youngest brother, a drummer, and the pianist Đặng Hữu Phúc, who was a folk music composer and did not play jazz at all, you could tell from the way he played. This was the group that provided the backup for my first solo recital. For the 1989 recital, I was able to recruit a few more young musicians to accompany me. By the 1994 concert, I had a totally different crew, the Sông Hồng Band [Red River Band].

For the 1988 and 1989 programs, I had to write out every single note on the music score for the musicians who agreed to play with me; there was no one who could improvise on their own. So any improvisation by them was really the result of industrious practice with a written score! I had to write out every single note. But it was clear that they really enjoyed playing, even though they were only playing as the rhythm section. Somehow, the sound of jazz gave them a sense of satisfaction.

Twenty years later, some of these players still tell me how memorable that performance was for them! Trung, the keyboardist from the 1989 gig, I saw him some time ago when he came in to attend class in the continuing education program at the conservatoire. Twenty years after the performance, he still remembered the atmosphere of that fateful day. He told me that he was honored to have been able to accompany brother Minh in this piece and that piece for the performance.

The Endorsement of Đàm Linh

Talent, industry, resourcefulness, perseverance, personality, and devotion to jazz were the qualities that Đàm Linh made reference to when endorsing Minh's recital programs on public television. It was an earlier, memorable, and personal encounter between Đàm Linh and Minh that allowed the former to witness the precocious talent that is Quyền Văn Minh.

For both the 1988 and 1989 solo recitals, after carefully selecting the repertoire, I presented the proposal to my troupe, the Thăng Long Song-and-Dance Troupe. My troupe signed a recommendation letter [giấy giới thiệu], which I submitted to the Hội Nhạc Sĩ. At that time, Đàm Linh was the deputy secretary-general of the association. He had already recognized me as a very capable musician by then; he respected my musicianship. That was after a most memorable encounter we had in 1984. Đàm Linh was very supportive of my solo recital programs at the Hội Nhạc Sĩ in 1988 and 1989. He advised me that such a recital program must be formally endorsed by all relevant agencies. I had official approval from my troupe to deliver the recital program, and the association agreed to host the performance, but the final repertoire still had to be endorsed by various agencies such as the Department of Culture, the Executive Committee of the Hội Nhạc Sĩ, and the Thăng Long Song-and-Dance Troupe (my own agency). Although I had the approval three months ahead of the performance date, endorsement of the repertoire could only be given the week before the performance. I submitted my schedule to all relevant agencies, the repertoire, details of the performance, and a definite list of dates clearly stating what and when all documents would be submitted for endorsement. I followed all due procedures for an official performance right from the beginning.

I came to know Đàm Linh personally during an incident that happened in 1984. When I met Đàm Linh, he was already a very famous and respected composer in Vietnam. The morning of the incident, Đàm Linh came to rehearse a performance with us at the Thăng Long Song-and-Dance Troupe. He had composed a ballet dance piece with parts that featured the saxophone, and we would be performing this piece with him personally conducting. Upon arriving at the theater, he asked, "Who is the best in this theater?" The band members told him, "Minh, the saxophonist." Well, that morning, the court had informed me that they would be hearing my case. That was in 1984, when I undergoing my divorce. So I went to the court that morning, and by the time I returned to the theater, I was late for the rehearsal. Đàm Linh, who was conducting, was very unhappy. He admonished me in front of everyone: "This fellow is ridiculous! I've never ever had to wait for a mere 'nhạc công' [music cadre], and now I've had to wait for you!" I immediately apologized and explained that the court had been hearing my divorce case that morning, which was why I had returned late, and I asked for his understanding. He said, "Alright then, get to your position in the orchestra and let's start the rehearsal." I went to my seat, but I had yet to copy the music score!

At this point, Đàm Linh was furious and said, "This is not acceptable!" I asked him to let me copy the score immediately, and in ten minutes we could play the piece as usual. Đàm Linh told the orchestra to take a break while I copied the saxophone part from the conductor's full score. And he added, "I will personally check your part; if you play one note wrong, I will have to punish you. But if you can play every note correctly from beginning to end, I will reward you with a bottle of wine." A bottle of wine at that time was a huge thing! Although it was just domestically made rice wine, in those days who could afford to buy a whole bottle? We could only afford to drink a cup or two on normal days! Anyway, I agreed to his challenge. As I was copying my part from the full score, a few guys who walked past the window of the room where I was copying the music remarked, "Gosh, that must be scary, huh?" To which I replied, "You are very fortunate, because you are going to have some free wine soon!" By the time I finished copying the saxophone part, I knew straightaway that I would have no problem playing it. I was already practicing to play jazz at that time, so to me the music written for that piece was rather easy.

After copying the music, I went back to the rehearsal room, and Đàm Linh said, "Well, start playing." I was thinking to myself, "How does he want me to play it?" As a musician in an orchestra, I knew very well that the conductor leads the orchestra, and the musicians must wait for him to indicate the tempo and direct everything else. So I asked him politely, "Sure, could you please let me know the tempo you want?" The piece that day was a ballet suite that Đàm Linh had written to commemorate the thirtieth anniversary of the liberation of the capital. He was both the composer and the conductor of the piece, meaning that he knew the music extremely well. Đàm Linh went ahead and gave me the tempo. You know, when you perform this kind of composition, a ballet suite, after playing the main parts with the rest of the orchestra, the saxophone might have to rest for thirty bars or even more! So, when I reached the extended section where I was supposed to rest, I continued counting the beats and played when it was time to play, waited when it was time to rest, counted the beats, and came in to play when it was my part again. As for Đàm Linh, after indicating the tempo, he sat down to listen and to observe me.

Three-quarters of the way through the score, Đàm Linh, said, "Alright, you got your bottle of wine. Thank you! There is no need to listen anymore, because you totally understand the music." He noticed that even for the most complex part of the piece, I had no problem at all; and he observed that I kept to the tempo, stayed precise even when playing on my own without the orchestra, and did not miss a beat even when there were extended rest sections for my part. Since it was just myself playing my own parts, I had to keep my own time. "Thằng này được" [This fella is good!], Đàm Linh commented, and he ordered someone to immediately run out and buy a bottle of wine for me to enjoy straightaway. I politely told him, "No, it's okay, thank you. I could not drink this wine. I am a good drinker, but I could not drink this bottle of wine, because it is associated with a punishment." After this incident, Đàm Linh and I got along well with each other. Because of the incident, the maestro recognized that I was a good musician. That was a memorable incident. In the 1989 concert broadcast on television, it was Đàm Linh who introduced the recital. He was one of the reasons for the success of the two solo recitals in 1988 and 1989.

After the 1988 and 1989 Concerts

For likely the first time in communist Vietnam, the term "jazz" was spoken in a positive sense in the public sphere. For the first time since reunification, jazz was publicly performed by a Vietnamese musician in two major events and broadcast on national television.

During the 1989 performance, I played within what I thought were the confines of the extent that the audience present at the hall could accept jazz improvisation. But in 1994, it was different. I could try more. I could go as far as I wanted, to show them what was jazz. Later in the concerts, for example the first Father, Son, and Jazz *concert, I could just let out the ideas. I could just play.*

But what Minh did in the 1989 recital was sufficient to impress the audience. In a brief review of the 1989 recital, Quang Nghi concluded: "Ninety minutes [were] filled with the beautiful sound of the saxophone by Quyền Văn Minh, with an enthusiastic atmosphere among the audience: a beautiful moment in the musical life of the capital."[8] Little did they know, those privileged to witness these two watershed recitals live at the Hội Nhạc Sĩ, those who saw it on television, and those who supported the materialization of these two performances; little did they know that the seeds of original Vietnamese jazz were being sown. But the country would have to wait until 1994 to hear the original sounds of Vietnamese jazz at the prestigious Hà Nội Opera House.

The Cold War came to an end in the late 1980s. In 1989, Vietnam completed its withdrawal of troops from Cambodia, and the Berlin Wall fell. But Quyền Văn Minh's successful introduction of the sound of jazz in the public sphere was no triumphant cultural moment to be claimed by any side. For Minh, it was the artistic possibilities that he could realize through jazz that mattered. After all, he had no idea what America was like, having only learned what even a US dollar looked like when he started giving saxophone lessons to foreigners in the late 1980s. Perhaps Rüdiger Ritter's conjecture about jazz and notions of freedom in socialist Europe could just as well be applied to Minh's endeavor to play jazz:

> [T]he members of the jazz scene associated the concept of freedom not so much with political freedom and possibly even a system change, but with spaces of freedom which were beyond any kind of control, such as the freedom pupils enjoy away from their teachers, youths enjoy away from their parents, and adults enjoy away from the state. Freedom means improvisation, the joy of playing and the willingness to experiment.[9]

With the 1988 and 1989 solo recitals, Minh realized his immediate objective of playing jazz on the public stage in Vietnam. Jazz was not *âm nhạc phản động* (reactionary music), and Minh demonstrated *chả có gì tội lỗi* (there was nothing criminal) about jazz music. In these two recitals, Minh successfully steered clear of any controversy about performing the "music of the enemy" as the Cold War came to a gradual end. Minh played jazz in Vietnam.

TRACK 8

Vietnamese Jazz

The 1990s was a significant decade in the story of jazz in socialist Vietnam. By 1991, Quyền Văn Minh was teaching saxophone and jazz full time at the national conservatoire. At the tail end of the decade, the first jazz club in socialist Vietnam, Minh's Jazz Club, opened its doors. The highlight of these years came in the middle of the decade, however, when Minh premiered three original jazz compositions on the stage of the Hà Nội Opera House, marking the birth of Vietnamese jazz as a nuanced genre of music.

Hà Nội, 1994

Quyền Văn Minh gave his third solo concert on April 12, 1994, which was also his first at the Hà Nội Opera House.[1] This concert marked the emergence of Vietnamese jazz as a musical genre in the soundscape of Vietnam, as three original Vietnamese jazz compositions premiered. Composed and performed by Minh, the tunes were "Tiếng Khèn Gọi Bạn" (The Call of the *Qeej* [Hmong reed pipe]), "Vấn Vương" (Meditations), and "Xuân Trên Cao Nguyên" (Spring in the Highlands).[2] Each tune was inspired by the sounds of different ethnic folk musics Minh heard during his travels as a musical cadre with various state song-and-dance troupes (*đoàn ca múa*) in socialist Vietnam during the 1970s and 1980s. Minh wrote original melodies and made room for improvisation in his compositions, to tell the stories he had in mind with his music. Jazz echoed from the main hall of the Hà Nội Opera House on the night of April 12, 1994. The concert marked a double "first" in Vietnam. For the first time, a Vietnamese musician performed jazz on the stage of the prestigious Hà Nội Opera House in socialist Vietnam. Also for the first time, original jazz pieces composed by a Vietnamese musician, blending elements inspired by Vietnamese traditional folk sounds and jazz improvisation, officially premiered in socialist Vietnam.

By the late 1980s and early 1990s, musicians in Vietnam were given a little bit more room to showcase their art forms. Prewar music was slowly rehabilitated

QUỸ PHÁT TRIỂN VĂN HÓA-THỤY ĐIỂN VIỆT NAM
CÂU LẠC BỘ ÂM NHẠC HỘI NHẠC SĨ
NHẠC VIỆN HÀ NỘI

TRÂN TRỌNG KÍNH MỜI ÔNG BÀ ~~DUY MINH~~
Tới dự: Đêm biểu diễn của Nghệ sỹ SAXO PHONE
QUYỀN VĂN MINH
Vào hồi 19h30 ngày 12 tháng 4 năm 1994
Tại: Nhà hát Lớn Thành Phố

với sự tham gia của BAN NHẠC SÔNG HỒNG

- Vương Tử Lâm — Guitare Solo
- Văn Dũng — Bass
- Yến Dung — Organ
- Ngọc Quân — Drum
- Văn Hào

và tốp đàn dây Nhà hát Giao hưởng Quốc gia

- Quốc Khánh — Violon I
- Hải Đăng — Violon II
- Thế Cường — Viola
- Quốc Dũng — Cello
- Thúy Hà — Piano

Dẫn chương trình: Nhạc sỹ Hồ Quang Bình
Dịch tiếng Anh: Tú Anh

Figure 8.1. Concert at the Hà Nội Opera House, April 1994.

and allowed to be heard in the public sphere. Yellow music (*nhạc vàng*) was tolerated, and one could hear these popular ballads from the 1950s–1970s period again in the cafés and restaurants of Sài Gòn. Besides Vietnamese music, Western popular music from the 1980s began to infiltrate the soundscape of Vietnam with the likes of ABBA, the Bee Gees, and Boney M. By the early 1990s, with the rise in tourism and the economic benefits that came along, tourist establishments such as hotels, restaurants, and music lounges began hiring musicians to play traditional folk music and instrumental Western music to entertain foreign visitors.[3] Quyền Văn Minh became the first Vietnamese musician in Vietnam to headline a regular performance at the Metropole Hotel in Hà Nội, playing jazz, in the 1990s. As recounted earlier, between 1993 and 1997, Minh was even regularly flown from Hà Nội to Sài Gòn by a wealthy overseas Vietnamese (Việt Kiều) businesswoman to perform with a band that tried to play jazz at a villa in Bình An village outside the city. Other than these limited occurrences, there was hardly any sound of jazz in Vietnam in the early 1990s.

Although the country had opened up more to the outside world by the early 1990s, at the same time the communist state was taking a closer look at the consequences of the Đổi Mới reforms. If prior to the reforms "modernity" according to the communist state was a straightforward vision driven by socialist ideals, the complications that arose when Vietnam actually opened up to a market economy and the capitalist world, as Philip Taylor argues, led to modernity's recharacterization as a threat due to its "unintended consequences."[4] Despite having more room to pursue their creative sensitivities, musicians were faced with a more subtle degree of uncertainty as well. Quyền Văn Minh's premier of original Vietnamese jazz compositions in 1994 was only made possible by opportunities presented by the political reforms. At the same time, it was also a significant gamble for Minh to count on the continued reception of jazz as a politically acceptable form of music in the communist state after his successful introduction of the genre in the public sphere in 1988 and 1989.

The 1994 Concert

The 1994 concert was very successful, judging from responses of the audience. The program was supported by a grant from SIDA [the Swedish International Development Cooperation Agency] to help develop the arts and cultural performances in Vietnam. With the support of the Ministry of Culture and Information, the conservatoire, and sponsorship from SIDA in Vietnam, I was able to put together this solo concert at the Hà Nội Opera House, my third solo recital in fact. The biggest achievement of this concert was the premier of my original jazz compositions. These were original melodies I had composed, and

MỞ ĐẦU:

SCHWER MIT DEN SCHAT ZEN – Rimsky Cooc sa cop

(do các học sinh của Nghệ sỹ **Quyền Văn Minh**)

NHẠC CỔ ĐIỂN:

SONATA

(CHƯƠNG III)   Solo Alto Sax   *W.A. Mozat*

AVE MARIA   Solo Tenor Sax   *J.S. Bach–CH.Gounod*

CONCERTO en Am

(CHƯƠNG I)   Solo Soprano Sax *J.S BACH*

STANDARD JAZZ:

– THE EN TER TAI NER Quartet Sax ScoH Jop lin

    QUYỀN VĂN MINH   Bariton Sax

    BẢO LONG   Alto Sax

    MẠNH TUẤN   Soprano Sax

    PHÚC KHANG   Tenor Sax

– Tuxedo–Junction Solo Tenor & Soprano Sax   *E.HAWKIN*

– Desafinado   Solo Tenor Sax   *A.C. JOBIN*

– The shadow of your smile Solo Bariton Sax

    ZOHNNYM ANDEL & T.F.WEBSTER

– Bloom di do   Solo Alto & Soprano Sax   *C. PARKER*

VIỆT NAM MUSIC:

- Tiếng khèn gọi bạn: Solo Tenor Sax   *Quyền Văn Minh*

  (phát triển dân ca Mèo)

- Vãn vương: Solo Soprano Sax   *Quyền Văn Minh*

  (phát triển dân ca quan họ)

- Xuân trên Cao Nguyên: Solo Alto Sax   *Quyền Văn Minh*

  (phát triển dân ca Tây Nguyên)

Figure 8.2. Concert program, April 1994.

the songs were inspired by ethnic folk sounds I had heard in Vietnam. In this concert, I also introduced the baritone saxophone as a solo instrument in order to further highlight the nuances among different types of saxophones. The program was recorded by VTV [Vietnam National Television] and broadcast nationally.

1994 was when I decided that I had to put together a big-scale performance program. And I did it at the Hà Nội Opera House. The opera house is the "dream theater" for any Vietnamese musician. It is the stage where every Vietnamese musician aspires to have the opportunity to perform for a live audience at least once in a lifetime. It is the grandest concert venue in the country; it is our sacred ground, our cathedral! Not every instrument can be allowed to perform on that stage. If you are not familiar with the imposing atmosphere of the opera house, you will totally freeze on stage! In 1994, I gave a solo saxophone concert at the opera house for the first time. I had in fact performed on that stage earlier, in 1987. That was after Đỗ Hồng Quân returned to Vietnam from his studies in Moscow. He invited me to perform two classical pieces with the National Symphony Orchestra. But this concert in 1994 was different. This was a featured performance starring the saxophone with classical music, jazz music, and my original compositions.

Minh's key objective in the 1994 concert was to give center stage to the saxophone as an instrument through both standard jazz tunes and his original compositions. In 1988 and 1989, Minh introduced jazz under the heading "International Music" to avoid any perceived association among the audience that he was playing the "music of the enemy." As a result of further political and cultural liberalization brought about by the Đổi Mới reforms, Minh felt sufficiently comfortable and confident to introduce jazz as simply "standard jazz" in the 1994 concert. Opening the "standard jazz" section with a Glenn Miller hit tune, "Tuxedo Junction," Minh was like the Pied Piper luring the uninitiated into a slow swing on the dance floor with the saccharine timbre of his tenor, reminiscent of Stan Getz. And he mesmerized his audience with an improvised solo that sounded so melodious, they could be forgiven for mistaking it as written beforehand and rehearsed note for note. Minh's attempt to entice the audience to follow him on this musical journey continued with Antônio Carlos Jobim's "Desafinado." Minh was not done wooing his audience with Jobim's masterpiece. With the ever-popular ballad "The Shadow of Your Smile," Minh introduced the baritone saxophone as a solo instrument in its own right to demonstrate the diverse timbre of the saxophone family of instruments and the possibilities of sounds with jazz. With a melancholic melody akin to the Vietnamese *tình khúc* (love songs) that were making a forceful comeback with the rehabilitation of popular music as a result of the Đổi Mới reforms, Minh had the audience enveloped in the embrace of his saxophone by the time the shadow of his sound faded into darkness with the dimming of the stage lights. He was then ready to jolt them into a frenzy with Charlie Parker's "Bloomdido." Quite possibly, this was the first time since independence, and definitely since the reunification of Vietnam under the communist regime, that a bebop tune was performed live by local Vietnamese musicians on the stage of the opera house. Minh had earlier performed "Bloomdido" in the 1989 solo recital at the Hội Nhạc Sĩ, but at that time the song was titled "Jazz and Jazz." In that earlier performance, Minh toned down the original intensity of the piece and kept his improvisation manageable for the audience. This time, however, Minh was unabashed in his intention right from the get-go with piano and drums playing off each other in a syncopated exchange before the bass announced Minh's off-the-block allegro on the alto saxophone. Accompanied by a capable and well-rehearsed rhythm quartet of swinging hi-hats with timely filling snare, brisk walking electric bass, and full-bodied syncopated interplays between keyboard and electric guitar, Minh tested the possibilities of chords planted by the original bebop master. At one point, Minh even switched to the soprano saxophone to elevate the register of his improvisation. Minh was telling the audience, "This is what jazz can sound like."

I was very honored by the award of that grant from SIDA. Earlier, a friend working at the Ministry of Culture informed me that the Swedish embassy had a grant program supporting the arts in Vietnam. I was teaching many foreign students at that time. One of my students was from Sweden, and the student's mother was working at the Swedish embassy. It just so happened that I was teaching this Swedish student! So I asked the student to guide me on how I should write my proposal, how to submit the proposal, and so on and so forth, which was very helpful. Many people submitted proposals for this grant. SIDA gave out only two grants in total, one for a recital program by Professor Tạ Bôn, the violinist; and the other for a program by Quyền Văn Minh, lecturer of saxophone [breaking into a smile as he exhales after a puff on the pipe].[5] *So we had two disciplines, one of which was already very established and in fact deeply rooted in Vietnam, the violin; and the other, the saxophone, which was a relatively new discipline at that time. The Swedish program provided up to US$4,000 for each project grant. In the grant proposal, I had to describe the repertoire I would be performing, where I planned to perform, and so on. A friend, having observed the poor condition of my saxophones, suggested that I put in the budget plan a request to purchase better instruments and other equipment for the concert. Guess what? The grant conditions did not allow the purchase of equipment; it was only for supporting the performance! So, out of the $4,000 I requested, they only approved $2,500! Seeing my situation, Professor Tạ Bôn suggested that I perform at a smaller venue, which would be less costly, and I could still invite representatives from various embassies and Vietnamese dignitaries. However, I did not want to compromise the plan I had in mind. I wanted to prove something. So, if the funding was not sufficient, I told myself, I would take money from my* own pocket to hold the performance. If required, I would have borrowed from friends and asked them for support. It was the dream of a lifetime to be able step onto the stage of the Hà Nội Opera House to give my own solo concert! And now I could bring onstage the saxophone, an instrument that Vietnamese had never perceived as a serious and proper instrument worthy of a featured program at a respected venue such as the Hà Nội Opera House!

I invited international guests, my fellow lecturers, the conservatoire's directors, and people who have a passion for music and wished to know more about jazz. As I knew there would be both Vietnamese and foreign dignitaries attending the concert, I wanted to avoid a situation in which people could criticize me for favoring foreign dignitaries by putting them in the front rows, the VIP seats, simply because I had received support from a foreign organization. I arranged for the invited Vietnamese and foreign VIPs to be seated in two column blocks instead of according to rows. The Vietnamese attendees were seated in one column block, and international guests in another. This way, both sets of dignitaries were evenly distributed in the front rows. No one could start any gossip or raise an accusation that I was pro-foreign and therefore was playing all this foreign music to please the foreigners! I did not want anyone to bring up this kind of nonsense at all! That was one thing I really insisted on for the concert. It was the right thing. People could focus on the music. The performance was really successful, even in the eyes of the lecturers and directors of the conservatoire. I was glad and proud that I was able to bring a big entourage of respected musicians to the opera house to witness the value and musical capacity of the saxophone and to listen to the premier of my original jazz compositions.

There were only about three months between the time I submitted the grant proposal and the actual day of the performance. You see, at that time I had already decided to put together a solo performance program that could feature my own compositions, so I had been practicing with the supporting musicians for a while. Whether or not SIDA supported the program by giving me the grant, I would still have put up the solo concert. If there was no monetary support, I could still do it at a less costly venue such as the Hội Nhạc Sĩ. I was practicing for such a performance anyway. I got the grant and, in the end, I was able to put together two nights of concerts at the opera house. The first night was solely my own program, as proposed in the grant application. The second night was held in conjunction with a program to support young talents in Hà Nội. I did the second night's program because I felt that it was a good contribution to the music scene in Hà Nội. It was for the good of the community, supporting young talents in my own children's generation. I treated it as my voluntary contribution. I did not take any honorarium for the second night's performance, so the opera house could sell tickets exclusively to raise funds for the program. For the second night, I performed popular songs as well as my *own compositions. But the first night was entirely my own, for which I invited dignitaries, friends, and students.*

One of the popular tunes that Minh performed on the second night was Trịnh Công Sơn's "Hạ Trắng" (White Summer). Trịnh Công Sơn was one of the most popular composers and lyricists of modern Vietnamese music, whose songs were philosophical musings on life, social commentary, and criticism of the wars in Vietnam.[6] His songs, branded as *nhạc vàng* (yellow music) during the collectivization era by the communist regime for not being ideologically aligned with revolutionary goals, were making a forceful comeback in the early 1990s.

Sơn wrote "Hạ Trắng" in 1961 after recovering from a bout of illness during that particularly hot summer in Huế. Sơn himself recalled how the fragrance of *dạ lý hương* (night-blooming jasmine) lured him out of an almost astral dream back to a corporeal, lived existence that was, ironically, in his own words, "hot as hell." Soon after this illness, Sơn visited a friend, whose father was sick and soon passed away. To keep a long story short, the friend's father had fallen sick with sadness after his spouse had passed away. Unable to bear the loneliness of an existence without his lifelong partner, the old man passed away soon after.[7] "Hạ Trắng" is one of Trịnh Công Sơn's most alluring masterpieces telling of his meditations about life. The unique assemblage of imagery from seasons (golden sunlight amid a clear blue sky in the summer), landscape (endless pathways toward the horizon on the plains), and love (in this case, the enchanting gentle flutter of the white *áo dài* [Vietnamese long dress] in the summer breeze) to ponder over how one might transcend the dualities of sadness-happiness, separation-reunion, and life-death is one of the key characteristics of Sơn's music, or rather, poetry. Minh gave a meditative recital of "Hạ Trắng" without flair or pomp, the sound of his saxophone gently fluttering amid the gentle breeze and serene blue sky engendered by his capable rhythm section. As can be observed in Minh's later albums featuring popular Vietnamese songs, namely *Đoàn Chuẩn & Hà Dũng với NSUT Quyền Văn Minh* and *Hà Nội, Autumn and You*, Minh always stays faithful to the original phrasings of the poetic lyrics when performing Vietnamese songs but delivers the tune in his own subtle expression of poignancy. Minh does not write lyrics to songs, as do popular and revered Vietnamese composers/lyricists such as Trịnh Công Sơn; Minh's poetry is in the music he produces on the saxophone and clarinet.

Around 1992 or 1993, when I was writing my own music, I was trying to imagine what I could perform in a future solo concert, which turned out to be this 1994 concert at the Hà Nội Opera House. From my experience of playing on stage for more than two decades and delivering the 1988 and 1989 solo recitals, I knew at that time when planning a concert, I had to ask myself, "What was the objective of that program?" In 1988 and 1989, I wanted to show that the saxophone should be respected as a mainstream and serious instrument, just like any standard musical instrument in the symphony orchestra. Only then, I was convinced, could people begin to be more receptive to jazz. In those two concerts, I played classical music, "chính thống" [mainstream and proper] music, and I played Vietnamese chamber music, our country's very own modern instrumental music. Then, in the third section, I introduced music from outside of Vietnam, jazz. When I played "Méditation" (from Thaïs) in 1989, I wanted to show that Quyền Văn Minh could play classical music on the saxophone, and it would sound just as serious as other orchestral instruments. When I played Bach's violin concerto in 1988, which was extremely difficult, I wanted to show the extent to which I could perform classical music.

Minh delivered a stellar performance of the first movement of Bach's Violin Concerto no. 1 arranged for a string quartet and solo soprano saxophone in the first part of the 1994 concert. Clearly this was the most challenging piece in the classical repertoire presented that night, and Minh was determined to showcase his ability to perform a most complex masterpiece by Bach on the saxophone, on the big stage. He had earlier performed it with piano accompaniment in the very first solo recital program at the Hội Nhạc Sĩ in 1988. Then, it was not exactly the breathtaking delivery he had hoped for, having to restart the performance after a few bars into the introduction due to extreme dryness of the mouth. This time, Minh returned to the big stage with a string quartet and emerged victorious. If the audience was just getting comfortable hearing his perfect and unfazed classical delivery of "Ave Maria" and Mozart's Sonata in C, then Minh certainly had them sitting straight up with adrenaline pulsing when the string quartet and his soprano saxophone unleashed the first few notes of the violin concerto. It was a delicate, clinical, and regal execution of Bach's famous composition. Minh made his point. The saxophone was a serious musical instrument to be treated with respect. At this point, he already had the conservative musical dignitaries from the Vietnamese music scene totally won over, as far as his ability as a performing musician and the status of the saxophone were concerned.

Audience who came to the 1994 recital, they had yet to know Quyền Văn Minh as a jazz musician. They only knew that I was an accomplished saxophonist. I followed the structure of the 1988 and 1989 programs but with some adjustments. Similarly, there were three parts in the 1994 program. In the first part, I performed classical music on the saxophone. In the second part, I performed "international jazz" music, meaning jazz music that originated from outside of Vietnam. In 1988 and 1989, I could only introduce jazz as "international music," but in 1994 I simply printed it as "standard jazz" in the program. In the third part, I played my own compositions, which I printed as "Vietnam music" in the program. I wanted the audience to recognize my compositions as Vietnamese music and as pieces that were uniquely Quyền Văn Minh's creations. When speaking to the audience, I introduced these tunes as "âm nhạc dân gian Việt Nam với phong cách jazz" [Vietnamese folk music in jazz style]. It was a really long title, but I had to explain in the title what I was playing in this section. I wanted the performance to speak for itself, so it was necessary to use a title that was self-explanatory. I have to say, the foreign guests really loved it, and the lecturers in the audience witnessed something new. I was the pioneer in doing something like that. It was a huge success!

When Minh gave the breakout solo concerts in 1988 and 1989 introducing the sound of jazz in the Vietnamese public sphere, he had to persuade his siblings and close friends to accompany him on stage as his makeshift rhythm section. Fellow professional musicians refused to take part in these "risky" performances for fear of ruining their reputations and because of discomfort with the musical genre that Minh was trying to perform. After forming his own small jazz groups to play at the French embassy and various gigs, including at the Metropole Hotel and the Cuban-designed Thắng Lợi Hotel, Minh learned what it took to have a tight ensemble accompany him on the jazz stage. And if Minh were to premier his original Vietnamese jazz compositions, he had to be certain that these musicians were both musically capable and agreeable to his avant-garde brand of music. After all, they would be performing at the "cathedral" of all concert halls in the north, if not in the whole of Vietnam. Everyone's musical reputation was at stake. Bringing in younger and capable musicians in Vương Tử Lâm (guitar), Văn Dũng (bass), Yến Dung (keyboards), Ngọc Quân (drums), and Văn Hào, Minh formed his very own jazz band, which he called the Sông Hồng Band (Red River Band). Minh was ready to swing to his own creations. Indeed, the real feature of Minh's 1994 concerts at the opera house was his original Vietnamese jazz compositions. Three original songs, each with a distinct character in sound, premiered on the stage of the Hà Nội Opera House that night.

Writing Original Vietnamese Jazz Compositions

When preparing for the 1988 and 1989 recitals, I worked with excellent composers such as Hoàng Vân, Đặng Hữu Phúc, and Đỗ Hồng Quân. I actually commissioned these three composers to write tunes for the recitals. Their compositions were very good, and the performances of these tunes were very successful. After the recital, I studied how existing melodies in Vietnamese folk music were adopted by Vietnamese composers to write Vietnamese chamber music. They basically followed the structures of classical music. Having performed these compositions for the 1988 and 1989 recitals, I was convinced that Vietnamese chamber music could not break out of the structures taken from classical music. In jazz music, it is all about improvisation. After I started teaching at the conservatoire, I really began to focus more on studying jazz in order to teach better. When the conservatoire invited me to teach there, I had already collected a substantial amount of materials on my own, but I went about to find more materials to enable me to teach the subject better. Throughout that period, I deliberated and thought very carefully about the way we played Vietnamese chamber music. The outcome was not ideal and definitely could not lead on to jazz. This was because the composers already wrote out every single note. Even for cadenza parts where we could improvise a tiny little bit, it was still very much restricted by the written notes. To play jazz, I must have the space to improvise.

The consecutive recitals in 1988 and 1989 echoed each other, highlighting a limitation I faced when performing the Vietnamese chamber music compositions; there was no space in the music to develop my ideas. I realized the need to write my own music in order to play jazz. I was convinced that I had to write my original music to bring jazz, especially Vietnamese jazz, to the Vietnamese public and to an international audience. In some ways, I felt that I had to do this all the more because I was already a lecturer of saxophone and jazz at the conservatoire. So, after the second recital in 1989, when I started teaching, through 1993, I thought about the need to write my own music for me to play, so that I could give a more effective performance. Some standard jazz pieces, for example Coltrane's "Blue Train," the melody and the sound, if you play it according to the Vietnamese style, it could sound like a Vietnamese composition. If you just look at the framework of the melody, it resembles the pentatonic scale found in Vietnamese folk music and Asian music. But when you come to the solo part, you could break free and play out your ideas; it becomes more complex. Studying that piece made me think, could I improvise from a melody in such a framework? Could I write my own melody of our own music? Could I do something like that and take back my own artistic agency like he, Coltrane, did?

Vietnamese folk music is indeed a very rich resource that I could use to develop our original brand of jazz. I could follow in the footsteps of many Vietnamese chamber music composers and borrow from Vietnamese folk music to develop jazz. But somehow, I knew that I should not adopt an existing folk tune to develop into a jazz composition. I knew I could not simply pick up an ethnic folk tune and jazz it up. This was simply because I had not studied at the conservatoire. Students who studied at the conservatoire could follow the directions of their teachers or their colleagues, and the school would always support and defend their work. There is a precedent for them to follow. But not me. I studied on my own and pioneered my own path. I am basically a self-taught musician. I have to think carefully about what I can do, what I cannot do, what others have done, and make sure that I go in a different direction. Yes, we have folk music to borrow. I could adopt or borrow an existing folk melody, improvise, and create a composition. But I knew at that time, when I was writing my first few original tunes, I should not do that and could not do that. People could say, and would definitely say, that I desecrated Vietnamese folk music by doing so! If anyone ever accused me of desecrating Vietnamese folk music, I might never get rehabilitated in the music circle! I was very certain that this kind of criticism would emerge if I had done that.

I knew very well from my experience as a musician and as a person who had pioneered his own path that such accusations could easily come about, and they would totally ruin my credibility. That was the reality then and I would say even now. There was no one and nothing to defend me. I had to protect myself. I had to be alert. I told myself, I must find ways to use these themes, Vietnamese folk music themes, to write my own music. When I started writing my own songs, I knew I had to do it differently from composers of Vietnamese chamber music. I wrote my own melodies, so I did not have to adopt or borrow any existing folk songs in my compositions at all. I wrote new, original melodies, and set these melodies in appropriate scales and in appropriate moods. Melody, scale, my thoughts, the stories, and my feelings, I put these together to form my compositions. I made sure when writing my music that it was jazz I was bringing to the audience. I made sure in my compositions that there was enough space in the music to solo and to improvise. I wrote three original tunes.

Minh's First Three Original Compositions

I am a northerner, so I wanted to write something about the north. The first song I wrote was "Tiếng Khèn Gọi Bạn" [The Call of the Qeej (Hmong reed pipe)]. When I started learning guitar and clarinet, I began to really pay attention to what was playing on the radio. I heard revolutionary songs [songs, marches, and symphonic tunes written to propagate the socialist revolution], classical music, and ethnic folk music played on the radio. Those days, I could only listen to what was played on the radio; it was not like I could access information from any other sources. So, I listened to what was being broadcast. When it was time for the music program, I turned on the radio. The radio station broadcast a lot of ethnic folk songs because we have so many ethnic groups in Vietnam, fifty-something or over sixty. The genre of ethnic folk music was already very well developed at that time. I guess it is because ethnic diversity is the soul of this nation. I tried to imagine the story behind the music, how composers wrote the music and how the musicians played the sounds. When I joined the military song-and-dance troupe and went up to the Việt Bắc military region, I heard a song played by the Mèo [Hmong] people in the uplands. Every now and then I had heard folk tunes played on the radio that sounded similar. But when I first heard this tune in person in the mountains, it was just different from what I had usually heard on radio! The sound of that tune stayed with me. The scale I heard

Figure 8.3. Ethnic Hmong playing the *khèn* in Sapa Town, 2013 (photo by Nguyễn Trường Giang).

in the melody and the timbre of the khèn I heard in the hills stayed with me. When I started thinking about composing my own music, I thought I could use that. I remembered very clearly how it sounded in my memory. I was inspired by this memory, so I wrote a three-part composition about the courtship process of the Mèo people. I composed an original melody to illustrate the courtship process, how the boy expresses his feelings for the girl, emulating sounds and melodies played by the khèn. Successful in getting her attention, he saddles her on the horse with him, and they gallop into the forested mountains, which is the second part. And they go through a whole process of affirmation of their relationship as lovers. Finally, they return as lovers, which is the third part, to the lush romantic melody of the khèn.

"Tiếng Khèn Gọi Bạn" is a tonal recollection of Minh's early venture out of the *miền xuôi* (downstream plains region) to the contrasting *miền núi* (mountainous region) in northern Vietnam. In 1970, Minh joined the Việt Bắc Military Region Song-and-Dance Troupe as an apprentice musician. In the Việt Bắc uplands, Minh for the first time in his life encountered the diversity he had first heard on radio. The scenes and sounds were different from what he had heard earlier. Professionally employed as a music cadre, Minh could fully focus on his ambitions to become a capable artist. He practiced relentlessly in his free time, and he woke up earlier than others to practice before roll call. To avoid disturbing his fellow comrades who were still sleeping, Minh climbed further up into the hills beyond the barracks and practiced his clarinet on an isolated hilltop at the break of dawn. It was a formative phase of his life as a professional musician, one defined by industry, persistence, and curiosity. It was the beginning of a life much traveled, exposing him to the kaleidoscope of sounds contained in the inclusiveness of the term *âm nhạc dân gian Việt Nam* (Vietnamese folk music).

With the piece "Vấn Vương," Minh returned to the plains, taking inspiration from the antiphonal lyricism of *quan họ*, a traditional folk music genre originating in Bắc Ninh Province in northern Vietnam. In "Vấn Vương," Minh tells his own story as a musician in Hà Nội striving to bring jazz to the public sphere in the midst of the current ideological climate, which was changing from conformity under intense socialist revolution to the possibilities unleashed by Đổi Mới. He took inspiration from his own lived experience. Like a *quan họ* song, "Vấn Vương" is a conversation, but one between Minh and himself.

"Vấn Vương" was really a melancholic piece, the lament of a musician. I played music because of my parents, especially my mother. I could do all this because of the support of my family. When I started working, practicing the clarinet and later the saxophone, it was a lonely road. Vấn vương, if you understand Vietnamese, is a kind of melancholy, being lost in thought, not a deeply depressive kind of sadness. It describes my own state of thought, my meditations, during the early 1990s, looking back at the different kinds of difficulties I had to overcome to play jazz and establish my career. So I wrote the song "Vấn Vương." It's a melancholy song. I asked questions about my own pathways while writing this song. I felt that I was on my own in my pursuit of music, jazz. Sure, I was playing music with other people, but I felt that I was sequestered in my own space. I was alone in the crowd. I never experienced the phase of being a student, like a music student; I did not have the experience of camaraderie from a cohort of fellow students because I was basically a self-taught musician; I only had colleagues who happened to play on the same stage. That was all. I was on my own. So I wrote "Vấn Vương" to tell of the times when I felt lost and entangled in my own thoughts. I composed "Vấn Vương" using both the saxophone and the guitar. I used the guitar mainly to arrange the music and develop the harmony I had in mind. I was also inspired by the timbre of the soprano saxophone when writing "Vấn Vương." I used the soprano when performing this piece, because I was imagining myself walking on the streets of Hà Nội trying to find a way out of that entanglement, to walk out of that melancholy, and I just kept going. It was written in 3/4 time signature because I wanted to tell the story of my own road to play jazz; I had to do this, I had to do that, just so I could play jazz.

By the early 1990s, Minh had accumulated considerable mileage traveling as a musician. In 1970, he was stationed in the Việt Bắc Autonomous Region,

Figure 8.4. Ethnic minority communal house (*nhà rông*) in Tây Nguyên, 1999 (photo of author).

home region of the ethnic Thái, Hmong, Dao, and Nùng, among others, as an apprentice musician venturing out of Hà Nội. Returning to Hà Tây in the plains in 1971 with the Hà Tây Song-and-Dance Troupe, Minh gradually gained traction across the neighboring provinces of Hà Nội in the early 1970s as an outstanding young musician, receiving allowances at the level of *bậc 3* (grade 3) as a recognized soloist in the ensemble. Soon after reunification of the country in 1975, Minh even visited Sài Gòn with the arts group of Hà Nội City Youth League. Even during the brief period in the late 1970s when Minh was working at the Propaganda Department of the Từ Sơn College of Physical Education and Sports, he found an opportunity to perform in the New Economic Zones of Lâm Đồng Province in the Central Highlands. As a member of the Golden Bell of the Capital Troupe from 1980 to 1981, Minh toured extensively across almost every province in northern Vietnam performing in the troupe's avant-garde New and Old Crossover program. Joining the Thăng Long Song-and-Dance Troupe, Minh's career as a musical cadre peaked, and he performed in almost every corner of a reunified Vietnam under the communist regime.

For the third composition, I wrote an entirely different piece, something livelier; I took inspirations from Tây Nguyên. I performed in Tây Nguyên during my time with the Thăng Long Song-and-Dance Troupe. There were many people who studied their music [of ethnic minorities in Tây Nguyên]. I also wish to be able to spend some time in the field studying all this different music. Maybe after I retire, I can devote some time to doing this. Anyway, at that time, I wrote "Xuân Trên Cao Nguyên" for the concert. I felt that there was a more festive element to the sounds of Tây Nguyên. "Xuân Trên Cao Nguyên" was written using a rock rhythm. I used rock to transit into swing in the solo improvisation section because I wanted to showcase the blues foundation of jazz. When I composed the opening motif, I wrote a melody reminiscent of folk songs from Tây Nguyên, but I wrote it in a blues scale. And it went well together. When I wrote these three pieces, I wanted to demonstrate the different moods of jazz. In "Vấn Vương," the second composition, I used a different rhythm to contrast with the intense sounds of "Tiếng Khèn Gọi Bạn" and "Xuân Trên Cao Nguyên." It's like eating. We cannot be eating the same dish in a multicourse dinner. So my compositions should not all sound similar. I made sure the pieces sounded distinct from one another.

When I was composing the songs, I wanted to use melodies and sounds that have a natural affinity with Vietnamese people so that they would try to understand the music. This should be something, when they listen, they can identify and say, "Hey, this is Vietnamese! That is from Vietnam!" I wanted to use that kind of melody to play jazz. So, for example, when I composed "Tiếng Khèn Gọi Bạn," the melody, when played on its own, Vietnamese could identify it as belonging to Vietnam's ethnic folk music traditions. When people hear that, when Vietnamese hear that, they will be able to tell that it sounds like the Hmong folk tunes found in Vietnam. It was, and would be, natural for them to react as such. And when you listen to Vietnamese folk sounds, you can hear the potential for developing that music into jazz just as well. When I listen to certain standard jazz pieces, I can hear the musical scale of Vietnamese folk music in the melody. If I play that melody with a Vietnamese ballad rhythm, it can sound generically like a Vietnamese ballad tune, too. So, you see, international audiences can see a connection in Vietnamese folk music with jazz, and vice versa, there is a connection in jazz with Vietnamese folk music, too. Vietnamese folk sounds can act as a bridge in the cultural exchange between Vietnam and other countries. There is a connection between others and us. If these compositions are successful, then when international musicians hear the songs, they can see that we have our own music, Vietnamese music, to play jazz. What I am trying to do here is to combine the best of developments in international music with the rich musical traditions in Vietnam. The different scales used in different ethnic folk music traditions in Vietnam are so diverse and rich, even if I spend my entire life studying it, I would not be able to understand everything! Vietnam's traditional folk music is a huge treasure trove that could really help develop an original sound for jazz, Vietnamese jazz.

The primacy of lyrics is ingrained in the conception of music in Vietnam. We have lyrics about war, the nation, ethnicity, the revolution, and about love. Don't get me wrong; we have many talented composers in Vietnam. Many! But with music in Vietnam, lyrics drive the melody! This has been a concern for the Hội Nhạc Sĩ, too. Some time back, the Hội Nhạc Sĩ even tried to promote the composition of instrumental music by giving out support and grants, but I was not considered as belonging to that inner circle of composers. I was basically categorized as a performing artist in our system, even though I was teaching at the conservatoire. You see, most of the composers, they studied and graduated from schools and conservatoires. They studied how to compose sonatas, symphonies, and concertos. The irony is that after graduation, when they started working, they realized that there is no demand for instrumental music in the market! Even today, instrumental music only makes up a very small proportion of the compositions by musicians in Vietnam. Instrumental music is like the thin layer of husk wrapped around the rice grain, unattractive and minimal. The music scene is flooded with love songs; everyone wants to write songs because our audience loves these love songs. All this means that introducing jazz to the Vietnamese audience has been a most daunting task. And certainly, jazz is not of interest at all to everyone. Besides, in Vietnam we have a saying, "không hiểu thì không đi nghe" [one will not listen if one does not understand]. Jazz has often been seen as complicated and different. Difficult to understand, too. And in the earlier days, when I started, there were no educational resources about jazz as a musical genre in Vietnam. So that made it all the more difficult.

Jazz is seen as something strange and foreign in this country. Jazz is not commonly found in Vietnam, but it is my work and passion. The story about me playing jazz in a country where people did not know about jazz, having to find my own way to play music and learn about jazz, you could find many of these stories in the world, and many of these people went on to achieve greater things than me. But the most important thing for me has always been about opening a pathway to develop Vietnamese jazz music, about using jazz to create an original musical genre on the basis of traditional folk sounds in Vietnam. Creating an original road to develop jazz that carries our nation's characteristics [bản sắc dân tộc] for the next generation of musicians, that has been my primary concern. What I am saying here is nothing new. If you look at the great jazz masters elsewhere, like John Coltrane and his compositions, that is what they did to create their own paths. They could find inspiration from their traditional cultural foundations and develop something great to conquer their critics. Naturally, every musician composes in their individual way, and every musician would market their music in their own way. As for me, I only have to ask, "What can I do to attract an audience to come away with me on this journey of discovery?"

For Quyền Văn Minh, Vietnamese jazz is about original melodies and original sounds developed through the spirit of jazz on the basis of existing soundscapes found in the cultural diversity captured by the term "Vietnam"—the hills and plains; the north, south, and central regions; and the city and the country—and, most crucially for him, the stories found within.

I did not study composition. Sure, I would like to learn how to write better so as to develop my music better. There was no one who advised me about what I could do or should not do to write my own jazz compositions. I had to find my own way. I wanted to be able to tell a story with the music. For example, when I wrote "Tiếng Khèn Gọi Bạn," I was trying to tell a story. But that story is told differently each time we play, and when played by different musicians and with a different ensemble. **But the key thing is this: the story itself is something unique from Vietnam.**

When composing these three tunes, Minh did not borrow any existing melodies from the great treasure trove of folk songs found among the fifty-four officially categorized ethnic groups of Vietnam. He consciously avoided improvising from any such melodies. Minh wrote original melodies inspired by existing soundscapes to tell the stories he had encountered, imagined, and lived through jazz. In other words, he made no attempt to mimic or borrow. Minh heard the possibilities of jazz in the traditional sounds of Vietnam. He heard the traditional sounds of Vietnam folded within the complexities of jazz. The encounter between these two broad genres gave Minh the creative space he needed to tell his stories. "Tiếng Khèn Gọi Bạn," "Vấn Vương," and "Xuân Trên Cao Nguyên" were only teasers to the full album he would release five years later, *Birth '99*.

All three tunes that premiered on the stage of the Hà Nội Opera House in 1994 were rearranged and recorded for *Birth '99*, Minh's debut jazz album. Minh wrote another five tunes inspired by soundscapes found in a diverse range of Vietnamese folk music to tell his stories using original melodies he composed. Minh wanted to help his listeners find "Vietnam" in the brand of jazz he composed, and jazz in the brand of Vietnamese music he performed. He did not take the path of "jazzing" existing folk music, like some early attempts at creating a "Japanese jazz" identity that E. Taylor Atkins discusses in his majestic story of jazz in Japan.[8] Instead, Minh's initial conception of jazz might bear some similarity to the "own jazz" that Rüdiger Ritter speaks of with respect to the development of an original genre of jazz in Poland and other parts of socialist Europe, a recombinant product of the encounter between jazz as invented in America and the soundscapes of the host country rather than a mere jazzifying of existing melodies.[9]

Minh's premier of original Vietnamese jazz compositions in his 1994 concert marked the beginning of an achievement comparable with Krzysztof Komeda Trzciński's contribution to the creation of Polish jazz as a distinct genre in socialist Poland during the 1960s.[10] Minh would properly define his own musical language with *Birth '99* and the follow-up album, *Đồng Cảm* (*Identify*, released in 2002) after this successful experiment in 1994. When presenting his original creations, Minh was determined to persuade the audience that jazz has a place in the diverse ethnic folk music soundscape of Vietnam, a position not too far from Atkins's daring suggestion of "indigenous musics as adaptive yet resilient enough to absorb jazz."[11] Elsewhere in Eastern Europe, Slovakian jazz musicians such as Matúš Jakabčic were convinced that "they had something to offer to Western jazz" even though jazz had developed in "relatively isolated conditions."[12] Minh shared similar beliefs, as demonstrated by the tunes he premiered in 1994. He was convinced that, with further development, Vietnamese jazz could just as well have a say in adding to the already rich and globally diverse texture of jazz.

Minh's attempt to develop an original Vietnamese jazz genre with these three compositions in 1994 was fundamentally, at a personal level, a "renewed appreciation of local traditions" (to borrow the words of Atkins) in order to freely express his musical ideas and tell his stories through jazz.[13] And he did so by treading carefully along the changing ideological contours of a socialist Vietnam undergoing the tension of reforms in the early 1990s. Quyền Văn Minh's development of an original Vietnamese jazz sound takes no side in the ideological debates of his era. He successfully navigated the ideologically sensitive context of the early Đổi Mới years to present an original experiment of a distinctive Vietnamese jazz sound to a Vietnamese audience with this public premier in 1994.

TRACK 9

Teaching Jazz

Quyền Văn Minh began teaching saxophone at the Hà Nội National Music Conservatoire of Vietnam in 1989. From 1991 onward, jazz was formally included as part of the *chính thống* (proper mainstream) professional music education curriculum at the most prestigious music education institution in socialist Vietnam, culminating in the formation of a Faculty of Jazz in 2013. When Minh formally had his tenure transferred from the Thăng Long Song-and-Dance Troupe to the conservatoire in 1991, he essentially changed vocation from being a *nghệ sĩ biểu diễn* (performing artist) to a *nhà giáo* (teacher).

A Teacher

Looking back, the concert in 1994 was really a huge success. Even the director of the conservatoire remarked to me, "This concert is essentially the college graduation recital of Quyền Văn Minh; in fact, a most outstanding graduation recital!" I thought that they would really award a college degree to me after the recital, just like when they awarded an ad hoc accreditation of "trung cấp đạt cách" [intermediate level proficiency achieved; a high school qualification] to me after the 1989 recital, so that I could officially teach at the conservatoire. This time, however, government regulations dictated that I had to complete all necessary courses at the college level in order to qualify for a degree certificate. They could not just grant me a degree based on the concert I had delivered. I worked very hard in order to finally earn that degree. While teaching at the conservatoire, I continued to study for a degree outside my working hours. I had to take classes about music as an academic discipline, classes about harmonization, and all kinds of other classes related to music just so I could receive a college degree. The audience viewed the 1994 concert as a distinct model, albeit a strange one. To many, it was viewed as a way of developing folk music through jazz, and it later inspired many young musicians in their own compositions.

The birth of Vietnamese jazz at the 1994 concert demonstrated Minh's passion as a teacher who would nurture generation after generation of jazz musicians in Vietnam. Even though this was a major concert for Minh to premier his original compositions, he was happy to share the stage with his students. Readers familiar with the Vietnamese music scene after the turn of the millennium would immediately focus on the name Trần Mạnh Tuấn, featured in the saxophone quartet performance of Scott Joplin's classic piece, "The Entertainer." Playing soprano in the saxophone quartet, Tuấn was one of Minh's earliest, albeit informal students of the saxophone before Minh even formally started taking in students. Tuấn has since become a household name known for his flamboyant showmanship in performances of Vietnamese popular music, and he has his own music lounge in Hồ Chí Minh City. Trần Mạnh Tuấn, Nguyễn Bảo Long, and Phúc Khang were Minh's most outstanding students of that era. But Minh also created an opportunity for a group of his younger students as well as less advanced learners of the instrument to experience the atmosphere of performing at the Hà Nội Opera House.

I opened the concert with a large saxophone ensemble playing a march composed by [Nikolai] Rimsky-Korsakov to welcome the guests. This ensemble was composed of my Vietnamese students from the conservatoire, including my son, [Quyền Thiện] Đắc, and foreign students I taught outside the conservatoire. There were more than ten of them, I remember. The saxophone ensemble opened the concert for me, welcoming all the guests to the night's performance.

Among members of the saxophone ensemble and saxophone quartet were indeed future stars such as Quyền Thiện Đắc, Trần Mạnh Tuấn, and Nguyễn Bảo Long. Tuấn and Đắc later had their respective sojourns at the Berklee College of Music in Boston and returned to make a name for themselves in the music scene. In a way, the concert foretold the future of the jazz scene in Vietnam. With this showcase, Minh proved his dedication as a teacher in his heart and soul. Such mentorship was something that Minh never had when he was learning the ropes as a budding musician. Minh himself never thought that he would end up as a teacher.

The Early Years of Teaching Saxophone

In the early years when I became a professional performing artist [nghệ sĩ biểu diễn], I never thought that I would teach the saxophone to generate more income. It was because people heard my playing, were impressed, and came to ask me to teach them. I did not even know how much I should ask to be remunerated for each lesson given! I was like, "Up to you!" That was the case when the brother-in-law of Trần Mạnh Tuấn came to ask me to teach Tuấn, back in 1979. Trần

Figure 9.1. Café opposite 31 Lương Văn Can.

Mạnh Tuấn, as you would know, is now a famous saxophonist in the Vietnamese pop music scene. I met Tuấn's brother-in-law in Hà Đông when I brought my daughter, Chi, along to play for a gig. When I started teaching Tuấn, I had no idea how much money I should accept for payment. I told his brother-in-law that it was entirely up to him, so he gave me some money and a gift of a few packets of cigarettes, because his family was selling cigarettes at that time.

Trần Mạnh Tuấn would climb up here to the rooftop at Hàng Giấy to study with me. Initially, my neighbors were not too happy with the sound of the saxophone invading their personal space. But the sound of our music overcame their resistance and displeasure. One of my neighbors even let her son study with me at the end of the day, telling me, "Listening to the sound of the saxophone when you were teaching, it was beautiful!" The son loved music. My neighbor could have let the son study with the guitarist who lived on the second floor, but she chose to have him study saxophone with me. In the morning, after waking up, I would make breakfast for my children. My student, the neighbor's son, would come up and practice with me. After that, my children would come up and eat their morning meals with me, then they went to school while I went to work. This student of mine, he would take me to work on his bicycle because I had already sold my own bicycle after my divorce! My workplace, the Thăng Long Song-and-Dance Troupe, was located at 31 Lương Văn Can, which was not too far from Hàng Giấy, where I lived. Arriving at 31 Lương Văn Can, we would sit at the café opposite my troupe's building and have some coffee. In fact, I drank regularly at that café for a good ten years! The student worked as a carpenter on Lương Văn Can Street. Although he was a carpenter, he was really interested in music. With the little income he had, he would treat me to coffee as a way of remunerating the music lessons I gave him. For musicians like us, morning coffee was a luxurious enjoyment; our salary was used mainly to buy food, that was all. Those were difficult days. I remember on days when it was raining, this student and I would pool together what little money we had to buy some rice wine—we called it "quốc lủi" [common rice wine] in those days—and pickled vegetables, and chatted over these simple "delicacies." These simple things we did those days remain a beautiful memory of the past. We were happy with these simple things. The small wooden shelter on the rooftop was a reminder of how I overcame the first difficult period in my career. The rooftop was the first place where I could practice playing music. When I learned the guitar, I had to go to the rooftop, because it would be too noisy to do so in the apartment. When I started learning the clarinet, I had to go to the rooftop, too. No one is staying there now, but that place is a quintessential part of my memory.

After I started teaching Trần Mạnh Tuấn, I began to take in more students. I organized my time very well. I worked, I performed, and I taught. And from there I began to see the value of teaching. When I started teaching more students, I knew that I had to continue to improve myself in order to teach better. From 1983 onward, I taught many students privately and helped to groom musicians for various troupes in Hà Nội and other provinces, as well as other government departments such as the Ministry of Internal Affairs and the People's Army of Vietnam. Some notable students of mine during the 1980s, while I was still a member of the Thăng Long Song-and-Dance Troupe, included:

Phan An Dũng, Ministry of Internal Affairs Song-and-Dance Troupe
Nguyễn Quốc Tuấn, Trung Hiếu Cải Lương Troupe of the Department of Public Security, Hồ Chí Minh City
Nguyễn Hồng Sơn, Army Headquarters Political Affairs Song-and-Dance Troupe
Trần Văn Dật, Army Headquarters Political Affairs Song-and-Dance Troupe
Nguyễn Đang Thọ, Customs Office Song-and-Dance Troupe
Lê Việt Tiến, Military Region 7 Song-and-Dance Troupe
Nguyễn Văn Vinh, Thái Bình Song-and-Dance Troupe
Đặng Huy Khiêm, Hà Nội Circus Troupe (Đoàn Xiếc Hà Nội)
Trần Mạnh Tuấn, Golden Bell of the Capital Cải Lương Troupe
Quốc Thịnh, Border Defense Regiment Song-and-Dance Troupe

Việt Hùng, Air Force Regiment Song-and-Dance Troupe
Nguyễn Phúc Khang, Nghệ Tĩnh Song-and-Dance Troupe
Lương Việt, Lào Cai Song-and-Dance Troupe

At the same time, I also taught many students from the Nam Hà Song-and-Dance Troupe and many other amateur ensembles in Hà Nội, Hải Phòng, Quảng Ninh, Thanh Hoá, Huế, Đà Nẵng, and elsewhere.

Joining the National Conservatoire

The Hà Nội National Music Conservatoire of Vietnam was established in 1956, called Trường Âm Nhạc Việt Nam (the Vietnam School of Music) until 1982. The conservatoire was formed with a group of seven musicians, among whom only the pianist, Thái Thị Liên, having studied in Paris and Prague, had a music degree. When it was first formed, the school only had an upright piano; a few violins, cellos, and accordions; and a few odd brass instruments left behind by the French. The school soon received support from socialist allies in Eastern Europe, who sent instructors, teaching materials, and musical instruments. The objective of the school was to provide professional music education of the highest level at international standards. In addition, the school was also tasked to develop among musicians the capacity to create an original repertoire of Vietnamese works.[1] From very humble beginnings, the conservatoire had by the 1980s became the home institution of the most respected and famous musicians in Vietnam. Notable Vietnamese violin professors such as Tạ Bôn and Ngô Văn Thành, both of whom graduated from the Tchaikovsky Conservatoire in Moscow, taught at the national conservatoire.[2] Only the most musically talented students could study at the conservatoire to become professional musicians, and studying there meant studying with the leading musicians of the country.

Minh's decision to join the prestigious national conservatoire to teach saxophone and jazz after the 1988 and 1989 recitals marked a significant turn in the story of jazz in Vietnam. Teaching saxophone and jazz at the conservatoire completed the triangle of making jazz a proper mainstream part of the Vietnamese soundscape. When Minh presented his solo concerts in 1988 and 1989, jazz was effectively endorsed by the powerful Hội Nhạc Sĩ, which was tasked to steer the development of music in accordance with the communist party's ideological prescription in socialist Vietnam. With the solo concert at the Hà Nội Opera House in 1994, Minh had brought jazz to the holy ground of performance venues for any serious musician in Vietnam. When jazz was included in the national conservatoire's professional music education curriculum, there was no denying its new status as a serious and respectable music art form. Beginning in 1991, jazz was allowed to be taught as a subject major under the newly formed Department of the Organ (Electric Keyboard) in the recently expanded Faculty of Accordion, Guitar, and Organ. By 1992, this new department, which also included the saxophone and jazz drums disciplines, was informally referred to as the jazz department. In 2007, the conservatoire began offering a major in jazz at the bachelor's degree level, and in 2013, it was formally established a Faculty of Jazz.[3]

After my first solo performance in 1988, the Hà Nội National Music Conservatoire of Vietnam invited me to teach at the school. The dean of the Faculty of Wind Instruments and Percussion at that time, Phúc Linh, had studied in Hungary, so he understood my recital. He was among the audience at the performance, and later, coincidentally, we went to the same session to record music for the soundtrack of a film. He told me, "I want to invite Minh to teach at the school, but I understand that it would be difficult because the salary is quite low. However, if Minh is passionate about music and wishes to help future generations, then Minh should teach." I told him, "I would really love to do so, and I have collected a lot of materials. We should discuss the concrete details of how this can be done, but a primary condition would be that I must be allowed to teach jazz." He was very positive and assured me, "Sure, sure. Jazz music of course, and classical as well! Just like the model you performed at the recital, that should be the way to teach our students." I loved that idea, and I agreed. But I asked the conservatoire to give me one week to consider before properly accepting the invitation. In the past, people would always consider very carefully the available opportunities and would "bite on one" to give it more consideration before actually taking it up. I finally agreed because to be able to give birth to a new field of music in Vietnam, the worth of that is much greater than any material gain in life.

After that, when it came to the 1989 recital, it was like a solo audition to see if I was qualified to teach at the conservatoire. The leadership of the conservatoire was there among the audience. When the recital was over, the director of the conservatoire, Trọng Bằng, told me that in principle the conservatoire would require some kind of paper qualification for someone to be able to teach there, because it was a state regulation. Although I did not have the paper qualification, my performance proficiency was way above any stipulated criteria at the conservatoire. They decided to give me an ad hoc accreditation of "trung cấp đạt cách" [intermediate level proficiency achieved; a high school qualification], so that I could officially teach there. I understood their constraints and thought that the decision was reasonable. When I started out to become a musician and applied to join the professional music troupes, people always asked me, "Where did you study?" My reply was invariably, "I studied at home." And this would be followed by the next question, "Do you have a diploma?" To which I could only answer, "No." How could I have a diploma if I learned by myself at home?

It was only when they really needed me and recognized my ability to play music, then they would put aside the issue that I did not have any diploma to certify that I could play. That was how I got to join the Thăng Long Song-and-Dance Troupe. When they really needed the saxophonist and the clarinetist in Quyền Văn Minh, then they would be willing to go around the organizational structure, rules, and regulations to give me the position. That was why I could accept the fact that the conservatoire only gave me a trung cấp đạt cách certificate just so that I could start teaching formally there.

There had never been anyone in Vietnam with anything like my case. All the professors at the conservatoire had studied music formally in school; some had even received formal training overseas and were retained by the conservatoire to teach music. For me to be able to teach saxophone at the conservatoire, it was an unusual case. I had studied on my own and so had no formal paper qualifications. I was totally on my own, but the directors and deans at the conservatoire recognized that I was a serious, capable musician. And with the recitals in 1988 and 1989, they could see that the saxophone was indeed an important instrument that should be included in the curriculum. There never was anyone teaching students to play classical music on saxophone, or anyone using the saxophone to play Vietnamese chamber music, and definitely no one playing jazz with the saxophone at the conservatoire. In the past, yes, there were people who played saxophone, but they had learned the instrument outside of the conservatoire. In fact, most people in the past learned informally with other musicians who knew how to play the saxophone. So, there had been a few people playing saxophone in the past. They played in the tea lounges, a few songs for the joy of it and for the fun of it, so to speak. That was it. For a very long time in Vietnam, people really did not perceive the saxophone as a serious instrument. When I picked up the instrument, I found that there was so much depth and possibility in the sound of the instrument; maybe I would never uncover every possibility of what this instrument could do in my life.

At that time, I was still with the Thăng Long Song-and-Dance Troupe. I only transferred out my tenure formally in 1991. In that year, the people at the troupe wanted me to work solely at the troupe and not teach at the conservatoire anymore. They even promised to promote me! I told them, "That would be impossible, because the school started a new discipline and that required the permission of two ministries, the Ministry of Culture and the Ministry of Education. If you make me abandon the work now, that would not be possible; my reputation would suffer." That was what I told the troupe chief. And I continued, saying, "When I went over to the conservatoire to start teaching, that was approved by the director of the Department of Culture. Only with his approval then could I start teaching there." The new troupe chief, who had just been promoted to that position, began to pressure me to concede. The director of the Department of

Culture at that time had worked at the conservatoire earlier; he was formerly the head of training there. He felt that the new troupe chief was shortsighted and immediately signed the papers for me to teach at the Hà Nội Vocational College for the Arts, so that not only could I formally teach, I could teach anywhere; I could even teach concurrently at two schools, and there would not be any problem at all! When I went over to the vocational college, the principal was hesitant about my appointment there. So I went back to the Department of Culture to explain the problem I faced, and they finally agreed to transfer my tenure completely to the conservatoire. By 1991, I had fully transferred to the conservatoire. In the past, there were only state institutions, and we were all cadres of the state. It was the same for me; for thirty-six or thirty-seven years, I was a tenured state cadre, except for a short period of time when I was unemployed.

When I was invited to join the conservatoire, I felt a little bit of hesitation. Partly, it was because I had to consider whether taking up that role would allow me to afford to take care of my two children. It was a big decision. Life, at the end of the day, is also about how much income one can bring home to take care of one's family. By the late 1980s, life was already very different from the earlier Thời Bao Cấp [Subsidy Period]. During Thời Bao Cấp, your official job basically determined your overall income and how well you lived. By the late 1980s, after Vietnam opened its doors, if you did not have any lucrative source of income outside your main job, then there was very little that you could do to improve life for your family. Everyone had to find additional work outside one's main job in the day.

Before joining the conservatoire in 1989, I had a stable job and a stable income working at the Thăng Long Song-and-Dance Troupe. And I had time that allowed me take up extra gigs to earn extra income, which paid a lot better than my official salary. You see, by 1989 the cultural and arts environment in Vietnam had changed from the pre–Đổi Mới period. It was a time when the government began to loosen control over cultural activities, creating an environment that made it possible for artists like us to have a very good income. When I agreed to teach at the conservatoire, I knew that I would have to cut back on my "work in the market economy," which was how people used to describe these paid external gigs. I could not do that anymore. The first few years after joining the conservatoire were a period of economic difficulty for my family. We somehow overcame that difficulty. Taking care of my children was indeed a very important responsibility. Going through all those difficulties in life, having less of this and having less of that, we could bear with those kinds of difficulties. I told myself, this was the right path. Even if this was going to be a long and winding road, as long as I believed it was the right path, I should just do it.

I also knew that from the day I joined the conservatoire, I had to put aside all the knowledge about putting on a good show as a performing artist that I'd accumulated over two decades as a cadre of various song-and-dance troupes, apart from giving up all the lucrative sources of income from taking up gigs as a very reputable performing artist. I knew right from the beginning that I would be in a very different working environment at the conservatoire.

The first year moving out of the Thăng Long Song-and-Dance Troupe to join the conservatoire was the most difficult. Life was tough. I continued to receive many invitations to take up gigs, and these were very lucrative opportunities to earn good money, but I could not take them up. Let me put it this way: I could have taken up all these extra opportunities that came along, no one was stopping me. But, how could I? How could someone carry the respected status of a teacher at the conservatoire and still go out and do all kinds of gigs unbefitting the respected status of a teacher? It would be crazy of me to do that! I could take up other gigs outside of Hà Nội, but I could not travel too far or for too long. I could do overnight gigs outside of Hà Nội, so long as I could return the next day. The salary at the conservatoire was indeed low at that time. I had to take on more external assignments beyond my official duties at the conservatoire that could bring in a little bit more income for the family. I could only take up "proper projects" such as studio recording sessions for other artists, soundtracks, television, and other proper assignments that came along. At that very juncture, at that very opportune moment, I knew that if I did not do all those things and if I did not start to teach at the conservatoire, then students who wished to study the saxophone and play jazz would not have the same rights as students who studied other instruments. If they study at the conservatoire, they can receive a diploma to help them find work. If they did not have the opportunity to learn the saxophone and jazz properly at the conservatoire, then they would encounter problems when they looked for work.

Joining the conservatoire was not an easy decision for another reason. I knew that from the moment I joined the conservatoire to start teaching, I would have to forgo the time I could spend practicing and performing the saxophone. I would have to compromise some of my goals as a performing artist, as a saxophonist. When I put together the 1988 and 1989 solo recitals, I did not imagine that I would go into teaching. I only wanted to demonstrate to everyone that the saxophone should be respected as a proper mainstream instrument, just like other orchestral instruments. I wanted to show that it is a very versatile instrument that can be used for different kinds of music. I wanted to introduce jazz. The instrument that I love, although people at that time felt that it was not "chính thống" [proper mainstream], I wanted to prove that it was chính thống. That was all. I did all this, even though I was just a self-taught musician. I never thought that I would be invited to teach at the conservatoire. So immediately after 1989, I stopped thinking about putting up another recital or concert. I focused on teaching so that I could prepare a proper curriculum for students at the conservatoire. And in

1991, the Department of Culture approved my full transfer from the Thăng Long Song-and-Dance Troupe to the conservatoire to allow me to fully concentrate on one set of official responsibilities, teaching.

In those days, I worked according to the requirements of the conservatoire. Outside my official working hours, I also gave lessons to students, for example people who worked in other companies or government departments but wanted to learn the saxophone or clarinet as a hobby; I did that as well, it was work. Teaching foreign students was a source of income, a good one. And doing that also meant that I had more friends to play saxophone with me! During this period, I found myself more occupied in the work of teaching saxophone, as more foreigners came to Vietnam to work, and some of their children wished to study the saxophone. Through the introduction of the external relations office of the conservatoire, I was able to teach foreign students who came from England, France, the United States, Germany, Sweden, Indonesia, Canada, Japan, Finland, Nepal, and other countries. This rich teaching experience gave me much inspiration and encouragement because I am a Vietnamese and yet I could teach them, an international group of people, the beauty and sophistication of the saxophone as a musical instrument! I even presented a saxophone recital featuring two foreign students and one Vietnamese student for a program called Blooming Flower *organized by the Vietnam National Television Broadcasting Station in the early 1990s.*

Teaching at the Conservatoire

Being able to start teaching saxophone and jazz at the conservatoire in 1989 marked a significant change in the musical environment in Vietnam for jazz. When I was invited to teach at the conservatoire in 1989, it was about including the saxophone as a proper discipline of study at the top music conservatoire of our country! Saxophone and jazz were finally allowed and finally approved by the top musical establishment in Vietnam. It was a huge thing! As a result of our war with America, Vietnamese people in those days tended to think of jazz as the music of the enemy. They overlooked or did not understand that jazz actually developed from the Black people and their complicated history with the white people. It was a cultural creation generated by the history of the United States and the world. Some lecturers who had studied in Eastern Europe and the Soviet Union such as Lưu Quang Minh, who later became deputy director of the conservatoire and the most ardent advocate for jazz education at the conservatoire, had heard jazz in socialist countries. There was jazz in these countries, and you could hear jazz all over the world. The head of the Faculty of Wind Instruments [and Percussion], who had invited me to join them in 1989,

Figure 9.2. Teaching at the conservatoire (photo by Dương Hà Linh).

also understood this. 1989 was a watershed for jazz in Vietnam. I have to say this again: for that to happen, to be able to teach saxophone and jazz at the national conservatoire of Vietnam, that was a huge thing!

The first year I started teaching at the conservatoire, I remember we recruited eight students for the saxophone program. Over time, we expanded into two classes. By 1997, three schools in Hà Nội were offering the saxophone as an academic discipline: the national conservatoire, the Hà Nội Vocational College for the Arts [Trường Cao Đẳng Nghệ Thuật Hà Nội], and the Military School for the Arts and Culture [Trường Quân Đội Văn Hoá Nghệ Thuật]. In 2014, we had twenty-two students in the saxophone program!

Even though I could teach jazz at the conservatoire, the learning environment for students was not ideal for a long time. Jazz was not treated as a specialized discipline because we did not have a specialized jazz faculty then. It was taught as a subject, then a major, but together with classical music. There is a certain common foundation in music, we can agree on that. Yes, in school you have to study music theory, harmony, the instrument, improvisation, and so on, with the respective teacher. But chord changes in jazz are a lot more complicated and elastic, so if you only study with a classical musician, you might not see that.

A few years after I joined the conservatoire, the saxophone program was transferred from the Faculty of Wind Instruments and Percussion to the Faculty of Accordion, Guitar, and Organ in 1992. The saxophone program was placed in the organ [electric keyboard] department, which everyone called the Department of Jazz. Twenty years later, in 2013, the conservatoire finally opened a separate Faculty of Jazz.

When it comes to recruiting students for the conservatoire, my personal take is that we should select students who are absolutely passionate about music. I say this based on more than twenty years' experience of teaching at the conservatoire. It is only when the students are really passionate that they then put in the effort to learn and to practice. Of course, natural talent for music is always a primary consideration. These naturally talented students learn very quickly. However, naturally talented students who are not passionate can easily waste away that gift, and everyone's time and effort. Certainly, when I teach, I hope that my students, at the end of the day, will attain the standards of a solo artist comparable to those of musicians overseas. But I understand that my students will individually embark on very different paths when they graduate. Some might become very reputable solo artists, some might go into teaching at various music schools, some might join existing musical ensembles and song-and-dance troupes, and many might go to a province to serve in provincial art ensembles and cultural departments. Not everyone will become a solo artist performing music professionally for a living. But they are all good musicians, and they serve the public with their music.

Life at the conservatoire, it was a normal working life. Everybody knew me. They knew that I had not gone to school to formally study music, but they all knew that I had studied my instrument very hard and had attended the necessary classes to get my degree, to properly qualify as a faculty member at the conservatoire. They knew that I was competent, so they respected me. However, I cannot say that I have had a totally fulfilling and happy working life as a musician and teacher at the conservatoire.

The conservatoire has its own rules, regulations, and policies to govern and teach the students: taking attendance, giving tests, checking whether they can play from a musical score, and so on and so forth. But I want the students to be able to realize in their own way what they are learning with me; a kind of self-realization. I want my students to know that when they come into a class, it is an important and serious occasion. I am there to listen to how they play, offer advice, and provide guidance so that they can progress to the next level of playing. Whenever a student tells me that they have something at home and wish to study at home, that they will practice on their own and be ready for the next class, that is fine with me. What is the point of forcing the student to come to class and take attendance when they cannot concentrate? I do not think this is necessary. Yes, not every student can be so disciplined. But the school insists on such a disciplinary regime. You must put a mark on the attendance sheet and everything. It is not good to be too dogmatic in our approach to teaching students. Yes, there are certain rules and foundations in music that students have to learn, but that does not mean that there is only one way to learn it. They may come in and check all the boxes, but what about the quality of their music? Let us really pay attention to that.

Teaching is an art. You need to be hard and soft. When Đắc studied at Berklee, he knew how important and valuable each lesson was because I had to sell my saxophones just so he could afford to study there. Students in Vietnam also have to pay school fees and other expenses to study at the conservatoire. But often they do not realize that when they do not prepare properly for each lesson, they are wasting time and money. Students do need discipline. But they also need guidance. It is the same with my own children. There was once, when Đắc was still very young, he went out to play until quite late. I scolded and punished him when he finally came home. In the midst of our argument, Đắc put on his jacket and said, "I am going back to Hà Đông." I let him go, but I followed him all the way to Hà Đông. I thought that he would turn back, but he kept walking! I stopped him midway, explained to him why I had to scold him, and brought him home. Just like when you send a student out of the classroom, you have to call them back in, too! Otherwise, they might not dare to come back in; they might just give up on music. We have to be more flexible in our approach when it comes to teaching.

Every teacher is different. Having worked at the conservatoire for more than twenty years, I can guarantee that most of the teachers there are very good, they live with music. When I hear my students play well, I am honestly impressed. I often ask myself, "When I was that age, could I play like that?" At the end of the day, I know that with the path I have taken to play jazz in Vietnam, to teach saxophone and jazz at the conservatoire, and to develop jazz in Vietnam, it has been like blazing a path across a field with my bare feet, all muddy, dirty, and difficult; bare feet in the mud. But I know that because I have already opened a new path for current and future students, they can wear nice shoes, run, and take off!

When I started out, I had no one to guide me. But I was aware of what I was doing; I was aware of what other people were doing; and I compared the differences. Why must I compare? Because I never had a chance to study. So if I hear anything different, anything strange, I immediately ask "how" and "why," and I practice to try to be able play the same thing. And I tell myself, "Oh, if I do it this way then it might be more interesting!" So I improved. As for a teacher, a proper teacher in heart and in soul, given my circumstances, I did not and could not have had a proper teacher. In the past, when I was younger, I asked the older players, "How did you do this and how did you do that?" The answers I got would often be, "Oh, come on, this is so easy!" But they did not teach me. They would not teach me. I heard people use the vibrato when they were playing, and I asked, "How did you do that?" I got the remark, "You are young, you can pick it up very fast!" But they would not teach me. I could only *imagine from listening. When I heard the music played from the radio and later from vinyl records, I could not see anything; I could only listen. I had to imagine how they produced that sound.*

In 2000, at the death anniversary of my mother, Trần Mạnh Tuấn and all my other students came to "ăn giỗ" [a memorial get-together].[4] *And we started talking about the future of jazz and the future of the saxophone in Vietnam. By then, a number of my earlier students such as Trần Mạnh Tuấn, Nguyễn Bảo Long, Nguyễn Hồng Kiên, and Phan An Dũng had already begun to establish themselves in the music scene in Vietnam. Some of them took up formal teaching positions in various colleges in Hà Nội, and almost all of them took in students informally. I said to the different generations of students present that day: "Please pass on fully what you have learned to your students. If you have embarked on the learning journey ahead of others, but you hide the things you have learned and refuse to pass them on, you are failing in your responsibility as a senior to the juniors. As for the students and the juniors, it is your responsibility to listen and learn what is being imparted to you." Let me put it this way: "teachers" and "seniors" in Vietnam do not always teach everything they know to their students and juniors. On the one hand, jealousy often prevents people from sharing what they know for fear that others might surpass them! On the other hand, the competitive nature among musicians is such that people might not always be ready to listen and learn from the experience of others as well. Sadly, I know this is a fact. You might be a good musician, but you might not be a good teacher. To be a good teacher, you have to think bigger than yourself.*

My own experience in music also taught me something very important. When I tried to join the Thăng Long Song-and-Dance Troupe for the first time, I was not successful, because I did not have a diploma in music. When I finally joined the troupe in late 1980, it was my second attempt. I was successful the second time around because this time they really saw my ability to play music. When I accepted the teaching position at the conservatoire in 1989, I had already begun to enjoy teaching. From teaching Long, who came back to find me at the jazz club after thirty years, when I was doing the wedding gigs as a young boy; teaching Tuấn when I became a professional musician; and later teaching so many other musicians when I was with the Thăng Long Song-and-Dance Troupe, I gradually learned to enjoy teaching, understand the meaning of teaching, and appreciate the importance of teaching what I know to others and the next generation.

From the time I joined my first song-and-dance troupe, I was very clear about one thing: there is a big difference between someone who has a diploma and someone who does not—you are treated differently. From the social system we live in to how organizations are governed, having a diploma or not is a fundamental basis of how a person is treated. It creates a certain mentality among Vietnamese that those who have a diploma are naturally superior to those who do not have a diploma. It is important to earn a diploma, but that is not everything.

All those years as a performing artist, I came to realize that people who possess a music diploma might not be better than me at all, at least musically speaking. So I came to one fundamental life philosophy: I could only survive by means of my own true ability to play music. We might not have had the conditions to learn music really properly during the war period and the years before Đổi Mới. But musicians of my generation persevered, continuously developed ourselves, and made real contributions with our music to Vietnamese society. If you compare life now with life in the past, the present might feel like a paradise. However, that does not mean that with better conditions, musicians can necessarily learn music better or learn the value of music better. And it does not mean that if we did not have those conditions, we could not achieve our musical ambitions. I try to teach my students this basic ethos toward music with my own stories.

The 1994 concert at the Hà Nội Opera House was an early showcase of Minh's dedication as a teacher of saxophone and jazz in socialist Vietnam. But Minh faced two greater challenges after 1994.

First, how was Minh going to create regular opportunities for his disciples and future jazz musicians to perform in the public sphere of socialist Vietnam when he had to work so hard to create such precious few opportunities for himself? Henceforth, Minh devoted body and soul to creating opportunities for his students to play for a live audience and for jazz to be a part of the soundscape in Vietnam. And he did so by nurturing wave after wave of jazz musicians, not just skilled saxophonists per se, to sustain a live jazz scene by opening Minh's Jazz Club in 1997. This jazz club became the key venue for budding jazz musicians to hone their craft. In fact, it is *the place* to play jazz in Vietnam. For Minh's students and other budding jazz musicians who came along the way, Minh's Jazz Club became a professional, live gig training ground.

Second, what sound could these budding jazz musicians aspire to achieve? With what sound was Minh going to cultivate an audience among the Vietnamese public that was more receptive to jazz? After successfully experimenting with his own conception of Vietnamese jazz as a genre in its own right in 1994, Minh endeavored to fully develop an original sound for Vietnamese jazz by writing and recording his own original compositions, and by touring with his own band and his own sound.

TRACK 10

Interlude II

Unlike most other countries in Asia, Vietnam's fate with jazz was put on hold for more than thirty years; only in China was the situation comparable. While North Vietnam was undergoing a fervent socialist revolution, fighting a bloody war with the Americans and their South Vietnamese allies and singing songs of revolution and patriotism, the rest of Asia was experimenting with jazz and trying to find its own individual voice in the world of jazz.

Shanghai was the first jazz capital of the Orient, attracting the services of jazz musicians from the United States, Europe, Japan, and the Philippines from the 1920s to the 1940s. While popular with the cosmopolitan crowd in Shanghai, jazz was resisted by Chinese conservatives and nationalists because of its association as something foreign and liberal. The story of jazz in China resonates with what happened in the European socialist states when their respective communist parties came into power. At the same time, the Shanghai example also bears some similarity to how jazz was introduced in other parts of Asia during the age of colonialism. Jazz, or rather its early dance music renditions, came to Shanghai as early as 1910, primarily for the entertainment of Europeans, Russians, and Americans based there. And it was enjoyed by the Chinese gentry class, which was benefiting from economic relations with the Western powers.

By the 1920s and 1930s, with the rising number of dance halls opening in Shanghai, jazz bands were in huge demand. However, there was a great shortage of Chinese musicians proficient in Western instruments and American dance music. As a result, Western musicians were hired from the United States and Europe to fill the gap.[1] Some notable African American jazz musicians who came included the likes of Buck Clayton, Teddy Weatherford, and Valaida Snow. Musicians who could play jazz from the Philippines, Russia, and Japan also landed in Shanghai with stints as resident musicians.[2] By the mid-1930s, Chinese bands began to emerge on the scene.[3] Yu Yuezhang (余约章) was perhaps the first person in Shanghai to organize a Chinese jazz band. The Yu Yuezhang Orchestra (余约章乐队), consisting of only Chinese musicians, played regularly at the Lao Dahua Dance Hall (老大华舞厅).[4] However, Filipino bands were considered the premium musical combos in Shanghai's dance hall circuit, followed by European, American, and Russian bands, while Chinese ensembles took the lowest position.⁵ Among the numerous Filipino musicians playing in Shanghai, the most notable was Apolo Dila. According to fellow musician Angel Peña, who played in a big band led by him, Dila was reputedly the best Filipino jazz trumpeter of the 1930s.⁶

Scholar Li Mo, however, is skeptical about the "jazz" that was being played and consumed. The term "jazz," apparently, only referred to instrumentation consisting of percussion, piano, brass, and woodwinds playing cabaret music.⁷ Citing the work of Chen Chen, Li Mo notes that "old Shanghai jazz," as this genre of music popular in Shanghai later came to be called, contained little or no improvisation or swing.⁸ Using video clips from the reunion performances of elderly musicians formerly active in the old Shanghai jazz scene at the Peace Hotel as evidence, Li Mo concludes that Chinese popular music rather than jazz best describes this genre of music. Jazz that contained elements of swing and improvisation was primarily played by a very small group of musicians such as Buck Clayton's band and the Yu Yuezhang Orchestra. By 1937, war had arrived in Shanghai, and these bands, together with jazz, disappeared from the scene (resurfacing only briefly after 1945).⁹

Among Chinese musicians active in the Shanghai music scene during the 1920s and 1930s was Li Jinhui (黎錦暉), an educator and composer. Li Jinhui is noted in the story of jazz in China for creating a hybrid genre referred to as "modern songs" that blended jazz, American film music, and Chinese folk music.¹⁰ He recorded these modern songs for major recording labels such as Pathe-EMI, RCA Victor, and Great China. At the same time, he is also remembered for composing the film music for fifteen popular entertainment films. Most significantly, Li Jinhui led his own all-Chinese jazz big band in the vibrant, cosmopolitan music scene of Shanghai.¹¹ While his music was popular with general audiences, critics labeled it "yellow music" (黄色音乐) or "pornographic" music. Both nationalist (under the Kuomintang) and communist cultural ideologues condemned Li Jinhui's music as a "decadent sound" (靡靡之音) that seduced "citizens away from the pressing tasks of nation building and anti-imperialist resistance."¹² When Mao Zedong's Communist Party took control of China in 1949, all things jazz and Western were shut down. Li Jinhui was singled out as the founder of yellow music and became a victim of political persecution during the Cultural Revolution of the 1960s.

After Mao's death, China gradually opened up to the rest of the world. Similar to the story in socialist Vietnam, an era dominated by "serious" music in the forms of classical music, traditional music, and revolutionary songs (革命歌曲) soon accommodated the return of easy-listening music, or rather "light music" (轻音乐). By the early 1980s, light music bands had emerged on the Chinese music scene. With this change, jazz slowly began to make its way back to the country.¹³ Beginning with Willow Ruff, a bass and French horn jazz musician who taught and performed in Shanghai in 1981, internationally renowned jazz musicians began to include China, especially Shanghai, as a key stop on the Asian leg of their tours. From Wynton Marsalis to Bob James, jazz musicians of different persuasions have performed in China.[14] Chinese musicians also began to take an interest in jazz. After the reemergence of jazz in the 1980s and early 1990s, Eugene Marlow argues that "jazz as a music style was not only of interest to Westerners coming to China's urban centers, such as Beijing and Shanghai . . . , but also to a growing number of indigenous Chinese who find in jazz that 'individual freedom of expression' long suppressed under Mao."[15] Older musicians who had been exposed to jazz in their youth before communist rule, such as Beijing saxophonist Fan Shengqi (范圣琦), reemerged and continued with their exploration of musical forms interrupted by three decades of ideological radicalism.[16] Enamored by the new sounds they heard as jazz entered the country by way of cassette tapes in the 1980s, a new generation of musicians began to pick up jazz. In Beijing, Huang Yong (黄勇), a bass player who first heard jazz on tape in 1989, not only organized his own band to play jazz but also began organizing jazz festivals from as early as 2005.[17] Dennis Rea, a guitarist who played in China, was impressed with the proliferation of Chinese jazz soloists who could improvise just a short decade after the release of a CD album called *Jazz in China* by the China Record Company, recorded by the pianist Gao Ping—an album Rea considered only "marginally jazz."[18]

Jazz also began to appear on Chinese radio channels, such as the program *Beijing Music Radio*, hosted by Zhang Youdai (张有待), and the station FM94.7 in Shanghai, hosted by Guchao (顾超).[19] By the end of the first decade of the twenty-first century, there was already a significant demand for jazz in China that was attracting the interest of major names in the business. In 2017, Jazz at Lincoln Center Shanghai opened in the vibrant commercial city, while Blue Note opened shop in Beijing, the political capital of the country.[20]

Despite the gradual growth of jazz in China since the 1980s, Liu Yuan (刘元), perhaps the first Chinese musician to perform jazz as a professional musician, feels that Chinese jazz musicians have yet to develop a kind of jazz that is uniquely Chinese.[21] As Fiach Ó Briain, an Irish jazz drummer who has been playing in Beijing since 2015, notes, Chinese jazz musicians are more comfortable emulating traditional jazz forms from the United States in the 1950s and 1960s.[22] Liu Yuan himself reportedly believes that "traditional jazz is the real jazz" and is critical of attempts to create "Chinese Jazz" without a thorough understanding of both traditional Chinese music and traditional jazz music.[23]

Jazz took off in a number of Southeast Asian countries in the early to mid-twentieth century. In the Philippines, jazz blossomed in the 1920s, a few decades after American troops first set foot in the archipelago, with phonographs and 78-rpm vinyls grinding out blues and early recorded jazz.[24] In 1921, Luis Borromeo (later known as Borromeo Lou), who was from Cebu, returned to the Philippines after spending time in the United States and Canada. He formed a jazz band and introduced classic jazz to the Philippines. According to Peter Keppy, when Borromeo staged his debut performances in Cebu, Iloilo, and Manila, he called the shows *A Review of the Evolution of the Classical Jazz Music, Operatic, and Classical Song*.[25] Soon, Borromeo Lou came to be called the "King of Jazz" in the Philippines.[26] It did not take long for Filipino musicians to pick up the genre and export their talents across the Asia-Pacific region, taking up gigs in major European enclaves in the cities of Japan, China, French Indochina, the Dutch East Indies, and British colonies in Southeast Asia.[27] By the 1930s, people in the Philippines were dancing to swing music, and jazz could be heard at fiestas and on the local radio. Among some of the most notable Filipino jazz bands were the Cesar Velasco Band, the Mabuhay Band, the Mesio Regalado Orchestra, the Pete Aristorenas Orchestra, the Shanghai Swing Masters, and the Trio Cruz Orchestra.[28] Although wildly popular, jazz music was despised by cultural critics such as Raymundo Bañas, who, according to Keppy, once stated that jazz would not have "a lasting life in the Philippines."[29]

By the 1950s, jazz had risen to become one of the most popular music genres in the Philippines. Jazz concerts such as those organized by the Upsilon Sigma Phi fraternity at the University of the Philippines were well attended.[30] These concerts at the university were especially significant; according to Richie Quirino, Pinoy jazz was born at the *Jazz 2* concert held at the university's theater in 1956. This concert had two main parts. The first part featured three original tunes composed and arranged by Narding Aristorenas, while the second part featured tunes by Angel Peña.[31] The highlight of Peña's contribution was a piece called "Bagbagtulambing" (Igorot Jazz Fantasy), which was inspired by a lullaby of the Igorot people, an ethnolinguistic group living in the mountainous regions of northern Luzon. This was the first time a piece of music that infused jazz with Philippine folk music was performed in public. And it was no mere rearrangement that jazzified an existing folk melody, but a completely new sound. This song marked the official birth of Pinoy Jazz.[32] In Peña's words, "Pinoy jazz is not just using indigenous music instrumentation or using Bahay Kubo [nipa hut] as thematic material. We should have our own ideas."[33] By the 1960s, prominent Filipino jazz musicians such as Peña, Exequiel "Lito" Molina and the Jazz Friends, Fred Robles, Piding Alava, Romy Katindig, and Romy Posadas were contributing in various ways to the creation of a distinct Pinoy jazz sound that was a blend of jazz and traditional folk tunes.[34]

Jazz in the Philippines caught up with the fusion trend in America that developed in the 1970s. Eddie Munji and Ryan Cayabyab were among the pioneer musicians who led this charge into a style that mixed jazz, rock, and popular music. Popular Filipino jazz artists who came to fame in the 1970s include Bob

Aves, Bobby Enriquez, Boy Katindig, Eddie Katindig, John Lesaca, Menchu Apostol, Pete Canzon, Rudy Lozano, and Tots Tolention.[35]

In 1978, the University of the Philippines Jazz Ensemble was formally established. However, for twenty-three years after its establishment, the ensemble played mainly music from the United States and Europe. Richie Quirino argues that the ensemble should be playing Pinoy jazz instead: "I felt that we are Filipinos and it is about time that we know our own identity, compose and arrange our own music, and offer it to the whole world."[36] Beginning in 2002, through the collaboration of Angel Peña and Professor Rayben Maige, the ensemble began giving concerts that featured Pinoy jazz composers, especially Peña's compositions. And since 2006, Candid Records, a British label, has been exporting Pinoy jazz albums overseas. The label also helped to launch the international career of jazz musicians and singers such as Mishka Adams and the Affinity Group.[37]

In Thailand, jazz blossomed under the tutelage of King Bhumibol Adulyadej, who inherited the crown in 1946 and passed away seventy years later, in 2016. Educated in Switzerland, King Bhumibol was a huge fan and promoter of jazz in Thailand. He was known as the "Jazz King," and many people claimed that it was the king who introduced jazz to the people of Thailand. In an interview, Admiral Usni Pramoj, a privy councillor, shared, "We didn't know jazz. His Majesty introduced us to the music, and it was very lively, with endless improvisation."[38] Living in Europe, King Bhumibol learned to become an accomplished saxophonist and clarinetist who was also adept at the trumpet. Upon returning to Thailand to take up his role as king in 1950, he started a jazz band called Lai Khram.[39] The band was renamed the Au Sau Band when more people, including members of the royal family, military musicians, and professional musicians, joined.[40] The king also established a radio station in the early 1950s called Au Sau Amporn Satharn, which broadcast jazz to a Thai audience. Every Friday, the Au Sau Band would perform live for their listeners.[41] It was reported that the king even participated in the live broadcasts every Friday, selected music for the radio program, and encouraged listeners to phone in with song requests.[42] King Bhumibol also enjoyed composing jazz music. In 2006, a selection of his compositions was recorded by Larry Carlton for the album *Jazz King* in celebration of the sixtieth anniversary of the king's accession to the throne (2006) and his eightieth birthday (2007).[43]

King Bhumibol personally received the first "jazz ambassador" to visit Thailand in 1957, namely Benny Goodman and his orchestra, and even invited the band to join him at the palace for four jam sessions.[44] In the early 1960s, the king invited West German musicians to visit Thailand. The Albert Mangelsdorff Quintett came and performed a piece written by the king himself, an original composition based on *ramwong*, a Siamese dance.[45] In 1964, the Mangelsdorff Quintett recorded an adaptation of this composition, which they called "Now Jazz

Ramwong," on an album that also included their interpretations of Vietnamese folk songs heard during the group's visit to South Vietnam.[46]

King Bhumibol also used jazz as a means to deepen connections between university students and the monarchy.[47] Eventually, jazz departments were formed in three of Thailand's prestigious universities, namely the Mahidol University College of Music, the Rangsit University Conservatory of Music, and Silpakorn University. These departments have actively promoted jazz in Thailand. The Thailand International Jazz Conference, which began in 2009, is organized annually by Mahidol's College of Music. The conference is aimed at "presenting top quality jazz music to the public and also offering jazz education to interested musicians."[48] There is also an annual Thailand Jazz Competition organized by Silpakorn University with prizes amounting to around US$11,000, jointly sponsored by Icon Siam, Silpakorn University, Yamaha, Theera, and other donors.[49] Additionally, the Rangsit Conservatory of Music organizes a five-day jazz camp, the first of its kind in Southeast Asia, which features international jazz artists and teachers from the United States and Thailand. Jazz festivals are also held yearly in Bangkok (since 2003), Hua Hin (organized by Hilton Hotel since 2001), and Chiang Mai (since 2011).

As early as the 1920s, musicians from the Philippines were hired to play jazz at clubs and lounges in major cities of British-ruled Malaya (Malaysia, after independence). From the time of its emergence in Malaysia, jazz was associated with modernity and the freedom to think independently.[50] Soon, local bands were formed that went around giving jazz music performances across the British colony. Some of these local bands introduced the use of small lutes to produce "interlocking rhythmic structures," thus injecting elements of *keroncong* musical stylings in the jazz they played.[51] Despite such attempts to adapt the music to local sounds, jazz was fundamentally perceived as Western music and also as a genre associated with modernity. Jazz thrived after independence, but only for a short while. Sectarian rioting in 1969 between ethnic Chinese and Malays ultimately led to a more ethnically conscientious cultural environment centered around reverence to the national religion, Islam. And jazz, an art form perceived as Western and foreign, quietly retreated into the background.[52]

Jazz can be heard in Malaysia today, especially in the country's capital city, Kuala Lumpur. But there is no "perceived rootedness" of jazz in the musicians' musical identity in Malaysia.[53] As Gisa Jähnichen reports, a jazz club owner lamented that musicians who play jazz in Kuala Lumpur have "no . . . spontaneity, no interaction, and . . . no sensitivity" in the music![54] Jazz is simply one of many genres played by musicians who are capable of playing in that style, but who can "switch style[s] without reflection on musically represented meanings."[55] Nonetheless, a small handful of Malaysian musicians have demonstrated attempts to develop a more pronounced local sound.[56] For example, Lewis Pragasam, a Punjabi drummer who founded the group Asiabeat, is seen as a "key influence of jazz in Malaysia" for his fusing of diverse ethnic elements to create innovative rhythms in his music.[57] Meanwhile, noted Malaysian guitarist Farid Ali is known for using the *gambus*, a short-necked lute that is considered a "highly symbolic instrument for Malaysian culture," as a jazz instrument. According to Jähnichen, Ali's music is a "successful hybridization of local and global sound colors," taking the *gambus* beyond its original identity as merely a local ethnic musical instrument.[58]

In Indonesia, Batavia under Dutch colonial rule had an active jazz scene. During the 1920s, the Batavia Band, the Batavia Syncopaters, Brown's Sugar Babies, the Melody Makers, the Silver Queens, and the Royal Jazz Band were some of the renowned jazz ensembles. Members of these bands consisted of young men, many of whom were still in school, who had learned jazz tunes just from listening to recordings. There were also Dutch musicians performing jazz such as Harry Braun, Piet, and Wim Bruyn van Rozenburg. These musicians were playing jazz alongside local musicians who included Aroef, George Tjoh, Jacob Sigalarki, and Rohadi. By the mid-1920s, Philippine jazz performers began to arrive and make their presence felt in Batavia. In 1928, jazz musicians from the United States such as Jack Carter, Noble Sissle, Valaida Snow, and most notably Teddy Weatherford began performing in Batavia.[59] Peter Keppy, however, maintains that jazz in Indonesia during the 1920s was mainly available to the middle and upper classes of the colonial society, who could access gramophone recordings and attend live performances at theaters and clubs.[60]

After Indonesia gained independence, Western musical genres were basically categorized as *hiburan* (entertainment) and seen by President Sukarno as indulgent, neocolonial cultural ills.[61] It was a difficult time for jazz during Sukarno's presidency. Legend has it that when Jack Lesmana, the guitarist, and Bibi Chen, the pianist, were performing for President Sukarno, they were asked not to improvise! It is also interesting to note that the US State Department did not organize any jazz tours to visit Indonesia prior to 1966.[62]

Following the rise of Suharto's regime in 1966, jazz was seen as "a form of upwardly mobile cosmopolitanism" and openly celebrated as a progressive cultural art form.[63] In 1967, Indonesian jazz was introduced to the world when the Indonesian Jazz All-Stars band toured Europe and played at small jazz clubs in the Netherlands, Switzerland, and West Germany. According to Oki Rahadianto Sutopo and Pam Nilan, "the band adapted Indonesian folk songs, made use of the *kacapi* (zither), and improvised using Indonesian indigenous scales."[64] By the late 1970s, it was clear that jazz not only appealed to the elites but had evolved into a popular musical art actively played in universities and even broadcast on national television (Televisi Republik Indonesia, or TVRI). In the 1980s, jazz fusion arrived in Indonesia, and musicians began to embrace the new sound, synthesizing jazz with rock, punk, and pop. Some musicians even developed their own brand of jazz fusion by injecting a variety of traditional and indigenous sounds from Sunda and central Java.[65] According to Andrew McGraw, by the 1980s, "many young Indonesian jazz musicians responded by self-consciously localizing the form, authenticating their expressions as overtly hybrid through the melding of local traditions (such as *gamelan*) with jazz."[66]

The sound of jazz in Indonesia took a turn in the late 1990s when musicians and critics began to react against the feverish convergence of "commodified jazz fusion" and mainstream popular music and rock. As a result, musicians active in the live jazz scene began returning to classic jazz roots.[67] According to Sutopo and Nilan, this was a period when jazz performance was characterized by "little originality and a great deal of conformity," and in reaction to this situation, established jazz musicians in Yogyakarta began to create "jazz-hybrid forms" by combining local Javanese musical elements into their music.[68]

Djaduk Ferianto, founder of the Kua Etnika Music and Theater Studio, is recognized as one of the pioneers who led this syncretism of jazz and local traditional musical and art forms that were supposedly "fully Indonesian, Javanese, and 'jazzier.'" Ferianto was trained in classical Javanese dance and had studied fine arts at the national conservatoire. Upon founding his Kua Etnika studio, Ferianto brought together performers of different ethnic artistic forms, and musical genres including jazz, rock, and theater. In 1997, his eclectic ensemble gave collaborative performances with Aminoto Kosin, a Javanese jazz musician trained at the famed Berklee College of Music in Boston. Ferianto organized "open" jam sessions that eventually expanded into the annual Ngayogjazz Festival, which celebrates this syncretism between jazz and local traditions.[69]

Of all the formerly colonized territories in Asia, it is perhaps India that really stamped its mark in the world of jazz beyond Asia.

Jazz first arrived in India in the 1920s through foreign music ensembles that performed at the famous European hotels in Calcutta, Bombay, Madras, and Delhi.[70] In the 1930s and 1940s, beside the Europeans, several maharajahs were also attracted to jazz after encountering the music during their travels in Europe. During this time, Goan musicians, Anglo-Indian musicians, and musicians from Nepal and the British colony of Burma also began performing jazz at the hotels in India alongside musicians from Europe and the United States. Frank Fernandes, a trumpet player from Goa, was among the noted Indian jazz musicians active in the scene. Fernandes traveled to Bombay at the age of sixteen in 1936 with the hope of working in one of the city's famous dance bands. Unsuccessful initially, Fernandes ended up working for Bata, a foreign shoe company, and was moonlighting as a musician at Green's Hotel after work. He was finally hired by an Italian pianist, Beppo di Siati, who led a band composed of musicians from Germany, the United Kingdom, and the United States.[71] Among the noted American jazz musicians playing in India was Teddy Weatherford, who had had stints in China and Indonesia. Weatherford in fact migrated to India, where he actively recorded with big and small ensembles in Calcutta from 1942 to 1944.[72]

Indian musicians generally played second fiddle to the imported musicians from the United States, Europe, and the Philippines. In 1942, when the US government decided to evacuate its citizens from India due to the war, many foreigners, including most of the American bandleaders, left the country. However, there was still a demand for jazz as entertainment for the remaining Allied soldiers based in India.[73] Indian musicians saw this as an opportunity to rise from mere sidemen to bandleaders in their own right.[74] One example of a jazz band that consisted entirely of Indian musicians that came to fill this gap left by the departing Americans was Sonny Lobo and His Nite Club Boys, who performed at the Taj Hotel in Bombay.[75]

By the late 1940s and 1950s, Anglo-Indian musicians dominated the jazz scene in India. At the same time, jazz was increasingly associated with the Indian upper class.[76] However, this changed in the 1950s when India, after independence, started the Prohibition movement. According to Tanya Kalmanovitch, "the Prohibition movement of the 1950s prompted many jazz venues such as the Bombay Club to close. Drinking establishments—such as those bars and nightclubs where jazz was performed—were considered morally low, as were the Anglo-Indian women and men employed by them."[77] Many Anglo-Indians migrated to England during this period. From 1947 onward, Indian cinema flourished, and film music grew in popularity and demand. As the jazz scene declined with the departure of the expatriate community and the start of the Prohibition movement, local Indian jazz musicians had to transition to film music to make a living. It was at this time that Frank Fernandes, one of the pioneer Indian jazz musicians in Bombay, became more involved in producing music for film studios.[78]

While jazz was in a state of decline in India during the 1950s, the US State Department's sponsored tours and Willis Conover's Voice of America jazz program helped dedicated jazz listeners and musicians in India to stay in touch with jazz.[79] Nightlife in Bombay gradually revived by the late 1950s, although the Prohibition Act was still enforced. Restaurants such as Gaylord's, Napoli's, Bombellis's, and Berry's on Churchgate Street Extension (Veer Nariman Road) in Bombay began to include live performances by jazz bands as part of the evening program. By then there were few foreign jazz musicians around, and most first-generation Indian jazz musicians such as Frank Fernandes had made their venture into film music. A younger generation of musicians who listened to and were influenced by bebop and the cool jazz of the 1950s such as Hecke Kingdom, Richie Marquis, Perry Isaac, Max Mascarenhas, and Edward Saldanha (also known as Dizzy Sal) gradually came onto the scene.[80]

Dizzy Sal is remembered as one of the most noted Indian jazz musicians in the late 1950s and 1960s who played in the "most modern and intellectual of jazz forms."⁸¹ Dave Brubeck was so impressed by Sal's talent that he arranged for Sal to study at the Berklee College of Music with a scholarship. Unfortunately, Sal's stint at Berklee and his time in Boston were unrewarding for him, and he left without completing his studies. After Sal returned to India in 1967, he gave a few concerts in Bombay, Delhi, and Bangalore and retired quietly. After his death in 1998, Sal's siblings revealed that Sal had moved away from the jazz scene as he had contracted leukoderma and, after that, Parkinson's disease.⁸²

The 1950s was also a time when jazz musicians in the United States began to look to India for inspiration, in particular the spiritualism one could draw from Indian classical music.⁸³ John Coltrane's recording of the song "My Favorite Things" for Atlantic Records is perhaps one of the most famous Western tunes that carries obvious Indian influences. By the 1970s, Kalmanovitch notes, "Indian music was a prominent note in the jazz-rock fusion that captured much of the jazz audience" in the United States, the home of jazz.⁸⁴ According to Warren Pinckney, there are two categories of Indian-influenced jazz music. In the first category, musicians "play modern jazz but incorporate Eastern scales in their solos, or use Eastern sounding instruments such as the oboe or the soprano saxophone."⁸⁵ In the second category, or "Indo-jazz" as its proponents call it, the music is characterized by the twin employment of Indian melodies and a mixed ensemble of Western and Indian instruments such as the sitar, *shehnai*, and tabla.⁸⁶

Niranjan Jhaveri, a businessman, jazz enthusiast, publisher of *Jazz Yatra* (an Indian jazz periodical), and one of the founders of the Jazz Yatra Festival, has championed a particular conception of Indo-jazz. He has called for "Indian vocalizing to be employed in jazz arrangements in which the singing and jazz elements would maintain their own purity of style and form."⁸⁷ Braz Gonsalves, who formed the very successful Jazz Yatra Sextet, was one of the first saxophonists to apply raga-based improvisation in modern jazz in the 1980s. Naresh Fernandes describes Gonsalves as "the ace saxophonist with shaggy sideburns," and "the most sophisticated jazz musician India had ever produced."⁸⁸ Gonsalves is generally seen as having helped develop the genre of Indo-jazz.

The first Jazz Yatra Festival was organized in 1978. For its tenth anniversary in 1988, the festival was held in Bangalore, Goa, and Delhi. Pinckney suggests that live performances seem to be a primary avenue for jazz champions to bring the genre to the masses in India.⁸⁹ While the Indian government was still skeptical about jazz in the 1970s and 1980s, by the 1990s Indian government agencies and business organizations in the country began to support the Jazz Yatra Festival and started to sponsor tours for jazz musicians in India.⁹⁰

Jazz arrived in Japan when Japanese who traveled to the United States returned home with jazz records.⁹¹ The first commercial dance hall, Kagetsuen (花月園), which staged live swing music for people to dance, opened in Yokohama in March 1920.⁹² By the 1930s, dance halls could be found in most major cities of

Japan, especially in Osaka, which by itself housed around twenty dance halls.[93] In the 1920s and 1930s, American and Filipino jazz bands that traveled to Japan to perform in these dance halls played a key role in bringing jazz to the Japanese public. The Conde brothers, Vidi, Raymond, and Gregorio, were among the earliest and most notable Filipino jazz musicians active in Japan during this era.[94] These dance halls of the 1930s gave jazz pioneers of Japan such as Nanri Fumio (南里文雄) and Taniguchi Matashi (谷口またし), who were only sixteen or seventeen at that time, the opportunity to perform for a live audience.[95] In 1934, foreign musicians such as the Conde brothers and Japanese musicians playing in the four biggest dance halls in the Kansai region, namely the Tiger, King, Palace, and Amagasaki, came together to form the Four Dance Hall Alliance Orchestra (四ホール連盟ダンス・オーケストラ), which also recorded for the Osaka music label Teikoku Chikuonki Shōkai (帝国蓄音機商会) (Imperial Records, which was later known as Teichiku Entertainment). The eldest of the Conde brothers, Vidi, served as conductor of this early multiethnic orchestra. Raymond Conde later also started playing jazz, chanson, and other adapted traditional Japanese music in an all-star ensemble called the Shōchiku keiongaku-dan (松竹軽音楽団) (Shochiku Light Music Orchestra). At the same time, the presence of these foreign jazz musicians provided firsthand opportunities for early Japanese musicians to play jazz in live settings instead of just learning from records.[96]

Filled with dance halls playing jazz to swinging crowds, Osaka's rise to prominence as a center for jazz in Japan in the 1920s was primarily due to two reasons. First, the Kansai region had been a major cultural center since the Edo period even though Tokyo became the political center of Japan. It helped that Osaka was a major center for industrial and commercial development during Japan's modernization drive, contributing to the city's bustling entertainment sector and, with that, cultural change.[97] Second, massive destruction caused by the great Kanto earthquake on September 1, 1923, leveled Tokyo's major entertainment districts, namely Shinjuku and Asakusa, leading to the relocation of surviving musicians to dance halls elsewhere, especially in western Japan.[98]

Jazz, however, was widely perceived as an un-Japanese music; it was simply treated as American music. The subsequent failure of dance halls in Osaka to properly mourn the death of Emperor Taisho in 1926 led to the closure of all the dance halls in that city on December 26, 1927.[99] As a result, some jazz players moved to other cities such as Tokyo to continue their career in jazz. And fifteen years later, during the war, Western cultural exports from the Allied powers, perceived as the culture of the enemy, were heavily restricted in Japan. However, cultural products from the Axis alliance, such as from Germany and Italy, were acceptable. Although clearly a cultural product of American origin and therefore supposedly "the music of the enemy," jazz, deemed the popular music of that time, was in fact appropriated for propaganda purposes. The Japanese government attempted to erase the "Americanness" and "foreignness" of jazz by, for instance, even coining Japanese words for the musical instruments used! At the same time, musicians of foreign origin during this period also took on Japanese names.[100]

Some Filipino musicians playing in Japan, such as Raymond Conde, took up Japanese citizenship before the war. With his new citizenship, Conde adopted a Japanese name, Yoshiba Reimondo (吉場レイモンド). Following the outbreak of the Pacific war, many foreign musicians who had not taken up Japanese citizenship earlier were either deported or put in detention camps. Although not conscripted into the Japanese military, some of these musicians were recruited to provide music for Japanese troops that was broadcast on shortwave radio, and to contribute to propaganda materials for the government. After the Pacific war ended, during the US occupation of Japan, Filipino jazz musicians as well as both professional and amateur jazz musicians from the United States performed with local Japanese jazz musicians for American troops and jammed at small Japanese clubs.[101] As for Yoshiba Reimondo, the Filipino jazz pioneer in Japan, his contribution to jazz in Japan was eventually recognized with several major national awards, including the Player Award in the twenty-second annual Japan Record Awards in 1980 (the fifty-fifth year of Shōwa [昭和]) and the Geidankyo (芸団協) Distinguished Service Award to the Entertainment Arts in 1998–1999 as a performing artist on the clarinet.[102]

Beginning in the 1930s, some Japanese musicians, such as Hattori Ryoichi (服部良一), who composed the beautiful "Suzhou Nocturne" (蘇州夜曲), tried to play down the "Americanness" of jazz by performing "jazzified" Japanese folk songs. As E. Taylor Atkins puts it: "For Hattori, creating Japanese jazz usually meant writing arrangements of traditional folk songs for jazz band, or composing original compositions with native themes or associations."[103] While Ryoichi was trying to create a form of Japanese jazz in the 1930s and after the war, many other jazz musicians were simply imitating and replicating jazz pieces played by famous jazz musicians in America. The predominance of this trend is evident in the recordings made by Japanese musicians in the decades following the end of the war.[104] However, up to the 1970s, many jazz musicians in Japan were still trying to imitate jazz musicians from overseas who were popular in Japan. According to jazz pianist Terai Hisayuki (寺井尚之) in an interview with William Minor:

> I turned to jazz from classical music in 1972. At that time in Japan, McCoy Tyner was the most popular pianist. All the jazz journalists talked and wrote about him—only McCoy Tyner. After him, Chick Corea came onto the scene, and everybody in Japan was raving about him. Every Japanese pianist became, first, McCoy Tyner, and then, Chick Corea. . . . The musicians don't have enough faith in themselves.

So everyone tries to be a McCoy Tyner or a Chick Corea—whoever is it from time to time.[105]

It was only from the late 1960s that Japanese jazz musicians began to "indigenize" jazz and forge a "national style."[106]

By the 1970s, jazz had staked a significant foothold in Japan's cultural and entertainment industry. Japan had grown to become a major producer and consumer of jazz recordings.[107] Jazz clubs and jazz coffeeshops (ジャズ喫茶店) (cafés that played only jazz records for their in-house music) at that time were thriving in the major cities of Yokohama, Osaka, and Tokyo. Soon, American musicians found another major stop for their overseas tours other than Europe. Hisayuki recalls:

> Before 1970, there were not so many concerts. American musicians started coming to Japan while the coffeeshops were still booming. They started coming one after the other. From 1972 until 1977, so many groups came to perform that it was known as the golden age of American jazz musicians. They didn't just play at festivals. They would give concerts with their own groups. Tommy Flanagan. Ella Fitzgerald. Sarah Vaughan. Johnny Griffin. Barry Harris. Jimmy Raney. . . .[108]

At the same time, a few Japanese jazz musicians such as Watanabe Sadao (渡辺貞夫), Yamashita Yosuke (山下洋輔), and Akiyoshi Toshiko (秋吉敏子) began to emerge as recognized musicians who developed their original styles from a variety of sources, including Japan. Atkins succinctly describes the rise of these musicians:

> [B]y the 1970s a number of globe-trotting Japanese musicians had garnered well-deserved reputations as jazz originals. From Watanabe Sadao's forays into pop, Latin American, and African musics, and Akiyoshi's masterly blend of Asian musical textures with an Ellingtonian approach to composition and arranging, to Yamashita Yosuke's energetic and startlingly original approach to improvisation, a number of Japanese jazz musicians demonstrated a new found and hard-won confidence that was conducive to creativity.[109]

Akiyoshi Toshiko, the world-acclaimed jazz pianist and big band leader, successfully blended traditional forms of Japanese music with jazz. In a documentary film, *Jazz Is My Native Language,* Akiyoshi reveals:

> I decided that perhaps I would look upon my heritage. . . . [T]raditionally to be Japanese was a handicap to becom[ing] a jazz player, because you were not American. But I decided that was a rather positive quality. . . . I'd been playing

long enough to have some experience at that time, and [I am] non-American, so I have a different heritage, and perhaps I can utilize this and infuse some of my heritage into jazz."[110]

But, as Kevin Fellezs sensitively notes, for Akiyoshi, it was more about "opening a creative space she could claim as her own, separate and yet connected to the musical traditions she would blend in large ensemble jazz compositions."[111]

The jazz pianist Yamashita Yosuke, well known for his free jazz playing style, is another prominent Japanese musician who has made a significant jazz foray into traditional Japanese sounds. In 1965, when he was around twenty-one years old, he was part of Watanabe Sadao's first session band. At that time, he was, in his own words, "playing like a 'straight' musician." Yamashita later formed his own trio, together with Nakamura Seiichi (中村誠一) and Moriyama Takeo (森山威男), that emulated the style of John Coltrane. In 1969, Yamashita began his long journey into free jazz after a chance discovery that playing "free" sounded interesting in a different way from what he had been doing.[112] At that time, it was difficult for audiences in Japan to accept his version of jazz, but Yamashita persisted. As he revealed, "I've continued to play my way for more than twenty-five years.... People finally came to think, 'Let him go. It's okay.'"[113] Despite being a freestyle jazz musician, Yamashita recognizes a resonance between Japanese traditional melodies and the blue notes of jazz. In 1990, Yamashita made an album featuring "'sakura-style' jazz with Japanese melodies" entitled *Sakura*.[114] According to him, "[s]ome Japanese traditional melodies do behave in the same way as the blue notes in jazz. When we first started to play freely, I believed that if you played that way, you could express everything including the entire history of your own nation, of your own land. All history in fact!"[115] Hino Terumasa (日野皓正), perhaps Japan's most famous jazz trumpet and flugelhorn player and also once Yamashita's bandmate, concurs: "We don't have harmony in Japan; traditionally, only a melodic line and rhythm. The African pentatonic scale, like John Coltrane played, modes, and the blues scale, remind me of Japanese folk and traditional songs."[116]

Jazz critics Kawano Ryuji (川野竜司) and Yui Soichi (油井正一), however, imposed on the notion of Japanese jazz a rather essentialist characteristic. To them, playing "jazzified" Japanese folk music is not the same as playing Japanese jazz. It merely means that the music is "somehow recognizably 'Japanese.'"[117] Accordingly, Japanese jazz is a feeling requiring the sensitivity that "only Japanese" could manifest.[118] Atkins provides one such example from Soichi's review of the All Japanese Jazz Festival in 1969:

> What impressed me as an example of a Japanese jazz performance in which that element appeared was Kikuchi Masabumi's [菊地雅章] piano solo on Charlie

Mariano's composition, "Rock Garden of Ryoan Temple" [from Charlie Mariano and Watanabe Sadao's 1967 LP *Iberian Waltz*]. That is a Japanese person's piano solo. Kikuchi's solo on this song has the so-called Japanese sense of "space," and constitutes a performance that the world's best pianist probably couldn't imitate if you made them.[119]

In contrast to attempts elsewhere in Asia to create an original voice in the world of jazz by borrowing from an existing repertoire of heritage sounds, Japanese jazz, according to this particular conception, requires no incorporation of ethnocultural aesthetic frills. You have to be one (i.e., a Japanese!), and deeply immersed, socioculturally speaking, to even have a chance of successfully playing Japanese jazz.

Watanabe Sadao is known as the "father of Japanese jazz." After studying at the Berklee College of Music, Watanabe passed on what he'd learned when he started managing Yamaha's Institute of Popular Music in February 1966. Together with pianist Yagi Masao (八木正生), Watanabe developed a comprehensive jazz curriculum covering jazz composition, harmonic theory, arrangement for jazz ensembles, instrumental technique, and jazz improvisation. Watanabe effectively developed a formal jazz education program in Japan for budding jazz musicians.[120] But Watanabe was more than a revered teacher; he had risen to become a very respectable alto saxophonist (as well as a soprano saxophonist) beginning in the 1960s. In that decade, Watanabe released a string of highly rated albums, starting with his self-titled album, *Sadao Watanabe*, in 1961 and ending the decade with *Live at the Junk* in 1969. In the 1970s, Watanabe released a number of live albums featuring his exploration of African music and his original compositions, such as *Mbali Africa* (1974) and *Swiss Air* (1975). Watanabe also started a radio program called *My Dear Life* in 1972 to help promote jazz. The program ran for a solid nineteen years in Japan.[121] In 1985, he produced *Bravas Club '85*, a record-setting twenty-three-day jazz festival in Tokyo.[122] Perhaps the most notable aspect of Watanabe's contribution to jazz, as demonstrated by his seventy-six-album discography, is his belief that if there is such a thing as Japanese jazz, then it should be about how musicians develop their own unique individual styles that are "not necessarily rooted in nationality or ethnicity."[123] Clearly, then, Watanabe does not quite agree with the strict conception of Japanese jazz expounded by Kawano Ryuji and Yui Soichi.

This brief interlude through the stories of jazz in Asia reveals a few common motifs. As jazz entered Asia during the age of colonialism, its consumption by the local populations, when they listened to the music and danced to the swinging rhythm, was associated with a perceived experiencing of modernity.[124] By consuming jazz, locals could in some ways imagine themselves as cultural equals to consumers of jazz in the homelands of the westerners, who had come to represent things "modern" in Asia. However, the popularity of jazz could also be interpreted as a foreign assault on the integrity of local cultures and values. In China, jazz was branded as decadent, yellow music. In Sukarno's Indonesia, jazz was lumped together with other Western art forms as *hiburan* and frowned upon. In Malaysia, with the rise of Islamic fundamentalism, jazz simply retreated into the background. Even in the Philippines, where jazz flourished, paying attention to one's own cultural heritage to develop an original voice in jazz was deemed undesirable. In Japan, jazz was simply treated as foreign and un-Japanese by conservatives. The pursuit of jazz by local musicians invariably resulted in attempts to create their own language to speak in the world of jazz by using "indigenous folk repertoire, melodic scales, rhythmic patterns, or instrumentation" rather than simply mimicking what was blowing in from the United States, the original home of the genre.[125] Even King Bhumibol, who could not be criticized or belittled because of Thailand's strict lèse majesté laws and therefore could have taken jazz in any direction he pleased, consistently took inspiration from the rich and diverse musical colors found in Thai traditions. Japanese musicians initially jazzified existing traditional music to alleviate jazz's association with a foreign, American culture. But emulating American jazz masters became the norm after World War II. It was when Japanese musicians began to break out of Japan, in particular the case of Akiyoshi Toshiko, that they gradually found an effective source through traditional folk sounds to develop their own musical language. However, this search for an original sound swung to an extreme, according to one school of thought: one needs to be Japanese and deeply immersed in Japanese culture in order to even be able to play Japanese jazz! Non-Japanese trying to imitate it would at best sound "recognizably Japanese." In this sense, these stories of jazz in Asia bear a good degree of resonance with how jazz developed its unique characteristics with respect to the former socialist European countries. Yet, right from the beginning, local Asian musicians who played jazz were perceived as "second fiddle" to Americans and Europeans. Among the Asians, only Filipinos were placed high up in the hierarchy as musicians who could play jazz, and they took their talents to jazz venues in other parts of Asia. As Japan developed its reputation as a jazz center in Asia after World War II, Japanese jazz musicians gradually earned the right to be recognized as bona fide jazz practitioners not just within their own country but also globally, including in the United States. Although not even coming close to the reputation of the Japanese jazz scene, Indonesia is known for its well-received annual Java Jazz Festival, which widely features both Indonesian and international acts.

Outside of Japan, jazz, in general, remains an exception in Asia.

TRACK 11

Birth '99

Quyền Văn Minh released his first two solo jazz albums of original compositions in 2000 and 2001, respectively. With this repertoire of original compositions, Minh brought his brand of Vietnamese jazz to Singapore for a nine-day performance tour sponsored by the Philip Morris Group with the official endorsement of relevant Vietnamese government agencies. In the following years, Minh participated in several key jazz festivals in Asia, presenting a mix of original compositions and standard jazz tunes. From 2001 to 2003, Minh was a key participant in the European Jazz Festival in Vietnam series held in Hà Nội, with his jazz club serving as one of the host venues for each festival. In just a decade after Minh's concerts in 1988 and 1989, an original Vietnamese jazz sound, very much inspired by the ethnic folk music sounds of Vietnam, emerged on the scene and gave Vietnamese jazz a nascent identity.

Singapore, 2001

On May 2, 2001, the minister of culture and information of Vietnam issued official approval for Quyền Văn Minh and his entourage of musicians and support staff, including a cadre responsible for public relations and interpretation, to travel to Singapore. Minh was scheduled to travel from May 4 to May 14 for a series of performances at the invitation of the Philip Morris Group. In the official document, Minh, as leader of the entourage, was tasked to submit a trip report and ordered to return his *hồ chiếu ngoại giao* (diplomatic passport) to the ministry on the conclusion of the trip. In the approval letter, the minister directed the chief of staff, the respective heads of the Departments of Planning Affairs, Finance, and Accounting in the ministry, the director of the Hà Nội National Music Conservatoire of Vietnam, and the named cadres participating in the trip to make the mission a success.[1] As representatives of the country, they carried the pride and honor of Vietnam on their shoulders. Minh's release of his debut album of original jazz compositions, *Birth '99*, in 2000 affirmed the nascent genre of Vietnamese jazz as an accepted component of the musical soundscape of Vietnam. And he was bringing the new sounds of Vietnamese jazz to an audience in the most economically developed, modernized, and globalized country in Southeast Asia, Singapore.

Minh would not have signed the agreement with the Philip Morris Group to accept this major overseas gig nor have had his band members rehearse, organize travel documents, and prepare wardrobes if he had no confidence of receiving official approval. And while it was an anxious wait for the final official document of approval to be issued by the ministry, at the same time final approval was merely a formality. As early as March 2001, the *Saigon Times* had already announced: "The first Vietnamese jazz band will perform abroad in a ten-day trip to Singapore on May 4–15."[2]

By 2001, Minh was already a prominent figure in the Vietnamese music scene. He was recognized as the premier saxophonist in Vietnam by the late 1980s when he delivered two solo recital programs back to back in 1988 and 1989 for the Hội Nhạc Sĩ. He was the first self-taught musician to become a tenured lecturer at the prestigious Hà Nội National Music Conservatoire of Vietnam in 1991, having been invited to start a saxophone program and teach jazz improvisation there in 1989. In 1994, he was one of two recipients of a major grant program to promote the arts sponsored by the Swedish International Development Cooperation Agency (SIDA), the other being the famous violinist Tạ Bôn. Minh's concert at the Hà Nội Opera House in 1994 saw the birth of Vietnamese jazz when he premiered three of his original compositions on the stage. In 1997, Minh had earned enough official accolades, acceptance by the official circle of artists, and respect by audiences and fellow artists to receive the prestigious Nghệ Sĩ Ưu Tú (Eminent Artist) award.

Jazz was already an audible albeit nominal part of the nighttime music scene in Hà Nội in late 1997, when Minh opened the first Vietnamese jazz music club, Minh's Jazz Club. Minh's reputation as a jazz musician expanded to encompass the milieu of foreign diplomats, expatriates, and tourists.

The Singapore Tour

The program booklet for the Singapore gig had printed in bold, "Vietnam's Godfather of Jazz," declaring the status of Quyền Văn Minh, the star of the Vietnamese jazz band brought to Singapore for a series of performances by the Philip Morris Group. The program was called *Jazz Moods with Quyền Văn Minh*, featuring original compositions by Minh recorded for his debut album, *Birth '99*, and a second jazz album that he was working on, as well as a selection of standard jazz tunes such as "Take Five," "Lullaby of Birdland," and "Take the

Figures 11.1a, 11.1b. The Singapore Tour.

A Train." Joining Minh on stage was the Red River Band consisting of Quyền Thiện Đắc (saxophone), Phạm Tuấn Hùng (piano), Đào Minh Pha (bass), Lê Hoàng Long (drums), and Nguyễn Thị Hồng (vocals). Quyền Văn Minh and his Red River Band performed variations of this program for seven nights, one matinee concert, and a special session at a local jazz bar for nine days during May 5–13, 2001.

The sounds of Vietnamese jazz could be heard at the H2o Zone, an outdoor event plaza located just outside Orchard Point shopping mall, an iconic building found along the high-traffic shopping belt of Orchard Road. Minh also played at the classy atrium of Liang Court, a shopping mall popular with the Japanese expatriate community; the compound of the Singapore Ministry of Information and the Arts, located in a colonial heritage building; and the newly constructed University Cultural Centre of the National University of Singapore (NUS). They were heard by the seaside at the East Coast Recreation Centre, adjacent to the road leading to Singapore's Changi Airport. Channel News Asia announced: "Self-taught Vietnamese saxophonist Quyền Văn Minh is bringing his brand of jazz music to the HDB [Housing and Development Board] heartlanders in Singapore."[3] Vietnamese jazz even penetrated the residential heartland of Singapore as Minh performed in the event hall of the Siglap Community Centre and the open area in front of Clementi Central Food Centre. Perhaps the highlight of the tour, for people familiar with the cultural scene in Singapore, was Minh's combined concert with the NUS Jazz Band on the Shaw Foundation Symphony Stage at the world-famous Singapore Botanical Gardens, which has hosted the likes of the New York Philharmonic Orchestra, the Brecker Brothers, and other luminaries of the music world. During a brief two-day break from this grueling tour, Minh and his Red River Band took the stage at Harry's, located at 28 Boat Quay, on the evening of May 7, 2001. Harry's was one of the few watering holes for good live jazz music in Singapore during those years. For a short time, Minh even became a minor celebrity in Singapore; a minidocumentary about Minh's rise to become the "Godfather of Jazz in Vietnam" was played and replayed in reruns on TVMobile, an early experiment with digital video broadcasting in Singapore to bring televised programs to commuters on the public bus system. Singapore heard Quyền Văn Minh's creation, Vietnamese jazz.

In his message for the concert program, Lê Tiến Thọ, then director of the Bureau of the Arts in Vietnam, acknowledged the contribution of the Philip Morris Group in supporting the development of Vietnamese arts and culture by sponsoring Minh's trip to Singapore. Thọ wrote:

> In Vietnam, jazz music as performed by Vietnamese musicians is still something very new. Quyền Văn Minh is one of the few musicians performing jazz in Vietnam and has achieved several feats of success that are worthy of our respect, especially his unique combination of traditional melodies in the style of modern

jazz. The invitation and sponsorship by the Philip Morris Group that brought Quyền Văn Minh and his band to Singapore, a center for the arts in Asia, is a major recognition of the success by the international community of Vietnamese jazz music in contributing to the development of modern jazz. This trip by Quyền Văn Minh and his band is also an absolutely meaningful cultural exchange that brings plenty of opportunities for musicians from different countries to learn from the experiences of one another. At the same time, it also helps the community in Singapore to understand more about the culture and peoples of Vietnam. We sincerely respect and hold in high regard the efforts by the Philip Morris Group in supporting this absolutely meaningful cultural exchange activity.[4]

Six years after his breakthrough jazz concert at the Hà Nội Opera House in 1994, Minh was officially recognized as a jazz musician in Vietnam and the region.

Vietnamese Jazz in Asia

From 2000 onward, Minh brought his brand of jazz to different parts of Asia. On August 30, 2002, Minh performed at the Vietnamese National Day reception organized by the Vietnamese consulate in Hong Kong at the invitation of the Hong Kong Press Club and Vietnam Airlines. The Vietnamese consul, Nguyễn Hồng Hải, kindly wrote to the board of directors of the conservatoire to thank them for endorsing Minh's trip: "The presence and participation of Quyền Văn Minh's jazz band contributed tremendously to the success of the reception. Our Hong Kong friends, international friends, and the Vietnamese community in Hong Kong were full of praise for his performance."[5] Soon after, at the invitation of Pedro Ascensão, organizer of the Macau International Jazz Festival, Quyền Văn Minh and the Red River Band participated in the twelfth edition of the festival, performing on the evening of September 27, 2002, at the Macau Tower Auditorium. Ascensão invited Minh after having heard him perform at Minh's Jazz Club in Hà Nội and receiving a copy of Minh's album, *Birth '99*. To end a busy year, in December 2002, Minh and his jazz band were invited by the Canadian embassy in Phnom Penh, Cambodia, to perform in a program called *A Treasure of Music and Culture*. This was a four-day art exhibition and music program headlined by the world-famous opera singer José Carreras with the Singapore Symphony Orchestra, and Quyền Văn Minh with his Red River Band in separate concerts. Minh's performance on December 5, 2002, entitled *Jazz by the River*, was organized as a benefit concert for victims of land mines in Cambodia. Afterward, Minh's Vietnamese jazz continued to travel widely. In 2004, he took his compositions to San Francisco. In 2005, Minh played at the Jazz Festival for Peace in Okinawa. For this performance, Minh brought along

Figure 11.2. The Hong Kong Press Club.

Quyền Thiện Đắc (saxophone), Vũ Đức Tân (piano), Phan Trung Kiên (bass), and Phạm Đức Duy (drums). On October 18, 2008, Minh and the Red River Band were featured as key artists in the Taichung Jazz Festival, performing at 99 Musical House in Taichung, Taiwan.

For every one of these trips, Minh was required to complete all necessary bureaucratic procedures and to submit all necessary documents to the conservatoire and the Vietnamese Ministry of Culture and Information for official permission to travel out of the country for the purpose of "cultural exchange." As an official cadre under the conservatoire and at the same time reporting to the Ministry of Culture for activities relating to the arts, Minh traveled with a diplomatic passport during these trips. He was an official cultural ambassador of Vietnam. Vietnamese jazz, or specifically Minh's tunes, were heard across Asia and beyond.

Even up to today, I am still really proud about the trip to Singapore in 2001. Before that trip, people outside of Vietnam did not know that there was jazz in Vietnam. In 2000, I was thrilled to be able to play a couple of jam sessions with local Japanese jazz musicians when I went to Japan with a friend from the Japanese embassy in Hà Nội. I thought that was it, just playing with some local musicians in a simple overseas social visit. I did not imagine that anything bigger in scale or more formal could be possible. After Japan, the trip to Singapore happened, followed by Hong Kong, Macau, Okinawa, Cambodia, and so on. I was able to bring a group of young Vietnamese musicians who played and rehearsed with me at 16 Lê Thái Tổ [Minh's Jazz Club] and had recorded with me on my debut album to participate in these tours and international jazz festivals. We played my original Vietnamese jazz compositions during these international performances. I was really proud of what we accomplished with those trips. This group of musicians and the music we played, I had hoped at that time, would be something that people around the world would want to hear. I am proud to be a Vietnamese. No matter where I go, I always tell people I am Vietnamese. I want to prove that although I am Vietnamese, I can play jazz. I can play music like that. I can play these international standard jazz tunes; I can play our original Vietnamese jazz compositions; and we are all playing jazz. I always hope that the generation of musicians after me can do more and achieve more than I've been able to.

Birth '99 and Đồng Cảm

After the 1994 concert, I asked myself, "What could I do to introduce jazz in Vietnam to both Vietnamese and foreigners?" I decided to record my own jazz albums. I continued to compose more original jazz tunes using inspiration from Vietnamese folk music. I did it this way because I wanted to use sounds familiar to ordinary Vietnamese people so that they could hear something that has Vietnam in it. Let me put it this way: jazz is difficult for ordinary Vietnamese to understand, so starting with something familiar could encourage them to listen and try this new genre of music. That was one of my fundamental objectives.

A second objective of mine at that time was to have our own "language" that I could use to play alongside international musicians. Of course, we could easily introduce Vietnamese folk music to the world in its original forms using traditional instruments such as the "đàn bầu" [monochord zither], "nguyệt" [moon-shaped lute], and "đàn tranh" [sixteen-chord zither]. However, I wanted to be able to bring the sounds of Vietnam through modern, Western instruments. I wanted to show that these traditional sounds that we have could come together with the musical essence of the world, such as jazz! I know, in recent years, there are musicians in Vietnam, including some of my former students, who have performed traditional compositions in the style of jazz with traditional Vietnamese musical instruments. Not that there is anything wrong with that. But I prefer to create original compositions inspired by these traditional sounds. Traditional Vietnamese folk music and Vietnamese popular songs have their own frameworks that limit the possibility of improvisation, which is the fundamental thing about jazz. Sure, you could make some adjustments, but bear in mind, others might accuse you of desecrating traditional folk sounds! The best way, in my mind, is to create something original based on these scales, based on these sounds. Write something original. Write something new.

When composing, I was not entirely influenced by the kind of music I was listening to or was able to listen to at that time. When I was young, when I was learning how to play the clarinet and play the guitar, I listened to a lot of music broadcast over the radio. The sounds that I heard, I saved them in my head and I practiced them so that I could play these tunes for gigs I picked up to earn some money. Then there were tunes that might not be useful for these gigs, so I did not pay much attention to them. When I started to compose my own music, I really had to use my imagination. I had to "drive according to my own imagination," so to speak; no one in Vietnam had driven these same roads before me.

When composing, I use both the guitar and saxophone. With the guitar, I can try out the arrangement I have in mind to go with the melody. With the saxophone, I develop the melody. My original compositions are found mainly on two albums, Birth '99 and Đồng Cảm; and later rerecorded in the Father, Son, and Jazz *live albums that featured both my original compositions and my son's original compositions. In the* Father and Son *concerts, we played international jazz standards in the first half, while the second half featured mainly our original compositions. In the albums* Birth '99 *and* Đồng Cảm, *I really wanted to bring out the sounds of different folk music from various parts of Vietnam.*

At that time, I could have set the trend that got really popular later by playing the music of Trịnh Công Sơn and songs about Hà Nội. I could play guitar and saxophone to perform all these ballads, and I would totally satisfy the Vietnamese listeners of that period. But I did not want to take that path then.

My first CD was an album of my original folk-music-inspired compositions. It included the piece "Sống Hay Là Chết" [To Live or to Die]. When I suggested using "Sống Hay Là Chết" as the title, the manager at the production studio discouraged me from doing so. It would frighten away listeners, he felt. When the album was pressed, I decided to put the piece "Sống Hay Là Chết" as the last track on the album. For me, this track would either have to go to the top or to the bottom of the track list on the CD. The studio manager told me that using this as the opening title was too intimidating, so I put it last.

I decided to just name the album '99: Âm Nhạc Dân Gian Việt Nam Với Phong Cách Jazz ['99: Traditional Vietnamese Folk Music with Jazz Style]. A Japanese friend suggested that I should add the word "Birth" in front to symbolize the birth of Vietnamese jazz. At that time, I had to consider carefully, very carefully, how I should name my album. Sure, I hoped that it would be well received. '98 or '99 as a title was easy to remember. Birth, *an English word, was simple. But I knew* that I had to avoid a situation in which people could accuse me of recording an album of foreign music and using a foreign title. I still remember, in the past when I was young, that people accused me of listening to and playing American music, the music of the enemy! There was another time when I was listening to a vinyl record printed with Russian words [i.e., printed in the cyrillic script], produced in Bulgaria, a jazz album featuring tunes by Charlie Parker, Dave Brubeck, Benny Goodman, and others. I would put on the record and play along to practice. One fine day, a public security officer [công an] came up and interrogated me: "Are you listening to capitalist music? American music?" I had to show him the sleeve, printed with Russian [cyrillic] lettering, before he believed that the record actually originated from our socialist allies, from Bulgaria, because it had a jacket printed with Russian letters! I put in a lot of thought before deciding on the title of the album. I made sure that the title included Vietnamese words, Âm Nhạc Dân Gian Việt Nam Với Phong Cách Jazz. I made sure that there were more Vietnamese words than foreign words in the title.

Birth '99 featured my compositions. At that time, Hiroki [Koichi] and his New Vision Band came to Hà Nội, and they performed at the Daewoo Hotel. I played with him, and our performance was recorded live. Hiroki requested that I include the song "Misty," which we played together as a bonus track on the CD. I thought, why not? Musicians from two different countries, two different ethnicities, playing jazz, and playing a Western composition together in Vietnam! In that sense, no one could accuse me of recording a Western, foreign song on a Vietnamese jazz album. Although the song was not in my original concept, I thought it was not a bad idea, so I agreed to his request. Besides, he helped me mix the recording for CD pressing. Initially, I must admit that there was some criticism about including a foreign track on the album. I had to pre-empt any possible complications concerning the release of the album. After all, playing jazz, people had already decided that we were playing foreign music. We put in so much effort to produce it. All you needed was some silly nonsense accusing me of doing something improper, and the project would be stopped prematurely in its tracks. All our efforts would be wasted. So, I had to find a way to make the album proper and open [đàng hoàng].

I wish that I could have done better. I wish that we had rehearsed more. We had to work every day, and so we had little time to rehearse. But that was the situation. We just had to put it out; if not, the album would still not be released! I still remember, when the jazz club was at 16 Lê Thái Tổ [the club's second location], we rehearsed the pieces we would be recording during the day and played the usual repertoire at the club in the evening. We practiced intensively. When the album was finally released, I felt that 1998 was a very fulfilling year because we practiced and rehearsed for the recording. The year before, 1997,

Figure 11.3. *Birth '99.*

was a year of loss, when I had to close the jazz club after opening for only three months at the Giảng Võ venue. In the eight months at 16 Lê Thái Tổ, so many musicians honed their art at the club. We practiced every day and recorded this album. It was during the summer of 1999 that we recorded the tracks. Although I paid the musicians, what made the album possible was that the musicians believed in what I was doing, in what we were doing. I tried to make sure that musicians who recorded on the album were featured in the CD artwork. We finally released the album in 2000. I felt a sense of fulfillment, and I affirmed one thing, that I must keep trying.

Birth '99, Ngẫu Hứng: Âm Nhạc Dân Gian Việt Nam Với Phong Cách Jazz (*The Traditional Folk Music of Vietnam with Jazz Style*) contains eight tracks of original compositions by Quyền Văn Minh and a bonus track featuring a live duet performance of Minh and Hiroki Koichi (廣木光一), a Japanese jazz guitarist.

Birth '99, Ngẫu Hứng: Âm Nhạc Dân Gian Việt Nam Với Phong Cách Jazz
(*The Traditional Folk Music of Vietnam with Jazz Style*)
Track 1: "Giai Điều Sapa" (A Melody of Sapa), by Quyền Văn Minh
Track 2: "Mùa Xuân Kinh Bắc" (Spring in Kinh Bắc), by Quyền Văn Minh
Track 3: "Ngẫu Hứng Tây Nguyên" (Tây Nguyên Improvisations), by Quyền Văn Minh
Track 4: "Chiều Thôn Quê" (Afternoon in the Countryside), by Quyền Văn Minh
Track 5: "Hô Kéo Lưới" (Chants of the Fishermen), by Quyền Văn Minh
Track 6: "Vấn Vương" (Meditations), by Quyền Văn Minh
Track 7: "Ngày Hội Mùa" (Festival of the Harvest), by Quyền Văn Minh
Track 8: "Sống Hay Là Chết" (To Live or to Die), by Quyền Văn Minh
Bonus Track: "Misty," by Erroll Garner
Musicians:
Quyền Văn Minh: Alto and Baritone Sax
Quyền Thiện Đắc: Soprano and Tenor Sax
Phạm Lê Phương: Piano
Phạm Tuấn Hùng: Piano
Phan Trung Kiên: Bass
Đào Minh Pha: Bass
Hà Đình Huy: Drums
Lê Việt Hùng: Drums

Birth '99 features a diverse texture of sounds inspired by the contrasting landscapes of Vietnam. Opening the album with "Giai Điều Sapa," Minh deliberates with a haunting melody that gradually picks up momentum to launch into a passionate gallop across the forested mountains of northern Vietnam. As the gallop slows back to a ballad and fades off, Minh signals a graceful celebration of spring in the old North with "Mùa Xuân Kinh Bắc." The end of spring opens a new season of sunlight and festivity with "Ngẫu Hứng Tây Nguyên," creating a new swinging sound for the Central Highlands, known for its distinct, colorful inhabitants such as the Mnong, Ede, Jarai, and Bahnar, dwelling amid the rolling hills and mountainous valleys. Then Minh plants us in the tranquility of gently swaying rice fields in the deltaic plains with "Chiều Thôn Quê" before sending us off again with the mesmerizing chants of fishermen in the open seas through "Hô Kéo Lưới." Minh has a moment of self-reflection as he engages in a meditative conversation with himself, finding peaceful pockets of space amid the increasingly bustling streets of Hà Nội overrun by the motorbikes of Đổi Mới. Just as farmers reap their seasonal harvest during a time of celebration, so, too, Minh finally releases his very first CD of original Vietnamese jazz compositions, with an ensemble display of musical technicality and creative impulse in the album's seventh track, "Ngày Hội Mùa." There must be light at the end of the tunnel, as Minh ponders over the present and future of jazz in Vietnam in "Sống Hay Là Chết." Eight different tracks inspired by eight different soundscapes found in the diverse ethnic and cultural expanse that is Vietnam, all connected through the spirit of jazz, the freedom of improvisation. Rich and rooted, it is a package that will take many listenings before one is truly able to appreciate the stories and fully feel the textures tied together by Minh's thoughtful saxophone.

Over the years, I think that we have managed to put behind a certain phase. In that phase, it was impossible to do more. It was too new. Even if I wanted to do more, I did not have the kind of imagination at that time. But it was sufficiently radical and new for listeners in that era. The 1989 performance was already at a level more sophisticated than 1988's. And 1994 was a step even further, performing at the opera house and featuring, for the first time, my three original jazz compositions. After the 1994 concert, I started writing more pieces, finding inspiration from different folk sounds, such as quan họ, and different regions of Vietnam, such as the plains and the hills, and the city and the villages. I composed eight tunes. The first album carries certain elements of different Vietnamese regions, and it also features certain philosophical musings, in this case, about my life, my musical pursuit, and my career. My compositions were influenced by my own philosophy of life.

In Birth '99, *I showcased the different sounds that inspired me from the different regions of Vietnam so that a Vietnamese audience could identify with the songs and experience the sounds of jazz. I also hoped that foreign audiences could have a taste of the diversity of Vietnamese sounds through jazz. When I released* Birth '99, *it bore some influence on the next generation of musicians and composers in Vietnam. In 2001, I recorded my second album of original jazz compositions,* Đồng Cảm *[Identify], with the help of Lưu Quang Minh. With this title, I asked people to empathize with what I am doing. I asked listeners to try to understand and find that empathy between jazz and Vietnamese folk music. When I was preparing for* Đồng Cảm, *I wanted to develop a different approach. I wanted to bring myself to the next level. When I produced* Đồng Cảm, *I was trying to further explore the sounds from different regions of Vietnam through jazz. I tried to imagine the landscape through the sounds I created. Through this model of Vietnamese jazz sounds found in the recordings, I hoped to open a road for the next generations of Vietnamese jazz musicians. The Vietnamese audience might not be familiar with jazz, even finding it strange, but I knew that these sounds could help bridge the gap a little.*

The album *Đồng Cảm* contains eight tracks, with seven composed by Quyền Văn Minh and one, "Chợ Xa" (Distant Market Place), composed by Lưu Quang Minh.

Figure 11.4. Đồng Cảm.

Đồng Cảm
Track 1: "Hội Làng" (Festival in the Village), by Quyền Văn Minh
Track 2: "Núi Rừng Quê Ta" (Mountains and Forests of Our Homeland), by Quyền Văn Minh
Track 3: "Vũ Điều Thăng Long" (Dance of Thăng Long), by Quyền Văn Minh
Track 4: "Lời Mẹ Ru" (Mother's Lullaby), by Quyền Văn Minh
Track 5: "Tiếng Sáo Gọi Ai?" (Who Is the Flute Calling?), by Quyền Văn Minh
Track 6: "Chợ Xa" (Distant Market Place), by Lưu Quang Minh
Track 7: "Nhớ Về Hậu Giang" (Missing Hậu Giang), by Quyền Văn Minh
Track 8: "Quan Họ Giao Duyên" (Quan Họ Interplay), by Quyền Văn Minh

Musicians:
Quyền Văn Minh: Alto and Baritone Sax
Quyền Thiện Đắc: Soprano and Tenor Sax
Phạm Lê Phương: Piano (Tracks 1, 2, 3, 4, 7, and 8)
Phạm Tuấn Hùng: Piano (Track 6)
Trần Hải Lý: Piano (Track 5)
Đào Minh Pha: Bass
Lê Hoàng Long: Drums (Tracks 1, 2, 3, 4, 6, and 8)
Nguyễn Mạnh Cường: Drums (Tracks 5 and 7)

Đồng Cảm is essentially a continuation of the unfinished anthology of stories that Quyền Văn Minh started with *Birth '99*. This time, Minh opens with "Hội Làng" (Festival in the Village), a piece inspired by *chèo*, a traditional lively satirical musical genre usually performed in the open plazas of rural towns in northern Vietnam in the past. It is perhaps appropriate to open the new album with a festive piece to celebrate the success of *Birth '99*. Jazz by this time has formally arrived in Vietnam. Never one to stray too far from the experiences that inspired his musical start, Minh brings us back to the forested mountains where he started his professional musical career with Đoàn Ca Múa Quân Khu Việt Bắc in Thái Nguyên. "Núi Rừng Quê Ta," inspired by the folk sounds of the ethnic Thái, is a joyful remembrance and delightful celebration of the majestic hills and crowns of trees of the Tây Bắc and Việt Bắc Mountains. This is a contrast with the next piece, "Vũ Điệu Thăng Long," which subtly uncovers the regality and decorum of a dance befitting the royal heritage of the capital that only a local could convey with pride and confidence. There are many songs about mothers composed by Vietnamese musicians, and there is Quyền Văn Minh's "Lời Mẹ Ru," a hidden gem that could only be unveiled by his deep-thinking improvisation. This is perhaps the only original composition of his that was not influenced by any traditional folk sounds. It is a piece Minh wrote for his late mother. Minh rerecorded "Giai Điệu Sapa" here but used a variation of its original title, "Tiếng Sáo Gọi Ai." This version is closer to the debut performance delivered in the 1994 live concert at the Hà Nội Opera House. With "Chợ Xa," an original composition by Lưu Quang Minh, then deputy director of the national conservatoire, Quyền Văn Minh demonstrates his rhythmic chops, telling of the winding road leading to that distant market place, a journey familiar to anyone who has spent some time in the Vietnamese uplands. No story of Vietnam is complete without a trip down either the Tiền Giang or Hậu Giang, as the great Mekong River fans out into the deltaic plains that define southern Vietnam. Remembering his boat ride along the majestic Hậu Giang, Minh wrote "Nhớ Về Hậu Giang" to capture that tranquil glide on the great river. A northerner at heart, Minh returns to the antiphonal tradition of *quan họ* with the piece "Quan Họ Giao Duyên," striking up a conversation between jazz and the traditional soundscape of the north. *Đồng Cảm* is Minh's confident reaffirmation of the original sounds he first debuted on the stage of the Hà Nội Opera House in 1994.

My Songs

I composed the piece "Sống Hay Là Chết" for Birth '99 because many Vietnamese told me at that time, to play jazz in Vietnam was like taking a pathway to death. 1997, I opened the jazz club and invested all my resources, time, and effort in it, but I had to close down the place after only three months. It was a failure. It was a haunting failure! I had people telling me, "See, you walked onto the path of death!" People would tell me, "Don't try that again! That was a mistake, don't walk the path of death again!" To play jazz was to choose a road to death, a dead-end road. When I was sitting with my friends drinking and chatting, I would retort by singing, "Chết đâu, đang ngồi đây!" [Dead? I am still sitting here!].

In 1998, I reopened the jazz club over there, at Lê Thái Tổ, but had to close it again after eight months! Then we moved to 31 Lương Văn Can, where we stayed open for a solid ten years. By the time I was forced to relocate out of Lê Thái Tổ in 1999, I had already finished writing eight tunes, all fully completed for my band to practice. Right to the last day of the lease, we practiced by day, we opened for business in the evening, and we played as usual in the evening. Then we started moving things out of the place. From the day I reopened the jazz club until the day we had to move and later went into the studio to record the first CD, people were telling me that I had chosen the path to death. I wanted to show them that I would survive; I would live, and jazz would live.

When composing that tune, I wanted to bring out a philosophy I had in my mind. When a person is alive but nobody knows that person, it is as if the person has already died. But a person who died, who did something good or great, people would talk about that person all the time; it is as if a person who is already dead is still living! It is okay to die. To be dead with honor is better to be alive without honor. I was alone in my pursuit to play jazz. That was how I felt. Instinctively, I believe that there is life on this path; it will be very tough, but jazz can live.

I used a particular motif found in Vietnamese funeral traditions. When a person passed away, a particular motif would be played at the funeral wake to help people remember that person. A remembrance to honor the dead. But I developed it differently to show that something alive could be born out of it, so it was not just about death. The main theme was arranged for the saxophone, played by Đắc, a melody to honor the dead, to accompany the crying at a funeral. Then I come in with another saxophone, and I take that theme to a different place, a place filled with life. I wanted to bring out my own thoughts as a musician trying to play jazz, alone. I wanted to tell of how a sound could be brought to the public. Could that sound be lifted up from nothing and be accepted among the public? I wanted to say through my music that, yes, it is difficult, and I might even have to experience failure and loss, but I can still rise up and live.

The song reflected my thoughts and emotions at that time. I always say that I wrote that piece for myself, but in fact, I wrote it for the next generation so that they can understand the challenges of playing jazz, why we have to continue to play jazz, why we play jazz even when it is in such a difficult context. I knew that I was the only one doing this then, that I was a pioneer, and it would always be difficult. But I still play. I wrote that song to remind myself that I must live to fulfill my mission.

"Giai Điệu Sapa," the first track on Birth '99, *is essentially a reincarnation of "Tiếng Khèn Gọi Bạn," the first tune I wrote and debuted in the 1994 concert. In 1970, I formally joined the Việt Bắc Military Region Artists' Troupe in Thái Nguyên. We played revolutionary songs and a lot of ethnic folk songs because we were in the uplands inhabited by our ethnic minority compatriots. That period of time really influenced my music a lot. In fact, my very first composition, "Tiếng Khèn Gọi Bạn," was a result of this deep impression of the sounds of the uplands during those years in Việt Bắc. I put "Tiếng Khèn Gọi Bạn" as the first track. But a Japanese friend suggested to me that this track reminded people of the Hmong sounds people could hear in Sapa. Listeners would be able to identify it instantly if I changed the title to "A Melody of Sapa" [Giai Điệu Sapa]. So, I used that title instead of "Tiếng Khèn Gọi Bạn" to encourage potential listeners to try the album. Of course, I encountered that sound during the time I was in the Việt Bắc Mountains, not Sapa, which is located in the Tây Bắc Mountains. The opening melody was to emulate someone playing the "khèn" [qeej, a Hmong reed pipe] by the riverbank, trying to attract the attention of the girl who has captured his heart. After he succeeds, together they hop onto his horse and embark on a journey of courtship through the forested mountains. Becoming lovers, they return to live in the village. Personally, I still prefer the title "Tiếng Khèn Gọi Bạn" more than "Giai Điệu Sapa."*

Like "Tiếng Khèn Gọi Bạn," I premiered "Vấn Vương" on the stage of the Hà Nội Opera House in 1994. You might remember that in early 1988, I managed to buy a soprano saxophone produced in the Democratic Republic of Germany that I used in the 1988 and 1989 solo recital programs. Before that, people usually only played alto and tenor saxophones here in Vietnam. I chanced upon a cassette featuring the music of Felix Slováček, a jazz musician from Czechoslovakia. That was the first time I heard the soprano saxophone. In those days, when we listened to foreign music, we were mainly listening to music from socialist countries, especially Eastern Europe. Czechoslovakia was one of those countries. *Unfortunately, I had to sell that soprano to someone else later on. It was a particularly memorable saxophone for me, so it was most unfortunate that I had to sell it. But I managed to buy another soprano after that, a Selmer Paris. Because of the sound of the soprano, I was inspired to compose "Vấn Vương." "Vấn Vương," as you already know, is a rather melancholic piece. When I wrote this piece, I wanted to tell my own story of the process by which I have to overcome, alone, the challenges of playing jazz in Vietnam. When writing this piece, I drew inspiration from quan họ, a rich folk musical tradition in the northern deltaic plains of Vietnam. It was my own soulful expression of the cultural context I come from and live in. "Vấn Vương" refers to a kind of melancholic meditation, not a depressive kind of sadness. Every time I play this piece, I feel that I am overcoming the loneliness I felt in the process of bringing jazz to Vietnam. It is probably my favorite composition, if you ask me.*

"Mùa Xuân Kinh Bắc" was inspired by "ả đào" music.[6] *But when I was writing the music, I did not have the opportunity to actually sit down and watch an ả đào performance. In the 1990s, this would have been most difficult! But I remember that sound from the time I was a child. Not from the radio; I do not recall hearing it on the radio. But I remember hearing it during my childhood. So, I researched it in the library of the conservatoire. I found written scores of this genre of music, arranged by the researchers, and I studied the music. Taking that as inspiration, I wrote my own melody and developed it into a jazz composition. I have to be careful to avoid people accusing me of desecrating ả đào music. I modified the rhythm. When you mention the term "Kinh Bắc" nowadays, people tend to think of Bắc Ninh. But in the past, it was also used as a reference to the old capital, Thăng Long, that is, Hà Nội. I was imagining a scene from the past in Hà Nội: someone riding a cyclo on the street, passing by someone singing ả đào. People standing around the singer, listening and being mesmerized by the sound. It was a scene on the streets of the capital in the old days. If you walk into the old alleys, when you see little makeshift tea stands with those short stools, the old folks serving "chè chén" [strong green tea served in traditional cups] and "thuốc lào" [traditional tobacco smoked with a "farmer's pipe"], it still carries a little bit of nostalgia from the past.*

With "Chiều Thôn Quê," I wanted to tell about the momentous tranquility of life. Music is rhythmic; it makes you move. But music is also about tranquility [em đềm]; there is that natural contradiction. When I was a member in the troupes, in between the stage performances and mealtimes, we had free time. By eight o'clock, the performance program would be over. During those blocks of free time, people in the troupe would often fall into bad social habits like gambling, "nhậu" [drinking alcohol in leisurely fashion over conversation], smoking, and the like. In that free time, you could also do something serious like reading a book or practicing music. And I would often go out and practice in the tranquility amid the rice fields during my free time in the day. "Chiều Thôn Quê" has a backstory. I tried to tell the story of a farmer, who, having worked in the fields the whole day, returns home in the late afternoon, but wife has yet to cook dinner. So he goes back out and sits amid the rice fields to enjoy the view of the sun setting behind the houses and wood-fire smoke rising into the clouds as dinner is being prepared. There is no hurry. It is a leisurely, beautiful scene. Imagine that, lying down on the ground by the fields, crossing your arms behind your head like a pillow, enjoying the view of the sky, and daydreaming. I told this backstory to the musicians during practice and recording. I really love this song. It might not get famous, but it is a memory of the scenes I remember when traveling with the troupes. A memory that I treasure. Like the farmers, we practice, we perform, and we return to our quarters. The next morning, the same routine starts all over again.

I used a samba rhythm for the song "Hô Kéo Lưới." Vietnamese songs have always been ballads about sadness. I wanted to write a song about people working. So I thought about the fishermen, pulling in the nets on their boats in the sea, "Zo-ho-zo!" I remember films depicting these scenes of the Vietnamese fishermen on television. I thought that it would be nice to write a song about the working life of fishermen. "Ngày Hội Mùa" follows this thought, a song about people working. I remember seeing the happiness on faces of the farmers coming home during harvest season. When the rice stalks were ripe, farmers cut the stalks, threshed out the grains, dried the grains, filled sacks with harvested rice, and stacked sacks after sacks of rice in the grain store. It was a festive time, with real happiness emanating from peoples' hearts. So I wrote the song in the style of chèo, in a fast staccato, to showcase the techniques of the musicians. I arranged it this way, the piano and the saxophone playing this opening part in unison, featuring Đắc on saxophone and Tuấn Hùng on piano. You could compare this with the unison section in Chick Corea's "Spain." If you have the chance to observe farmers, it is very hectic during harvesting time: from going out to the fields early in the morning to harvesting the rice and returning home in the evening with sacks and sacks of harvested rice. But in that hectic rhythm, there is a natural joy, happiness emanating from the heart.

I created our own style of swing with "Ngẫu Hứng Tây Nguyên," which was composed earlier and performed at the 1994 concert. It was originally called "Xuân Trên Cao Nguyên." There is no swing in Vietnamese music. But through the sounds found in ethnic folk music, we could create our own swing. That was how I composed "Ngẫu Hứng Tây Nguyên." The folk sounds I heard in Tây Nguyên, I feel there is a festive element to them, a rock element. Just as rock had its foundation in blues, I created an original type of Vietnamese swing. In the first album, Birth '99, I wrote about the north, about the uplands. But I did not write any songs about the south. After releasing the album, I thought of writing more songs about *the south. I wrote a ballad about the south called "Nhớ Về Hậu Giang." In 1998, I traveled to Hậu Giang in the Mekong Delta for a performance. We sat on a boat for a short cruise on the Hậu Giang. It was relaxing and beautiful, as if gliding along a current of harmonious virtuosity. Hopefully, later, when I have more time and resources, I can produce another album that tells more of these stories with the different sounds of the different regions and different ethnicities in Vietnam. "Lời Mẹ Ru" is the only song in* Đồng Cảm *I wrote that took no inspiration from Vietnamese ethnic folk music. It was a song I wrote for my mother. When I performed this song in Singapore, Ms. Hồng [Nguyễn Thị Hồng] sang the tune. But in the album* Đồng Cảm*, I recorded it as an instrumental piece.*

With the release of Birth '99 and Đồng Cảm, Minh had a full repertoire of original jazz compositions in his bag. In Vietnam, Minh was able to present his compositions to an appreciative audience of expatriates and foreign visitors, and a small number of Vietnamese receptive to jazz through specially organized concerts such as the first European Jazz Festival in Hà Nội held in 2001. The festival took place from November 24 to December 7, 2001, and featured mainly invited jazz artists from Europe. Minh and his quintet performed in a "Special Vietnam Evening" program on November 28. In this concert, Minh featured several new tunes from Đồng Cảm, namely "Vũ Điệu Thăng Long," "Núi Rừng Quê Ta," and "Hội Làng."[7] Joining Minh for the "Special Vietnam Evening" was the Sông Hồng (Red River) Big Band and the Voeten/Bernal Quintet. The latter included two Vietnamese musicians, one of whom was Lê Thành Long, a regular player at Minh's Jazz Club. The Sông Hồng Big Band was composed of Vietnamese musicians and expatriates living in Hà Nội. In fact, there were fifteen Vietnamese musicians in the band, namely Quyền Văn Minh, his students, and his friends![8] By the second edition of the festival held from November 22 to December 5, 2002, Minh, playing with his Quyền Văn Minh Group this time, was joined by two other Vietnamese ensembles, the Âu Cơ Band and the Hà Nội Jazz Band, as well as the Voeten/Bernal Quartet for the "Jazz of Vietnam" evening on November 29 at the Youth Theater (Nhà Hát Trẻ). The Hà Nội Jazz Band was led by Trần Mạnh Tuấn, Minh's former student. The Âu Cơ Band featured the Vietnamese guitarist Nguyễn Lương Bình, who studied at the national conservatoire.

Minh was no longer just an in-demand saxophonist and lecturer of saxophone in Hà Nội, but an in-demand jazz musician with his own repertoire of original jazz compositions. He was recognized as the *bố già nhạc jazz* (godfather of jazz) in Vietnam, an accolade lavished on him by reporters writing in local newspapers and magazines about the changing music scene in Vietnam. Quyền Văn Minh had become an iconic figure symbolizing the existence of jazz in Vietnam, and Vietnamese jazz as a minor but integral fiber of the soundscape of Vietnam. In fact, by the third European Jazz Festival in Vietnam held during November 9–13, 2003, it was reported that there were some ten jazz bands active in Hà Nội.[9]

Birth '99

liên hoan nhạc jazz châu Âu lần II

jazz

2nd European jazz festival
22 November – 5 December 2002

Hanoi: Youth Theatre – Nhà hát Tuổi trẻ
Hochiminh City: Conservatory – Nhạc viện

Figures 11.5a, 11.5b, 11.5c. The first, second, and third European Jazz Festivals in Vietnam.

Our Songs

Quyền Văn Minh started his career playing polkas and dance tunes at weddings and patriotic songs and marches at community events. He developed into a professional musician in the various state song-and-dance troupes and rose to become the top saxophonist with the Thăng Long Song-and-Dance Troupe, the premier troupe in Vietnam. Minh could literally play any standard pieces (and, I might add, many obscure pieces as well) found in the extensive repertoire of *nhạc tiền chiến* (prewar music), *nhạc đỏ* (red music), *nhạc vàng* (yellow music), and songs about Hà Nội by the exclusive circle of composers who specialize in writing music about the capital such as Phú Quang. If there was anyone who would have had privileged access to music, in terms of equipment and media during the difficult 1970s and early 1980s, it would be musical cadres in the state song-and-dance troupes such as Minh. Minh knows the music of his time. In fact, he built his career as the preferred saxophonist to accompany the vocals of many reputable and famous singers in the music scene of Vietnam during the late 1970s and through the 1980s. As a performing artist (*nghệ sĩ biểu diễn*) in the inner circle of musical cadres in the state song-and-dance troupes, Minh fully grasped the delicate official sensitivity and audience receptiveness to the music he should play and the music he could play. He paid due attention to the political and cultural context of the times to successfully deliver his 1988 and 1989 solo recital programs in the wake of the Đổi Mới reforms. Minh continued to tread with care in 1994, when he held his first solo concert at the Hà Nội Opera House, even though Đổi Mới was already in full swing.

After the Subsidy Period, the music scene in Vietnam also started to change, and popular love songs were rehabilitated. During the Subsidy Period, songs by Trịnh Công Sơn, the ballads, were prohibited. When these songs started coming back, especially after Đổi Mới, I was quite influenced, too. That was why I decided to record an album of ballads. I wanted to provide a comparison between Vietnamese and international ballads, to show where they converged and where they were different. I have a passion for both clarinet and saxophone. I use the C clarinet and bass clarinet. But this alto clarinet that I have, it is quite a special instrument. I do not know of too many people who actually used this for solo performances, so not too many people are familiar with the alto clarinet. I chanced upon this alto clarinet when I performed in Hồ Chí Minh City many years ago. The timbre of the sound just sat really well with me. I had to have it, even though I knew it was not easy to fit into most gigs I was doing at that time.

Những Tình Khúc với Quyền Văn Minh: Jazz Style
Solo with Clarinet in B♭, Alto Clarinet in E♭, Bass Clarinet, Soprano Sax, Alto Sax, Tenor Sax, and Baritone Sax

Figure 11.6. Quyền Văn Minh at Minh's Jazz Club (photo by Deborah Jan Aronson).

Figure 11.7. *Những Tình Khúc với Quyền Văn Minh: Jazz Style*.

Track 1: "Nghìn Những Mùa Thu Đi" (With Each Passing Autumn), by Trịnh Công Sơn
Track 2: "My Way," by Paul Anka
Track 3: "Nỗi Lòng" (Letting Go), by Nguyễn Văn Khánh
Track 4: "Georgia on My Mind," by Hoagy Carmichael
Track 5: "Hoài Cảm" (Remembrance), by Cung Tiến
Track 6: "The Shadow of Your Smile," by Johnny Mandel
Track 7: "Gửi Gió Cho Mây Ngàn Bay" (Wind among the Clouds), by Đoàn Chuẩn
Track 8: "As Time Goes By," by Herman Hupfeld
Track 9: "Dư Âm" (Echo), by Nguyễn Văn Tý
Track 10: "Mona Lisa," by Jay Livingston
Track 11: "Lỡ Chuyến Đò" (Missing the Boat), by Anh Việt
Track 12: "Em Đến Thăm Anh Một Chiều Mưa" (I Came to You One Rainy Day), by Tô Vũ
Track 13: "Chiều Hải Cảng" (Evening at the Harbor), by Vasily Solovyov-Sedoi

In 2000, when I recorded a selection of "tình khúc" [Vietnamese ballads], as well as international ballads, I featured the C clarinet as one of the solo instruments. The album was called Những Tình Khúc Với Quyền Văn Minh: Jazz Style. *I recorded Trịnh Công Sơn's "Nghìn Những Mùa Thu Đi" and another song, "Mona Lisa," with the C clarinet. "Nghìn Những Mùa Thu Đi" is a classic tune in Vietnam, a tune that Vietnamese could easily recognize. "Chiều Hải Cảng" is a Russian song that is very well received in Vietnam, especially for people of my generation. The composer, Vasily Solovyov-Sedoi, also wrote the song "Moscow Nights" [Chiều Mát-xcơ-va], which was extremely popular in Vietnam. "Mona Lisa" is another one of my favorite ballads. In this album, I tried to introduce to the general listener the art of jazz improvisation through the sounds of "tiền chiến" [prewar] songs, performed with seven different types of saxophones and clarinets in total.*

In 2003, Minh continued his attempt to subtly introduce Vietnamese listeners to jazz through instrumental music, measured improvisation, and the sound of the saxophone by covering familiar Vietnamese popular songs. This time, he recorded a selection of tunes by two Vietnamese composers, Đoàn Chuẩn and Hà Dũng.

Đoàn Chuẩn, Hà Dũng với NSUT Quyền Văn Minh (*Vietnamese Songs with Jazz and Blues Styles*)[10]

Figure 11.8. *Đoàn Chuẩn, Hà Dũng với NSUT Quyền Văn Minh.*

Track 1: "Falling Autumn Leaves" (Lá Đổ Muôn Chiều), by Đoàn Chuẩn
Track 2: "Autumn Reminiscence" (Thu Hoài Niệm), by Hà Dũng
Track 3: "Port Transfer" (Chuyển Bến), by Đoàn Chuẩn
Track 4: "Announcing the Night with a Feast" (Tiếng Ram Đêm), by Hà Dũng
Track 5: "Feelings of an Artist" (Tình Nghệ Sĩ), by Đoàn Chuẩn
Track 6: "Quietness" (Lặng Lẽ), by Hà Dũng
Track 7: "Lyrical Mood" (Khúc Tự Tình), by Hà Dũng
Track 8: "The Blue Skirting of a Dress" (Tà Áo Xanh), by Đoàn Chuẩn
Track 9: "Rain" (Mưa), by Hà Dũng
Track 10: "To the Girl in the South" (Gửi Người Em Gái Miền Nam), by Đoàn Chuẩn
Musicians:
Quyền Văn Minh and the Red River Band

Figure 11.9. *Hà Nội: Autumn and You.*

Not exactly a prolific composer like Trịnh Công Sơn, Đoàn Chuẩn's small repertoire of some nineteen compositions is well remembered by musicians and artists, in particular the tunes "Thu Hoài Niệm," "Gửi Người Em Gái Miền Nam," and "Tình Nghệ Sĩ." Đoàn Chuẩn had passed away earlier in 2001. Always respectful of the pioneers who came before him, this was Minh's personal tribute to the respected musician. To Quyền Văn Minh, Đoàn Chuẩn's songs carry a natural blues feel, and Hà Dũng's songs carry a feel akin to jazz. This was a selection that suited his continued attempt to bring the sound of jazz to Vietnamese listeners.[11]

Minh dedicated an album of Hà Nội songs to his friend Bùi Kim Dung in 2007. It was also an album recorded for all his supporters in Hà Nội who were not exactly jazz aficionados.

Hà Nội: Autumn and You
Specially dedicated to Kim Dung Bùi, March 19, 2007
Track 1: "I Miss the Autumn in Hà Nội," by Trịnh Công Sơn
Track 2: "Hà Nội, the Day of Return," by Phú Quang
Track 3: "Memory Sea," by Trịnh Công Sơn
Track 4: "Hà Nội, the Season without Rain," by Trương Qúy Hải
Track 5: "Sữa Flower," by Hồng Đang
Track 6: "Hà Nội and I," by Lê Vinh
Track 7: "Charming Autumn," by Đoàn Chuẩn and Tư Linh
Track 8: "Past Memory" (Diêm Xưa), by Trịnh Công Sơn
Track 9: "Darling, Hà Nội's Corner," by Phú Quang
Bonus Track: "Mona Lisa," by Jay Livingston
Musicians:
Arranged and Performed by Quyền Văn Minh

Ever since Minh first opened his jazz club on Giảng Võ Street, his friends would frequent the club to support him, even if they were not exactly fans or aficionados of the genre. Even today, it is not uncommon to hear Minh's friends requesting a song or two about Hà Nội, such as "Em ơi, Hà Nội Phố" by Phú Quang or "Tôi Nhớ Mùa Thu Hà Nội" by Trịnh Công Sơn. And Minh would always oblige his friends by going to the stage to play these requests. These are songs familiar to Vietnamese listeners, so this was an album he recorded for his friends. Minh believes that the album helps, even in a small way, to make his friends a little more receptive to jazz. These are their songs. These were also the songs that built Minh's career as a musician. And he would give them a big band spin, later in the DVD era of his discography, with a series of live recorded concerts at the Hà Nội Opera House.

When Quyền Văn Minh first brought jazz to the officially sanctioned public sphere in his solo recital programs in 1988 and 1989, he was a professional musician aspiring to play jazz and bring respectability to the saxophone as a serious musical instrument in Vietnam. His main job was to play music. Wish granted, Minh could now play jazz, form his own jazz ensembles, and teach saxophone and jazz at the prestigious Hà Nội National Music Conservatoire of Vietnam. He had to play two roles rather than just focus on one as a performing artist playing jazz. Now he was both teacher and musician. To push his agenda of bringing jazz to Vietnam, Minh created a new sound through his compositions, Vietnamese jazz, which he premiered at the 1994 concert at the Hà Nội Opera House. He added on the role of composer to his already hectic life as a musician and a teacher. His achievements were nationally recognized when he was awarded the title of Eminent Artist by order of the government of Vietnam in 1997. In the same year, Minh took on yet another role as club owner, opening Minh's Jazz Club, something entirely beyond his comfort zone. While Minh had done plenty of recordings as a session musician, he finally emerged as a solo recording artist with the release of *Birth '99* in 2000. His CD albums released in the years between 2000 and 2007 affirmed his status as a solo recording artist, with the albums being regularly featured in rotation on Vietnam Airlines' in-flight entertainment program. But it was *Birth '99* and *Đồng Cảm*, containing his original Vietnamese jazz compositions recorded amid the hectic end-to-end schedule that came with all these multiple roles he had taken on to bring jazz to Vietnam, that really cemented Quyền Văn Minh's status as the "godfather" of Vietnamese jazz and jazz more generally in Vietnam.

There is no doubt that a musician is usually very single minded and devotes all his attention to his music. The musician strives to reach the pinnacle of his art. Unfortunately, my life is different. I wished to be able to focus on my art, too! Even in the albums I recorded, when the band was rehearsing for the recording, I had to run all kinds of errands so that we could actually walk into the studio and record the music to produce the album. It was the same for all the performance programs; I had to organize everything by myself, even though I was the musician taking center stage. I just did not have the means to hire a company or someone to do these things on my behalf. Furthermore, at the end of the day, I had to decide on the direction of how things should turn out. I just had to do it myself. I could really only practice and rehearse for maybe one or two hours, then after that I had to see to other things. I had no choice. I had to take on many different roles concurrently in order to realize my vision. It was rather ironic. When I started learning the clarinet as a child, that was the only thing I had to do; I could focus and practice. But by the time I really got into jazz as a professional musician, I had less and less time to focus on my art. What an ironic turn!

TRACK 12

Minh's Jazz Club Reprise

For more than twenty years, Minh's Jazz Club has been the venue where Vietnamese musicians in Hà Nội have their first experience playing jazz for a live audience, where they first listened to live jazz, or where they wanted to be on stage to indulge in a night of playing pure jazz. In 1997, Minh's Jazz Club opened its doors at Giảng Võ Exhibition Center but had to close after three months when the venue was slated for redevelopment by the government. The club then moved into the heart of Hà Nội's city center at 16 Lê Thái Tổ in 1998, but again, it had to close after less than a year when the building was designated for other purposes. Minh's Jazz Club finally found a long-term home at 31 Lương Văn Can, a site coincidently owned by the Thăng Long Song-and-Dance Troupe, Minh's former employer. Staying there for about ten years, the club had to move again when its lease expired and the troupe took back the site for redevelopment. In 2010, the club moved to Trấn Vũ Street overlooking scenic Trúc Bạch Lake adjacent to Tây Hồ (West Lake) for a very brief few months before relocating to 65 Quán Sứ, just outside the Old Quarter of Hà Nội. In 2014, Minh's Jazz Club finally moved into the cultural arts hub in the city center at 1 Tràng Tiền, behind the majestic Hà Nội Opera House.

Jazz Seven Days a Week

I want jazz to not merely exist in the soundscape of Vietnam; I want jazz to be accepted as a proper mainstream [chính thống] genre of music in Vietnam. Minh's Jazz Club is the place where we play jazz seven days a week, every day of the year. The musicians who play on stage every night at the jazz club, their overall capacity to play jazz, I have to say, is quite good. These musicians can play. They can improvise individually and play in a group. However, I am not comparing their standards with musicians in other countries around the world. This jazz club has nurtured generation after generation of some of the best young musicians in Vietnam.

Figure 12.1. Minh's Jazz Club, 1 Tràng Tiền (photo by Deborah Jan Aronson).

It was really difficult when I started the jazz club in 1997. Other genres of music in Vietnam such as ethnic music, classical music, and traditional music could receive all kinds of support from the state. Mainstream music ensembles in the country such as song-and-dance troupes and classical music orchestras could recruit music students who had been properly trained to play classical music, ethnic music, and traditional music. But there was little government support for jazz until a small Department of Jazz was formed at the conservatoire in 1991 and a Faculty of Jazz was established in 2013. Even then, I still had to do everything on my own with almost no state support. I had to source my own funds to operate the jazz club as a place for musicians to experience playing for a live audience, organize my own recordings, and put together my own concerts. For jazz music, I even had to nurture musicians through the jazz club! At the jazz club, many musicians came to play, honed their skills, and gained the experience of playing jazz for a live audience. Many came. Some stayed on, and some left. Some left and came back. Some continued to develop their career in music and continue with jazz. Some left jazz behind to develop their musical career. And some gave up music altogether to pursue a different livelihood.

With my students, I always encouraged them to try playing with me at the jazz club. I would have them practice two or three tunes really well. They learned the form of the tune, then the chords, the rhythm, and they learned to listen to what others were playing in the band and be able to improvise a solo. I also let them sit with me at the jazz club in the evenings. But I have a simple rule: make no more than three mistakes in one night! When the jazz club opened at Giảng Võ, I gave Đắc the opportunity to play on stage every night, too. This way, students could get the experience of playing with professional musicians and for a live audience. I also encouraged students to develop their own style and not just follow the way I played. It was a most valuable platform for Đắc and other younger musicians to learn about playing jazz, improvising on the stage and performing in front of a live audience, every night. Before I had the jazz club, I would let my students follow me to evening gigs to get some experience. As a musician, I place a lot of emphasis on practice and real gig experience. You can talk about theory later.

During the SARS [severe acute respiratory syndrome] epidemic in 2003, the jazz club suffered big-time. It was empty night after night. But we survived. I remember, for a whole week, almost all the live music venues in Hà Nội stopped playing live music because there were no guests! Music lounges and bars lost revenue, and musicians lost gigs. But we continued with our double live sessions every single night at the jazz club. At best, we received only six or seven guests sitting at the tables each night during that week. But we had to live up to our promise of "live jazz seven nights a week, every week of the year!" I continued to pay the musicians even when the club had no guests. I want our jazz musicians to have self-discipline. Guests or no guests, the music plays on. At the end of the day, they must understand that our passion to play jazz comes from within.

Musicians at Minh's Jazz Club

Minh's Jazz Club is where some of the finest and most creative musicians in Hà Nội congregate, either onstage or among the audience, whether they play jazz or not. Among the Vietnamese musicians who have played or continue to play at Minh's Jazz Club is tenor saxophonist Hùng Sơn of Đoàn Ca Múa Quân Đội (Army Song-and-Dance Troupe), who won a gold medal for his performance of Minh's composition "Giai Điệu Sapa," in the *Biểu Diễn Múa và Âm Nhạc Dân Tộc Lần Thứ 2* (Second Ethnic Song-and-Dance Show) in 2003. Hùng Sơn was among the earliest in the group of musicians who played at Minh's Jazz Club when it opened in 1997, and he continues to play there regularly. One of Minh's early students, Nguyễn Bảo Long, a Vietnamese saxophonist who leads his own group, Jump for Jazz, played at the jazz club for an extended period of time. Bảo Long was also one of the saxophonists featured in the saxophone quartet in Minh's concert at the Hà Nội Opera House in 1994. Bùi Xuân Hoà, another former student of Minh's and current lead saxophonist at Minh's former employer, the Thăng

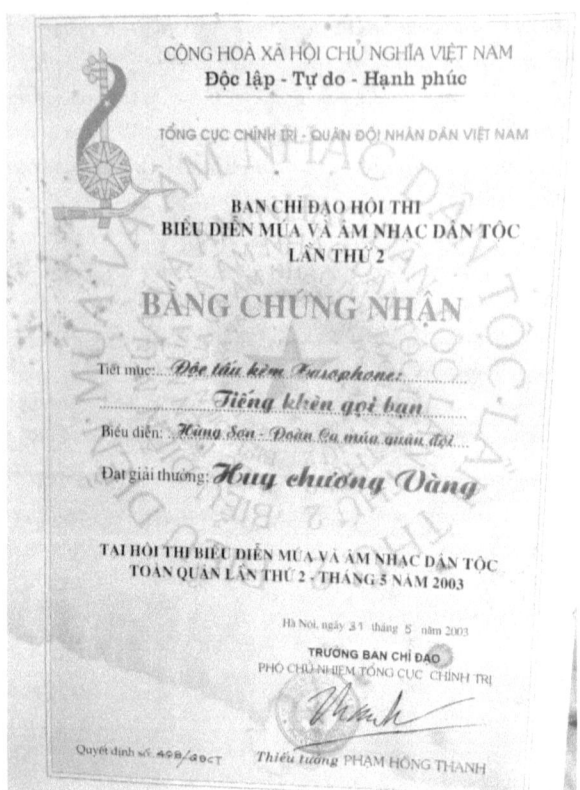

Figure 12.2. Hùng Sơn's award certificate.

Long Song-and-Dance Troupe, as well as adjunct lecturer at the conservatoire, has cast his familiar shadow in the limelight of the jazz club since its early days.

Nguyễn Minh Đức, bassist for Vietnam's most well-known rock band, Bức Tượng, plays regularly at Minh's Jazz Club, even though he is already a rock celebrity in his own right. Đức joined Bức Tượng during the last phase of the band's active years and wrote a few songs for the group, including the hit "Những Chuyến Đi Dài" (The Long Journeys). Lê Thành Long, a reputable and versatile bassist/cellist and vocalist in the music lounge scene of Hà Nội, has been a regular bassist at the jazz club. Đào Minh Pha, the current premier jazz bassist in Vietnam, recorded on Minh's *Birth '99* and *Đồng Cảm* albums as a very young musician and was one of the regular bassists at the jazz club before he moved to teach in Sài Gòn in the middle of 2018. Pha taught jazz at the national conservatoire before his move to the South. Pha, an ethnic Tày, is probably the only Vietnamese jazz musician of his generation who hails from one of the ethnic minority groups in the northern uplands of Vietnam.

Among the notable Vietnamese pianists who have played at the jazz club are Vũ Tú Cầu, Phạm Tuấn Hùng, Nguyễn Tuấn Nam, Nguyễn Đình Phúc, Bạch Ngọc

Figure 12.3. Scene from Minh's Jazz Club.

Vượng, and Phạm Lê Phương, most of whom participated in the recording of various albums or concerts by Quyền Văn Minh and Quyền Thiện Đắc. Lê Quốc Hưng, Lê Việt Hùng, Lê Hoàng Long, and Hà Đình Huy are among the notable Vietnamese drummers and percussionists who contributed to jazz performances organized by Minh over the years as well as having drummed at Minh's Jazz Club. Nguyễn Thu Hương, Nguyễn Diêu Thùy, and Lai Thị Phương Thảo are three of the very few female Vietnamese jazz vocalists singing at the jazz club.

Quyền Thiện Đắc, Minh's son, has been playing at the jazz club almost every night since 1997. Đắc leads the saxophone discipline at the Faculty of Jazz of the conservatoire and is currently the most respected jazz saxophonist in the country. Each week, Minh's Jazz Club has between sixteen to twenty musicians rotating in quartets or quintets for the double nightly sessions, seven days a week. As for Quyền Văn Minh, he has been the resident artist ever since the club opened in 1997.

In the beginning, most of the guests at the jazz club were foreign tourists. Gradually more Vietnamese listeners started coming in. There are foreign tourists who play some music; some even play some jazz. They are surprised to find that jazz actually exists in Hà Nội, in Vietnam. Quite often, foreign visitors who play jazz bring along their instruments and jam along with the musicians onstage. I welcome them all the time. It is a good thing. We come from around the world, but we can play jazz together on the same stage in Vietnam.

Figure 12.4. Rehearsing at Minh's Jazz Club (photo by Deborah Jan Aronson).

At the jazz club, I could not afford to pay a high salary. But the jazz club really helped the musicians to improve their ability to play jazz. At the end of the day, in order to earn a living, many jazz musicians who played at the club had to leave for better pay elsewhere. They left to play regular, popular music gigs. Some even changed profession altogether. Many of the musicians also had to take up gigs to play in the lobbies of hotels or fancy restaurants in the city. But they are not really playing jazz at these venues. Playing in hotel lobbies or fancy restaurants is simply playing music that is pleasing to the ears of the guests; nothing more. That is not jazz. There is no pressure on the musicians to lift their music to a higher level. But it is good income. I did that myself in the past, too. At the end of the day, many stopped playing jazz altogether. Many had to switch to playing popular music at other places. Simply put, even the guests at these extravagant places just want simple music with a catchy melody. Many who have worked with me know that I like to produce large-scale, serious performances like the jazz concerts I organized at the Hà Nội Opera House. I want to raise the standard of music. When they play nightly sessions at the jazz club, I always ask them to try something different from their usual engagements elsewhere, something of a higher quality. It is not like I am being too demanding, but I do ask for a higher quality, a higher level of music. But not too many musicians want to bear with this kind of pressure.

It is a little bit sad, to be honest, because it is indeed quite often that many talented jazz musicians have to give in to the pressure of earning a decent livelihood at the end of the day. It is a pity for jazz, but I know they have no choice. Managing the jazz club and presenting live jazz every single night is no simple thing. Musicians come into the jazz club to train themselves to be better jazz musicians, not because I can pay them a high wage. I cannot afford that. There have been occasions when musicians decided to take up gigs elsewhere at the last minute because other places offered them higher pay, so they canceled a session or two that was already scheduled. I have to be understanding and let them go; it is their right to try to have a better income, too! For a session or two, I have to be understanding, so these musicians might come back to jazz. I totally understand, and I totally empathize with them. When I started playing jazz, I was in a most difficult situation as well.

With the musicians playing at the jazz club, I am totally fine with it when they inform me beforehand, even at the last minute if they are going to be late or are unable to turn up for their scheduled sessions. But I do ask them to be honest with me. I understand that they have to try to earn more money to take care of their family. Me, too. I went through the same difficulties as them. In the past, there were occasions when I had to rush off on my bicycle to play an additional gig, and I ended up late for another scheduled rehearsal or gig. I would give lame excuses such as, "Oh, I had a toothache." People knew that it was a lame excuse; everyone in the circle knew the usual lame excuses when musicians were late or canceled a gig at the last minute! Thus, I ask musicians at the jazz club to be honest with me. If they are really having a hard time, I am always willing and ready to help.

But when musicians have a better life, do they naturally become more devoted to jazz? Not necessarily so. Quite often, I know, they spend more time playing popular music gigs or work unrelated to music. They have to fulfill their responsibilities to their full-time employers. They might start a family, get married, and have kids; then they have a family to take care of, too! These are real and proper responsibilities. We need to have a decent livelihood. People need to bring money home to support their families. They have to find gigs that pay well. We are controlled by our economic conditions. I pay all the musicians on time; I never owe them a single Vietnamese đồng. But it is difficult to keep them at the jazz club for long. They love jazz, but they also have to earn a decent livelihood. I simply cannot afford to keep these musicians at the jazz club to just play jazz and become better jazz musicians.

Indeed, besides Minh's Jazz Club, there have not been any commercial venues in Hà Nội where jazz musicians can indulge in playing jazz as a paid gig for a live audience. Over the years, since the early 1990s, there have been restaurants such as Gustav's and the Press Club, and lounges and bars at luxurious hotels such as the former Plaza Sofitel (now the Pan Pacific), the Hilton Opera, the Marriott, and the Metropole that have called for musicians to play easy-listening music, popular music, and sometimes light jazz to entertain customers. These venues and the gigs at these venues come and go. Musicians are expected to play music to suit the ambience of the venue. These gigs pay well, but musicians do not always have the freedom to indulge in sophisticated improvisations. Music is merely part of the setup to give an element of "upper-class" ambience to the venue. In comparison, while Minh's Jazz Club has always emphasized playing jazz and allowing musicians to really indulge in jazz, Minh simply could not afford to pay comparable rates to the musicians. Playing in other venues, as any of these musicians would readily concur, has always been about earning a livelihood. Minh's Jazz Club is where they play jazz. And while they may play at Minh's Jazz Club in the evening, it is not uncommon to find these musicians working a more stable, regular paid job in the day or on other evenings when they are not scheduled at the jazz club. Some teach music at the national conservatoire, local colleges, or international schools in the city. A few of these talented musicians even work as realtors and insurance agents. Several run their own small retail businesses. There are others who work at radio and television broadcasting stations. Some manage to secure full-time day jobs as members of music ensembles such as song-and-dance troupes and professional symphony orchestras. Many of the exceptionally talented and more flexible musicians earn a rather comfortable living just playing as sessionists for popular and rock music shows in the city. All of these musicians invariably call Minh's Jazz Club their jazz home.

I have guided many young music students and Vietnamese artists onto the path of jazz. They are very disciplined, and they are very good musicians. Excellent musicians, in fact! They do very well in the music scene in Vietnam. The younger musicians, after apprenticing with me, often find stable gigs at other places that pay better. They can have some stability, but it is only stability in terms of having a better income; musically speaking, maybe not. These higher-paying venues need better-quality musicians, so they come and hire these young jazz musicians. And as soon as the young musicians start playing in other places, they inevitably compare themselves with the other musicians, their audience, and the environment. It does not take too long for them to realize that, musically speaking, they are more competent. And that is when the attitude starts to change. Thinking they are "number one," "the best," they stop practicing as hard as before, and they stop practicing to improve themselves further. And some of them start behaving like "stars." Vietnamese love the words "ngôi sao" [star] and "số một" [number one]; and this kind of mentality is detrimental for music.

In life, after we are born, we grow up, we start working, and we see all these dazzling five-star hotels, people driving their flashy automobiles and riding their expensive motorbikes; it is natural for people to wish that they could have all this. But they might not be able to have it there and then. So, we accept our fate, we ride our bicycles or very ordinary motorbikes. We work hard, hoping that one fine day, we can achieve our goals. That is natural. It is similar to playing jazz in Vietnam. Listen to a CD, and one would naturally wish to be able to play like these jazz masters. But if you really want to be able to play as well as the jazz masters, you must be willing to pay the price; you must be willing to pay with your labor and hard work! To buy a nice automobile, there are many ways, you can adopt underhanded means or engage in illicit activities to get the money quickly. You can take shortcuts. But in music, there is no other way. If you can't play, you can't play. You have to work hard to be able to play well! I always tell my students and all the musicians playing at the jazz club, "Pop in any CD and listen. Even listening to the not-so-famous artists, you will find that you have a lot to learn from them. Can you be satisfied with where you are right now, musically speaking? No way. Even I am not satisfied with myself, musically speaking. I want to constantly improve."

Managing Minh's Jazz Club

I wish I could just focus on playing music. But I have to organize all these things so that future generations of musicians can play and improve jazz, and bring jazz in Vietnam to a higher level, to a higher standard. Managing the jazz club means that I do not really have the luxury of investing in my personal development, to do things like devoting a few hours each day to just listen to music and practice my saxophone! I have had to sacrifice my own personal development so that the generations of musicians after me can develop. That is fine with me. I have to take care of many things, like teaching in and out of the conservatoire and repairing instruments for other musicians to make more income, playing at the jazz club and managing the jazz club. There was a period of time, during evenings when there were not too many guests at the jazz club, that I would let Đắc know after playing a few songs that I was going home to repair instruments to make more money, to support the operation of the jazz club. Over the years, the club changed locations so many times, and each move meant that I lost more money, in fact, quite a lot of money. Where could I find a stable financial source to ensure that the club was able to function with each new move? I have been fortunate, and that is due to jazz. I play jazz, and there are many foreigners in Vietnam who love the music and want to study the saxophone with me. In the beginning, I only charged US$7 to $10 per session of coaching, then it slowly rose to $12, $15, and then to $20 per session by 2015. I saved up all that money; I did not spend a single cent. I was determined not to spend a single cent of that money, just so I could use the money to support the jazz club.

To keep the jazz club in operation, I have to be honest, I had no choice but to accept gigs specifically inviting me to play popular music. People might even pay VND15 million [around US$720 at the time of this conversation] for me to play just two popular Vietnamese songs! I wish I could tell them that I only accept gigs to play jazz. But if I were to accept this gig, I could use the money to invest in the jazz club, to ensure that the club can survive. When the young musicians at the jazz club asked me, "What was the gig?," I can only say, "Just another gig." But I am also known as an "on-call" musician. People like to call me up for gigs, even at the last minute. Every night, I come back to the jazz club even if I've had other engagements. If I'm not too tired, I always get on stage to play a few tunes with the musicians. There is not a day that goes by without me wishing that I could just focus on playing jazz on the stage at the jazz club.

All these things take up all my time. But doing these things helps to sustain the operation of the jazz club. I still remember, there were days when I was holding the saxophone, performing at the jazz club, but only 30 percent of my attention was on playing the saxophone, and for the other 70 percent I would be thinking about other things. I would be worrying about all kinds of things. Were the guests properly attended to by my staff? Did we order enough supplies to ensure the smooth operation of the club? Can we break even for the month? And before moving to Tràng Tiền [Street], I was constantly thinking about if there might be a better venue for the jazz club! I could only play with 30 percent of my attention at times like this! In the early days, guests complained about the quality of service at the club and even the quality of drinks served at the club! From the wine served having already gone bad, to cocktails not being mixed right. These were quite complicated matters for me, because I did not know much about such things! For a while, the club even served food with its own kitchen, when we were still located at the Lương Văn Can venue. But I could not provide professional food and beverage service training for staff working at the jazz club. I might have been a club owner, but I really didn't know anything or even have the time to be able to see to such details. I could only focus on the music.

There are days when the club is crowded, and there are days when we only have a few customers. On nights when the club is empty, I do feel very disappointed and sometimes a little discouraged. This often happens during public holidays in Vietnam when there are all kinds of activities on the street, such as open-air performances or night markets. Foreign tourists are often attracted by these exotic activities, which are the things they came to see in Vietnam. They do not come here especially to explore the local jazz scene. It is only when all these activities have ended that foreign tourists begin looking for venues that are still operating, such as a jazz club. So, there are days when the place is almost empty, but on other days, the club might be totally packed!

I finally gave in and paid for advertisements in the first year of operation at 31 Lương Văn Can in 1999. But they were not very effective, so I decided not to waste that money. Instead, I invested that money to cultivate my musicians. I have

Figure 12.5. Minh's Jazz Club ninth anniversary flyer (photo by Deborah Jan Aronson).

always just wanted these kids to be able to play jazz really well and to be able to play jazz naturally. In Vietnam, we have a saying, "hữu xạ tự nhiên hương" [where there is musk, there is naturally fragrance], so if the music is good, then it will naturally attract people to come. And we acquired that reputation in the decade at 31 Lương Văn Can. That is the reputation of Minh's Jazz Club we have built up over the years. We try to play good music, good jazz.

When I hire staff for the jazz club, the waitstaff, I usually only hire males. This is how I see it; jazz is never inferior to anything such that it would require additional sweeteners or perks. I do not need to hire young, pretty female waitresses to attract customers to the jazz club. Many restaurants and music lounges do that. Good music will ultimately attract a good audience. If you want to give jazz a try, come. If not, that is fine. There is no rush. I do not want to sell it to you with other incentives. No, I do not want to do that. I want people to come of their own accord. I want them to come for the music. This is not an easy principle to uphold when operating a jazz club, trust me! The pursuit and development of jazz in Vietnam is my mission in life. Even if I only have a tiny little place, and even if every night I only have thirty or forty customers, I will have a band on the stage playing jazz. Sure, I wish I had a bigger venue or even a nicer place. But that is not possible, financially speaking.

At the point when I had to move out of Lương Văn Can in 2009, it cost me at least around US$2,000 [~VND36 million in 2009] a month to operate the jazz club. The rent itself was only VND10.5 million, but I had to add in this thing and that thing, and the cost of the venue came to about VND20 million! There are many random things that you have to do and many informal expenses to take care of in order to get things done in Vietnam. I have to accept that and abide by that.

There are also all kinds of social relationships, from the most superficial and minute to the most deep-rooted and ingrained, that I have to foster and maintain to ensure that things can get done. I have had to take on all these engagements in order to keep the jazz club going. Quite often, friends and acquaintances will just want to meet up with me, and have a few drinks or dinner. They might not know anything about jazz or even care about jazz, but I am always more than happy to bring along my saxophone and play for them. This is to help them understand a little bit more about what we are trying to do, musically speaking. It's like having one more person know what jazz is about. Maintaining all kinds of relationships in Vietnamese society is of the utmost importance. You have to invest time in building and maintaining these relationships. You need all kinds of help and support to get something, even something very simple, done in Vietnam. Even a simple word of support from the right person can go very far in helping me get something done. All these years, never once did the cultural police or local police from the ward administration come to the jazz club to demand to see a license or a permit. I have full official endorsement for the jazz club. But there was one occasion when a newly transferred officer came and demanded to see our license for playing live music! I told him to go back and check with his superiors first. He never came back to ask for such a thing again. That was how things worked in Vietnam, and it is still how things work now.

The jazz club is more than just another significant milestone in Minh's jazz life story, as the solo concerts in 1988, 1989, and 1994 were. From the day Minh opened the club, it has grown to become an integral part of his life. He is there every day, unless he has other gigs to perform or social engagements that he is obliged to attend. Rarely is Minh not talking to someone at one of the tables at the jazz club. Old friends, new friends, friends of friends, and newly met acquaintances visit Minh at the club frequently. Usually, these friends are quite willing to spend at the club, opening bottles of wine, whiskey, or cognac, paying for imported cigars or buying his CDs and DVDs to support his endeavor. They are there to catch up with Minh. To not disappoint his visitors, Minh takes to the stage and joins the musicians for the next tune in their repertoire. Following that, he accedes to requests from his friends and plays a Vietnamese popular song or two. Quite often, among his entourage of visiting friends are a few old friends in the music circle. In fact, sometimes they are quite famous singers such as Quang Thọ, who sang with Minh in the program *Quyền Văn Minh và Bạn Bè Với Jazz III* (*Quyền Văn Minh and Friends with Jazz III*) at the Hà Nội Opera House on January 10, 2012. It is not unusual for these musician friends of Minh to take to the stage and sing a song or two of Vietnamese classics. There are also friends who are just not that interested in music, and definitely not jazz, visiting Minh to show support for his work. And during these occasions, the conversations and drinking take center stage and continue through the night, impervious to the focused, loud jazz playing onstage.

Often, my Vietnamese friends come and support us at the jazz club. They might even open a bottle or two of wine or whiskey to support the operations of the club. And, you know, after a copious amount of alcohol people start to talk loudly among themselves and even ask to sing a song or two that they like with the band, totally oblivious to the jazz music being performed live at the jazz club! As for foreign guests at the club, we do get a wide range of people as well. Some really love jazz. Some are just looking for a place to hang out. In the early days, foreign visitors to the jazz club were not willing to spend a lot. They would sit there the whole night after ordering just one beer. Many were just traveling through the country for a budget holiday. At 31 Lương Văn Can, it happened a few times that some of the guests, foreign tourists, tried to leave the club without even paying for their drinks! At the Lương Văn Can venue, along the passageway leading to the club's toilet, there was a door that allowed one to exit the club. Once, a club security guard had to hold back a group of these young foreign tourists who tried to leave without paying. It was disappointing. But these things do happen. Well, I have to accept the complexity of the guests and friends who come to the jazz club.

In Vietnam, at every particular juncture, if you want to introduce something new, you have to be patient and wait. There is no way you can immediately introduce something here simply because the world out there is doing it. No way. Not even if you know it deeply and have mastered it. You have to think about how it should be done and, more importantly, how it could be done. Quite often, after taking one step forward, you have to take two steps back. To introduce jazz to my audience, I have to do it through popular music, too. I do not deny it. Sometimes at the jazz club, I play popular tunes at the request of my friends. It is a way of gradually introducing them to jazz. You cannot force jazz on Vietnamese. No way. When I gave the solo recitals in 1988 and 1989, I included Vietnamese ethnic folk music in the repertoire so as to introduce jazz to the Vietnamese listeners. If I only play jazz that is entirely strange to them, then they might not be receptive, and the outcome might not be so good. Through ethnic folk music, we can gradually try to help them accept jazz. But even then, we have to do it with a balanced approach. When I gave the 1994 concert to introduce my original jazz compositions inspired by ethnic folk music, I prepared a repertoire that had something familiar for the audience. I introduced my original jazz compositions through these familiar tunes, so that they could enjoy the show and at the same time have a taste of something new. Imagine playing a full concert of these original compositions, original Vietnamese jazz, inspired by ethnic folk music sounds: it will certainly be a most interesting concert for us. But for the audience, not necessarily so. This is something that is different and difficult about playing jazz in Vietnam. It is a headache, to be honest. But there is no other way to do it. In Vietnam, I have to say, it has been difficult to develop jazz.

I have performed in many different places in the world; it is not as if every foreigner likes jazz! But people in other countries have a more diversified range of musical tastes, such as jazz, classical, popular music, world music, and so on. In Vietnam, we have yet to develop that kind of diverse cultural appreciation. The difference is that in Vietnam, the audience for jazz is still minuscule. Vietnamese in the 1990s mainly relied on what was broadcast on television and radio. These public broadcasting programs actively introduced music to the people. I have to record my music and make my music available. But I also understand that not everyone can afford to buy my CDs, so I have also tried to hold live concerts to bring my music to an audience, and I've given out a lot of complimentary tickets to get people interested in jazz! Of course, now we have the internet, so things are a fair bit different. At the end of the day, it is not easy to play jazz as a Vietnamese in Vietnam. People do compare, to see if we are as good as Westerners. And people, both foreigners and Vietnamese, are still surprised that Vietnamese can play jazz!

Managing the jazz club means I can create paid gigs for musicians to come and play jazz, even if some of these musicians are still at the level of just learning to play jazz. It is okay that I lose money every month. And I do lose money every month operating the jazz club! For more than twenty years! If I did not have the jazz club, that is, if I had to close it down, we would not die of hunger, because we earn most of our living outside of the club. Musically speaking, we could still practice on our own. But if you practice on your own, will you improve more than actually having to play live gigs regularly? Playing real gigs, there is that moment of adrenalin rush that helps you bring out an idea in your music; now that is good! We have guests who understand jazz, who love jazz. But they are mainly foreigners. We also have some Vietnamese guests. Maybe they do not know anything about jazz. That is okay. If you ask me, and some readers might strongly disagree with me, having one Vietnamese walk into my jazz club is more valuable than having ten foreigners sitting at the club. That is one more Vietnamese who has been exposed to jazz.

Throughout the past twenty-plus years since I opened the jazz club, other people have tried to open other jazz clubs or bars, too. These businesses employed some of the musicians from my jazz club to play for them. Unfortunately, these "jazz" venues never last long. They cannot stay in business. The jazz club is a business entity; we have to pay for rent, pay the staff, and pay the musicians. Guests who come have to pay for drinks, but they do not have to pay a cover charge to enter the club. At Minh's Jazz Club, I always focus on the music rather than the business. Let me put it this way: I choose to sustain the music.

Musicians playing jazz on the stage might not be really top-notch jazz musicians in the world, maybe not yet, but they are very good musicians, and some of them are indeed excellent musicians. Most importantly, they love jazz. At the same time, guests sitting at the tables might not really be informed listeners. But they are there to give jazz a chance. This is my job as jazz club owner. My job is to bring them to the same place. A place where musicians can really play jazz. A place where the general public can encounter real jazz and try listening to jazz. It is okay that I have to deal with guests who do not appreciate jazz or even appreciate music. When they come to the club, they are exposed to real jazz. This is how I see it. And this is the only thing I am concerned about. I am a musician playing at the club, and I am the club owner. I am also a friend of many of the guests. I have to take on all these roles, all at the same time. It is tough. But I see it as my mission in life to pursue and develop jazz in Vietnam.

The Past, Present, and Future of Jazz in Vietnam

Often, I have to stop and check, did I veer from my path? My words and actions, did they go together? I have to be honest with myself. In life, there is always a certain degree of stifling. When we follow all these rules, regulations, expectations, and conventions in the society that we live in, in some ways, we are already stifled. On the stage, you always have to look vibrant and dazzling. Backstage, you cannot deny that there is still a certain degree of conformity to societal expectations just because you are not in front of any audience. Because this is the environment we are born into, and not everyone gets the advantage of the kind of desirable musical environment that we wish was more available. In the past, in the environment that I grew up in, to speak well of the United States was to risk being criticized, persecuted, and even imprisoned! Many conservative figures, during a certain period of our history, thought that speaking well of jazz was to some extent equivalent to speaking well of the United States, so that was not acceptable! I am older than my students by at least a generation, so they call me "bố" [father]. Developing jazz in Vietnam, as I see it, is like a conversation between the aged father and the young child: two different sets of mentalities of two different generations doing different things.

I want people to remember me as a jazz musician. They see me at the jazz club, playing jazz every day. Recently, after playing "Take Five," a foreign guest came to me and said, "Fantastic, that totally sounded like Paul Desmond!" I was very happy to hear that; after all, I am a Vietnamese musician playing "Take Five." Sure, I might sound like Paul Desmond, but I know that the solo improvisation was my own. I know that I have my own sound. I want my students to be able to find their own sounds. I love it when the kids try their best and experiment with new stuff on the stage. Even though they might bring out maybe only one or two nice ideas when they play, or only produce a nice lick or two when they improvise, I continue to encourage them. At least they are trying to do something new, something different. And this is where the jazz club comes in. They try it here.

To me, the jazz club is really a training school for aspiring jazz musicians to play on a real stage for a live audience. Musicians here in Hà Nội, in Vietnam, I know they will always have this jazz club to play jazz. In that sense, my financial loss over the years from operating the jazz club has been a worthy sacrifice. I could do this for so long and keep doing it because I believe in what I am doing. I believe in my ideals. With this jazz club, I have helped nurture generation after generation of jazz musicians in Vietnam, as a result of my persistence and their own individual dedication to jazz, hard work, and sacrifice. Many of them still play jazz. You can see my imprint in the story of jazz in Vietnam, here at this jazz club.

TRACK 13

Postlude

Quyền Văn Minh took the sound of his saxophone (and clarinet) all over Vietnam as a music cadre during his days in the song-and-dance troupes. As a lecturer of saxophone at the national conservatoire, Minh traveled to the provinces, from Sơn La Province in the Tây Bắc Mountains to Quảng Ninh by the Tonkin Gulf, to recruit students for the conservatoire. As a respected musician in the country, Minh is regularly invited to perform at events in different provinces and in the national capital, Hà Nội. Minh has joined goodwill visits in the mountains, such as in mid-2016, when he brought the sound of his saxophone to students staying at the newly opened dormitory of Nậm Trà Boarding School in mountainous Lai Châu. He has participated in remembrance events, such as a memorial service for a friend on February 20–21, 2019, at Sơn La Prison, where the French colonial government imprisoned a large number of Vietnamese patriots. Minh is always ready to serve with his music.

The ultimate highlight of Minh's travels across Vietnam was his trip to the Trường Sa Islands in 2014. The Trường Sa (Spratly) Islands, together with the Hoàng Sa (Paracel) Islands, are territories in Biển Đông (the East Sea, referred to as the South China Sea by China), hotly contested by multiple countries, including China.[1] In May 2014, Vietnamese citizens took to the streets in massive numbers to protest against China, following two earlier incidents in which Chinese patrol boats fired shots against Vietnamese oil exploration ships and fishing vessels. Things came to a head when China deployed the oil rig *Haiyang Shiyou* (海洋石油) 981 to Hoàng Sa waters in early May 2014, triggering the massive anti-Chinese protest.[2] His trip to Trường Sa was a way for Minh to express patriotic sentiment for his motherland with his music.

For Minh, promoting jazz in socialist Vietnam has always been about bringing this highly innovative art form to different quarters of Vietnamese society, and most importantly developing an original voice to play on "planet jazz" (to borrow E. Taylor Atkins's term). Minh's modus operandi has always been a blending of familiar Vietnamese musical sounds, the timbre of the saxophone, and his subtle, melodic improvisations on stage to coax the uninitiated Vietnamese listener to be a little more receptive to the sound of jazz. He would play for anyone in any setting, anywhere.

Figure 13.1. Nậm Trà Boarding School, Lai Châu.

Figure 13.2. Memorial service at Sơn La Prison (with permission of Ngô Ngọc Lâm).

Figure 13.3. Trường Sa Islands, 2014.

I visited the Trường Sa Islands in 2014. The trip, organized by the Ministry of Foreign Affairs, brought some fifty Việt Kiều [overseas Vietnamese] to visit the islands. We had to travel over a very long distance by ship to get to Trường Sa! But still many people tried to register to join the trip. The Association for Việt Kiều, which coorganized the trip, invited me to perform on the islands to give encouragement to the soldiers stationed there, protecting the sovereign territory of our motherland. I was very fortunate to be able to join them for ten days. It was a ten-day trip. I was very touched by the dedication of the soldiers the moment I landed on one of the islands. It was just a bare island; there was nothing there. The soldiers stationed there were basically surrounded by the sea, covered by the sun and totally exposed to the rain and wind! The moment you opened your eyes in the morning, you could only see the sea. Every morning. And every time a delegation came visiting, it felt like the atmosphere of Tết Spring Festival! And there they were, stationed to protect our sovereign territory.

I carried my saxophone everywhere I went during the visit. Every time I sat down to chat with the soldiers, I happily took out my saxophone to play a few Vietnamese songs for them. Some of the soldiers knew what a saxophone was; some did not, and that encounter with me was the first time they had ever seen or heard a saxophone. Some knew about Trần Mạnh Tuấn. And some had heard of Quyền Văn Minh. But most of them did not know about the music we play, and had never heard of jazz. I gave a formal performance on the central stage set up by the organizers for the soldiers stationed on the Trường Sa Islands. The next day, during our visit to other stations, one of the younger soldiers I met told me that it was a pity he had to miss the performance because he was on duty at the cookhouse. So I went to the cookhouse with my saxophone and played a few tunes for him and his friends. In total, I visited more than ten islands. It was unforgettable.

I wonder, how would I live if I were stationed on one of these islands? I live in a much more comfortable environment than these soldiers tasked to defend our motherland; how could I not work harder to develop jazz for Vietnam? I was honored to be able to play for these warriors. I played songs about "quê hương" [the homeland] and about the islands for them.

We made the trip during the third month of the lunar calendar, so the voyage there was relatively smooth because the sea was rather gentle. In Vietnam, we have a saying, "tháng ba, bà già đi biển" [the third month (of the lunar calendar) is when the old ladies take to the sea]. But on the islands, it was extremely hot! In the later months of the year, the weather gets rough, and the soldiers have to spend most of their time in shelters underground. I gave my all to play for these brave warriors, to give encouragement to them. I wanted to express my appreciation and to thank them for defending our country. I tried my best to bring them some joy through my music for the ten days I was visiting the islands. Sometimes, I feel, if my life were not as comfortable as it is now, perhaps I might have even worked harder! I might even be more motivated. Sometimes, when life is too comfortable, people start to find excuses and complain, why are things not like this or if only things were like that. I am in my sixties now, but I still find life meaningful and I still find life beautiful. And I still find that I have things to prove, so I know I still have to work harder.

With this trip, Quyền Văn Minh literally brought his music to the final frontier of Vietnam's sovereign territory.

As we step into the third decade of the twenty-first century, thirty years after Minh publicly introduced the sound of jazz with his first solo concert in 1988, jazz is fundamentally recognized as *chính thống* (proper mainstream) music in Vietnam, not as something one can only find in hidden alleys and underground pubs. Jazz, played by Vietnamese musicians, can be heard every night at Minh's Jazz Club, located just behind the Hà Nội Opera House. And almost every year, jazz fans in Vietnam look forward to Quyền Văn Minh's annual large-scale jazz concert. Played to a full house every time, Minh's annual concerts are held at the Hà Nội Opera House, the ultimate concert venue for any serious musician in Vietnam.

On April 6, 2008, Minh presented the first *Father, Son, and Jazz* concert at the Hà Nội Opera House. Celebrating the return of his son, Quyền Thiện Đắc, from the Berklee College of Music in Boston, this concert featured a repertoire containing compositions by Quyền Văn Minh, Quyền Thiện Đắc, and Lưu Quang

Figure 13.4. *Father, Son, and Jazz*.

Minh. More significantly, Quyền Văn Minh was no longer the lone Vietnamese name headlining a concert organized by himself to bring jazz to Vietnam, such as in 1988, 1989, and 1994. Minh was most proud and pleased to share the headline with another Vietnamese musician, namely his own son. The concert was recorded live and later released in both CD and DVD formats.

Father, Son, and Jazz: Live at the Hà Nội Opera House, April 6, 2008,
   DVD edition
Disc 1
Track 1: "St. Louis Blues" (Dixieland)
Track 2: "My Shining Hour" (Swing)
Track 3: "My Little Suede Shoes" (Bebop)
Track 4: "Line for Lyon" (Cool School)
Track 5: "The Night Has a Thousand Eyes" (Hard Bop)
Track 6: "Turn Out the Stars" (Ballad)
Track 7: "La Fiesta" (Contemporary)

Disc 2
Track 1: "The Horn Calling" (Tiếng Kèn Gọi Ai?), by Quyền Văn Minh
Track 2: "Jazz Girl" (Cô Gái Nhạc Jazz), by Lưu Quang Minh
Track 3: "Northern Wind" (Gió Bắc), by Quyền Văn Minh and Quyền Thiện Đắc
Track 4: "Inconstant Love Shore" (Bến Phải Tình), by Hà Dũng
Track 5: "Inclined to the Heart and Mind" (Hướng Tâm), by Quyền Thiện Đắc
Track 6: "Experience" (Cảm Nhận), by Quyền Văn Minh
Track 7: "A Vietnamese Traditional Character" (Chú Tễu), by Quyền Văn Minh
Musicians
Quyền Văn Minh, Saxophones
Quyền Thiện Đắc, Saxophones
Phạm Tuấn Hùng, Piano
Đào Minh Pha, Contrabass
Hà Đình Huy, Percussion
Lê Việt Hùng, Drums

In the first half of the concert, Quyền Văn Minh was able to present for the first time on the stage of the Hà Nội Opera House a comprehensive array of jazz styles, from classic Dixieland to bebop, ending with Chick Corea's fusion classic, "La Fiesta." Featuring original jazz compositions by three Vietnamese composers, namely Quyền Văn Minh, Lưu Quang Minh, and Quyền Thiện Đắc, the second half of the concert was a demonstration of the gradual growth of jazz in Vietnam in the decade after the 1994 concert, which saw the birth of Vietnamese jazz.

To outdo himself, Quyền Văn Minh organized two concerts at the Hà Nội Opera House the following year. The first, *Quyền Văn Minh with His Friends and Jazz*, held on April 6, 2009, featured the very first concert by a Vietnamese big band at the opera house. Minh had always dreamed of leading his own big band of Vietnamese musicians, to show that jazz had finally reached a certain level of proficiency and acceptance in Vietnam. With a band of Vietnamese musicians filling in complete saxophone, trumpet, trombone, and rhythm sections, and performing on the stage of the Hà Nội Opera House, this was a dream come true for Quyền Văn Minh. He spent months writing his own arrangements of standard big band tunes, adapting available scores, and arranging a few classic Vietnamese popular tunes for his band. With the jazz club still located at the spacious Lương Văn Can venue, Minh paid the musicians to come in for regular rehearsals on weekend mornings and before club operation hours on some weekdays. Minh was determined to deliver a successful concert. If *Father, Son, and Jazz* was a

Figure 13.5. *Quyền Văn Minh with His Friends and Jazz.*

fourth breakthrough concert (after the 1988, 1989, and 1994 concerts) with the featured joint participation of Quyền Thiện Đắc, this big band concert was an even bigger statement for Minh, demonstrating that one could assemble a good crowd of proficient musicians capable of playing ensemble jazz in Vietnam.

Quyền Văn Minh with His Friends and Jazz, Live at the Hà Nội Opera House, April 6, 2009, DVD edition
Disc 1
Track 1: "Night Shadow" (Big Band)
Track 2: "New York, New York" (Big Band)
Track 3: "In the Mood" (Big Band)
Track 4: "Body and Soul" (Big Band)
Track 5: "Le Soleil et Chachacha" (Big Band)
Track 6: "Sentimental Journey" (Big Band)
Track 7: "Muskat Ramble" (Big Band)

Track 8: "In a Mellow Tone" (Big Band and Đặng Nhật Quang)
Track 9: "Summertime" (Kristin and Combo Jazz)
Disc 2
Track 1: "All of Me" (Big Band and Kristin)
Track 2: "I've Got You under My Skin" (Big Band)
Track 3: "Những Phút Giây Qua" (The Passing Minutes and Seconds) (Big Band and Quốc Trường)
Track 4: "Moonlight Serenade" (Big Band)
Track 5: "Thu Hoài Niệm" (Remembrance) (Big Band and Diêu Thùy)
Track 6: "Don't Get Around Much Anymore" (Big Band and Diêu Thùy)
Track 7: "A Night in Tunisia" (Big Band)
Track 8: "Just a Gigolo" (Big Band)
Musicians
Quyền Văn Minh and the Sông Hồng Big Band

Quyền Văn Minh, Hoàng Xuân Vượng, Nguyễn Quốc Trường, and Laurent Schwab came together in 2000 to form the Sông Hồng Big Band, composed mainly of Vietnamese musicians. The band gave its first major performance at the first European Jazz Festival held in Hà Nội in 2001. After that, the Sông Hồng Big Band was assembled occasionally for major events in Hà Nội, including playing at the tenth anniversary celebration of the reestablishment of US-Vietnamese diplomatic relations. April 6, 2009, was the first time the band gave a featured performance on the stage of the Hà Nội Opera House. Minh selected a repertoire of easy-listening big band favorites and included two Vietnamese tunes. "Những Phút Giây Qua" is an original composition by band member Nguyễn Quốc Trường, while "Thu Hoài Niệm" is a popular tune written by Hà Dũng and arranged for big band by Quyền Văn Minh.

Immediately after the big band concert, on April 27, 2009, Minh presented *Father, Son, and Jazz II* at the Hà Nội Opera House. This concert was dedicated in memory of his mother.

Father, Son, and Jazz II, Live at the Hà Nội Opera House, April 27, 2009, DVD edition
Disc 1
Track 1: "Work Song"
Track 2: "Here's That Rainy Day"
Track 3: "I Can't Get Started"
Track 4: "Fly Me to the Moon"
Track 5: "Litha"
Track 6: "The More I See You"
Track 7: "Four Brothers"

Figure 13.6. *Father, Son, and Jazz II.*

Track 8: "Recado Bossa Nova"
Disc 2
Track 1: "Chợ Xa" (Distant Market Place), by Lưu Quang Minh
Track 2: "Núi Rừng Quê Ta" (Mountains and Forests of Our Homeland), by Quyền Văn Minh
Track 3: "Nhớ Về Hậu Giang" (Missing Hậu Giang), by Quyền Văn Minh
Track 4: "Winter Love," by Quyền Thiện Đắc
Track 5: "Chèo," by Quyền Thiện Đắc
Track 6: "Một Nét Huế" (A Touch of Huế), by Quyền Thiện Đắc
Track 7: "Ngẫu Hứng Nam, Bắc" (Northern and Southern Improvisations), by Quyền Thiện Đắc
Track 8: "Vũ Điệu Thăng Long" (Dance of Thăng Long), by Quyền Văn Minh

Following the format of *Father, Son, and Jazz* the year before, this concert demonstrated how jazz had continued to persist and grow in Vietnam. Not only

Figure 13.7. *Jazz with Vietnamese Lyrics.*

was it a sold-out concert, guests traveled from as far away as Sơn La Province to listen to Quyền Văn Minh and his band play jazz. Minh had planned to play his favorite original composition, "Vấn Vương," but he chose to replace this tune with "Núi Rừng Quê Ta," a song inspired by ethnic Thái folk sounds, to express his gratitude for a guest who had come all the way from Sơn La, the heartland of the ethnic Thái people in Vietnam.

In the following four years, Quyền Văn Minh kept the big band active with successive annual concerts that paid tribute to well-known Vietnamese popular songs, which he adapted and arranged. On April 12, 2010, Minh performed his sensitive arrangements of such songs for big band and vocals in the concert *Jazz with Vietnamese Lyrics* (*Jazz với ca khúc Việt Nam*) at the Hà Nội Opera House. Featuring songs of notable composers from Trịnh Công Sơn ("Hà Trắng" [White Summer], "Phôi Pha" [Fading Away], "Cát Bụi" [Sand and Dust], and "Một Cõi Đi Về" [My Own Lonely World]) to Hồng Đăng ("Hoa Sữa" [Milk

Figure 13.8. *Quyền Văn Minh and Friends with Jazz II*.

Flower]) and Trần Tiến ("Thành Phố Trẻ" [City of Youth]), this was an attempt by Minh to make jazz more endearing to Vietnamese listeners. After playing to a full house in Hà Nội, Minh took the show on the road to Hải Phòng and Hồ Chí Minh City later in the same month.

Figure 13.9. *Quyền Văn Minh and Friends with Jazz III.*

Encouraged by the enthusiastic reception of Vietnamese listeners to his big band renditions of Vietnamese popular songs, Minh organized yet another concert in late 2010. *Quyền Văn Minh and Friends with Jazz II* was held on November 29, 2010, featuring the participation of noted Vietnamese singers Tùng Dương, Mai Lan, Như Quỳnh, and Minh Biên. Joining in the celebration of the one-thousandth anniversary of Thăng Long City (Hà Nội), Minh created a program consisting of songs about Hà Nội, popular classic Vietnamese songs such as Đoàn Chuẩn's "Gửi Người Em Gái Miền Nam" (For a Girl in the South), and big band favorites. Once again, the Sông Hồng Big Band was assembled for a feature concert on the stage of the Hà Nội Opera House.

But tragedy struck when trumpeter Nguyễn Quốc Trường, a close friend of Minh's, passed away after a freak accident at home not too long after the 2010 concert. On January 10, 2012, Minh dedicated the concert *Quyền Văn Minh and Friends with Jazz III* to the memory of Nguyễn Quốc Trường. Soon after, Hoàng Xuân Vượng, a trumpeter who had released the first solo trumpet album in Vietnam and was one of the founding members of the Sông Hồng Big Band, also passed away. Hoàng Xuân Vượng's album, simply entitled *Trumpette: Hoàng Xuân Vượng*, was released in 2008 and featured a selection of popular classical pieces (e.g., "Ave Maria"), jazz tunes, and two Vietnamese popular songs about Hà Nội.[3] On October 8, 2013, Minh again gathered the members of the big band for a special concert in remembrance of Hoàng Xuân Vượng. Nguyễn Quốc Trường, Hoàng Xuân Vượng, and Quyền Văn Minh had been playing together since the early 1980s when Minh joined the Thăng Long Song-and-Dance Troupe as the lead saxophonist. A host of notable Vietnamese singers joined Minh and the Sông Hồng Big Band on stage to pay tribute to the two trumpeters. Noted vocalist Quang Thọ, who had been conferred the title of Nghệ Sĩ Nhân Dân (the People's Artist) by the government and was former dean of the Faculty of Vocals at the national music conservatoire, was one of the featured singers at both concerts.

For Quyền Văn Minh, these big band concerts held at the Hà Nội Opera House from 2009 to 2013 were significant milestones for jazz in Vietnam. In 1988 and 1989, when Minh delivered his first two solo concerts at the Hội Nhạc Sĩ to introduce jazz to the Vietnamese public, his colleagues, who were all professional musicians, pulled out of the performances for fear of being associated with the strange sound that was jazz. He had to engage the help of his brothers and friends who were merely amateur players, to accompany him on stage to perform for dignitaries of the Vietnamese music circle. Twenty years later, musicians who had made their names in classical and Vietnamese popular music joined him on stage to play and sing jazz, for five concerts in succession.

The year 2017 marked the twentieth anniversary of Minh's Jazz Club and Minh's fiftieth year of a life in music. On October 27, 2017, more than sixty musicians took turns playing on the stage of the Hà Nội Opera House to pay tribute to Quyền Văn Minh. The concert opened with "Giai Điệu Quê Hương" (Melody from Home), an original composition by Minh, performed by nine-year-old Tuệ Anh on soprano saxophone and backed by an ensemble of sixty saxophones. Tuệ Anh had only been studying with Minh for ten months when he performed at this concert. This young boy, coincidentally, is the grandson of the very friend

Figure 13.10. *Fifty Years of a Life in Music* concert.

Figure 13.11. Filming *Sắc Màu Của Jazz*.

who had let Minh listen to a vinyl record brought back from Eastern Europe that marked Minh's second encounter with jazz. True to its name, *20 năm Nhạc jazz và 50 năm Cuộc đời Âm nhạc NSƯT Quyền Văn Minh* (*Twenty Years of Jazz and Fifty Years of a Life in Music of the Eminent Artist Quyền Văn Minh*), the concert was a walk down memory lane for Quyền Văn Minh, his friends and students, and the audience. Minh began his life in music by playing at weddings in the late 1960s. He took his audience back in time with a solo performance of a polka often played at weddings in the 1960s and 1970s. With an old friend, Trần Quang Vũ from the Thăng Long Song-and-Dance days, Minh played "Spanish Eyes," another nostalgic favorite often heard at weddings in the 1970s and early 1980s. Besides these musical throwbacks, the three-and-a-half-hour extravaganza featured a good mix of standards, Minh's original compositions (played by former students and friends), and original compositions by his former students.

The concert clearly demonstrated four things about the state of jazz in Vietnam. First, Vietnamese jazz pioneers such as Minh had started out in a musical context in which jazz was fundamentally absent. Second, twenty years after Minh opened his jazz club, Vietnamese jazz musicians were able to improvise, were technically competent, and were entirely capable of playing jazz standards. Third, in the space of twenty years since Minh released his debut album of original Vietnamese jazz compositions, *Birth '99*, these individual tunes had become the standards of Vietnamese jazz, as demonstrated by Bùi Xuân Hoà's delivery of "Ngày Hội Mùa," Hùng Sơn's extended improvisation on "Giai Điệu Sapa," and Hồng Kiên's thoughtful interpretation of "Nhớ Về Hậu Giang." Fourth, the generation of Vietnamese jazz musicians after Minh are ready to take over the

Figure 13.12. *All In Live: Jazz and Friends* (photo courtesy of the Faculty of Jazz, Vietnam National Academy of Music).

work of developing jazz in Vietnam. This was most convincingly demonstrated by Quyền Thiện Đắc's soulful performance of his own composition, "Một Nét Huế" (A Touch of Huế), backed by the sophisticated piano of Nguyễn Tiến Mạnh, the new associate dean of the Faculty of Jazz at the conservatoire.

Filmmaker Manouchehr Abrontan attended the 2017 concert and was so enchanted by Minh's music that he immediately set about making an hour-long documentary about jazz in Vietnam. The documentary was funded and produced by the VTV Documentary Film Center, and Manouchehr and the production unit started filming in March 2017. In a whirlwind two-week schedule, the production crew finished filming interviews with a host of active Vietnamese jazz musicians in Hà Nội and Hồ Chí Minh City, captured live footage of nightly sessions at Minh's Jazz Club, and recorded Minh's emotional tribute to his mother at the apartment on Hàng Giấy Street. Finally airing on VTV1 during prime time on October 21, 2018, *Sắc Màu Của Jazz* (*Colors of Jazz*) is the first full-length (fifty-six minutes long) documentary about jazz in Vietnam, and the first documentary about jazz produced by the national television station's documentary film unit. Thirty years after the broadcast on national television of Quyền Văn Minh's first solo saxophone concert in 1988, in which he snuck in the sound of jazz by introducing it as "international light music," a full-length documentary about jazz in Vietnam with the word "jazz" in the title was actually made in Vietnam.[4]

On November 30, 2018, the Faculty of Jazz at the national conservatoire celebrated its fifth anniversary with the concert *All In Live: Jazz and Friends* at the conservatoire's very own concert hall. The concert was effectively a musical history of how jazz had grown into a full-scale faculty at the conservatoire. Beginning with a high-energy percussion ensemble of multiple drum sets playing in unison and exchanging fills and solos, the concert had the audience's attention right from the start. After the mandatory introduction and speeches, the main program opened with Quyền Văn Minh, introduced as the "godfather of jazz" in Vietnam, playing his original composition, "Nhớ Về Hậu Giang," first recorded some eighteen years earlier on the album *Đồng Cảm*. Minh played only one song, because the night belonged to all jazz musicians teaching and studying at the conservatoire. One after another, faculty members came out with their own groups to perform either rearranged, jazzified folk tunes or original compositions. It was a full-house concert. It would be tempting to imagine that on a stage filled with scores of professional and aspiring Vietnamese jazz musicians gathering to celebrate only the fifth anniversary of the first jazz faculty in Vietnam, this would be the only spot in Hà Nội alive with jazz played by Vietnamese musicians on that evening. But across town, behind the Hà Nội Opera House, Minh's Jazz Club was bustling as usual with its nightly double live sessions.

In the third decade of the twenty-first century, jazz is without a doubt already a part of the mainstream soundscape of Vietnam.

My name is Văn Minh, which means "to civilize," and my family name is Quyền, which means "rights," so I believe that I have the "right to lead a civilized life." I have led a dignified and civilized life in spite of the difficulties and challenges in my journey to play jazz. From the days in the song-and-dance troupes to my time at the conservatoire, I have worked in two very different types of professional musical environments. But there was always one thing that connected the two: I always asked how I could play jazz better. I never gave the excuse that I had other things to attend to and therefore wasn't able to perform to my own expectations. These two extended phases of my life, in the song-and-dance troupes and at the conservatoire, were filled with challenges. But I managed to overcome the challenges. I overcame them simply because of my love for jazz. You could say that I overcame myself because of jazz! Many times, people have asked me, "You could have done so many other things, why did you choose a path that was so steep and winding?" I was born, to put it colloquially, like a weed, deep rooted and persistent. You can cut it down, and it will still grow back. Yes, because of my love for music, I could still have had a fruitful career just playing Vietnamese popular music and ethnic folk music. To be able to play with all these great fellow Vietnamese musicians, it would have indeed already been a most fruitful and rewarding career! I would have been honored just to be able to play music among my fellow musicians in Vietnam. But I had a dream, a dream about playing jazz in Vietnam. Because of jazz, I encountered a lot of difficulties. Because of jazz, I also received a lot of happiness and enjoyment. Now I have retired from the conservatoire. That was my work with the state. But my work with the saxophone, it never ends. In 2017, I handed over ownership of Minh's Jazz Club to my son, Quyền Thiện Đắc. I hope he can continue with the work I have done to develop jazz in Vietnam and bring it to the next level.

As for myself, I have a lifelong debt to jazz. To develop jazz in Vietnam remains my ultimate mission in life.

Quyền Văn Minh is a key figure in the story of jazz in Vietnam. He is a pioneer, but he was by no means alone as the story progressed. The narrative presented here merely seeks to flesh out how life was actually experienced as jazz *came into being* in socialist Vietnam. As Minh hardened his resolve to make jazz a part of the proper mainstream soundscape after his successful recitals in 1988 and 1989, jazz in socialist Vietnam indeed branches off into a story of multiple overlapping narratives. As the collection of essays edited by Nicholas Gebhardt and Tony Whyton, *The Cultural Politics of Jazz Collectives*, so persuasively demonstrates, jazz, generally speaking, is in many ways a collective endeavor in terms of music, social relationships, and interaction with larger fields of force such as social structures, politics, and even technological change.[5] The story of how jazz began to slowly *take shape* in socialist Vietnam indeed requires an examination of the collective effort of many musicians and the slowly growing jazz audience, a topic in itself worthy of a separate book-length analytical treatment.

Jazz in Vietnam, as in other Asian countries and the formerly socialist Eastern European countries, is mediated by the passion, tenacity, and innovation of devoted musicians who saw in jazz the power of artistic self-expression. In E. Taylor Atkins's words, these musicians are "non-American artists who heeded the jazz aesthetic's demand to constantly 'innovate' and transform the music, those musicians who became leaders within their communities and nations, who approached jazz performance in original ways by transcending the hegemonic 'influence' of America's jazz titans."[6] Atkins aptly calls them the "local heroes" of jazz planet. To develop jazz in Vietnam under socialism, Quyền Văn Minh navigated an ideological dogmatism more intensive and encompassing than what was experienced in socialist Eastern Europe because of the combined pressure of the Vietnamese revolution and the succeeding Indochina wars. To give jazz a place in the pantheon of sounds in Vietnam, Quyền Văn Minh had to work along the seams of tension between tradition and modernity, between local (national) and (Western) global, that continue to haunt postcolonial Asia. The state of jazz in Vietnam today speaks volumes on Minh's devotion, tenacity, passion, and creativity. He deserves a place in the chapter of "local heroes" in the book of jazz planet, too.

NOTES

Track 1: Prelude

1. Stan BH Tan-Tangbau and Quyền Văn Minh, "Quyền Văn Minh and the Birth of Vietnamese Jazz," *Jazz Perspectives* 11, no. 2 (2018): 173–99, doi:10.1080/17494060.2019.1616871.

2. Stan BH Tan-Tangbau and Quyền Văn Minh, "Excerpts from *Quyen Van Minh: A Jazz Life Story*, the 1988–89 Solo Recitals," *Journal of Narrative Politics* 3, no. 2 (2017): 70–96.

1. Nguyễn Thụy Kha, *Thế Kỷ Âm Nhạc Việt Nam: Một Thời Đạn Bom* [*A Century of Music in Vietnam: The Period of Bullets and Bombs*] (Hà Nội: Nhà Xuất Bản Văn Học, 2017), 23.

2. Vĩnh Phúc, "Sơ khảo lịch sử tân nhạc ở Thừa Thiên Huế" [A Brief History of New Music in Thừa Thiên Huế], *Tập Chí Sông Hương*, August 31, 2017, http://tapchisonghuong.com.vn/tin-tuc/p9/c29/n25896/So-khao-lich-su-tan-nhac-o-Thua-Thien-Hue.html.

3. Nguyễn Thụy Kha, *Thế Kỷ Âm Nhạc Việt Nam: Một Thời Hoà Bình* [*A Century of Music in Vietnam: The Period of Peace*] (Hà Nội: Nhà Xuất Bản Văn Học, 2017), 350–51.

4. Huỳnh Hiếu, "Jazz và Nhạc Sĩ Việt Nam" [Jazz and Vietnamese Musicians], n.a. I came across this article from the "collection" of old magazine and newspaper clippings that Minh had accumulated over the years. Unfortunately, we could not trace the magazine's name. See also Jason Gibbs, "Saigon-Palace-Hotel 1937," Tây Bụi, September 11, 2018, http://taybui.blogspot.com/2018/09/saigon-palace-hotel-1937.html.

5. Lonán Ó Briain, "Musical Cosmopolitanism in Late-Colonial Hanoi," *Ethnomusicology Forum* 27, no. 3 (2018), 265–85, doi:10.1080/17411912.2018.1521728.

6. Jason Gibbs, "Tại Nhà hát Tây đêm 8 Juillet (1937)" [The Night of the Eighth of July at the West Theater], Tây Bụi, December 2, 2018, http://taybui.blogspot.com/search/label/đĩa%20hát; and Ó Briain, "Musical Cosmopolitanism in Late-Colonial Hanoi," 4.

7. Jason Gibbs, "The West's Songs, Our Songs: The Introduction and Adaptation of Western Popular Song in Vietnam before 1940," *Asian Music* 34, no. 1 (Autumn 2003–Winter 2004), 70.

8. Gibbs, "The West's Songs, Our Songs," 57–83.

9. Gibbs, "The West's Songs, Our Songs," 74; John C. Schafer, "The Trịnh Công Sơn Phenomenon," *Journal of Asian Studies* 66, no. 3 (2007): 602; and Jason Gibbs, "Reform and Tradition in Early Vietnamese Popular Song," *Nhạc Việt* 6 (Fall 1997): 5–34.

10. Nguyễn, *Thế Kỷ Âm Nhạc Việt Nam: Một Thời Đạn Bom*, 28–30.

11. Nguyễn, *Thế Kỷ Âm Nhạc Việt Nam: Một Thời Đạn Bom*, 6.

12. Nguyễn Công Luận, *Nationalist in the Viet Nam Wars: Memoirs of a Victim Turned Soldier* (Bloomington: Indiana University Press, 2012), Kindle ed., loc 4747.

13. Nguyễn, *Thế Kỷ Âm Nhạc Việt Nam: Một Thời Đạn Bom*, 46–52, 168–72.

14. Nguyễn, *Thế Kỷ Âm Nhạc Việt Nam: Một Thời Hoà Bình*, 354.

15. Nguyễn, *Thế Kỷ Âm Nhạc Việt Nam: Một Thời Đạn Bom*, 314–15; and Nguyễn, *Nationalist in the Viet Nam Wars*, loc 4771.

16. Nguyễn, *Thế Kỷ Âm Nhạc Việt Nam: Một Thời Đạn Bom*, 8; and Nguyễn, *Nationalist in the Viet Nam Wars*, loc 4798.

17. Nguyễn, *Thế Kỷ Âm Nhạc Việt Nam: Một Thời Đạn Bom*, 14.

18. For a recent overview on the subject of "jazz diplomacy," see Yoshiomi Saito, *The Global Politics of Jazz in the Twentieth Century: Cultural Diplomacy and "American Music"* (London: Routledge, 2019).

19. Jason Gibbs, "Buddy Rich đến Sài Gòn năm 1961" [Buddy Rich in Saigon, 1961], Tây Bụi, December 26, 2013, http://taybui.blogspot.com/2013/12/buddy-rich-en-sai-gon-nam-1961.html.

20. Donald L. Maggin, *Stan Getz: A Life in Jazz* (New York: William Morrow, 1996), 233.

21. Barley Norton, "Music and Censorship in Vietnam since 1954," in *The Oxford Handbook of Music Censorship*, ed. Patricia Hall (Oxford: Oxford University Press, 2015), doi:10.1093/oxfordhb/9780199733163.013.29.

Track 2: Minh's Jazz Club

1. Howard Schultz claims this ambience of aroma, style, comfort, and jazz as the signature Starbucks experience in Howard Schultz and Dori Jones Yang, *Pour Your Heart Into It: How Starbucks Built a Company One Cup at a Time* (New York: Hyperion, 1997), 12–13, 175.

2. See, for example, the *Saigon Times*, September 10, 1999.

3. Friends of Vietnam Heritage, *Vignettes of French Culture in Hanoi* (Hà Nội: Gioi Publishers, 2008), 29.

4. Louis Cha (查良鏞), better known by his pen name, Jinyong (金庸), is perhaps the most famous Chinese novelist in the genre of heroic kung fu (chivalry, martial arts) (武俠) stories set in actual historical periods. Almost all of his novels have been translated into Vietnamese.

5. William Minor, *Jazz Journeys to Japan: The Heart Within* (Ann Arbor: University of Michigan Press, 2004), 165–74.

Track 3: Growing Up

1. Stan BH Tan, "Dust beneath the Mist: State and Frontier Formation in the Central Highlands under the First Republic of Vietnam, the 1955–1961 Period," PhD diss., Australian National University, 2006, chap. 4.

2. Philippe Pappin, *Lịch Sử Hà Nội* [*A History of Hanoi*], trans. Mặc Thu Hương (Hà Nội: Nhà Xuất Bản Thế Giới, 2016), 290.

3. Georges Boudarel and Nguyen Van Ky, *Hanoi: City of the Rising Dragon*, trans. Claire Duiker (Lanham, MD: Rowman and Littlefield, 2002), Kindle ed., loc 2080.

4. Pappin, *Lịch Sử Hà Nội*, 295.

5. Boudarel and Nguyen, *Hanoi: City of the Rising Dragon*, loc 2163.

6. Boudarel and Nguyen, *Hanoi: City of the Rising Dragon*, chap. 5; and Pappin, *Lịch Sử Hà Nội*, 295–98.

7. Đặng Phong, *Phá Rào Trong Kinh Tế Vào Đêm Trước Đổi Mới (Tái Bản Lần Thứ 6)* [*Fence Breaking in the Economy the Night before Đổi Mới*, 6th printing] (Hà Nội: Nhà Xuất Bản Trí Thức, 2017), 19–20.

8. Ngô Minh, *Sống Thời Bao Cấp (Tái Bản Lần Thứ 2)* [*Living in the Subsidy Period*, 2nd printing] (Hà Nội: Nhà Xuất Bản Hội Nhã Văn, 2018).

9. For further reading on the Second Indochina War, see William S. Turley, *The Second Indochina War: A Concise Political and Military History*, 2nd ed. (Lanham, MD: Rowman and Littlefield, 2009).

10. Pappin, *Lịch Sử Hà Nội*, 300–303.
11. Nguyễn, *Thế Kỷ Âm Nhạc Việt Nam: Một Thời Đạn Bom*, 450–52.
12. Edward Miller, *Misalliance: Ngo Dinh Diem, the United States, and the Fate of South Vietnam* (Cambridge, MA: Harvard University Press, 2013), Kindle ed., loc 3921; and Jessica Chapman, *Cauldron of Resistance: Ngo Dinh Diem, the United States, and 1950s Southern Vietnam* (Ithaca, NY: Cornell University Press, 2013), Kindle ed., loc 3952.
13. Nguyễn, *Thế Kỷ Âm Nhạc Việt Nam: Một Thời Đạn Bom*, 453.
14. Hữu Thọ, *Đi Khai Hoang Tây Bắc* [*Pioneering in the Northwest*] (Hà Nội: Nhà Xuất Bản Nông Thôn, 1963), 7.
15. For an insightful account of internal migration to the uplands, see Andrew Hardy, *Red Hills: Migrants and the State in Vietnam* (Copenhagen: Nordic Institute of Asian Studies Press, 2003).
16. For a biographical account of Willis Conover and the *Music USA: Jazz Hour* program, see Terence M. Ripmaster, *Willis Conover: Broadcasting Jazz to the World* (New York: iUniverse, 2007).

Track 4: Interlude I

1. Marta Domurat-Linde, "From 'Jazz in Poland' to 'Polish Jazz,'" in *Meanings of Jazz in State Socialism*, ed. Gertrud Pickhan and Rüdiger Ritter (Frankfurt: Peter Lang, 2016), 85.
2. Yvetta Kajanová, "Jazz Artists in the Former Czechoslovak Socialist Republic and Their Conflicts with the Socialist Ideology," in *Jazz from Socialist Realism to Postmodernism*, ed. Yvetta Kajanová, Gertrud Pickhan, and Rüdiger Ritter (Frankfurt: Peter Lang, 2016), 130.
3. Frederick S. Starr, *Red and Hot: The Fate of Jazz in the Soviet Union* (New York: Limelight Editions, 1994), 37–129.
4. Frederick S. Starr, "The Music of the Gross, 1928–1931," in *Jazz Planet*, ed. E. Taylor Atkins (Jackson: University Press of Mississippi, 2003), Kindle ed., loc 1844–49.
5. Starr, "The Music of the Gross," loc 1824.
6. Starr, "The Music of the Gross," loc 1805–910.
7. Penny Von Eschen, *Satchmo Blows Up the World: Jazz Ambassadors Play the Cold War* (Cambridge, MA: Harvard University Press, 2006), 95.
8. Domurat-Linde, "From 'Jazz in Poland' to 'Polish Jazz,'" 82.
9. Domurat-Linde, "From 'Jazz in Poland' to 'Polish Jazz,'" 84–86.
10. Jaroslaw Szurek, "Subversive Sounds: Music and Censorship in Communist Poland," *Music Reference Services Quarterly* 11, no. 2 (2008): 146.
11. Domurat-Linde, "From 'Jazz in Poland' to 'Polish Jazz,'" 84–86.
12. Keith Hatschek, "The Impact of American Jazz Diplomacy in Poland during the Cold War Era," *Jazz Perspectives* 4, no. 3 (2010), 260–61.
13. Domurat-Linde, "From 'Jazz in Poland' to 'Polish Jazz,'" 85–86.
14. Gergő Havadi, "Individualists, Traditionalists, Revolutionaries, or Opportunists? The Political and Social Constellations of Jazz in Hungary during the 1950s–1960s," in *Meanings of Jazz in State Socialism*, ed. Gertrud Pickhan and Rüdiger Ritter (Frankfurt: Peter Lang, 2016), 132.
15. Havadi, "Individualists, Traditionalists, Revolutionaries, or Opportunists?," 119–25.
16. Uta G. Poiger, "Searching for Proper New Music: Jazz in Cold War Germany," in *German Pop Culture: How "American" Is It?*, ed. Agnes C. Mueller (Ann Arbor: University of Michigan Press, 2004), 83.

17. Christian Schmidt-Rost, "Freedom within Limitations: Getting Access to Jazz in the GDR and PRP between 1945 and 1961," in *Jazz behind the Iron Curtain*, ed. Gertrud Pickhan and Rüdiger Ritter (Frankfurt: Peter Lang, 2010), 227–28.

18. Schmidt-Rost, "Freedom within Limitations," 230–31.

19. Danielle Fosler-Lussier, *Music in America's Cold War Diplomacy* (Berkeley: University of California Press, 2015), 77–100.

20. Hatschek, "The Impact of American Jazz Diplomacy," 270.

21. Schmidt-Rost, "Freedom within Limitations," 229.

22. Von Eschen, *Satchmo Blows Up the World*, 13.

23. For a detailed analysis of Willis Conover's *Music USA* program, see Mark A. Breckenridge, "Willis Conover's International Jazz Diplomacy through Fandom: The *Friends of Music USA Newsletter* (1964–1969)," *Jazz Perspectives* 7, no. 2 (2013): 91–109.

24. Hatschek, "The Impact of American Jazz Diplomacy," 270–71.

25. Lisa E. Davenport, *Jazz Diplomacy: Promoting America in the Cold War Era* (Jackson: University Press of Mississippi, 2009), 38–61.

26. Domurat-Linde, "From 'Jazz in Poland' to 'Polish Jazz,'" 87.

27. Hatschek, "The Impact of American Jazz Diplomacy," 270.

28. Rüdiger Ritter, "Broadcasting Jazz into the Eastern Bloc: Cold War Weapon or Cultural Exchange? The Example of Willis Conover," *Jazz Perspectives* 7, no. 2 (2013): 116.

29. Hatschek, "The Impact of American Jazz Diplomacy," 271.

30. Havadi, "Individualists, Traditionalists, Revolutionaries, or Opportunists?," 122.

31. Von Eschen, *Satchmo Blows Up the World*, 6.

32. Fosler-Lussier, *Music in America's Cold War Diplomacy*, 146–73.

33. Von Eschen, *Satchmo Blows Up the World*, 9–12, 67.

34. Von Eschen, *Satchmo Blows Up the World*, 27, 43, 47.

35. Fosler-Lussier, *Music in America's Cold War Diplomacy*, chap. 7; and Von Eschen, *Satchmo Blows Up the World*, 92–94.

36. Von Eschen, *Satchmo Blows Up the World*, 185–86.

37. Von Eschen, *Satchmo Blows Up the World*, 50.

38. Hatschek, "The Impact of American Jazz Diplomacy," 287–88.

39. Von Eschen, *Satchmo Blows Up the World*, 206–7.

40. Von Eschen, *Satchmo Blows Up the World*, 215.

41. Von Eschen, *Satchmo Blows Up the World*, 208–10.

42. Domurat-Linde, "From 'Jazz in Poland' to 'Polish Jazz,'" 95.

43. Von Eschen, *Satchmo Blows Up the World*, 250.

44. Gertrud Pickhan and Rüdiger Ritter, introduction to *Meanings of Jazz in State Socialism*, ed. Gertrud Pickhan and Rüdiger Ritter (Frankfurt: Peter Lang, 2016), 10.

45. Starr, "The Music of the Gross," loc 1862.

46. Domurat-Linde, "From 'Jazz in Poland' to 'Polish Jazz,'" 88–89.

47. Rüdiger Ritter, "Jazz in State Socialism: A Playground of Refusal?," in *Meanings of Jazz in State Socialism*, ed. Gertrud Pickhan and Rüdiger Ritter (Frankfurt: Peter Lang, 2016), 25.

48. Poiger, "Searching for Proper New Music," 87.

49. Poiger, "Searching for Proper New Music," 90–91.

50. Günther Huesmann, "After 1945: Jazz in Germany," Goethe-Institut, September 2009, https://www.goethe.de/en/kul/mus/gen/jaz/ruc/4932331.html.

51. Ritter, "Broadcasting Jazz into the Eastern Bloc," 127.

52. Starr, *Red and Hot*, 144–56.

53. Benjamin J. Beresford, "Rhapsody in Red: Jazz and a Soviet Public Sphere under Stalin," PhD diss., Arizona State University, 2017, 71–72.
54. Beresford, "Rhapsody in Red," 74.
55. Starr, "The Music of the Gross," loc 1895.
56. Beresford, "Rhapsody in Red," 66.
57. Beresford, "Rhapsody in Red," 76.
58. Beresford, "Rhapsody in Red," 78.
59. Domurat-Linde, "From 'Jazz in Poland' to 'Polish Jazz,'" 84.
60. Domurat-Linde, "From 'Jazz in Poland' to 'Polish Jazz,'" 88.
61. Domurat-Linde, "From 'Jazz in Poland' to 'Polish Jazz,'" 94.
62. For a detailed analysis of the development of Polish jazz, see Igor Pietraszewski, *Jazz in Poland: Improvised Freedom*, trans. Lucyna Stetkiewicz (Frankfurt: Peter Lang, 2014).
63. Domurat-Linde, "From 'Jazz in Poland' to 'Polish Jazz,'" 96.
64. Adrian Popan, "Jazz Revival in Romania, 1964–1971," in *Jazz behind the Iron Curtain*, ed. Gertrud Pickhan and Rüdiger Ritter (Frankfurt: Peter Lang, 2010), 201.
65. Popan, "Jazz Revival in Romania," 202.
66. Popan, "Jazz Revival in Romania," 213.
67. Kajanová, "Jazz Artists in the Former Czechoslovak Socialist Republic," 121.
68. Kajanová, "Jazz Artists in the Former Czechoslovak Socialist Republic," 128.
69. Kajanová, "Jazz Artists in the Former Czechoslovak Socialist Republic," 120–21.
70. Yvetta Kajanová, "Communism and the Emergence of the Central European Jazz School," *Journal of Literature and Art Studies* 2, no. 6 (June 2012): 630.
71. Domurat-Linde, "From 'Jazz in Poland' to 'Polish Jazz,'" 96.
72. Von Eschen, *Satchmo Blows Up the World*, 190.
73. Havadi, "Individualists, Traditionalists, Revolutionaries, or Opportunists?," 141.
74. Havadi, "Individualists, Traditionalists, Revolutionaries, or Opportunists?," 138.
75. Hatschek, "The Impact of American Jazz Diplomacy," 267.
76. Havadi, "Individualists, Traditionalists, Revolutionaries, or Opportunists?," 150.
77. Peter Motyčka, "The Jazz Section: A Platform of Freedom in Czechoslovakia," in *Jazz behind the Iron Curtain*, ed. Gertrud Pickhan and Rüdiger Ritter (Frankfurt: Peter Lang, 2010), 217.
78. Domurat-Linde, "From 'Jazz in Poland' to 'Polish Jazz,'" 80.
79. Domurat-Linde, "From 'Jazz in Poland' to 'Polish Jazz,'" 94.
80. Kajanová, "Jazz Artists in the Former Czechoslovak Socialist Republic," 130.
81. Havadi, "Individualists, Traditionalists, Revolutionaries, or Opportunists?," 141.
82. Schmidt-Rost, "Freedom within Limitations," 236.
83. Gergő Havadi, "An Individual Subculture Reflected in Domestic Spies' Reports: Hungarian Jazz in the Socialist Period," in *Jazz behind the Iron Curtain*, ed. Gertrud Pickhan and Rüdiger Ritter (Frankfurt: Peter Lang, 2010), 192.
84. Havadi, "Individualists, Traditionalists, Revolutionaries, or Opportunists?,"147.
85. Miroslav Zahradník, "Jazz Personalities after the Downfall of the Iron Curtain: Matúš Jakabčic and His Contribution to Slovak Jazz," in *Jazz from Socialist Realism to Postmodernism*, ed. Yvetta Kajanová, Gertrud Pickhan, and Rüdiger Ritter (Frankfurt: Peter Lang, 2016), 246–51.
86. Hatschek, "The Impact of American Jazz Diplomacy," 267.
87. Ritter, "Jazz in State Socialism," 25.
88. Havadi, "Individualists, Traditionalists, Revolutionaries, or Opportunists?," 141.
89. Havadi, "An Individual Subculture Reflected in Domestic Spies' Reports," 193.

90. Schmidt-Rost, "Freedom within Limitations," 232.
91. Popan, "Jazz Revival in Romania," 205.
92. Ritter, "Jazz in State Socialism," 21–22.
93. Ritter, "Broadcasting Jazz into the Eastern Bloc," 128.
94. Motyčka, "The Jazz Section," 216.
95. Motyčka, "The Jazz Section," 221–22.
96. Kajanová, "Jazz Artists in the Former Czechoslovak Socialist Republic," 133.
97. Havadi, "An Individual Subculture Reflected in Domestic Spies' Reports," 193–94.
98. Havadi, "An Individual Subculture Reflected in Domestic Spies' Reports," 192.

Track 5: Encountering Jazz Again

1. David Marr, "A Brief History of Local Government in Vietnam," in *Beyond Hanoi: Local Government in Vietnam*, ed. Benedict J. Tria Kerkvliet and David Marr (Singapore: Institute of Southeast Asian Studies, 2004), 45.

2. Grażyna Szymańska-Matusiewicz, "The Vietnamese Communities in Central and Eastern Europe as Part of the Global Vietnamese Diaspora," *Central and Eastern European Migration Review* 4, no. 1 (2015): 5.

3. Alena K. Alamgir, "Race Is Elsewhere: State-Socialist Ideology and the Racialisation of Vietnamese Workers in Czechoslovakia," *Race and Class* 54, no. 4 (2017): 71–72.

4. Christina Schwenkel, "Rethinking Asian Mobilities: Socialist Migration and Post-Socialist Repatriation of Vietnamese Contract Workers in East Germany," *Critical Asian Studies* 46, no. 2 (2014): 248, doi:10.1080/14672715.2014.898453.

5. Mike Dennis, "Working under Hammer and Sickle: Vietnamese Workers in the German Democratic Republic, 1980–89," *German Politics* 16, no. 3 (2007): 348–51, doi:10.1080/09644000701532700.

6. Jason Gibbs, "How Does Hanoi Rock? The Way to Rock and Roll in Vietnam," *Asian Music* 39, no. 1 (Winter–Spring 2008): 5–25.

7. Huỳnh, "Jazz và Nhạc Sĩ Việt Nam."

8. Nhu-Ngoc Thuy Ong, "Governing Music in Vietnam: From Socialist to Post-Socialist Use of Nationalism," PhD diss., University of California, Irvine, 2009, 87–104. See also Philip Taylor, "Music as a 'Neocolonial Poison' in Postwar Southern Vietnam," *Crossroads: An Interdisciplinary Journal of Southeast Asian Studies* 14, no. 1 (2000): 112.

9. For insightful background reading about Trịnh Công Sơn, see Schafer, "The Trịnh Công Sơn Phenomenon."

10. Taylor, "Music as a 'Neocolonial Poison,'" 104. See also Jason Gibbs, "Cấm lưu hành, phổ biến các bản nhạc, đĩa hát xuất bản trước ngày 30-4-1975" [Prohibiting the Circulation and Availability of Music and Records Published before April 20, 1975], Tây Bụi, January 6, 2019, http://taybui.blogspot.com/2019/01/cam-luu-hanh-pho-bien-cac-ban-nhac-dia.html.

11. Taylor, "Music as a 'Neocolonial Poison,'" 122.

12. Cửu Long Giang, "Thực chất của cái gọi là nghệ thuật âm nhạc Sàigòn cũ" [The Essence of So-Called Arts in Old Saigon], *Văn Hoá Nghệ Thuật* 6 (1977): 39; cited in Taylor, "Music as a 'Neocolonial Poison,'" 122–23.

13. Nhu-Ngoc, "Governing Music in Vietnam," 87–104.

14. Nguyen Long with Harry H. Kendall, *After Saigon Fell: Daily Life under the Vietnamese Communists* (Berkeley: Institute of East Asian Studies, University of California, 1981), 77–79.

Track 6: Berlin, 1987

1. Nguyễn, *Thế Kỷ Âm Nhạc Việt Nam: Một Thời Hoà Bình*, 259.
2. Gibbs, "How Does Hanoi Rock?," 12.
3. Norton, "Music and Censorship in Vietnam."

Track 7: Solo Recitals

1. *Báo Hà Nội Mới*, October 14, 1989, 4.
2. Nhu-Ngoc, "Governing Music in Vietnam," 94–100.
3. Trần Hùng, "Nhà soạn nhạc Đàm Linh" [Đàm Linh, the Composer], in *Tự Hào Nửa Thế Kỷ Hội Nhạc Sĩ Việt Nam (1957–2007)* [*Taking Pride in Half a Century of the Association of Musicians of Vietnam (1957–2007)*], ed. Cát Vận, Nguyễn Thụy Kha, Quốc Đông, and Phạm Phúc Hải (Hà Nội: Hội Nhạc Sĩ Việt Nam, 2007), 319–20.
4. Cát Vận, Nguyễn Thụy Kha, Quốc Đông, and Phạm Phúc Hải, eds., *Tự Hào Nửa Thế Kỷ Hội Nhạc Sĩ Việt Nam (1957–2007)* [*Taking Pride in Half a Century of the Association of Musicians of Vietnam (1957–2007)*] (Hà Nội: Hội Nhạc Sĩ Việt Nam, 2007), 722–23.
5. Hoàng Vân, "30 năm chặng đường đầu tiên của nền âm nhạc khí nhạc Việt Nam" [The First Thirty Years of Vietnamese Instrumental Music], in *Tự Hào Nửa Thế Kỷ Hội Nhạc Sĩ Việt Nam (1957–2007)* [Taking Pride in Half a Century of the Association of Musicians of Vietnam (1957–2007)], ed. Cát Vận, Nguyễn Thụy Kha, Quốc Đông, and Phạm Phúc Hải (Hà Nội: Hội Nhạc Sĩ Việt Nam, 2007), 398–401.
6. Cát Vận et al., *Tự Hào Nửa Thế Kỷ Hội Nhạc Sĩ Việt Nam*, 722–23.
7. Bùi Gia Tường, "Hội Nhạc Sĩ Việt Nam—Ngôi nhà chung của tất cả chúng ta" [Association of Musicians of Vietnam: Our Common Home], in *Tự Hào Nửa Thế Kỷ Hội Nhạc Sĩ Việt Nam (1957–2007)* [Taking Pride in Half a Century of the Association of Musicians of Vietnam (1957–2007)], ed. Cát Vận, Nguyễn Thụy Kha, Quốc Đông, and Phạm Phúc Hải (Hà Nội: Hội Nhạc Sĩ Việt Nam, 2007), 679–80.
8. Quang Nghi, "Nghệ Sĩ Quyền Văn Minh với vẻ đẹp của tiếng kèn saxo" [The Artist Quyền Văn Minh and the Beauty of the Saxophone], *Âm Nhạc* 4, no. 12 (1989): 11.
9. Ritter, "Jazz in State Socialism," 36.

Track 8: Vietnamese Jazz

1. Vietnamese musicians usually refer to the opera house as simply Nhà Hát Lớn (the Big Concert Hall).
2. *Khèn* refers to the *qeej*, a reed pipe used by the Hmong people, an ethnic minority who live in the uplands of northern Vietnam and other parts of the Southeast Asian massif. "Vấn Vương" was translated as "Sentiments" when Minh released the song on his debut album, *Birth '99*. I have translated it as "Meditations" in this book, based on my understanding of the story behind the song as told by Minh.
3. Trần Quang Hải, "Vietnamese Music in Exile since 1975 and Musical Life in Vietnam since Perestroika," *World of Music* 43, nos. 2–3 (2001): 110.
4. Philip Taylor, *Fragments of the Present: Searching for Modernity in Vietnam's South* (Crows Nest, Australia: Allen and Unwin, 2001), 119–32.
5. Tạ Bôn is perhaps the most famous Vietnamese solo violinist of his generation and

a respected professor of violin in the Socialist Republic of Vietnam. He was trained in prestigious music conservatoires in China (the Chinese Central Conservatoire of Music) and the Soviet Union (the Tchaikovsky Conservatoire in Moscow). Tạ Bôn was deputy director of the Hà Nội National Music Conservatoire of Vietnam from 1979 to 1988. See Nguyễn, *Thế Kỷ Âm Nhạc Việt Nam: Một Thời Đạn Bom*, 601–5.

6. For an insightful commentary on Trịnh Công Sơn's philosophy, see John C. Schafer, "Death, Buddhism, and Existentialism in the Songs of Trịnh Công Sơn," *Journal of Vietnamese Studies* 2, no. 1 (February 2007): 144–86.

7. Trịnh Công Sơn, "Giấc mơ Hạ trắng," June 16, 2015, https://trinhcongsonblog.word press.com/2015/06/16/giac-mo-ha-trang/.

8. E. Taylor Atkins, *Blue Nippon: Authenticating Jazz in Japan* (Durham, NC: Duke University Press, 2001), Kindle ed., chap. 6.

9. Ritter, "Broadcasting Jazz into the Eastern Bloc," 112–13.

10. Domurat-Linde, "From 'Jazz in Poland' to 'Polish Jazz,'" 94.

11. E. Taylor Atkins, "Toward a Global History of Jazz," in *Jazz Planet*, ed. E. Taylor Atkins (Jackson: University Press of Mississippi, 2003), Kindle ed., loc 189.

12. Zahradník, "Jazz Personalities after the Downfall of the Iron Curtain," 262.

13. Atkins, "Toward a Global History of Jazz," loc 154.

Track 9: Teaching Jazz

1. Deborah Rosen, "Music Training and Cultural Transmission: A Study of Piano Pedagogy and the Transmission of Culture in Vietnam and Thailand," PhD diss., Claremont Graduate University, 1998, 20–24.

2. Somjit Saysouvanh, Suphanni Luebunchu, and Athe Nantachak, "Research Brief: Instruction Process on the Violin Performances of Great Teachers at Vietnam National Academy of Music," *International Forum of Teaching and Studies* 10, no. 2 (2014): 44.

3. Lưu Quang Minh, "Đào tạo tài năng nhạc Jazz trong thời kỳ hội nhập quốc tế," *Tạp chí Giáo dục Âm nhạc* 3, no. 103 (2016).

4. A memorial meal organized in remembrance of a person who has passed away.

Track 10: Interlude II

1. Eugene Marlow, *Jazz in China: From Dance Hall Music to Individual Freedom of Expression* (Jackson: University Press of Mississippi, 2018), Kindle ed., loc 1055.

2. Li Mo, "A History of Jazz in China: From Yellow Music to Jazz Revival in Beijing," master's thesis, Kent State University, 2018, 99–100, 104–7.

3. Marlow, *Jazz in China*, loc 543.

4. Marlow, *Jazz in China*, loc 1431.

5. Gui Hu Zi [鬼虎子], "闻名上海的四大舞厅" [The Four Famous Dance Halls in Shanghai], World Show, April 11, 2018, http://www.worldshow.com.cn/frontViewInfo Action!news.htm?newsId=78094.

6. Richie C. Quirino, *Pinoy Jazz Traditions* (Pasig City, Philippines: Anvil Publishing, 2004), 20.

7. Li, "A History of Jazz in China," 107–9.

8. Chen Chen, "A Study of the Localization of Jazz in Shanghai," master's thesis, Shanghai Normal University, 2005; cited in Li, "A History of Jazz in China," 108.

9. Li, "A History of Jazz in China," 108–9.
10. Andrew Jones, *Yellow Music: Media Culture and Colonial Modernity in the Chinese Jazz Age* (Durham, NC: Duke University Press, 2001), Kindle ed., loc 155.
11. Jones, *Yellow Music*, loc 1358.
12. Jones, *Yellow Music*, loc 198.
13. Li, "A History of Jazz in China," 143–47.
14. Marlow, *Jazz in China*, app. I, app. II.
15. Marlow, *Jazz in China*, loc 1902.
16. Marlow, *Jazz in China*, loc 3263–3291.
17. Marlow, *Jazz in China*, loc 3298–3309.
18. Marlow, *Jazz in China*, loc 4775.
19. Marlow, *Jazz in China*, loc 4832–4838.
20. Marlow, *Jazz in China*, loc 4804.
21. Marlow, *Jazz in China*, loc 2653.
22. Li, "A History of Jazz in China," 240–41.
23. Ling Yun and Shi Er, "The Development of Jazz Should Start with the Tradition: Liu Yuan on Jazz," *News of Musical Lives*, December 6, 1996; cited in Li, "A History of Jazz in China," 241–42.
24. Quirino, *Pinoy Jazz Traditions*, 12–13.
25. Peter Keppy, "Southeast Asia in the Age of Jazz: Locating Popular Culture in the Colonial Philippines and Indonesia," *Journal of Southeast Asian Studies* 44, no. 3 (2013): 450.
26. Alex R. Castro, "Meet the Force Who Ruled the Philippine Jazz Age," *Town and Country*, July 1, 2018, https://www.townandcountry.ph/people/heritage/borromeo-lou-profile-a2087-20180701-lfrm2. See also Keppy, "Southeast Asia in the Age of Jazz," 449.
27. Atkins, "Toward a Global History of Jazz," loc 87.
28. Filipinas Heritage Library, "Jazz Music in the Philippines," Himig Collection, http://www.himig.com.ph/features/61-jazz-music-in-the-philippines; and Marlow, *Jazz in China*, loc 1062–1075.
29. Keppy, "Southeast Asia in the Age of Jazz," 454.
30. Filipinas Heritage Library, "Jazz Music in the Philippines."
31. Quirino, *Pinoy Jazz Traditions*, 193.
32. Richie C. Quirino and Collis Davis, dirs., *Pinoy Jazz: The Story of Jazz in the Philippines*, Culture Unplugged Studios, 2006, http://www.cultureunplugged.com/documentary/watch-online/filmedia/play/377/Pinoy-Jazz-The-Story-of-Jazz-in-the-Philippines.
33. Quirino, *Pinoy Jazz Traditions*, 37–38.
34. Filipinas Heritage Library, "Jazz Music in the Philippines."
35. Filipinas Heritage Library, "Jazz Music in the Philippines."
36. Quirino and Davis, *Pinoy Jazz*.
37. Quirino and Davis, *Pinoy Jazz*.
38. "The High Notes of a Musical Life," *The Nation* (Bangkok), October 17, 2016, https://www.nationthailand.com/life/30297811.
39. "The King of Jazz," *Bangkok Post*, October 25, 2016, https://www.bangkokpost.com/learning/learning-entertainment/1115037/king-of-jazz.
40. "The King of Jazz," *Bangkok Post*.
41. "The King of Jazz," *Bangkok Post*.
42. "The High Notes of a Musical Life," *The Nation*.
43. Larry Carlton, comp., *The Jazz King: The Musical Compositions of H.M. King Bhumibol Adulyadej*, 335 Records, 2018.
44. Von Eschen, *Satchmo Blows Up the World*, 45–46.

45. Mario Dunkel, "'Jazz—Made in Germany' and the Transatlantic Beginnings of Jazz Diplomacy," in *Music and Diplomacy from the Early Modern Era to the Present*, ed. Rebekah Ahrendt, Mark Ferraguto, and Damien Mahiet (New York: Palgrave Macmillan, 2014), 159.

46. Dunkel, "Jazz—Made in Germany," 160.

47. "The High Notes of a Musical Life," *The Nation*.

48. Mahidol University College of Music, "Thailand International Jazz Conference (TIJC) 2018," https://www.music.mahidol.ac.th/events/thailand-international-jazz-conference-tijc-2018/.

49. Silpakorn University Faculty of Music, "Thailand Jazz Competition 2015," https://www.music.su.ac.th/thailand-jazz-competition-2015-3/#pll_switcher.

50. Gisa Jähnichen, "Jazz in Kuala Lumpur," *Jazz Research Journal* 4, no. 2 (2010): 147.

51. Jähnichen, "Jazz in Kuala Lumpur," 147–48.

52. Jähnichen, "Jazz in Kuala Lumpur," 149.

53. Jähnichen, "Jazz in Kuala Lumpur," 150.

54. Elaine Lau, "In Conversation: Groove in Motion," Options lifestyle pullout, *The Edge*, no. 840 (January 10–16, 2011); cited in Jähnichen, "Jazz in Kuala Lumpur," 152.

55. Jähnichen, "Jazz in Kuala Lumpur," 151.

56. Jähnichen, "Jazz in Kuala Lumpur," 160.

57. Craig A. Lockhard, *Dance of Life: Popular Music and Politics in Southeast Asia* (Honolulu: University of Hawai'i Press, 1998), 246; cited in Jähnichen, "Jazz in Kuala Lumpur," 160.

58. Jähnichen, "Jazz in Kuala Lumpur," 162.

59. Andrew McGraw, "The Ambivalent Freedoms of Indonesian Jazz," *Jazz Perspectives* 6, no. 3 (2012): 276–77.

60. Keppy, "Southeast Asia in the Age of Jazz," 457.

61. Philip Yampolsky et al., "Indonesia," in Grove Music Online, http://www.oxfordmusiconline.com/subscriber/article/grove/music/42890pg8; quoted in McGraw, "The Ambivalent Freedoms of Indonesian Jazz," 282.

62. McGraw, "The Ambivalent Freedoms of Indonesian Jazz," 286.

63. McGraw, "The Ambivalent Freedoms of Indonesian Jazz," 287.

64. Oki Rahadianto Sutopo and Pam Nilan, "The Constrained Position of Young Musicians in the Yogyakarta Jazz Community," *Asian Music* 49, no. 1 (Winter–Spring 2018): 39.

65. Sutopo and Nilan, "The Constrained Position of Young Musicians," 39.

66. McGraw, "The Ambivalent Freedoms of Indonesian Jazz," 294.

67. Sutopo and Nilan, "The Constrained Position of Young Musicians," 41.

68. Sutopo and Nilan, "The Constrained Position of Young Musicians," 42.

69. McGraw, "The Ambivalent Freedoms of Indonesian Jazz," 302.

70. Warren R. Pinckney Jr., "Jazz in India: Perspectives on Historical Development and Musical Acculturation," *Asian Music* 21, no. 1 (Autumn 1989–Winter 1990): 36.

71. Naresh Fernandes, *Taj Mahal Fox Trot: The Story of Bombay's Jazz Age* (New Delhi: Roli Books, 2016), 77–78.

72. Pinckney, "Jazz in India," 37.

73. Stephane Dorin, "Jazz and Race in Colonial India: The Role of Anglo-Indian Musicians in the Diffusion of Jazz in Calcutta," *Jazz Research Journal* 4, no. 2 (2010): 134.

74. Tanya Kalmanovitch, "Indo-Jazz Fusion: Jazz and Karnatak Music in Contact," PhD diss., University of Alberta, 2008, 50–52.

75. Dorin, "Jazz and Race in Colonial India," 134.

76. Pinckney, "Jazz in India," 38.

77. Kalmanovitch, "Indo-Jazz Fusion," 52.
78. Fernandes, *Taj Mahal Fox Trot*, 141.
79. Kalmanovitch, "Indo-Jazz Fusion," 56.
80. Fernandes, *Taj Mahal Fox Trot*, 141.
81. Fernandes, *Taj Mahal Fox Trot*, 142.
82. Fernandes, *Taj Mahal Fox Trot*, 148–49.
83. Pinckney, "Jazz in India," 41.
84. Kalmanovitch, "Indo-Jazz Fusion," 66.
85. Pinckney, "Jazz in India," 46.
86. Pinckney, "Jazz in India," 46.
87. Pinckney, "Jazz in India," 49.
88. Fernandes, *Taj Mahal Fox Trot*, 15.
89. Pinckney, "Jazz in India," 43.
90. Pinckney, "Jazz in India," 56.
91. UNESCO, "Jazz in Japan: A History of Tradition and Modernity," UNESCO, http://www.unesco.org/new/en/unesco/events/prizes-and-celebrations/celebrations/international-days/international-jazz-day-2014/jazz-in-japan-a-history-of-tradition-and-modernity/#.XIhxhKeB3so.
92. Atkins, *Blue Nippon*, loc 1251, 1314.
93. Atkins, *Blue Nippon*, loc 1251, 1314.
94. 井上エイド, "Raymond Conde and Francisco Reyes: Profile of Naturalized Imperial Japan Subject Jazz Musicians," Becoming Legally Japanese, October 24, 2016, https://www.turning-japanese.info/2016/10/jazz.html.
95. Atkins, *Blue Nippon*, loc 1320.
96. 井上エイド, "Raymond Conde and Francisco Reyes."
97. Atkins, *Blue Nippon*, loc 1291.
98. Omori Seitaro, *Nihon no yogaku*, vol. 1 (Tokyo: Shinmon Shuppansha, 1986), 136; and Mitsui Toru, "Interactions of Imported and Indigenous Musics in Japan: A Historical Overview of the Music Industry," in *Whose Master's Voice? The Development of Popular Music in Thirteen Cultures*, ed. Alison J. Ewbank and Fouli T. Papageorgiou (Westport, CT: Greenwood Press, 1997), 156–57; quoted in Atkins, *Blue Nippon*, loc 1291.
99. Atkins, *Blue Nippon*, loc 1419, 1425.
100. 井上エイド, "Raymond Conde and Francisco Reyes."
101. 井上エイド, "Raymond Conde and Francisco Reyes."
102. 井上エイド, "Raymond Conde and Francisco Reyes."
103. Atkins, *Blue Nippon*, loc 2885.
104. Atkins, *Blue Nippon*, loc 897.
105. Minor, *Jazz Journeys to Japan*, 183–84.
106. Atkins, *Blue Nippon*, loc 897.
107. Atkins, *Blue Nippon*, loc 4685, 4691.
108. Minor, *Jazz Journeys to Japan*, 183–84.
109. Atkins, *Blue Nippon*, loc 4747, 4753.
110. Renée Cho, dir., *Jazz Is My Native Language: A Portrait of Toshiko Akiyoshi*, Rhapsody Films, 1983; cited in Atkins, *Blue Nippon*, loc 5038.
111. Kevin Fellezs, "Deracinated Flower: Toshiko Akiyoshi's 'Trace in Jazz History,'" *Jazz Perspectives* 4, no. 1 (2010): 39.
112. Minor, *Jazz Journeys to Japan*, 167.
113. Minor, *Jazz Journeys to Japan*, 168.

114. Michael Pronko, "Freedom at His Fingertips," *Japan Times*, September 7, 2003, https://www.japantimes.co.jp/community/2003/09/07/general/freedom-at-his-fingertips/#.XI-9ARoxWfA.
115. Minor, *Jazz Journeys to Japan*, 171.
116. Minor, *Jazz Journeys to Japan*, 194.
117. Atkins, *Blue Nippon*, loc 5089.
118. Atkins, *Blue Nippon*, loc 5189.
119. Atkins, *Blue Nippon*, loc 5150.
120. Atkins, *Blue Nippon*, loc 4941.
121. Sadao Watanabe, "Biography," http://www.sadao.com/en/biography/index.html.
122. Minor, *Jazz Journeys to Japan*, 275.
123. Atkins, *Blue Nippon*, loc 5097–5104.
124. Atkins, "Toward a Global History of Jazz," loc 71.
125. Atkins, "Toward a Global History of Jazz," loc 97.

Track 11: *Birth '99*

1. So 902/QĐ-BVHTT, Quyết Định của Bộ Trưởng Bộ Văn Hoá—Thông Tin Về Việc Cử Đoàn Ra Nước Ngoại [Decision by the Minister of Culture: Information about the Delegation Traveling Overseas], Hà Nội, Ngày 02 Tháng 05 Nam 2001.
2. "First Vietnamese Jazz Band Performs Abroad," *Saigon Times*, March 8, 2001. It was actually just a nine-day performance tour that lasted from May 5 to 14.
3. Channel News Asia, "Vietnam's Godfather of Jazz Plays for HDB Heartlanders," May 6, 2001.
4. Lê Tiến Thọ, "Về Chuyến Biểu Diễn của Nhạc Sĩ Quyền Văn Minh và Ban Nhạc tại Singapore" [Regarding the Performance Trip of the Musician Quyền Văn Minh and His Band in Singapore], Ngày 12 Tháng 3 Nam 2001, letter written for the concert program.
5. Nguyễn Hồng Hải, Tổng Lãnh Sự Việt Nam tại Hồng Công, "Kính gửi: Ban Giám Đốc Nhạc Viện Hà Nội" [Letter to the Board of Directors of the Hanoi Music Conservatoire], Tổng Lãnh Sự Quán Việt Nam tại Hồng Công, Ngày 6 Tháng 9 Nam 2002.
6. A traditional form of sung poetry found in northern Vietnam.
7. Mai Thủy, "NSUT Quyền Văn Minh với Liên Hoan Nhạc Jazz Châu Âu" [The Eminent Artist Quyền Văn Minh and the European Jazz Music Festival], *Lao Động*, November 23, 2001.
8. Quốc Phúc, "Nhạc Jazz Việt Nam đã đủ từ tin!" [Vietnamese Jazz Is Ready with Confidence], *Văn Hoá*, November 21–25, 2001.
9. "European Jazz Festival in Vietnam," *Saigon Times*, November 4, 2003.
10. The English translations are taken directly from the album's liner notes.
11. Hà Sơn, "Nghe Tình Nghệ Sĩ qua phong cách Jazz-Blues" [Listening to "Sentiments of an Artist" in Jazz and Blues Style], *Việt Báo*, October 14, 2003, http://vietbao.vn/Van-hoa/Nghe-Tinh-nghe-si-qua-phong-cach-Jazz-Blues/20032309/181/.

Track 13: Postlude

1. For a more detailed discussion of Vietnam's territorial disputes with China, Taiwan, and other Southeast Asian countries over the South China Sea, see Hãn Nguyên Nguyễn Nhã,

Vietnam, Territoriality and the South China Sea: Paracel and Spratly Islands, trans. Vinh-The Lam (New York: Routledge, 2019).

2. Kate Hodal and Jonathan Kaiman, "At Least 21 Dead in Vietnam Anti-China Protests over Oil Rig," *Guardian*, May 15, 2014, https://www.theguardian.com/world/2014/may/15/vietnam-anti-china-protests-oil-rig-dead-injured.

3. "Hoàng Xuân Vượng và album trompette đầu tiên ở Việt Nam" [Hoàng Xuân Vượng and the First Trumpet Album in Vietnam], *Việt Báo*, December 30, 2008, http://vietbao.vn/Van-hoa/Hoang-Xuan-Vuong-va-album-trompette-dau-tien-o-Viet-Nam/75204336/181/.

4. The documentary is available at https://vtv.vn/video/phim-tai-lieu-sac-mau-cua-jazz-330171.htm.

5. Nicholas Gebhardt and Tony Whyton, eds., *The Cultural Politics of Jazz Collectives: This Is Our Music* (London: Routledge, 2015).

6. Atkins, "Toward a Global History of Jazz," loc 181.

BIBLIOGRAPHY

Alamgir, Alena K. "Race Is Elsewhere: State-Socialist Ideology and the Racialisation of Vietnamese Workers in Czechoslovakia." *Race and Class* 54, no. 4 (2017): 67–85.

Atkins, E. Taylor. *Blue Nippon: Authenticating Jazz in Japan*. Durham, NC: Duke University Press, 2001. Kindle ed.

Atkins, E. Taylor. "Toward a Global History of Jazz." In *Jazz Planet*, edited by E. Taylor Atkins, xi–xxvii. Jackson: University Press of Mississippi, 2003. Kindle ed.

Beresford, Benjamin J. "Rhapsody in Red: Jazz and a Soviet Public Sphere under Stalin." PhD diss., Arizona State University, 2017.

Boudarel, Georges, and Nguyen Van Ky. *Hanoi: City of the Rising Dragon*. Translated by Claire Duiker. Lanham, MD: Rowman and Littlefield, 2002. Kindle ed.

Breckenridge, Mark A. "Willis Conover's International Jazz Diplomacy through Fandom: The *Friends of Music USA Newsletter* (1964–1969)." *Jazz Perspectives* 7, no. 2 (2013): 91–109.

Bùi Gia Tường. "Hội Nhạc Sĩ Việt Nam—Ngôi nhà chung của tất cả chúng ta" [Association of Musicians of Vietnam: Our Common Home]. In *Tự Hào Nửa Thế Kỷ Hội Nhạc Sĩ Việt Nam (1957–2007)* [Taking Pride in Half a Century of the Association of Musicians of Vietnam (1957–2007)], edited by Cát Vận, Nguyễn Thụy Kha, Quốc Đông, and Phạm Phúc Hải, 679–80. Hà Nội: Hội Nhạc Sĩ Việt Nam, 2007.

Carlton, Larry, comp. *The Jazz King: The Musical Compositions of H.M. King Bhumibol Adulyadej*. 335 Records, 2018.

Castro, Alex R. "Meet the Force Who Ruled the Philippine Jazz Age." *Town and Country*, July 1, 2018. https://www.townandcountry.ph/people/heritage/borromeo-lou-profile-a2087-20180701-lfrm2.

Cát Vận, Nguyễn Thụy Kha, Quốc Đông, and Phạm Phúc Hải, eds. *Tự Hào Nửa Thế Kỷ Hội Nhạc Sĩ Việt Nam (1957–2007)* [Taking Pride in Half a Century of the Association of Musicians of Vietnam (1957–2007)]. Hà Nội: Hội Nhạc Sĩ Việt Nam, 2007.

Chapman, Jessica. *Cauldron of Resistance: Ngo Dinh Diem, the United States, and 1950s Southern Vietnam*. Ithaca, NY: Cornell University Press, 2013. Kindle ed.

Chen Chen. "A Study of the Localization of Jazz in Shanghai." Master's thesis, Shanghai Normal University, 2005.

Cho, Renée, dir. *Jazz Is My Native Language: A Portrait of Toshiko Akiyoshi*. Rhapsody Films, 1983.

Cửu Long Giang. "Thực chất của cái gọi là nghệ thuật âm nhạc Sàigòn cũ" [The Essence of So-Called Arts in Old Saigon]. *Văn Hoá Nghệ Thuật* 6 (1977): 37–39.

Đặng Phong. *Phá Rào Trong Kinh Tế Vào Đêm Trước Đổi Mới (Tái Bản Lần Thứ 6)* [Fence Breaking in the Economy the Night before Đổi Mới, 6th printing]. Hà Nội: Nhà Xuất Bản Trí Thức, 2017.

Davenport, Lisa E. *Jazz Diplomacy: Promoting America in the Cold War Era*. Jackson: University Press of Mississippi, 2009.

Dennis, Mike. "Working under Hammer and Sickle: Vietnamese Workers in the German Democratic Republic, 1980–89." *German Politics* 16, no. 3 (2007): 339–57. doi:10.1080/09644000701532700.

Domurat-Linde, Marta. "From 'Jazz in Poland' to 'Polish Jazz.'" In *Meanings of Jazz in State Socialism*, edited by Gertrud Pickhan and Rüdiger Ritter, 75–96. Frankfurt: Peter Lang, 2016.

Dorin, Stephane. "Jazz and Race in Colonial India: The Role of Anglo-Indian Musicians in the Diffusion of Jazz in Calcutta." *Jazz Research Journal* 4, no. 2 (2010): 123–40.

Dunkel, Mario. "'Jazz—Made in Germany' and the Transatlantic Beginnings of Jazz Diplomacy." In *Music and Diplomacy from the Early Modern Era to the Present*, edited by Rebekah Ahrendt, Mark Ferraguto, and Damien Mahiet, 147–68. New York: Palgrave Macmillan, 2014.

Fellezs, Kevin. "Deracinated Flower: Toshiko Akiyoshi's 'Trace in Jazz History.'" *Jazz Perspectives* 4, no. 1 (2010): 35–57.

Fernandes, Naresh. *Taj Mahal Fox Trot: The Story of Bombay's Jazz Age*. New Delhi: Roli Books, 2016.

Filipinas Heritage Library. "Jazz Music in the Philippines." Himig Collection. http://www.himig.com.ph/features/61-jazz-music-in-the-philippines.

Fosler-Lussier, Danielle. *Music in America's Cold War Diplomacy*. Berkeley: University of California Press, 2015.

Friends of Vietnam Heritage. *Vignettes of French Culture in Hanoi*. Hà Nội: Gioi Publishers, 2008.

Gebhardt, Nicholas, and Tony Whyton, eds. *The Cultural Politics of Jazz Collectives: This Is Our Music*. London: Routledge, 2015.

Gibbs, Jason. "Buddy Rich đến Sài Gòn năm 1961" [Buddy Rich in Saigon, 1961]. Tây Bụi, December 26, 2013. http://taybui.blogspot.com/2013/12/buddy-rich-en-sai-gon-nam-1961.html.

Gibbs, Jason. "Cấm lưu hành, phổ biến các bản nhạc, đĩa hát xuất bản trước ngày 30-4-1975" [Prohibiting the Circulation and Availability of Music and Records Published before April 20, 1975]. Tây Bụi, January 6, 2019. http://taybui.blogspot.com/2019/01/cam-luu-hanh-pho-bien-cac-ban-nhac-dia.html.

Gibbs, Jason. "How Does Hanoi Rock? The Way to Rock and Roll in Vietnam." *Asian Music* 39, no. 1 (Winter–Spring 2008): 5–25.

Gibbs, Jason. "Reform and Tradition in Early Vietnamese Popular Song." *Nhạc Việt* 6 (Fall 1997): 5–34.

Gibbs, Jason. "Saigon-Palace-Hotel 1937." Tây Bụi, September 11, 2018. http://taybui.blogspot.com/2018/09/saigon-palace-hotel-1937.html.

Gibbs, Jason. "Tại Nhà hát Tây đêm 8 Juillet (1937)" [The Night of the Eighth of July at the West Theater]. Tây Bụi, December 2, 2018. http://taybui.blogspot.com/search/label/đĩa%20hát.

Gibbs, Jason. "The West's Songs, Our Songs: The Introduction and Adaptation of Western Popular Song in Vietnam before 1940." *Asian Music* 34, no. 1 (Autumn 2003–Winter 2004): 57–83.

Gui Hu Zi [鬼虎子]. "闻名上海的四大舞厅" [The Four Famous Dance Halls in Shanghai]. World Show, April 11, 2018. http://www.worldshow.com.cn/frontViewInfoAction!news.htm?newsId=78094.

Hãn Nguyên Nguyễn Nhã. *Vietnam, Territoriality and the South China Sea: Paracel and Spratly Islands*. Translated by Vinh-The Lam. New York: Routledge, 2019.

Hardy, Andrew. *Red Hills: Migrants and the State in Vietnam*. Copenhagen: Nordic Institute of Asian Studies Press, 2003.

Hatschek, Keith. "The Impact of American Jazz Diplomacy in Poland during the Cold War Era." *Jazz Perspectives* 4, no. 3 (2010): 253–300.

Havadi, Gergő. "An Individual Subculture Reflected in Domestic Spies' Reports: Hungarian Jazz in the Socialist Period." In *Jazz behind the Iron Curtain*, edited by Gertrud Pickhan and Rüdiger Ritter, 191–98. Frankfurt: Peter Lang, 2010.

Havadi, Gergő. "Individualists, Traditionalists, Revolutionaries, or Opportunists? The Political and Social Constellations of Jazz in Hungary during the 1950s–1960s." In *Meanings of Jazz in State Socialism*, edited by Gertrud Pickhan and Rüdiger Ritter, 109–55. Frankfurt: Peter Lang, 2016.

Hoàng Vân. "30 năm chặng đường đầu tiên của nền âm nhạc khí nhạc Việt Nam" [The First Thirty Years of Vietnamese Instrumental Music]. In *Tự Hào Nửa Thế Kỷ Hội Nhạc Sĩ Việt Nam (1957–2007)* [*Taking Pride in Half a Century of the Association of Musicians of Vietnam (1957–2007)*], edited by Cát Vận, Nguyễn Thụy Kha, Quốc Đông, and Phạm Phúc Hải, 396–401. Hà Nội: Hội Nhạc Sĩ Việt Nam, 2007.

Huesmann, Günther. "After 1945: Jazz in Germany." Goethe-Institut, September 2009. https://www.goethe.de/en/kul/mus/gen/jaz/ruc/4932331.html.

Hữu Thọ. *Đi Khai Hoang Tây Bắc* [*Pioneering in the Northwest*]. Hà Nội: Nhà Xuất Bản Nông Thôn, 1963.

Jähnichen, Gisa. "Jazz in Kuala Lumpur." *Jazz Research Journal* 4, no. 2 (2010): 141–70.

Jones, Andrew. *Yellow Music: Media Culture and Colonial Modernity in the Chinese Jazz Age*. Durham, NC: Duke University Press, 2001. Kindle ed.

Kajanová, Yvetta. "Communism and the Emergence of the Central European Jazz School." *Journal of Literature and Art Studies* 2, no. 6 (June 2012): 622–40.

Kajanová, Yvetta. "Jazz Artists in the Former Czechoslovak Socialist Republic and Their Conflicts with the Socialist Ideology." In *Jazz from Socialist Realism to Postmodernism*, edited by Yvetta Kajanová, Gertrud Pickhan, and Rüdiger Ritter, 119–37. Frankfurt: Peter Lang, 2016.

Kalmanovitch, Tanya. "Indo-Jazz Fusion: Jazz and Karnatak Music in Contact." PhD diss., University of Alberta, 2008.

Keppy, Peter. "Southeast Asia in the Age of Jazz: Locating Popular Culture in the Colonial Philippines and Indonesia." *Journal of Southeast Asian Studies* 44, no. 3 (2013): 444–64.

Li Mo. "A History of Jazz in China: From Yellow Music to Jazz Revival in Beijing." Master's thesis, Kent State University, 2018.

Lockhard, Craig A. *Dance of Life: Popular Music and Politics in Southeast Asia*. Honolulu: University of Hawai'i Press, 1998.

Lưu Quang Minh. "Đào tạo tài năng nhạc Jazz trong thời kỳ hội nhập quốc tế." *Tạp chí Giáo dục Âm nhạc* 3, no. 103 (2016).

Maggin, Donald L. *Stan Getz: A Life in Jazz*. New York: William Morrow, 1996.

Marlow, Eugene. *Jazz in China: From Dance Hall Music to Individual Freedom of Expression*. Jackson: University Press of Mississippi, 2018. Kindle ed.

Marr, David. "A Brief History of Local Government in Vietnam." In *Beyond Hanoi: Local Government in Vietnam*, edited by Benedict J. Tria Kerkvliet and David Marr, 28–53. Singapore: Institute of Southeast Asian Studies, 2004.

McGraw, Andrew. "The Ambivalent Freedoms of Indonesian Jazz." *Jazz Perspectives* 6, no. 3 (2012): 273–310.

Miller, Edward. *Misalliance: Ngo Dinh Diem, the United States, and the Fate of South Vietnam*. Cambridge, MA: Harvard University Press, 2013. Kindle ed.

Minor, William. *Jazz Journeys to Japan: The Heart Within*. Ann Arbor: University of Michigan Press, 2004.

Motyčka, Peter. "The Jazz Section: A Platform of Freedom in Czechoslovakia." In *Jazz behind the Iron Curtain*, edited by Gertrud Pickhan and Rüdiger Ritter, 215–22. Frankfurt: Peter Lang, 2010.

Ngô Minh. *Sống Thời Bao Cấp (Tái Bản Lần Thứ 2)* [*Living in the Subsidy Period*, 2nd printing]. Hà Nội: Nhà Xuất Bản Hội Nhã Văn, 2018.

Nguyễn Công Luận. *Nationalist in the Viet Nam Wars: Memoirs of a Victim Turned Soldier*. Bloomington: Indiana University Press, 2012. Kindle ed.

Nguyen Long with Harry H. Kendall. *After Saigon Fell: Daily Life under the Vietnamese Communists*. Berkeley: Institute of East Asian Studies, University of California, 1981.

Nguyễn Thụy Kha. *Thế Kỷ Âm Nhạc Việt Nam: Một Thời Đạn Bom* [*A Century of Music in Vietnam: The Period of Bullets and Bombs*]. Hà Nội: Nhà Xuất Bản Văn Học, 2017.

Nguyễn Thụy Kha. *Thế Kỷ Âm Nhạc: Một Thời Hoà Bình* [*A Century of Music in Vietnam: The Period of Peace*]. Hà Nội: Nhà Xuất Bản Văn Học, 2017.

Nhu-Ngoc Thuy Ong. "Governing Music in Vietnam: From Socialist to Post-Socialist Use of Nationalism." PhD diss., University of California, Irvine, 2009.

Norton, Barley. "Music and Censorship in Vietnam since 1954." In *The Oxford Handbook of Music Censorship*, edited by Patricia Hall. Oxford: Oxford University Press, 2015. doi:10.1093/oxfordhb/9780199733163.013.29.

Ó Briain, Lonán. "Musical Cosmopolitanism in Late-Colonial Hanoi." *Ethnomusicology Forum* 27, no. 3 (2018): 265–85. doi:10.1080/17411912.2018.1521728.

Pappin, Philippe. *Lịch Sử Hà Nội* [*A History of Hanoi*]. Hà Nội: Nhà Xuất Bản Thế Giới, 2016.

Pickhan, Gertrud, and Rüdiger Ritter. Introduction to *Meanings of Jazz in State Socialism*, edited by Gertrud Pickhan and Rüdiger Ritter, 1–17. Frankfurt: Peter Lang, 2016.

Pietraszewski, Igor. *Jazz in Poland: Improvised Freedom*. Translated by Lucyna Stetkiewicz. Frankfurt: Peter Lang, 2014.

Pinckney, Warren R., Jr. "Jazz in India: Perspectives on Historical Development and Musical Acculturation." *Asian Music* 21, no. 1 (Autumn 1989–Winter 1990): 35–77.

Poiger, Uta G. "Searching for Proper New Music: Jazz in Cold War Germany." In *German Pop Culture: How "American" Is It?*, edited by Agnes C. Mueller, 83–95. Ann Arbor: University of Michigan Press, 2004.

Popan, Adrian. "Jazz Revival in Romania, 1964–1971." In *Jazz behind the Iron Curtain*, edited by Gertrud Pickhan and Rüdiger Ritter, 199–214. Frankfurt: Peter Lang, 2010.

Quang Nghi. "Nghệ Sĩ Quyền Văn Minh với vẻ đẹp của tiếng kèn saxo" [The Artist Quyền Văn Minh and the Beauty of the Saxophone]. *Âm Nhạc* 4, no. 12 (1989): 11.

Quirino, Richie C. *Pinoy Jazz Traditions*. Pasig City, Philippines: Anvil Publishing, 2004.

Quirino, Richie C., and Collis Davis, dirs. *Pinoy Jazz: The Story of Jazz in the Philippines*. Culture Unplugged Studios, 2006. http://www.cultureunplugged.com/documentary/watch-online/filmedia/play/377/Pinoy-Jazz-The-Story-of-Jazz-in-the-Philippines.

Ripmaster, Terence M. *Willis Conover: Broadcasting Jazz to the World*. New York: iUniverse, 2007.

Ritter, Rüdiger. "Broadcasting Jazz into the Eastern Bloc: Cold War Weapon or Cultural Exchange? The Example of Willis Conover." *Jazz Perspectives* 7, no. 2 (2013): 111–31.

Ritter, Rüdiger. "Jazz in State Socialism: A Playground of Refusal?" In *Meanings of Jazz in State Socialism*, edited by Gertrud Pickhan and Rüdiger Ritter, 17–38. Frankfurt: Peter Lang, 2016.

Rosen, Deborah. "Music Training and Cultural Transmission: A Study of Piano Pedagogy and the Transmission of Culture in Vietnam and Thailand." PhD diss., Claremont Graduate University, 1998.

Saito, Yoshiomi. *The Global Politics of Jazz in the Twentieth Century: Cultural Diplomacy and "American Music."* London: Routledge, 2019.

Saysouvanh, Somjit, Suphanni Luebunchu, and Athe Nantachak. "Research Brief: Instruction Process on the Violin Performances of Great Teachers at Vietnam National Academy of Music." *International Forum of Teaching and Studies* 10, no. 2 (2014): 42–46.

Schafer, John C. "Death, Buddhism, and Existentialism in the Songs of Trịnh Công Sơn." *Journal of Vietnamese Studies* 2, no. 1 (February 2007): 144–86.

Schafer, John C. "The Trịnh Công Sơn Phenomenon." *Journal of Asian Studies* 66, no. 3 (2007): 597–643.

Schmidt-Rost, Christian. "Freedom within Limitations: Getting Access to Jazz in the GDR and PRP between 1945 and 1961." In *Jazz behind the Iron Curtain*, edited by Gertrud Pickhan and Rüdiger Ritter, 223–38. Frankfurt: Peter Lang, 2010.

Schultz, Howard, and Dori Jones Yang. *Pour Your Heart Into It: How Starbucks Built a Company One Cup at a Time*. New York: Hyperion, 1997.

Schwenkel, Christina. "Rethinking Asian Mobilities: Socialist Migration and Post-Socialist Repatriation of Vietnamese Contract Workers in East Germany." *Critical Asian Studies* 46, no. 2 (2014): 235–58. doi:10.1080/14672715.2014.898453.

Seitaro, Omori. *Nihon no yogaku*, vol. 1. Tokyo: Shinmon Shuppansha, 1986.

Starr, Frederick S. "The Music of the Gross, 1928–1931." In *Jazz Planet*, edited by E. Taylor Atkins, 129–50. Jackson: University Press of Mississippi, 2003. Kindle ed.

Starr, Frederick S. *Red and Hot: The Fate of Jazz in the Soviet Union*. New York: Limelight Editions, 1994.

Sutopo, Oki Rahadianto, and Pam Nilan. "The Constrained Position of Young Musicians in the Yogyakarta Jazz Community." *Asian Music* 49, no. 1 (Winter–Spring 2018): 34–57.

Szurek, Jaroslaw. "Subversive Sounds: Music and Censorship in Communist Poland." *Music Reference Services Quarterly* 11, no. 2 (2008): 143–51.

Szymańska-Matusiewicz, Grażyna. "The Vietnamese Communities in Central and Eastern Europe as Part of the Global Vietnamese Diaspora." *Central and Eastern European Migration Review* 4, no. 1 (2015): 5–10.

Tan, Stan BH. "Dust beneath the Mist: State and Frontier Formation in the Central Highlands under the First Republic of Vietnam, the 1955–1961 Period." PhD diss., Australian National University, 2006.

Tan-Tangbau, Stan BH, and Quyền Văn Minh. "Excerpts from *Quyen Van Minh: A Jazz Life Story*, the 1988–89 Solo Recitals." *Journal of Narrative Politics* 3, no. 2 (2017): 70–96.

Tan-Tangbau, Stan BH, and Quyền Văn Minh. "Quyền Văn Minh and the Birth of Vietnamese Jazz." *Jazz Perspectives* 11, no. 2 (2018): 173–99. doi:10.1080/17494060.2019.1616871.

Taylor, Philip. *Fragments of the Present: Searching for Modernity in Vietnam's South*. Crows Nest, Australia: Allen and Unwin, 2001.

Taylor, Philip. "Music as a 'Neocolonial Poison' in Postwar Southern Vietnam." *Crossroads: An Interdisciplinary Journal of Southeast Asian Studies* 14, no. 1 (2000): 99–131.

Toru, Mitsui. "Interactions of Imported and Indigenous Musics in Japan: A Historical Overview of the Music Industry." In *Whose Master's Voice? The Development of Popular Music in Thirteen Cultures*, edited by Alison J. Ewbank and Fouli T. Papageorgiou, 152–74. Westport, CT: Greenwood Press, 1997.

Trần Hùng. "Nhà soạn nhạc Đàm Linh" [Đàm Linh, the Composer]. In *Tự Hào Nửa Thế Kỷ Hội Nhạc Sĩ Việt Nam (1957–2007)* [*Taking Pride in Half a Century of the Association of Musicians of Vietnam (1957–2007)*], edited by Cát Vận, Nguyễn Thụy Kha, Quốc Đông, and Phạm Phúc Hải, xx. Hà Nội: Hội Nhạc Sĩ Việt Nam, 2007.

Trần Quang Hải. "Vietnamese Music in Exile since 1975 and Musical Life in Vietnam since Perestroika." *World of Music* 43, nos. 2–3 (2001): 103–12.

Trịnh Công Sơn. "Giấc mơ Hạ trắng." June 16, 2015. https://trinhcongsonblog.wordpress.com/2015/06/16/giac-mo-ha-trang/.

Turley, William S. *The Second Indochina War: A Concise Political and Military History*. 2nd ed. Lanham, MD: Rowman and Littlefield, 2009.

UNESCO. "Jazz in Japan: A History of Tradition and Modernity." UNESCO. http://www.unesco.org/new/en/unesco/events/prizes-and-celebrations/celebrations/international-days/international-jazz-day-2014/jazz-in-japan-a-history-of-tradition-and-modernity/#.XIhxhKeB3so.

Vĩnh Phức. "Sơ khảo lịch sử tân nhạc ở Thừa Thiên Huế" [A Brief History of New Music in Thừa Thiên Huế]. *Tập Chí Sông Hương*, August 31, 2017. http://tapchisonghuong.com.vn/tin-tuc/p9/c29/n25896/So-khao-lich-su-tan-nhac-o-Thua-Thien-Hue.html.

Von Eschen, Penny. *Satchmo Blows Up the World: Jazz Ambassadors Play the Cold War*. Cambridge, MA: Harvard University Press, 2006.

Yampolsky, Philip, et al. "Indonesia." In Grove Music Online. http://www.oxfordmusiconline.com/subscriber/article/grove/music/42890pg8.

Zahradník, Miroslav. "Jazz Personalities after the Downfall of the Iron Curtain: Matúš Jakabčic and His Contribution to Slovak Jazz." In *Jazz from Socialist Realism to Postmodernism*, edited by Yvetta Kajanová, Gertrud Pickhan, and Rüdiger Ritter, 243–63. Frankfurt: Peter Lang, 2016.

INDEX

Adderley, Nat, 3
Adulyadej, Bhumibol (king of Thailand), 170–71
Agrarian Land Reform policy, 51
Agricultural Pioneering (policy), 5, 65, 86
Akiyoshi Toshiko, 178–79
Armstrong, Louis, 75
artistic value, 73, 81
artists' troupe, 8, 10, 52, 84–85
Association of Proletarian Musicians (Soviet Union), 72
audience, 215, 220, 222–24, 225
August Revolution, 8

Babetta (moped), 110
Bắc Nam Tư (North '54), 50
Bằng, Trọng, 156
Bata, 173
Berklee College of Music, 163, 173, 175, 180, 230
bia hơi (local draft beer), 35
big band, 4, 32, 166, 167, 176, 200, 232–33, 234, 236–37, 238–39
birth, 52
Blue Note, 168
bombardment (of Hà Nội), 56–57, 59–60
Bôn, Tạ, 137, 155
Borromeo, Luis, 168–69
brass bands, 7
Brecker, Michael, 20
Brubeck, Dave, 75, 76, 79, 175

cafés (in Vietnam), 18, 153, 154
cải lương (reformed opera), 98–99
Cambodia, 102
Cao, Văn, 8, 93
Carlton, Larry, 170
cassette tapes, 29, 94–95, 121, 168
Catholic Vietnamese, 20, 121
censorship, 113–14, 116
children, 28, 35, 96, 163

Chinese language (Mandarin), 53
Chinese music, 68
choosing a vocation, 63
Chuẩn, Đoàn, 8, 206–8
circus troupe, 90
classical music, 7, 37, 73, 116, 117, 118, 124, 125–26, 140
Clayton, Buck, 166, 167
Cold War, 38, 56, 59, 71, 73, 74–75, 76–77, 82, 83, 131
Coleman, Ornette, 76
collaborative narrative, xii–xiv
Colors of Jazz (documentary film), ix, 242
Coltrane, John, 142, 148, 175, 179
COMECON, 79
concert program, 111, 113, 116, 117, 135
Conde, Raymond, 176, 177
Conover, Willis, 9, 69, 70–71, 74, 82, 174
Conservatoire Française d'Extrême-Orient, 7
cooperative, 53
Corea, Chick, 3
Cuban music, 68
cultural house, 58, 79
Czechoslovak Musicians' Union, 80, 82

Đắc, Quyền Thiện, ix, 3–4, 39, 96, 103, 105, 121, 152, 163, 185, 187, 192, 195–96, 199, 213, 215, 219, 230, 232–33, 235, 242
Đàm Linh, 114–15, 128–30
dance halls, 93, 166–67, 175–76
Đặng Hữu Phúc, 116, 117, 125
Davis, Miles, 18, 19
Déczi, Laco, 72
Democratic Republic of Vietnam (North Vietnam), 50
Diệm, Ngô Đình, 56, 61
Dila, Apolo, 167
divorce, 28, 103–5
Dizzy Sal (Edward Saldanha), 174–75
Đỗ Hồng Quân. *See* Quân, Đỗ Hồng
Đoàn Chuẩn, 8, 206–8

265

Đổi Mới, 10, 102, 113–14, 132–34, 136, 138, 150
Doky, Chris Minh, 44
DVD albums, 231–32, 233–35

East Berlin, 11, 109–10
Eastern European jazz albums, 80
electric combo band, 97–98, 100, 101
Ellington, Duke, 19, 75, 76
Eminent Artist award, 13, 24–25, 116
ethnic minorities (in Vietnam), 86, 143
ethnic Tày, 214
ethnic Thái, 5, 118, 236
European Jazz Festival in Vietnam, 44, 200, 201, 202, 203

Facebook, 20
family background, 52–53, 58
father, 52, 53, 59, 61, 62, 66–67, 69–70, 105
Filipino jazz bands, 169
First Indochina War, 8, 39, 50
Fitzgerald, Ella, 81
free jazz, 179
Freelon, Nnenna, 45
French colonialism, 6–7, 23
French Culture Day (in Hà Nội), 23
French language, 53
funerals, 196–97

Getz, Stan, 9, 20, 79, 136
Giảng Võ Exhibition Centre, 34–35
Gillespie, Dizzy, 76
Gonsalves, Braz, 175
Goodman, Benny, 75, 76, 170
Gorky, Maxim, 72
green music, 93

Hà Nội: bombardment of, 56–57, 59–60; French Culture Day, 23; Metropole, 22, 23–24, 29; Old Quarter, 26–28; parachute houses, 40; street scene, 18, 27–28, 38, 40, 43; summer, 28, 69
Hà Nội Children Palace, 58
Hà Nội Opera House, 3–4, 11–13, 44, 132, 136, 137, 138, 230, 232–33, 234–35, 236–37, 238–40
Hà Tây, 86–87, 90, 95
Hammer, Jan, 72
Hancock, Herbie, 19, 45, 48–49
Hattori Ryoichi, 177

Hino Terumasa, 179
Hmong, 143–44
Hoàn Kiếm Lake, 37–39
Hoàng Tùng, xii
Hồ Chí Minh, 8
Hồ Chí Minh City Municipal Theatre, 4
Hoàng Vân, 116, 117, 118, 124, 125
Hoàng Xuân Vượng, 239
Hong Kong, 186; television drama serials, 36
Honna Tetsuji, ix, 45
Honored Artist of the Russian Soviet Federative Socialist Republic, 78
Housing Development Board (HDB, Singapore), 185
Hungarian Association of Musicians, 73
Hungary, 107

Indian jazz bands, 174
Indo-jazz, 175
Indonesian jazz, 172, 173
Indonesian jazz bands, 172

Jakabčic, Matúš, 81, 150
jam sessions, 44, 76, 170, 173
Japanese jazz, 149, 177–78
jazz: ambassadors, 9, 75–76, 170; in China, 166–68; clubs, 12, 19–20, 21, 22 24, 32–34, 37, 39–41, 42–43, 65, 165, 211–12, 213, 226, 239–40; concerts, 3–5, 11, 12, 132, 133, 138, 140, 230–36, 243; in Czechoslovakia, 79–80; in East Germany, 74, 77, 110; education, xii, 11, 80–81, 155–56, 160, 161–62, 171, 180; festivals, 12, 44, 80, 186–87; free jazz, 179; fusion, 169–70, 172–73; gigs, 22, 24, 29–30, 216, 218, 224–25; in Hungary, 107; in Indonesia, 172–73; in Japan, 149, 175–78; jazz kissaten (coffeeshops), 178; in Malaysia, 171–72; and modernity, 167, 171, 172, 180–81; old Shanghai jazz, 167; in Poland, 73, 75, 79, 80; in Romania, 79, 80; in Soviet Union, 72–73, 76, 77–78; in Thailand, 170–71
Jazz at Lincoln Center, 168
Jazz Jamboree (Poland), 79
Jazz Section (Czechoslovakia), 80, 82
Jazz Yatra Festival, 175
Jobim, Antônio Carlos, 136

Kenychi Hirose, 32
Komeda, Krzysztof (Krzysztof Komeda Trzciński), 78–79, 80, 149–50
Kuhn, Steve, 19

labor booklet, 91
Lai Châu, 227
Laos, 101, 115
learning: clarinet, 62, 63, 66–67, 68; guitar, 57–58, 59–60; jazz, 69, 70, 88–90
Legrand, Michel, 81
Li Jinhui, 167
light music, 68, 93, 97–98, 99, 101, 116, 167
Linh, Đàm, 114–15, 128–30
Linh, Nguyễn Văn, 10
Louis Cha (Kim Dung), 36
Lưu Quang Minh, xii, 4, 160, 193, 194, 195

Macau, 186
management (jazz club), 217, 219–22, 225
Mangelsdorff, Albert, 170
marriage, 30, 95–96
Martoník, Ladislav, 79
Mekong River Delta, 195
Metropole (Hà Nội), 22, 23–24, 29
migration (to Eastern Europe), 53, 88, 107, 109–10
Miller, Glenn, 136
Mingus, Charles, 76
Minh, Lưu Quang, xii, 4, 160, 193, 194, 195
Mobley, Hank, 4
modern songs (China), 167
Monk, Thelonious, 76
Moscow, 23, 24
mother, 21, 22, 52, 54–55, 58, 59, 61, 62, 66–67, 69–70, 100, 106, 110, 195
motorbike headlight bulbs, 110
motorbike taxi, 20, 30
Mraz, George, 72
music: diploma, 90, 99–100, 125, 151, 156–57, 159, 164–65; gigs, 28, 62, 63–64, 66–67, 68, 87, 88, 96, 102, 107, 126, 158, 159, 216–18; instruments and accessories, 58, 59, 63, 120–21, 122, 123; literacy, 58; mentorship, 63, 212–13, 218–19, 220–21, 224–25, 226; and politics (in Vietnam), 8–9, 11, 60–61, 68, 93–94, 190; prewar, 93, 132, 204, 206; rehearsals, 84–85; scores, 84–85, 129

Nam Định, 20–21
Nanri Fumio, 176
National Assembly (Democratic Republic of Vietnam), 38
National Light Music Festival, 23
neighborhood speakers, 67
New and Old Crossover Program, 98–99
New Economic Zone policy, 5, 65, 92, 98
Nghĩa Đô Collective Residential Area, 28, 108–9
Ngô Đình Diệm, 56, 61
Ngô Văn Thành, 155
Nguyễn Quốc Trường, 4, 64, 239
Nguyễn Văn Linh, 10
Nhân Văn-Giai Phẩm affair, 51

Okinawa, 186
Old Quarter (Hà Nội), 26–28
overseas Vietnamese, 29, 229
"own jazz" (Eastern Europe), 76–77, 78–79, 150

parachute houses (in Hà Nội), 40
Paris, 24
Parker, Charlie, 19, 119, 137
Pastorius, Jaco, 19
patriotism, 227, 229–30
Philip Morris Group, 182, 185
Phú Quang, 204, 209
Phúc, Đặng Hữu, 116, 117, 125
Pinoy jazz, 169–70
Polish jazz, 78–79, 149–50
popular music: Vietnamese, 7–8, 19, 102, 205–6, 206–7, 209, 216, 220, 236–37, 238–39; Western/foreign, 7, 10, 19, 102, 134, 241
Prague Spring, 82
prewar music, 93, 132, 204, 206
professional musician (in Vietnam), 84, 87, 144–45, 152, 204
propaganda department, 92

Quân, Đỗ Hồng, 108, 116, 117, 118, 124, 125
Quang, Phú, 204, 209
Quyền Thiện Đắc. See Đắc, Quyền Thiện

radio, 7, 9, 19, 67, 68–69, 70, 74, 75, 81, 143, 168, 170, 180
Raffles Hotel (Singapore), 23

railway, 107
red music, 8, 61, 67–68, 93, 167, 197
Red River Delta, 86
repairing musical instruments, 30–32, 219
Republic of Vietnam (South Vietnam), 9–10, 50, 56, 93, 171
rice booklet, 104
Rich, Buddy, 9
Rollins, Sonny, 20
Rudorf, Reginald, 77
Russia: language, 53; music, 68

Sài Gòn, 29–30, 36, 92–93, 122
SARS epidemic, 213
saxophone program (conservatoire), 160–61
saxophones, 113, 114, 115, 117–19, 120, 121, 136, 152
schooling, 59–60, 68–69, 70
Second Indochina War, 9, 22, 56, 69–70, 92–93
self-criticism, 91
Shorter, Wayne, 45, 48, 49
siblings, 53, 84, 127
SIDA (Swedish International Development Cooperation Agency), 134–35, 137
Singapore, 182–83, 183–85, 187–88
Singapore Botanical Gardens, 185
Slováček, Felix, 44, 121
Snow, Valaida, 166, 172
Solovyov-Sedoi, Vasily, 206
Sơn, Trịnh Công, 93–94, 139, 189, 204, 206, 208–9, 236
Sơn La, 3, 5, 236
Sơn La Prison, 227
Song of Hope, 60–61
song-and-dance troupe, 5, 10, 11, 39, 41, 64, 65, 86–87, 89, 95–96, 99–102, 102–3, 103–4, 108–10, 111, 113, 115, 117, 127, 128–30, 153–55, 157–58, 164–65, 204
South China Sea, 227, 229–30
Sting, 16
street scene (Hà Nội), 18, 27–28, 38, 40, 43
Subsidy Period, 10, 21, 85, 87, 90, 96, 104, 106, 107, 109–10, 154, 158
Sukarno, 172
summer (in Hà Nội), 28, 69
Sweden, 137

Tạ Bôn, 137, 155
Taiwan, 187
Tây Bắc, 3, 5, 86
Tây Bắc University, 3
Tây Nguyên, 92, 146–47
Tchaikovsky Conservatoire, 115, 155
teaching music: adjunct lecturer, 21; conservatoire faculty, 152, 155, 156–57, 158, 159; private lessons, 21, 28, 30, 52, 57–58, 64, 152, 153–55, 160, 219
teaching philosophy, 159, 162–63, 164
television, 11–12, 110, 114–15, 117, 119, 136, 172, 242
Terai Hisayuki, 177–78
Tết New Year, 35–36
Thai jazz bands, 170
Thái Nguyên, 52, 65, 86–87
Thành, Ngô Văn, 155
Tiến, Trần, 113–14
tourism, 43, 134, 215, 220
Trần Tiến, 113–14
Trịnh Công Sơn, 93–94, 139, 189, 204, 206, 208–9, 236
Trnečka, Bohumil, 81
Trọng Bằng, 156
Tropp, Ladislav, 72
Trường, Nguyễn Quốc, 4, 64, 239
Từ Sơn, 91–92
Tùng, Hoàng, xii
Tuyên Quang, 6
TVMobile (Singapore), 185

Utesov, Leonid, 77–78

Vân, Hoàng, 116, 117, 118, 124, 125
Văn Cao, 8, 93
Van Heusen, Jimmy, 3
Việt Bắc, 85, 86, 143–45
Việt Minh, 8, 86
Vietnam: arts and culture system, 36–37; cafés, 18, 153, 154; chamber music, 116, 117, 118, 141–42; ethnic minorities, 86, 143; jazz, 24, 26, 39–40, 132, 140–41, 142–48, 149, 183, 196–200; jazz albums, 4–5, 12, 26–27, 39, 183, 188, 189–90, 192–94, 195–96; jazz musicians, 213–15;

music and politics, 8–9, 11, 60–61, 68, 93–94, 190; relations with China, 53; relations with Eastern Europe, 88, 122, 125; relations with Soviet Union, 53; religious practice, 40–41; traditional music, 142–43, 145
Vietnam Association of Musicians, 11, 61, 108, 111–12, 114, 115, 124–25, 128, 148
Vietnam National Academy of Music, xi, 11, 25, 67, 68, 125, 155–56, 243
Vietnam National Symphony Orchestra, vii, 31, 44, 108
Vietnamese Revolution, 8–9, 50–51
vinyl records, 7, 29, 88–89, 94, 168, 190
violin, 137
Vitouš, Miroslav, 72
Vượng, Hoàng Xuân, 239

Wall, The (Bức Tường), 214
Watanabe Sadao, 178, 180
Weatherford, Teddy, 166, 172, 173–74
weddings, 63–64, 65, 96
Western Christian missionaries, 6
White Nights café, 76
women's rights, 105

Yamashita Yosuke, vii–viii, ix, 44–45, 46–47, 178, 179
yellow music, 9, 93–94, 102, 134, 139, 167
Youth League, 92
Youth Theatre, 97
YouTube, 13
Yu Yuezhang Orchestra, 166, 167
Yui Soichi, 179

ABOUT THE AUTHORS

Stan BH Tan-Tangbau is a Southeast Asian Studies scholar specializing in cultural narratives and political and social change in Vietnam and the mountainous region across mainland Southeast Asia. He has been doing research in Vietnam since 1997 and has published widely on jazz in Vietnam, the Central Highlands of Vietnam, collaborative anthropology, and the historical geography of the China-Vietnam railway corridor. Dr. Tan-Tangbau has taught at Ritsumeikan University in Kyoto and the National University of Singapore.

Quyền Văn Minh is a recipient of the Eminent Artist award of the Socialist Republic of Vietnam. Minh has released more than ten albums, beginning with *Birth '99* in 2000. He founded Minh's Jazz Club in Hà Nội in 1997. Minh has performed in numerous jazz concerts and international jazz festivals since 1994. He started teaching at the Vietnam National Academy of Music in 1989, being the first lecturer of saxophone at the conservatoire.

www.ingramcontent.com/pod-product-compliance
Lightning Source LLC
Chambersburg PA
CBHW030612230426
43661CB00053B/1949